Building
Construction
Before
Mechanization

Although we may not arrive at a perfect knowledge of the facts, some advantages may be derived from the attempt, such as suggesting inquiries, and giving interest to an important and heretofore unexplored subject, or generalizing and arranging sound practical observations, so as to induce others to take it up.

(**C. H. Smith**, "Lithology; or, Observations on Stone Used for Building," p. 129.)

John Fitchen

Building Construction Before Mechanization

The MIT Press
Cambridge, Massachusetts
London, England

This book was set in Century Schoolbook by Achorn Graphic Services and printed and bound by Halliday Lithograph in the United States of America

Library of Congress Cataloging-in-Publication Data

Fitchen, John.
    Building construction before mechanization.

    Bibliography: p.
    Includes index.
    1. Building—History. 2. Civil engineering—
History. 3. Building materials—History. I. Title.
TH15.F58   1986   690'.09   86-10647
ISBN 0-262-06102-3

To E.N.F.

*in celebration of the common ground we've
shared throughout the years*

Contents

13

Native House Building 213

14

Building Cheops' Pyramid 227

Preface

This study is an attempt to identify the problems of building construction and to recover reasonable and likely answers to what procedures and techniques were adopted, here and there, throughout the ages. It stops short of dealing with the present, for the equipment utilized today and the methods by which the buildings of our own era are brought into existence are already documented. Rather, this study focuses on the centuries of building activity that stretch back from modern times into unrecorded history. Starting with the Architectural Year One, so to speak, it progresses not to the present but to the pre-present.

The latter is not to be understood as a precise calendar date, however; for the cut-off point of this study varies with the nature of the particular construction method under consideration. Thus it stops short of dealing with metal-frame construction, which began its major evolution and expansion with Chicago skyscrapers in the mid-1880s as a result of two principal circumstances: the discovery of a large new market for the expanded steel industry after it had supplied the rails and the bridges for America's transcontinental railroads and the development of the high-rise passenger elevator. Similarly, the story of Portland Cement and its constructional development, though dating back to the 1820s, is too well documented to need explanation or comment. On the other hand, some age-old processes are still practiced today—pisé or rammed earth, for example, and thatching. Because these are nonmechanized techniques of building that persist into our own time, they are considered without concern for their anachronistic survival. In general then, this study addresses essentially handicrafted practices. It follows that the time span dealt with here encompasses building types and operations prior to the takeover of modern methods and techniques of analysis, investigation, and mathematical computation, with their reliance on tables, formulas, and test results.

Inevitably, any such imprecise cut-off point can be a source of uncertainty and perhaps confusion to the reader who may be unaware that different methods and practices rarely emerge or come into general use all at once. Tardy developments in one phase (or one place), sudden breakthroughs in another, and long periods of static overlap have been facts of life throughout the history of building construction. The evolution of viable techniques of construction and the perfecting of some definitive scheme of building practices have varied from place to place, depending on many factors (such as materials, equipment, the labor force, the stage of technical development, the needs of a society, the state of the economy, warfare and the dissemination of prisoners). In any event, the criteria that have determined the cut-off points are not strictly chronological but functional, that is to say, whenever handicraftsmanship was superseded by the machine and its attendant attitudes, methods, and procedures.

It may be thought that this study gives more attention to the medieval than to any other historical period. If so, it is because the Gothic era gave rise to the most varied, unprecedented, and demanding problems to stretch the builders' inventiveness and capabilities. In addition, more records—such as they are—survive from the late medieval period than from any previous building era. Moreover, it is probably safe to assert that all the major constructional problems encountered had been solved when mechanization took command. The one remaining challenge to the imagination and the technical mastery, both structurally and constructionally, of Renaissance builders was huge masonry domes raised high aloft on window-pierced drums.

At the other extreme, this study examines building operations (and the conditions under which they took place) in relatively unsophisticated societies. Such examination allows us to perceive the starkest, least complicated aspects of many building-related problems as well as their perhaps rude but effective solutions.

The topics dealt with in this book are far more numerous than the table of contents would lead one to believe. As the occasion warrants, the study covers such constructional and building-related considerations as bridges; construction in mud, clay, and rammed earth; defensive structures and military devices; excavations and foundations; funerary and commemorative structures; quarrying, mining, and tunneling; types of roof covering; stone carving and polishing procedures; and water supply including dams. Many of the problems posed by these and other important categories of building construction are intricately complex and interdependent. Inevitably, a topic is best handled in the context of its particular circumstances. For only thus can we see how it pertains to other factors that may have determined the eventual solution.

A case in point is the use of pisé, or rammed earth, for building substantial walls. This has been a common practice in many parts of the world throughout untold centuries right up to the present day. Its discussion therefore appears in a number of chapters. On the other hand, ventilation constitutes a separate chapter. For this is a vital subject not previously dealt with in a comprehensive way historically. Moreover, its careful examination demonstrates the close interplay between building construction and such essential building services as heating and illumination. In any case, as all aspects of the construction process cannot be covered independently, a comprehensive index is included.

It has seemed both appropriate and necessary to include, prior to the major topics addressed in this study, a chapter on jerry-building. This subject is almost invariably ignored, in spite of the fact that jerry-building continues to represent—as it has throughout the ages—a considerable proportion of the built world. Its shortcomings and hazards point up the need for the regulation and supervision of building construction, and its practices clearly reveal many of the distinctions between the problems, contributions, and areas of competence and responsibility of the designer, on the one hand, and the builder on the other. Moreover, through their need for constant repairs and replacements as well as their high incidence of total failure and collapse, jerry-built structures serve as a negative example. Their study demonstrates the extensive range of the builder's decisions (and temptations!) in matters of materials selection, preparation, assemblage, and finishing to assure a reasonable life expectancy for a building and the safety of its users.

Following upon preliminary considerations that serve as position papers, as it were, most of the chapters of this book deal with universal (or once universal) aspects of construction: site selection and preparation; the order and sequence of operations; construction equipment such as falsework, rope, and ladders; permanent features used as aids in the erection of buildings; stresses during construction and in the finished building; conveyance of men and materials to the site, by water or overland. These considerations range widely across the spectrum of building types. Consequently, the coverage accorded them is selectively representative rather than exhaustively inclusive. Only two chapters concentrate on a single type of building, and are included because they demonstrate so emphatically the two extremes in the building efforts of former times. One addresses certain kinds of quickly built vernacular habitations of quite limited longevity, erected by nomadic or precariously situated peoples who lived very close to nature and whose lives were inescapably regulated by the imperatives of an environment in which their very survival was marginal. The other case in point focuses on the opposite extreme: the timeless, monumental Great Pyramid of Egypt. With a teeming population, largely insulated from external threats, their abundantly productive land annually watered and rejuvenated, the Egyptians could put the most stupendous building efforts into permanent, mammoth sealed tombs for their dead rulers.

Perhaps the findings of this study are erroneous (we will doubtless never know for sure). But they are the result of a careful sifting and piecing together of whatever clues have survived and an assessment of the conditions and the possibilities that were in effect at the time and governed the practices of production. Lacking ordinary types of documentation, authentication has had to rely to a large extent on inference and deduction, on reasoning and informed common sense. For unfortunately, contemporary accounts of the processes and procedures adopted in ancient and medieval times simply do not exist; and, of course, eyewitnesses to what actually transpired on the job during all those centuries are no longer available for interview.

Consequently, whether to a partial or an all-embracing degree, inference and deduction has had to be resorted to in many cases where the remaining evidence of former building practices is either incomplete or inconclusive. Prime examples of this approach include using constructional stairs on the Great Pyramid, shipping Egyptian obelisks by water, raising and setting the Parthenon's column drums, removing the Pont du Gard's centerings, tracing the route of an access roadway at Glasgow Cathedral, accounting for the mechanisms of Salisbury Cathedral's spire.

The investigative procedure followed by the historian of construction practices corresponds to that required of a physician, for example, when confronted with a patient's obscure or troublesome illness or of an automobile mechanic faced with an ill-functioning motor. In common with these practitioners, the investigator of former handicrafted methods of building construction cannot know all the facts of a given situation. Inevitably he plays the role of diagnostician, evaluating and interpreting whatever clues he can uncover, from which he determines his course of action. He must listen and observe, test and check, marshal and screen his data. When confronted by conflicting or equivocal clues, he must call on his experience and his reservoirs of related knowledge—even his hunches. He does well to consult with others; but in the end his own response, his own judgment are put on the line and are a matter of record in arriving at a plausible solution.

In the quest for enlightenment, we search for those windows in time that, however limited and elusive they may be, can unexpectedly reveal how a former practice of building construction was actually carried out. In trying to rediscover these elusive windows on the past, we become acutely aware of what took place at the far side of the breakthrough, when determined and resourceful men managed to devise answers to the same practical problems we strive to understand nowadays. When these revelations seem all too often impossible to recover, we turn to a more promising source: the testimony of later commentators. Here, some of the most perceptive assessors of early building practices made their discoveries and reported their findings long before they could depend on the camera or on the scientific data we take for granted today. But like the very builders whose works they commented on, they too were on their own, often in quite similar circumstances and conditions. Consequently, no one has improved upon or superseded Thomas Lennox Watson's 1901 coverage of Glasgow Cathedral, or Frederick Schwatka's 1883 account of Eskimo igloos, or Francis Price's 1753 inspection and analysis of the fabric of Salisbury Cathedral.

Granted we cannot entirely recapture the environment in which an Egyptian obelisk was quarried in one piece and transported hundreds of miles or in which a Parthenon, a Pont du Gard or even a prehistoric lake dwelling was erected. But we can try to reconstruct the problems encountered and the means then available for solving them. To do so, we must remove ourselves as far as possible from the stereotypes and the quick, impersonal uninvolvement of late-twentieth-century practices. In bringing about this transformation of attitude, we benefit from going back as far as possible in searching out information, consulting the writings of those who, if not contemporaneous with the buildings they discuss, were at least closer to the situation than we. It is with this intention in mind that so many of the citations and references in these pages are drawn from sources that appeared long before the methods and procedures of our own day had evolved.

The subject of this book has long been neglected, if not utterly ignored. This is largely because documentation in the usual sense is so sparse and sporadic, in many instances nonexistent. The neglect also exists because knowledge about the nature of building construction remains a minor part of the background and training of historians. Even those who in recent years have been working so diligently and productively in other areas of the broad field of technology seldom know construction history. Consequently, this book attempts to focus afresh on building construction throughout the past from the perspective of the actual builder. Insofar as it is possible to do in a single book, the study addresses itself to two audiences. The text proper speaks primarily to the first and presumably larger audience: the intelligent layman curious about how the built world of the past was constructed. For him, the book tries to clarify unfamiliar practices and to present some sort of order to the subject's formidable complexities and interdependencies. For the second audience—architectural historians and other scholars who want to go more deeply into any of the matters touched upon—the book provides rather voluminous notes. It also includes a bibliography that is fairly extensive considering the scant and scattered coverage previously given these matters.

In a general but fundamental way, my thanks go to many generations of students. For without their sometimes ingenuous but crucial questionings I would probably not have been pressured into seeking answers that are not to be found in any textbook. Nor would I have been spurred into figuring out how some unaccountable building procedure of the past might have been accomplished.

The search has involved library sleuthing, an evaluation of conflicting theories, a weighing of alternative possibilities, and a continuous regimen of speculative reasoning and skeptical testing. In short, this book has been in gestation for a long time. Thus, wittingly or not, many individuals have served in different ways and in varying degrees to clarify explanations, to enrich the book's coverage, and to simplify what is actually a very complex subject.

More immediately, the names of a few particularly outstanding contributors to the development of this book cannot be passed over in silence: my sons, Allen Nelson Fitchen and John Hardy Fitchen; my talented longtime neighbors and friends, Arthur and Betsy Meggett; my unobtrusive mentor and advocate, Joseph Slater; my always obliging librarians, Bruce Brown and Frank Dugan. Each knows the areas in which his or her help has been special, but probably I alone appreciate the degree to which that help has been indispensable and therefore invaluable. To each of them my perennial gratitude for services rendered, above and beyond.

John Fitchen
Hamilton, New York
April 1985

Building
Construction
Before
Mechanization

1

The methods of the constructor must necessarily vary according to the nature of the materials, the means at his disposal, the requirements which he must satisfy, and the civilization in the midst of which he is placed.[1]

The Role of the Builder

The concern of this book is construction as practiced in former times. Its intention is to describe, explain, and comment on the ways in which structures—primarily buildings—were actually put together.

In no way does this intention belittle or negate the sometimes stupendous achievements of the designer. Rather, it seeks to redress somewhat the imbalance of attention and adulation that has universally been bestowed on the architect to the eclipse of the resourceful and inventive, often courageous, men who implemented the designer's vision.

The distinctions between design and construction, particularly in the past, have not always been clear; the two were at times mutually inclusive. For, until the Renaissance, the master mason and master carpenter served in two capacities, at once (in modern terminology) both architect and contractor.[2] Consequently, it is sometimes difficult to differentiate the two functions. We will therefore need to treat some situations in which practical considerations significantly influenced what were primarily matters of engineering or architectural design.

Thus the way in which a feature or assemblage was actually *built* sometimes critically affected the *design*. A striking modern instance is that of the enormous Quebec Bridge. Huge traveling gantry cranes were used to erect the cantilever arms of this two-track railroad bridge. The exigencies of construction, however, brought about a significant modification in the engineering design. This modification involved a change in the disposition of the web members in each bay of the trusses, from an N pattern to a K pattern. As a result, more but shorter and far less cumbersome units had to be handled and accurately positioned. Hence as the framing progressed member by member out over the void, construction proved far less difficult and hazardous.

More often, however, the aesthetic design imposes restrictions not only on the use and disposition of the materials but also on the effectiveness of the design itself. The so-called onion domes—clustering above churches throughout the Slavic countries—exemplify structures whose shapes largely dictate the materials and methods used in their erection. In general, their bulging forms pro-

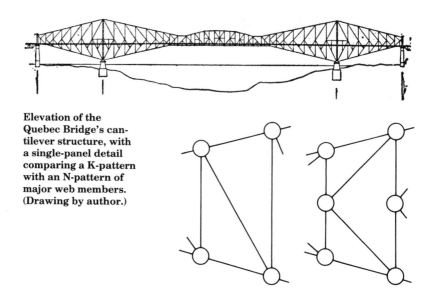

Elevation of the
Quebec Bridge's can-
tilever structure, with
a single-panel detail
comparing a K-pattern
with an N-pattern of
major web members.
(Drawing by author.)

hibit masonry construction throughout. Instead, they must be internally braced and strutted and tied together by timberwork. That is
why (unlike the usual form of domes in the Western world) the view
of them from within, from below, is sealed off. Their shapes, conspicuous in silhouette against the sky, do not contribute anything
whatsoever to the visual effect of the overhead space-volume from
within the building. Nor do they serve, as do almost all masonry
domes elsewhere, as either sources of natural illumination or means
of ventilation. Whether large or small, these decorative onion
domes serve solely to identify the building as a place of worship.

In any event, the major aim of this study is to investigate
banausic and operational practices rather than aesthetic or stylistic
criteria. Two or three clear-cut instances will illustrate situations
in which practical procedures are entirely unrelated to any computations of the engineer or any aesthetic concerns of the designer.

The distinction between design and construction

Anyone who has watched an ocean liner being berthed has seen a
deckhand throw a coil of light line many yards across intervening
water to a man on the pier who grabs it and hauls it in. Attached to
the line is a heavy hawser whose end-loop is heaved over a bollard,
whereupon an on-board power-winch draws the hawser taut and
thereby eases the great vessel in against the pier. No naval architect specified this ploy; it was evolved from necessity by those
charged with mooring the ship.

A similar but much larger building-related problem occurred when the first bridge was erected over the chasm of the Niagara River (long before the helicopter came on the scene). Here, the builder—who happened to be the designer as well—solicited the help of a local lad to fly a kite across the gorge. To the long, slender but strong kitestring was attached a light line that was used to haul across a larger rope and finally a cable. Direct contact was thus established between opposite sides of the chasm so that the construction of the bridge could proceed.

In ancient times nothing would appear to have been simpler, in erecting the stark geometrical mass of the Great Pyramid, than to pile thousands and thousands of stones, one on top of another. Yet so far no one has come up with a universally accepted scheme by which this operation was actually accomplished. Somehow, millennia ago, the Egyptian builders succeeded in doing the job with precision, though employing only minimal and crude devices. Though aesthetically simplistic in design, the project was an extraordinary triumph of construction.

Some years ago an elegant design was made for an urban fountain. Its chief feature was a granite monolith, many feet in diameter, fashioned as a shallow circular bowl to contain a pool of water; the constantly replenished water was intended to overflow the flaring rim of the bowl and fall like a translucent veil into a basin below. But this design created an installation problem for the contractor because the flaring lip of the bowl was too thin to be grappled by lifting slings. He solved the problem with a novel and unorthodox scheme. After nudging the monolith along skids onto the site exactly above the installation point, he transferred support for it from the skids to jacks and set blocks of ice between the jacks. The contractor then lowered the jacks in order to bring the unwieldy monolith to bear upon the ice. With the jacks removed, the monolith was supported exclusively by the blocks of ice. The melting ice enabled the heavy stone to descend onto the site, gradually and under precise control. As a result, the monolith was set level and without damage to its rim.

Functions outside the builder's authority

In the past, as indeed today, certain aspects of the construction process were often quite outside the contractor's realm or, at best, allowed but minor input on his part. *Financing* was one such consideration. The builder was seldom charged with raising money for a project. Instead funding came from princely gifts, wills or estates, general subscription or fees for indulgences, tithes or special taxes.

Yet the builder's work was indeed affected by both the amount and continuity of the project's financing. During the Middle Ages, for instance, considerable savings could often be made in the transport of stone by selecting a more distant quarry over one nearer the building site. This was so because the shorter distance could entail crossing many petty jurisdictions, each exacting transit fees. It should also be recalled that, due to sporadic funding most of the great medieval churches of Europe underwent long periods of building inactivity during their erection. Yet the builder had to maintain falsework lashings, temporary props and braces, and coverings for partially built features.[3] As well, he had to weatherproof those portions of the building that were sufficiently finished to permit church services.

Among primitive societies *site selection* was often an elaborate process that involved the whole community. An elected building committee consulted the omens, investigated the site's qualifications (particularly defensibility and an assured water supply), and tested such factors as the humidity, the degree of evaporation, the feasibility of growing crops and procuring firewood nearby. In medieval Europe, by contrast, the site was usually selected by the client, who may or may not have sought the advice of architect or engineer. The builder was also not directly involved in the prescribed *rituals* invariably connected with the genesis and production of building, large or small. Instead, these ceremonies of propitiation or dedication were administered by the priests and the headman or king.

Responsibilities of the builder

But many functions, both administrative and operational, clearly lay within the province of the builder, demanding special skills, expertise, and experience. It was the builder's responsibility, for example, if not always to assemble, certainly to assign tasks to and coordinate the efforts of a *labor force* that, in major projects, could number in the thousands. Where operations were carried on over a considerable period of time in remote or uninhabited sites such as quarries or logging camps (as for offshore oil drilling today), he had to provide barracks to house the workers, administrative personnel, and perhaps security forces. He also had to supply ancillary buildings for their tools, equipment, and food.

The establishment and upkeep of *access roads* to and from the sources of building materials devolved upon the builder as well. Near Athens, the skidways—used by the classical Greeks for easing blocks of marble down from the quarries on the slopes of Mount

Pentelicus—are discernible to this day. Evidence survives for the location of stone posts, set at intervals to left and right, around which ropes were snubbed to control and guide the blocks' descent. Centuries later, logging operations in North America depended on teams of horses or oxen to haul the logs out of the mountainside forests to river and sawmill. This traffic necessitated the removal of stumps and large rocks, a certain amount of grading and of cut and fill, and the corduroying of the road in swampy places. It also required unremitting maintenance, especially during the winter months.

Service roads to and within the actual building site were obviously the direct responsibility of the builder. In ancient Egypt, extensive causeways and ramps were constructed to haul myriad stone blocks from the river landing stage to the pyramid's site. Herodotus reports on the length of time it took the workmen to heap up and pave these construction-servicing embankments. Similarly, in medieval Scotland an on-site service road was established so that narrow-gauge carts could trundle large stones from the building yard to precise spots within the periphery of Glasgow Cathedral's already well-advanced lower story.

Roads inevitably bring to mind the larger, more complex matter of *transportation,* an extensive topic with numerous ramifications for the builder. All but the meanest and most transient structures were composed of materials that had to be brought to the building site, sometimes from considerable distances. Numerous types of transportation (already in operation) may have been available for a given project. Even so, the builder had to decide which alternative was most feasible, appropriate, and economical granted the nature of the loads to be carried and the distances to be covered. In addition, he had to arrange for the orderly, safe, and timely transmission of materials. For large projects the high costs of transporting building materials (particularly stone) from source to site demanded ingenuity on the part of the builder in scheduling shipments, devising routes, and reducing along the way the number of cargo transferences from one form of conveyance to another.

The builder had to provide certain essential items of construction *equipment* such as ropes and ladders. Lifting devices, too, have for centuries been featured in the arsenal of the builder, from simple gins fitted with a windlass, to cranes, to great wheels, depending on the size and cumbersomeness of the burden to be lifted and the distance it had to be raised.

Distinct from such standard reusable gear as ropes and ladders was the whole category of *falsework* assemblages, required especially in the construction of permanent masonry buildings. Most such buildings could not be erected at all without first establishing one or more of these temporary structures, assembled on the site as needed and fashioned to meet the specific requirements of individual projects. These structures—scaffolding, shoring, and formwork and arch centering for vaulting—were always constructed by the builder. Many builders eventually hired engineers to design critical shoring installations or the centerings for stone bridges of long span. But invariably the builder actually erected and, most critically, dismantled and/or removed them.

It was essential that the builder be intimately familiar with and competent in his understanding of *mechanical processes*—those that involved levers; grappling devices for lifting heavy stones and setting them in place with precision; tourniquets and pry-bars for inching heavy blocks into position; and equipment for loading and unloading wagons,[4] sledges, and ships. He had to know the *properties of materials*—different species of wood; different kinds and qualities of granite, limestone, sandstone, and marble;[5] the ingredients and proportions of mortar, stucco, and plaster; and techniques of installing, finishing, and preserving materials from weathering and decay. He had to understand both the *kinds and degrees of stresses* that might act upon the work before, after, and especially during the building process—forces that endangered the stability and integrity of the installations against dislocations or even outright failure due to foundation settlement, overloading, shrinkage, earthquake tremors, vibration and high winds.

Moreover, as the builder was in direct charge of the activities of the entire work force, he needed to have a thorough knowledge of all related building trades. For he was responsible for *the performance of each building mechanic:* the stonemasons,[6] the bricklayers,[7] the structural carpenters, and those whose expertise lay in iron and other metals,[8] decorative tiles, mosaic and inlay, carving, polishing marble, painting,[9] stained glass, and other finish work.

It should be noted that invariably the builder has had to ensure that the structure *as designed* would work—that it would not collapse of its own weight or from inadequate bracing or attachment, nor topple from the vibrating of high winds above or the scouring of river currents below. Thus he had to line and brace the sides of excavations to prevent cave-ins or mud slides; he had to supply and operate pumps of sufficient capacity to keep tunnels and below-grade areas of construction from flooding; he had to determine the most feasible and effective positions at which to locate cranes and other lifting devices; he had to anchor adequately all freestanding exposed features such as pinnacles and the capstones of spires; he had to have in mind from the start how to dismantle and remove falsework structures (notably arch centerings) without injury to completed work. These and innumerable other pragmatic

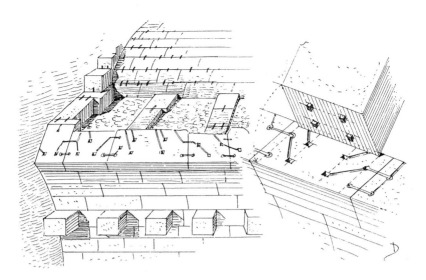

Scheme of molten lead
poured around metal
dowels and cramps
often used in Greek
and Roman dry-wall
masonry to assure the
permanent alignment
and security of the
stone blocks. (Josef
Durm, *Die Baukunst
der Römer,* 1905, fig. 9,
p. 15.)

matters demonstrate the comprehensive and critical nature of the builder's participation (now, indeed, as formerly) in converting two-dimensional drawings—or even small models—into full-scale, three-dimensional reality.

A comparison with the modern contractor

To do full justice to the scope and special nature of the builder's involvement in past construction, it can be instructive to comment on the contractor's role *today* (when architect and contractor are recognized as separate entities). Nowadays, the architect's work for any given project is recorded in the form of the contract documents: the specifications, in voluminously comprehensive and precise detail, and a set of drawings that includes a plot plan and various floor plans; elevations, sections and details; window and door schedules; electric, heating, plumbing and other layouts. The contract documents present the total record of *what* must be done and constitute the basis on which competitive bids are submitted and a contract awarded. But this total record seldom specifies *how* to execute the work. With few exceptions, that is left up to the successful contractor. Consequently the amount of the contractor's bid, rather than the architect's estimate, establishes the cost of the project.[10]

Herein lies a significant point of difference between the designer and the executor of the design. For in the case of the latter (at least until quite recently)[11] there has been nothing comparable to the architect's agenda as detailed in the complete package of contract documents. Instead, the contractor meets the pragmatic requirements of the work by the most direct and/or least expensive means, in a sometimes traditional, sometimes unorthodox manner. His methods take into account the training and skills of his labor force together with the possibilities and the limitations of each particular situation. These are flexible criteria of *procedure* that adapt to the exigencies of a given time, place, and set of circumstances. Less flexible is the absolute necessity for the contractor to determine the order and sequence of the steps that must be followed in executing the work. Here, too, he gets no significant directives from the contract documents. Instead, he must rely on foresight, judgment, and wide practical experience.

It should be noted that the very nature of his job obliges the modern contractor to take substantial financial risks against factors often quite beyond his control. Strikes of long duration, for example, may plague him in any one of a number of building trades as well as in the mills and factories that manufacture structural and finish materials. Like a farmer, the contractor cannot rely on clement weather. Much of the work takes place out-of-doors, exposed to rain, sleet, high winds, and frigid temperatures. Hence his costs may escalate as a result of lost time with respect to his labor force or the need to protect the labor force—and the work itself—within extensive cocoons of tarpaulins or plastic sheets. Moreover, particularly in large-scale urban projects, the contractor faces a multiplicity of often conflicting codes, ordinances, statutes, regulations, and prohibitions promulgated by various jurisdictions—federal, state, and municipal. Their reconciliation consumes many hours of his time.

Yet in the face of all these hazards, uncertainties, and conflicting restrictions, two essential functions need to be carried out in any substantial building project. One belongs to the architect who designs the building, working out what many centuries ago Vitruvius called its *utilitas, firmitas, venustas.* The other belongs to the builder who converts the design into permanent, full-scale reality. The following pages consider representative examples of the builder's challenges and successes before mechanization.

2

It frequently happens, however, that the most barbarous people possess, in particular branches of art, an accuracy of principle, or a dexterity of operation, even superior to their more polished neighbours; and hence it will be found of use to collect detached information of this kind from every part of the globe.[1]

The Nature of Building Construction and Sources of Information about Its Former Practices

Building construction, as addressed in these pages, may be defined in the aggregate as comprising all those undertakings and practices that are involved in the actual production of the man-made world of the past. This includes, of course, but is not limited to, what we think of as works of architecture, with their concern for and differentiation into one or another of the historical styles. In fact, however, building construction focuses on much more fundamental, universal, and down-to-earth considerations; namely, on how man *executed* the structures that provided shelter and a viable environment for him, his goods, his institutions and his life style. Thus we are concerned with African tribal huts and Bedouin tents as well as the palaces of kings and popes. We are concerned with such things (not usually associated in the public mind with architecture) as bridges and excavations, water supply and ventilation, devices for transporting and lifting materials. This book investigates the *pragmatic operations* attendant upon bringing the man-made environment into being, and any concern for *aesthetic design* is incidental. Rather than stylistic matters, it seeks to account for and explain technological procedures that are not generally understood nor widely noted and appreciated for their significance.

A few decades ago the public expressed a widespread upsurge of interest in the "home industries" and the handicraft techniques of a great variety of traditional crafts.[2] In America this interest was reflected in the exhibition programs of many county and state historical associations. It even transformed the entire concept of such sites as Old Sturbridge Village in Massachusetts, Old Bethpage Village on New York's Long Island, Upper Canada Village north of the St. Lawrence River, and many others across the land.[3] These complexes have become live presentations of folk arts, reviving the handicraft skills and industries of America's premechanized past. At the same time, scholarly research has produced technological studies that are concerned with one area or another of the whole range of former eras, cultures, and civilizations in a worldwide perspective. Such a work as Joseph Needham's monumental, many-volumed *Science and Civilization in China* is an extraordinarily comprehensive example of the new focus on technological history. But even here, there is a disappointing sparseness of information on the technology of former building operations and procedures.[4]

We are still, it would seem, in the early stages of a veritable revolution of thought about the world of past ages and cultures, particularly with respect to building construction. To date, there have been very few serious, scholarly attempts to reconstruct the building methods and procedures that were resorted to in various eras of the past. The delay in addressing a systematic inquiry into these matters has undoubtedly been due in large part to the paucity of contemporary records—a condition that has prevailed throughout history. To take a broader view of the matter, however, it can perhaps be illuminating to speculate for a moment on a universally applicable explanation for such partial and less-than-adequate coverage of one of man's most universal activities—providing shelter and accommodations for his multiple needs.

How building differs from other handicrafts

To be sure, other handicraft industries—basketry, weaving, pottery, tool and weapon making—were universal, too, and some achieved a phenomenal state of both technical and artistic excellence. But the same degree of perfection is evident in some of the architecture of the past, in such masterpieces as the Parthenon, Hagia Sophia of Byzantium, Chartres Cathedral and the Taj Mahal. Why, then, is so little information on record about how these buildings—and for that matter, countless quite humble and unpretentious buildings—were brought into being?

The reasons would seem to reflect the nature of the operations involved. In practically every other handicraft, actual production required constant repetition day in day out of the same procedures, the same sequences of operations; so the mechanics of production became ingrained in the hands of the skilled practitioners. This observation applies, of course, to masons and especially to carpenters quite as much as it does to potters and weavers. But the activities of building mechanics were far more varied than those of potters or weavers. In fact, all but the smallest and rudest buildings required the coordinated services of many different artisans. Buildings of any considerable size and complexity involved totally different materials and procedures. Above all, unlike other handicrafts, the erection of buildings took place at the site of the project, not in the home, shop, or atelier of the individual artisan.

And so the conditions of the building industry were multiple and often fundamentally different from those of other types of handicraft technology. Construction was a complicated, overall operation that could take months, sometimes years to complete. Along the way the varied but interdependent activities of a considerable company of men had to be strictly coordinated. Often, the need arose for extensive temporary equipment such as scaffolding, gins, and other lifting devices. It also required transporting both men and materials to the building site. The size of the undertaking (irrespective of the size of the building) invariably meant that its erection was conducted in the open; that is to say, its purpose was to *create* shelter from the elements, not to *make use of* shelter in order that artifacts might be produced.

The lack of writing on building construction

The foregoing may explain why information about the practices of building construction is too complex, too esoteric to be grasped and comprehensively recorded by those who deal in words rather than in bricks and mortar. With neither the manual skills nor the know-how of the expert artisan, the men adept with words—those who had been formally educated in philosophy and other polite studies, the "gentlemen" of each era—have traditionally shown their superiority by denigrating the artisan and relegating him to an inferior status in society. The intelligentsia—the philosophers and priests, along with the politicians, administrators, and men of affairs—have invariably dominated all media of the spoken and written word. What they did not understand they either ignored or belittled. This patronizing attitude toward artisans has prevailed everywhere, in almost all eras and civilized cultures, creating a major distinction, a social dichotomy, between those who worked with their hands, no matter how expertly, and those who talked and/or wrote.

Among a large number of examples confirming this attitude, a striking case—exceptional only because of the preeminent stature of the man involved and the fact that he fought back articulately—is that of Leonardo da Vinci.

Leonardo's greatest problems were caused by the contempt in which he was held by the humanists. . . . Having lacked the opportunity of attending a university to study the liberal arts, he had learned no Greek and very little Latin. This was to prove a major stumbling block in his life. The Renaissance humanists, who were his contemporaries, glorified the great culture of classical antiquity, but to him that culture was largely a closed book. He was probably never truly accepted in a humanist milieu, where discussions would often be carried on in Latin. . . . Thus, time and time again in his writings Leonardo returns to the scorn of the humanists: "Because I am not a literary man some presumptuous persons will think that they may reasonably blame me by alleging that I am an unlettered man. Foolish men! . . . They will say that because I have no letters I cannot express well what I want to speak of." He questions the right of these literati to judge him: "They go about puffed up and pompous, dressed and decorated with the fruits not of their own labours but those of others, and they will not allow me my own. And if they despise me, an inventor, how much more could they—who are not inventors but trumpeters and declaimers of the works of others—be blamed."

We have in these passages—and in others where Leonardo is outraged because the intellectuals consider him merely a manual worker, a technician—remarkable proof of the gulf that has always existed, wider at some times than at others, between the literary intellectual and the technologist, between what C. P. Snow, that rare combination of both types, has appropriately called the Two Cultures.[5]

Today we are just beginning to see a break in this perpetual attitude. It has not yet meant recognizing the craftsman himself and elevating him to a position of widely acknowledged respect and prestige, except in a few oustanding but isolated cases where an establishment such as the American Institute of Architects bestows a craftsmanship medal or citation. Rather, the break has taken the form of an absorbing, genuine interest in the artisan's craft and a penetrating inquiry into the processes and the details of his métier.

In the past there have been countless writings on the aesthetic basis of traditional styles, the distinctions between the sublime and the beautiful, the so-called laws of proportion, the expressiveness of ornamentation, and the principles of composition generally. These are unquestionably valid considerations (though an unconscionable amount of repetitious nonsense about them has glutted many a printed page, and too often the writing has been superficial, precious, or dilettantist). The exposition of technical processes, on the other hand, requires a different kind of perception, training, and observation—one that is no less precise and highly disciplined, but pragmatic and factual as well. Precise knowledge of the latter kind as formerly applied to architecture and to building in general consists of three distinct but related considerations; namely, building materials, structural systems, and, most important, construction techniques.

The source, manufacture or preparation, and properties of the various building materials that man has used at one time or another have on the whole been adequately covered in various publications.[6] Likewise, the structural systems employed by man—in foundations and walls, in roofs, above all in response to the major structural problem, spanning space—have been investigated, analyzed, and reported on quite thoroughly by knowledgeable engineers.[7] Previous techniques of erecting a broad range of buildings, however, have been written about sparsely and intermittently, instead of comprehensively and systematically from beginning to end. To the question, How was such and such a building of the past erected?, almost invariably contemporary accounts provide no factual, circumstantial answers whatsoever.

The meticulously kept building accounts of the Middle Ages—for example, the Fabric Rolls and Pipe Rolls of the English cathedrals[8]—list the nature and quantities of materials, who supplied them and what was paid for them, as well as the names and wages or other remuneration assigned to each category and grade of the labor force. But none of these accounts includes specific, detailed information about the procedures of erection. These latter were part of the "mystery" of the building trades, the jealously guarded secrets of master craftsmen that were worked out in the privacy of building lodges and discussed behind closed doors at periodic synods.[9] Even the secrets of *design* were disclosed only at the end of the medieval period;[10] the secrets of *construction* were never committed to writing. Oral not written tradition was followed in training apprentice and journeyman in the building trades. Construction skills were learned by example and by demonstration at the site.

This universal tradition of training in, and perpetuation of, craft practices by visual example and oral direction goes far in accounting for the virtual absence of written records that explain comprehensively and in detail the methods followed in building erection. (Only in recent years have a few large universities in America established degree-conferring programs that train students to become general contractors, capable of directing major construction projects.) Moreover, the practice of hands-on instruction has had significant and far-reaching effects on the entire history of building construction. The long history of timber-frame construction in Europe clarifies this assertion.

What we have come to realize, nowadays, is that undoubtedly timber construction, because of its very anonymity, represents a heretofore ignored but unexpectedly valid and unusually trustworthy index of unbroken continuity in architecture. The reason is clear enough: in timber building of the past there has been almost no self-consciousness of design, no attempt at ego-centric novelty, no arbitrariness of structural form for visual effect alone. Timber buildings of the past, like the timberwork portions of masonry buildings contemporary with them, have been assigned a practical role instead of being fea-

tured as the conspicuous primary interest and focus of the building's design. Hence the development of timberwork design through the centuries has not been tampered with; it has been free to meet the problems and adapt to the needs of its own nature, its own properties and peculiarities. Vernacular building in timber has been left to develop anonymously and naturally, undisturbed by academic prescription or the interference of aesthetes. . . .[11]

Clues to former building practices

In the absence of procedural textbooks and lacking eyewitness accounts of the details of former building practices, the historian is left perforce with speculation and deduction. He speculates what method *might* have been employed, granted the materials available, the work force that could be called upon, and the climate and other conditions that prevailed in a particular locality. He deduces the procedures and sequences that would logically have been followed from what he knows of the state of technology at the time and the tools available, and from whatever evidence the surviving structures themselves can reveal of the secrets of their execution, including falsework structures and other temporary auxiliary paraphernalia.

For the more primitive categories of buildings, clues to these operations can be derived from comparable structures built today by the people of societies as yet unaffected by modern, mechanized technology. This approach could be appropriate for many structures that utilize the organic products of nature as major building materials, with or without clay, animal skins, or thatching applied as the continuous weather-excluding surface.[12] For more sophisticated, monumental buildings—particularly those whose structure consists of masonry materials fashioned to enclose large areas of uninterrupted interior space (usually employing vaulted or domed construction)—one looks for more or less obscure clues that sometimes remain in the completed structures.[13] But the complexity of operations in buildings of this type and their high degree of specialized technology usually require a greater reliance on deductive logic to assess the most likely construction procedures.

Another source from which clues might be gained in recreating the building procedures of the past is that of the methods used, sometimes centuries later, in the repair or reconstruction of a building.[14] The danger here is in relying too much on later reconstructions. If a considerable time has elapsed between the original erection of the building and its rebuilding after injury or partial collapse, different and more modern methods may have been developed in the intervening years. So there is no positive assurance that the later techniques duplicated those that prevailed in the first instance. If approached with caution and some skepticism, however, this avenue of investigation can sometimes offer revealing leads.

A potentially rich source of information, as yet almost completely untapped, lies in how the builders of our own day—the practicing master masons or carpenters or other mechanics—would go about reproducing a given structure of the past if they had to do it. There is a tremendous reservoir, even today, of traditional skill and know-how on the part of the most experienced and resourceful of these men. They are the current practitioners and custodians of a building inheritance—former trade secrets, in fact—that goes back many centuries. Not all the secrets of a Gothic cathedral's achievement, for example, are lost to these men; not all the building techniques of the thirteenth century have disappeared from their repertory.[15]

These master builders no longer hold periodic, closed-door professional conclaves as they did during the medieval era; nor do they commit their practical expertise to writing. So, to learn from such a source, one would have to seek them out in England and France, in Germany and Spain—wherever the heritage of the Gothic world survives. Though the benefits of such a widespread investigation would be enormous, the assignment would be difficult and time-consuming. It would demand numerous talents and capabilities on the part of the researcher: a fluency in a number of languages; a knowledge of construction operations; a familiarity with historical precedents; a capacity to understand and visualize sometimes complex and intricate solutions to practical problems of operation, procedure, and sequence in building erection; and a facility in overcoming the reserve of master craftsmen who are naturally reluctant to reveal trade secrets on which their superior reputation and standing in their field are founded.

Photographic sources of construction information

Because written documentation is often nonexistent and in any case quite inadequate outside of Europe—even for the nineteenth century—it seems appropriate and useful to supplement the customary type of bibliographical references with those of a pictorial nature. One welcome source of illustrations of traditional native structures is to be found in those quarto volumes of photographs that appeared toward the end of the last century and were devoted to presenting anthropological studies of the native peoples of pre- or nonindustrial societies.[16] The illustrations in these albums are especially valuable not only because they are large and on excellent paper for reproduction but also, being early examples of photography from plates, they are exceptionally sharp in the delineation of detail. Thus even those illustrations where buildings are no more than background for human subjects nonetheless often reveal specific details that are very much in focus. Moreover, they were taken at a time when native construction was still "pure," uncontaminated by the adoption of foreign methods and imported materials (such as corrugated iron roofing as a more permanent and fireproof substitute for thatching). One drawback of these early, posed portraits of native peoples and their domestic environment is that few include scenes of buildings under construction. The characteristics of the finished structures are shown in such clarity, however, that it is possible to observe various clues to the procedures followed in their erection.

Here and there from miscellaneous sources, especially from long-run periodicals such as *Travel* and notably *National Geographic,* we have an extensive reservoir of photographic pictures, some of which illustrate works in progress. These photographs demonstrate the survival of handicraft techniques that have persisted with little if any change for untold generations: pit sawing,[17] rope making, excavating,[18] mud plastering,[19] and thatching.[20] Sometimes, too, the illustrations depict scaffolding or other falsework installations that utilize pre–Industrial Revolution techniques that have undergone but slight modification in recent times.[21] Their study provides useful insights into the nature and extent of their antecedent applications. Still other present-day illustrations can help to reveal the environmental and other contributory conditions of a given area, thus aiding us in assessing the steps that were necessary to erect former buildings of the sort pictured. These are surviving examples of types (such as pile-supported lake dwellings)[22] for which no installational data is on record. Photographs can also reveal obscure details, significant to the process of erection, that may have escaped the notice of even a knowledgeable person at the time he took the picture.[23]

Today, in America at least, one of the minor items covered in the contract documents requires that a pictorial progress report be made monthly of the state of any major building's erectional advancement. But the purpose of these periodic photographs is to record the nature and the *amount* of the work accomplished, as visual evidence on which to base payments to the contractor. Hence the *methods* by which the work has been achieved are incidental and often remain obscure in the progress photographs. So for a meaningful, visual record of building operations as practiced today, the camera's recording eye (supplemented wherever possible by pencil drawings) needs to be directed by an interested and knowledgeable person who photographs not merely *what* is being accomplished but *how*.[24]

The influence of materials and structure

Any investigations into the history of building *construction* are complicated by its close interrelation with the other two practical aspects of building; namely, the *materials* and the *structural systems*. A given structural system is fundamentally affected—even completely determined, in most cases—by the materials employed in its realization; and both considerations have an intimate bearing on the method of execution adopted. For example, vaulted buildings (representing a particular structural system) are invariably fashioned of masonry (stone or brick materials) whose assemblage is virtually impossible without some sort of temporary falsework (a technique of erection) or, at the very least, some form of scaffolding.

Hence, though many books and technical articles have described and analyzed the structural systems used in buildings, and though much has been written also about the source, preparation, and nature of different building materials, it is nevertheless virtually impossible to cover the actual erection of buildings as a similarly separate and discrete category of investigation. The construction of buildings is a dynamic, ongoing series of operations that is intimately tied in with both the materials and the systems it utilizes. The engineering principles that account for a building's enclosure of space and the stability of its structure, quite as much as the materials that make up its fabric, can generally be considered independently from the processes of assemblage. For data concerning them remain in place and are available for assessment throughout the entire life of the building. However, any attempt at recreating the multiple steps that had to be undertaken to realize the building in the first place must take into account both the materials and the structural scheme. Consequently, this study presents information on materials and structures that can be found elsewhere and is, in fact, already well known. But such information is included not for its own sake but as it can be shown to have influenced or modified the *execution* of buildings in the past.

Moreover, this attempt to recreate the erectional procedures of former times does not assume that the solutions proposed are necessarily those that were actually adopted in each individual case. The simple fact is that we do not know for certain what construction techniques were used (at least in ancient times) because no direct documentation survives—neither trustworthy eyewitness accounts nor formal reports and official records. The best we can hope to do is to suggest how a building *might* have been achieved at the time it came into being.

In this connection it is worth recalling what often happens today. At one time or another, every modern architect has experienced designing a feature that is complicated or intricate enough to have necessitated working out—often with the advice and collaboration of an engineer—the way in which the feature is to be installed or erected, only to find that the contractor proposes to build it in a quite different way. The contractor's change of *method* to achieve the same result is invariably proposed for economic reasons; that is, he can do the job more cheaply, perhaps more efficiently, by following his own scheme. And if the architect is satisfied that it is a viable alternative, the contractor's solution is approved and adopted. The point is that even today we have alternative solutions that are not always readily discernable even to professionals involved in building design and construction. We should therefore be wary of assuming that there is always but one unique solution to former problems of building erection.

In pursuing the history of building construction, the scholar becomes more and more deeply impressed by the resourcefulness and inventiveness of builders throughout the ages in solving the multiple problems they faced. Some of these problems were so demanding and formidable that today, with all our scientific apparatus, all our specialist knowledge, we are at a loss to figure out how they accomplished what they did with the limited means at their disposal. In the following chapters, we will investigate some of the builders' solutions, along with the conditions and the limitations they had to work with and overcome. Clearly, their works remain as evidence of their success; and it is embarrassing that we find it difficult, if not impossible at times, to reconstruct with confidence their methods.

Unexpected solutions from the natural world

Of the three physical considerations involved in the creation of buildings, materials and structural systems are static or passive in that they may be investigated, tested, and analyzed at will, even centuries after their original installation or application. But the third consideration—construction techniques—is the active ingredient in any building program. It is the immediately contemporaneous factor. Seldom if ever documented in the past, the details of construction are notoriously obscure and elusive for the historian to comprehend and recreate.

This situation can perhaps best be illustrated by examples drawn from the world of animal behavior. Various writers, foreign and domestic, have commented on the ingenious constructions of the beaver dam, the pendent, woven nest of the oriole, and the many-celled, insulated nest of the hornet, for example. But until quite recently there has been rather scant and only scattered notice of the actual operations of a structural or engineering nature that are sometimes undertaken by insects, fish, birds or mammals in the natural world. Two examples will illustrate the kinds of operations that cannot be deduced after the fact, but only ascertained at the time from lucky and unexpected on-the-spot observation of ongoing activities.

My bee-house is built of brick, without windows, and has only one small door. The hives are made of glass and covered with thick curtains of muslin. This renders observation very easy. On one occasion I noticed that from some cause a comb had become detached and was in danger of falling to the floor. The bees had noticed this before it had become apparent to me, and had begun to provide against disaster. They rapidly built a broad, thick support of wax between the endangered comb and the one next to it, thus securing it firmly. They then reattached the detached comb securely to the roof of the hive. When this had been done, they took away the temporary support and used it elsewhere. . . .[25]

I once saw a minute spider (hardly larger than the head of a pin) lift a house-fly, which must have been more than twenty times its weight, through a distance of over a foot. The fly dangled by a single strand from the cross-bar of a window-sash, and when it first caught my attention, was being raised through successive small distances, of something like a tenth of an inch each; the lifts followed each other so fast, that the ascent seemed almost continuous. It was evident that the weight must have been quite beyond the spider's power to stir by a 'dead lift'; but his motions were so quick, that at first it was difficult to see how this apparently impossible task was being accomplished.

I shall have to resort to an illustration to explain it; for the complexity of the scheme seems to belong less to what we ordinarily call instinct than to intelligence, and that in a degree we cannot all boast ourselves. The reader who questions the propriety of the last remark may be invited to pause, before hearing the spider's device, to consider how he would proceed to lift a whole ox hanging vertically beneath him at the end of a hundred-fathom cable, if he had no appliances whatever except some spare rope.

The little spider proceeded as follows (ab is a portion of the window-bar, to which level the fly was to be lifted from his original

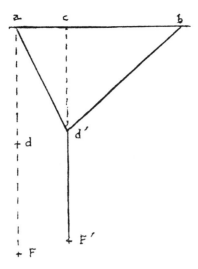

"A Spider's Device in
Lifting." (*Science*
3(January–June 1884):
432.)

position at F, *vertically beneath* a): *the spider's first act was to de-*
scend halfway to the fly (to d), *and there fasten one end of an almost*
invisible thread; his second, to ascend to the bar and run out to b,
where he made fast the other end, and hauled on his guy with all his
small might. Evidently the previously straight line must yield some-
what in the middle, whatever the weight of the fly, who was, in fact,
thereby brought into the position F′, *to the right of the first one, and*
a little higher. Beyond this point, it might seem, he could not be
lifted; but the guy being left fast at b, *the spider now went to an*
*intermediate point (*c) *directly over his victim's new position, and*
hence spun a new vertical line from c, *as before below* a, *but a little*
higher.

The same operation was repeated again and again, a new guy
being occasionally spun, but the spider never descended more than
about half way down the cord, whose elasticity was in no way in-
volved in the process. All was done with surprising rapidity. I
watched it for some five minutes (during which the fly was lifted
perhaps six inches), and then was called away.[26]

As the author was unfortunately called away before the job
of raising the fly all the way to the spider's nest was consummated,
some explanation and extrapolation of the data is in order. To displace the fly laterally as it dangled on its cord from the window-bar
above, the least effort would involve pulling on the drop-cord at a

point immediately above its attachment to the fly, and at approximately right angles to the cord. During the time he was being observed, the spider made the judicious compromise of attaching his pulling line halfway down the drop-line. Otherwise, if he descended all the way down to the fly and pulled on it from above, he would be pulling much more vertically upward, and that he did not have the strength to do. But as the incremental lifts of the fly, by successive lateral displacement to one side then the other, brought it closer to the window-bar, the spider undoubtedly did attach his later guy-lines to the body of the fly, for then he would be pulling it laterally almost exactly at right angles to the supporting drop-line. It is clear that, by following this procedure, the higher the fly was raised the easier it was to raise it farther, right up to the window-bar itself. In any case this eyewitness account relates enough to cause us to marvel at the spider's engineering sagacity in raising a relatively heavy load, without any evidence of the operation remaining after its successful completion.

It is important to present in some detail the foregoing examples of actual construction operations in nature. For such instances often parallel situations that have prevailed throughout the past in the building operations of humans. As the latter were accomplished with only the most meagre explanations and as contemporary accounts are totally incomplete, we are as much in the dark about them as we would be about the bees and the spider, were it not for the chance observations of those lucky enough to have witnessed them in action.

We do not know definitively how most of the significant buildings of past eras were actually brought into being. For example, no one today knows for certain how the stones of the Egyptian pyramids were raised to their destined positions in those colossal monuments. No one knows incontrovertibly how the pharaoh's engineers managed to erect the nearly hundred-foot-high granite obelisk of Queen Hatshepsut to the upright position it has maintained for nearly three-and-a-half millennia. No one knows how the classical Greeks raised and maneuvered into position with such nicety the column drums of the Athenian Parthenon, one on top of another, in erecting its thirty-four-foot-high columns.

Moreover, there were kinds of building practices in former times that are alien to our thinking nowadays. In stone buildings, for example, oversized blocks were widely used in one way or another as aids in building construction. And in timber buildings, joints were made without benefit of metal, using mortice and tenon, dove-tail, or other forms of all-wood connections—a practice that was universal even into the twentieth century (at least in the Western world).[27]

The lesson to be learned, then, from these instances of construction in the world of animal behavior is that we need to free ourselves of many customary and habitual thoughts about the construction of buildings in the past. So much of what we do today in building operations is conditioned by our machines, our scientific calculations, our technological advances, our use of steel, our utilization of and dependence on prodigious amounts of mechanized power. It takes a real effort to disabuse our minds of these familiar instrumentalities and expedients. But only by so doing can we expect to penetrate the veil of uncertainty and obscurity that shrouds so much of the picture of building procedures in preindustrial eras.

3

*One of the most important and far-reaching of
all the adaptations of nature [is] an adjustment that tends to cause variation when it is
needed, and to keep things as they are, so long
as no change is demanded. As the conditions
of life become unfavorable, variation becomes
desirable in order to restore the adjustment between the organism and its environment. . . .*[1]

Physical and Cultural Forces Affecting Building Construction

Because building construction involves considerable time and expense, and because most buildings are expected to be long-lived, frequent or sudden failure cannot be tolerated. So steps of development have usually been gradual, testing each innovation, trying out solutions in modest prototypes to assess their performance and feasibility before attempting large-scale undertakings. This sometimes tentative, sometimes daring progress in the development of building construction has resulted in the survival of the fittest or, at least, in the adoption of what worked, what met the conditions and fulfilled the requirements of the particular situation.

Of course there have been many failures along the way. For in all but the rudest and most minimal examples, building is a complicated activity that must accommodate many conditions and meet many requirements. Obviously, the primary, universal function of man's building has always been to ensure his survival by creating an environment that could shelter him from the hostile elements as well as from his human or animal enemies. Whether the hostilities of nature manifested themselves in excesses of heat, cold, wind, or rain, or any combination of these and other inimical forces, man as a builder has had to work out solutions that could protect him from their baneful effects and provide him with a viable interior habitat. As his state of civilization developed, he had to create a more and more ideally controlled habitation that went far beyond the stark needs of mere survival, preservation, and the perpetuation of life.

Throughout history builders have always learned, sooner or later, from mistakes and failures. It may therefore be instructive to list some of the causes of failure that have resulted in either partial or total collapse.

Failure from natural forces

The titanic forces of nature are one cause of destruction. Take, for example, the thick, smothering overburden of hot ash and mud from the A.D. 79 eruption of Vesuvius that embalmed Pompeii and Herculaneum respectively; the tidal waves that have drowned thousands from time to time in Bengal and East Pakistan; the periodic floods that have caused such widespread misery and devastation in China along the Yangtze River's erratic course; the earthquakes that have brought appalling ruin to so many places in the world over the centuries, such as Calcutta where hundreds of thousands of people reportedly lost their lives in the convulsions of 1737; the forest fires, out of control over hundreds of acres, that in this century have brought recurring desolation and wholesale property damage in the timbered mountain states of western America; and the earth slides in northern Italy that have repeatedly obliterated whole villages, created or eliminated lakes, and even changed the course of rivers.

One would think that localities susceptible to such catastrophes would be shunned by men, once and for all. But not so. Perhaps these cataclysmic disasters occur too infrequently in places that are otherwise highly desirable and/or productive. In any event, man seems to be a perennial optimist when it comes to building in dangerously vulnerable locations. And, at least when the devastation is not total and the damage is reparable, means have been devised to counteract some of the fury of destructive forces or to lessen the damage they cause, if builders will but heed the lessons of previous destruction and build accordingly.

With respect to one of these destructive forces—earthquake action—the following account comments on the inertia and the carelessness of those responsible for building in areas known to be at high risk.

In 1798, Spallanzani, an Italian traveler visiting Messina, which had been completely destroyed in 1783, wrote down as good a rule for earthquake-proof structures as I have ever read. He said that in order to meet the horizontal thrust directed at the base of a structure, it was necessary either to provide that the entire structure move as a unit under the thrust, or that it have elasticity enough to carry the thrust from its own center of gravity when the shock came. He advised against building structures more than two stories high (at that time of course the steel structures of today were not known). The brick buildings of that day and those of stone above two stories in height he knew would be dangerous in the severe earthquakes that visit the Calabrian Straits. He also recognized the increased danger to all structures erected upon the sandy shore. He then gave plain warning to those who should rebuild the city of Messina that certain building rules must be observed. The city of Messina has since been rebuilt and again destroyed, and it is now being rebuilt for the third time. . . . I venture to say that the structures of the third rebuilding will differ little from those which were in the mind of Spallanzani and against which he warned.

The account continues with an updating of the tendency to ignore the clear warnings of past experience:

After the great earthquake [of San Francisco] in 1906, the city build-ing code was revised to insure an increased wall strength through which to meet horizontal thrusts. There was no method then known to accomplish this except in terms of wind-load, and so the wind-load specification was raised in 1907 from 15 lb. to 30 lb. per sq. ft. In 1925, however, it is rather curious to note that without anybody being able to tell just when, why or how, the wind-load had somehow found its level at 15 lb. again. In addition to that, the allowable limit of maximum load for structural steel had also been increased in the meantime 12½ per cent, so that San Francisco, on that day of our visit last summer, was less well prepared to meet another shock of severity such as it had once been through, than it was in 1906. . . .[2]

Failure from human causes

A much more constant and common category of failure in build-ing construction consists of man-made predicaments, the result of misjudging the behavior of materials or miscalculating the degree of strain and stress that a building may undergo in the normal course of events. These problems include inadequate foundations, insufficient bracing against wind pressure, and unsatisfactory framework for meeting the structural requirements for strength and stability. Failure may result from vibration, caused by the ring-ing of bells in a lofty tower[3] or by the rhythmic tread of a military detachment (which contributed, along with the blasts of the priests' trumpets and the great shoutings of the Israelites, to the destruc-tion of the walls of Jericho).[4] Structures may collapse from the over-loading of walls and foundations due to the addition of stories they were not originally designed to receive.[5] Quite adequately designed structures may collapse because of inferior materials, as in the case of the original choir of Beauvais Cathedral whose failure was at least partly due to the poor quality of the stone that could not take the compressive loads of the lofty superstructure.[6] With respect to more universal conditions, too casual and infrequent maintenance[7] may result in failure where weathering, rusting, or rotting has been allowed to proceed unchecked,[8] where serious cracks or fissures in the fabric of the building have been ignored,[9] and where periodic cycles of expansion and contraction have weakened the fabric through metallic fatigue or the disintegration of proper adhesion between the components of the masonry.[10] Sometimes, moreover, drastic failures occur while the building is under construction, as when formwork is removed prematurely, when the mortar or concrete is still green.[11] Finally, failure may follow from the culpable negligence, outright dishonesty, or fraudulent practices of the builder.

Maintenance, repair, and reconstruction

In building construction of all sorts, a very considerable effort over the years goes into repairs and reconstructions. In buildings made of organic materials—such as thatched roofs of grass or walls of plaited palm fronds—the materials themselves dry out, become brittle, and are no longer effective protection against rain or wind. Clay or mud plaster extends the life span of these materials, but such coatings spall off in time and need to be patched. Wood-attacking insects (the deathwatch beetle in England, for example[12]) have caused serious damage to the timberwork of many medieval roofs, including the unique octagon at Ely Cathedral. In Japan the most ancient wooden pagodas have been periodically taken down, when the age and weathering of the old materials have threatened their survival, and then rebuilt in new materials as exact replicas in every minute detail.[13] In the case of lofty structures, high winds sometimes topple exposed features[14] and bolts of lightning cause major damage that requires extensive repairs.[15] The scouring of rivers, causing shifts in the channel, sometimes endangers the integrity of pier foundations and abutments, necessitating deeper and more protected footings.[16] In wintertime ice builds up and sometimes breaks man-made structures, which then need to be repaired.[17] Both fire and earthquake may cause very extensive damage, imposing the need for comprehensive repair, if not total rebuilding.[18] Movements or shifts in the subsoil water table may compromise the stability of foundations and require underpinning to forestall subsidence.[19] Particularly in jungle areas, the insinuating roots of vines and even great trees constantly disintegrate stone buildings.[20] To a lesser extent, weeds lodging in crevices in the walls and moss forming on the roofs of buildings, must be periodically removed and the affected areas repaired.[21] In our own day atmospheric pollution is not only fouling the appearance of but actually disintegrating stonework.[22] Shingled roofs need replacing at least every twenty years; clapboarded walls need repainting every few years, with cracked or warped or rotted clapboards replaced as required.

Very extensive repairs and rebuildings come about not only in consequence of the forces of nature but by man's own destructiveness, as in the seemingly interminable recurrence of warfare. An enormous amount of money has been expended for reconstruction necessitated by the devastation of World Wars I and II, particularly in Europe. Even cosmetic repairs to these buildings usually involve the use of equipment—such as scaffolding of some sort—and are both time-consuming and costly.

Over the years, as social needs and institutions have changed, repairs to some buildings have involved shifts in the buildings' use or occupancy. A well-known Roman example is the central concourse of Diocletian's great Imperial Baths, which became a Christian church, Santa Maria degli Angeli, in the fifteenth century. Again, the thick-walled donjon was built as the place of impregnable refuge in the castles of the early Middle Ages; later, its very indestructibility brought about its use as a prison when times became more settled and life on a medieval barony more civilized. Were it not for such changes in use, most of the monumental buildings of former eras would long since have perished through neglect and ruin or through the removal of their materials to build entirely different structures.

Architectural cannibalism and many-strata sites

The use in new structures of secondhand building materials appropriated from older structures has been more widespread throughout the past than is generally realized. Hence, any history of building construction should mention, at least in passing, the perennial practice of architectural cannibalism. This practice has prevailed throughout the ages, especially in the case of masonry structures. So it is difficult to assess how many buildings have been obliterated or at least extensively pillaged by serving as convenient quarries for the extraction of stone that had already been prepared and shaped. Michelangelo's extensive "borrowing" from the exterior façade of the Coliseum for reerection in the courtyard of the Farnese Palace in Rome comes immediately to mind, as does the widespread reuse in medieval St. Albans Cathedral of the bricks that had served so extensively in the Roman habitations of that community, then known as Verulamium.[23] During and after the Middle Ages, the Arabs stripped the entire casing of limestone blocks from the Great Pyramid at Gizeh to build the walls and mosques of Cairo's Citadel.[24] Throughout Asia Minor and the Fertile Crescent the land is dotted with the massive ruins of once substantial dynasties whose building materials have been purloined over the centuries, some to be fashioned into the coarsely built dwellings of subsequent inhabitants.[25] A similar fate has befallen some of the stone-building former civilizations of India, Southeast Asia, and China.[26]

A more lethal kind of architectural cannibalism than the pirating of stone blocks was practiced at times in the past. In this obliterating kind of destruction the fine and costly marbles of many a provincial Roman city—like those of Rome itself—were fed to kilns by barbarian conquerors in order to extract the lime. It is reported that for a considerable stretch of time during the medieval period two lime kilns were active in the Roman Forum, burning innumerable marble statues as well as columns and other architectural features of marble buildings.[27] It is a revealing indication of the sumptuous richness and splendor of the Eternal City's architectural and sculptural patrimony that this wholesale destruction could continue for so many years after the plundering incursions of foreign armies, the internecine depredations of contending city factions, and the widespread appropriations of antique columns and capitals for Early Christian churches.

A somewhat special case of the reuse of stones that had formerly been incorporated in completed buildings occurred after the Persians sacked Athens in the fifth century B.C. There the Athenians hurriedly built the "long walls" to connect the city with its port, making use of whatever stone was available (including column drums) from the buildings destroyed by the invaders.[28]

Somewhat related to architectural cannibalism was the common practice, particularly in ancient times, of rebuilding communities in recurring sequence on sites that had proved to be viable and desirable. Wherever the primary building material was clay or mud, this practice led to many-layered villages—sometimes whole cities. The successive strata of ancient Troy represented the dilapidated remains of earlier settlements going back many centuries.

In prehistoric times, many-layered villages developed quite naturally from the physical characteristics of the *terramaricoli* communities in northern Italy. These consisted of a ditch and dike which enclosed a basin where the huts of the inhabitants were erected on piles. A detailed account of the layout and original construction of one of many such "stations" winds up with these observations:

The village was now complete, and the inhabitants, in the course of their domestic avocations, threw the refuse of food and other debris into the space below, probably by means of holes, which gradually accumulated until the space became completely filled up. When this stage was reached the people did not change their chosen site, but proceeded to erect a new palafitte above the old one. They elevated the dyke by extending its base, placed new contrafforte along its inner side superimposed on the older one, and thus converted the surface of the first platform into the base of the new one. They then repeated the operation of planting it with piles, and over these a new platform and huts were erected, which were occupied as before until the accumulation of debris again drove the inhabitants to construct a third habitable area at a still higher level.[29]

A recurrent cause for many-layered accretions in communities of the past was the rebuilding that took place after the convulsions of warfare. Here is a striking example.

Still a third reason [for the lack of inscriptions and artifacts] is to be noted in the fact that Jerusalem has so often been destroyed. To say nothing of earthquakes, of which there have been several, George Adam Smith enumerates about 40 different sieges, occupations and devastations which the Holy City has had to endure. [The Romans not only destroyed the city, but they also tried to wipe every evidence of its former location from the face of the earth, "even sowing the site with salt"]. Following many of these destructions were also many attempts to rebuild and restore that which had been so ruthlessly destroyed. It is said that no less than eight Jerusalems have been built, each upon the ruins of all that preceded, so that the original city was, because of all this, in some places at least 100 feet below the streets of today. . . .[30]

The persistence of tradition in building

Tradition in native practices and customs has always been a dominant and very powerful force among peoples and cultures in former times. Innumerable examples come to mind, embracing language and its local dialects, dress and ornament, food and its preparation, social relationships—in fact, all those characteristics of belief and conduct, of attitude and habit, that particularize each human culture and distinguish one tribe or people from another.[31] Building has been no exception. It too has quite universally shown its own adherence to time-honored custom, and even more strongly so, perhaps, because of its constant and highly visible physical presence.

There have been, of course, significant breakthroughs from time to time; but most (as far as public acceptance is concerned) have been gradual and incremental rather than sudden and spectacular. Colored glass, for example, was produced and applied in tiny pieces to small, infrequent perforations in thick walls many centuries before the extensive, resplendent achievements of thirteenth-century stained-glass windows were created.[32] Again, the cantilever principle was utilized in native Himalayan bridges in stepped, overlapping projections of timber beams centuries before steel made possible the astonishing triumphs of the Firth of Forth and the Quebec bridges.[33] But at the very least, where change has indeed occurred, the record indicates that man has often taken a long time to accept innovation, to come to terms with and adopt practices, however advantageous, that defy conservative tradition and local custom. Until quite recently, even in the Western world, the building industry has reputedly been one of the most conservative businesses, least subject to progressive practices, least disposed to abandon traditional methods. In the past this persistent conservatism generally accounted for continuity in the life style of a people, even in the face of hostile invasion, constant warfare, or grinding exploitation. It gave to the inhabitants, perhaps quite unconsciously, an indispensable sense of community, participation, and shared identity.

It is important, then, to try to retrieve credible information on the construction methods and building techniques of the past. For the traditional native crafts and processes represented stable usages and time-honored practices. It is clear that they indicated an accepted and viable way of adjusting to the climate and of meeting the requirements of living in a particular community. Wherever these established practices had time to develop independently, they were perfected in terms of the materials employed, the tools developed to obtain, prepare, and fashion them, and the procedures followed in their assemblage or erection. The various steps and operations adopted in customary building operations were therefore recognized by the whole community. That is, each culture had one "style" of building, one way of creating a habitation or a temple, a storehouse or a means of defense. With tools, materials, and physical needs in common, the members of every native community in former times produced common results in the sphere of building activities. These shared building products identified and defined all such communities and their life style, both physically and visually. Certainly among what in modern times have been called "underdeveloped peoples," these indexes of sustained differentiation are clearly evident in the building forms they followed and the practices they perpetuated.

4

Thousands of human lives and millions of dollars' worth of property have been sacrificed by the criminal folly of erecting unsafe or defective buildings. So long as those in authority permit such buildings to be erected, neither life nor property can be safe. . . .[1]

Jerry-Building and the Unending Quest for Standards of Safety

Jerry-building may be defined as shoddy practices that result in unsafe or dangerously substandard structures, that flout existing building regulations by substituting faulty or inferior materials or by utilizing adulterated, damaged, inadequate or defective components, or that are the consequence of inept or incompetent workmanship. As no systematic coverage of this subject has ever found its way into print, there are only indirect and partial sources that reveal some idea of the nature and extent of jerry-building practices, despite their existence throughout the world and throughout history.

With respect to the past, building regulations or bylaws provide one source of information in standards that imply the existence of undesirable practices. Another source is the assessments that have now and then been made of the causes of a structure's collapse, particularly as a result of earthquakes. Occasionally, to be sure, there are even direct accounts that report on some specific instance of jerry-building practices.

Code compliance through laws, rituals, and self-policing standards

Apparently it is only in strongly organized and firmly established civilizations—and probably only in those dominated by the complexities of city culture—that building regulations were formulated in legalistic terms and written down. As centers of urban civilizations, Egypt, Rome, and medieval London, for example, had numerous building regulations that ostensibly assured good practices in building construction.[2] Instances of poor construction practices were penalized to prevent future abuses that were recognized as endangering the populace.[3]

In fact, some degree of control over building practices has been considered indispensable from very early times. Thus there are legal sanctions and penalties against malpractices with respect to building construction in the most ancient surviving code of laws: that of Hammurabi, king of Babylonia, dating from about 2250 B.C. Following are some of the paragraphs of this code that address the inadequate or unsafe construction of both buildings and ships:

#229: If a builder builds a house for anyone and does not complete it firmly, and the house that he has built collapses and kills the owner, then the builder shall be put to death.

#232: If it destroys property, he is to make good all that has been destroyed and, because he has not carried out finally the building of the house [contracted to be] built by him, so that it collapses, he is to build up the collapsed part and furnish his own materials therefor.

#233: If a building master builds a house for anyone and he has not carried out completely [his undertaking], and the wall threatens to fall, the builder is to make the wall firm out of his own money.

#236: If a shipbuilder builds a ship for anyone and does not make it strong, and the ship sails during that year [upon a journey] and suffers injury [by reason of its faulty construction], the shipbuilder shall take the ship apart and rebuild it firmly out of his own materials; and he shall build a firm ship for the shipowner.[4]

Other legislation covered by the Hammurabi Code reveals characteristics of life in very ancient Babylonia that somewhat relate to the matters under discussion. For example, the code designates penalties for anyone neglecting to keep his irrigation dike in good repair against flooding his neighbor's land (paragraphs 53, 55, and 56). It lists the rate of proper wages to be paid to the potter, tailor, carpenter, ropemaker, and mason. And it prescribes the amount of the fines to be levied for stealing from a field a water wheel, a dipping bucket, or a plow and for cutting wood on another's property.

One of the ways in which poor construction was guarded against, particularly in the case of important public buildings, was to specify exactly and in minute detail how such buildings were to be constructed and to enforce the prescribed execution of the work by accompanying it, step by step, with a mandatory series of rituals. The most elaborate protocol of this sort was worked out centuries ago in India and religiously adhered to. Thus in the building of Hindu temples, the texts enjoined such prescriptions as the depth of the foundation pit, the layers of different materials that went into it, their thickness, the way and time that they were wetted down and/or tamped (by trodding elephants!), and the level at which the masonry proper began. Similarly,

Detailed prescriptions are given how to make good baked bricks. . . . For instance, . . . soil free from gravel, stones, roots, bones and clods should be selected, having fine sand of uniform colour and pleasant to touch. First one should throw a lump of earth into knee-deep water, and then stir and knead it repeatedly forty times with one's feet. One should wet it with waters of pine, mango and tree bark and the water of the three fruits and go on kneading it for a month. Then the bricks . . . should be thoroughly dried and then evenly baked; after an interval of 1, 2, 3 or 4 months they should be thrown into water, by an expert; thereafter they should be taken out of the water and dried completely, and then used in the desired undertaking. The bricks must be freshly made and all the other building materials too must be hewn or quarried in due time, and used exclusively for the building for which they are destined.[5]

Complicated and ever-present ritualistic formulas (by which the proper procedures and operations were assured at every step) are particularly noteworthy in the practices of the ancient Egyptians.

The building of an Egyptian temple involved an elaborate series of ceremonies. . . . By Ptolemaic times, when the king and his priests decided to build a temple, they consulted the "Book of Foundations of Temples." . . . Every important Egyptian temple had its archives in which were preserved the instructions and precedents of those who had gone before. . . . These formulas were rigidly observed because the priests, at least, demanded that their buildings should conform with regulations laid down at the earliest times. . . .[6]

In the case of less sophisticated, less complex cultures, the material evidence of their buildings makes clear that they, too, have always recognized and adhered to a body of regulations governing activities, operations, and conduct (including building practices). These laws are nonetheless binding—and probably even more so—for being sanctioned by custom rather than by written legal statute. Where the natives of a vernacular culture have built in a shoddy or slovenly fashion (which tends to be a relatively rare occurrence), they have compromised their own living accommodations or means of livelihood and have therefore exposed themselves to discomfort and communal disgrace. In general, the inveterate mores of the tribe, through sanctions and taboos, act powerfully to assure the policing of the community's traditional forms and standards.[7]

As a rule, then, urban areas were more susceptible to jerry-building practices throughout the past than were rural or other nonurban localities. This was undoubtedly so because the crowded conditions of cities and large towns engendered pressure from an expanding population for physical growth—both vertical and horizontal. Concomitantly, building contractors were tempted to realize quick profits at the expense of both safety and long-term durability.

In the past, at least, human habitations and other structures erected in nonurban localities were generally substantially built. Instance, for example, the time-defying granite farmhouses of northern Portugal; the traditional squared-log habitations of Sweden, the Balkans, and Switzerland; the corbelled stone *trulli* of southeastern Italy;[8] the solidly built, eighteenth-century Dutch barns of eastern New York State.[9] Undoubtedly a major reason why these and other vernacular structures were so well built was that they were constructed by local artisans—probably in part by the owner himself. The owner may not have been a trained carpenter and/or mason, but he certainly would have been accustomed to working with his hands. He would therefore have recognized quality in craftsmanship and have known from direct, painstaking experience that the only way to do a job was responsibly and properly, for posterity as well as for himself.[10]

Shoddy building practices: poor workmanship and inferior materials

Consequently, the representative examples of dangerous or shoddy building practices that follow are generally of the sort perpetrated by professional contractors rather than by nonspecialized members of the community undertaking their own building operations. Most of these examples involve masonry construction and date from relatively modern times. Significantly enough, the first of these accounts was written by a practicing building contractor. He may not have written very well, but he had firsthand experience with the distinction between quality and poor workmanship.

Stucco is among the oldest in some form or other of man's early attempt at the artistic. With all the possibilities and, despite the fact, that there can be found to this day portions of stucco in a good state of preservation after standing the wear of many centuries, there is no other form of building material that has fallen more into disrepute than stucco. This is especially so in the United States. The causes can be largely traced to the slipshod methods of procedure that has gradually crept into our building industry. Today the main point of view or achievement that is looked for is whether a contractor can complete in sixty days what should take three or four times longer. Short cuts are taken wherever they can; things that appear small in the successful completion of the work are sacrificed for time. The boy learning the business does not learn how good to do it but how fast to do it. The view he sees as a successful craftsman is not to do better and try to improve on the specifications for the work but just how much he can scamp and get away with.

Some contractors govern their cost by these methods and we get the results so often noticeable in modern construction, competition in price instead of competition in value or good work. The good contractor who tries to figure at a price that will permit good work, in many cases is forced out of business leaving the field open to the cheaper man and cheaper methods. The old school of craftsman had a different view; they tried to make their work masterpieces just as much so as the artist did his canvas. They wanted to look at it years afterward and be able to say "I did that", or "I worked on that", and feel the pride that comes from viewing a masterpiece.[11]

Scamping in the case of materials—that is, the production and/or use of inferior building units such as poorly fired bricks, crooked tiles, green lumber, and friable or insufficiently consolidated stone—has plagued architecture, and cheated the client, throughout the ages. In ancient Egypt, for example, sun-dried bricks were customarily made with straw as a binder; omitting the straw produced bricks of inferior quality.[12] Elsewhere, kiln-baked bricks that had been insufficiently fired rapidly deteriorated, becoming a friable clay when exposed to cycles of heat and cold and alternating periods of moisture and dryness.

Sometimes jerry-building results from the use of irregular and poor-quality roofing tiles—a particularly unfortunate circumstance as the roof is always such a vulnerable part of any structure. The following account reports on this situation in England in the later Middle Ages:

During the fifteenth century complaints were made of the lack of uniformity in the size, and still more in the quality, of the tiles. It was said that many of the tiles then being produced would last only four or five years instead of forty or fifty, and this is borne out by many series of manorial accounts, which show that a surprising amount of tiling repairs had to be carried out every year on the farm buildings. To remedy these defects, an Act was passed in 1477 regulating the process of manufacture and the size of the products. . . . In 1488 John Goldray of Caversham agreed to supply 24,000 tiles for Thomas Englefield's new buildings at Englefield, such tiles to be "of the best, and that he shall deliver hym no crokyd tyle, crop tyle nor grounde tyle," every tile "to be at the lest of the leynth of xj inche, of brede vij inche, and of thyknesse iiij quarter of an inche at the lest. . . ."[13]

In fact, the improper preparation of building materials and their ingredients—as in the case of mortar—is a prevalent factor in jerry-building, negating what may otherwise be skillful work. A case in point:

There are several varieties of sandstone; the most common has a yellow or ferruginous tinge,—the layers are of sufficient thickness for all the masonry on the whole line of road, and for this purpose it has been used in the numerous bridges, culverts and embankments, which are constructed with skill; but the cement has entirely failed, owing probably to substituting loam for sand, which appears to be rare in these regions; I have never been able to discover a pebble, or a handful of silex, except in the beds of water courses, or that which is coherent in the sandstone, on any of these mountains,—the soil being a fine friable loam. The parapet walls of all these constructions exhibit a mortifying appearance of dilapidation, they are all fast crumbling, some already even with the pavement, and fatal accidents may soon be expected to follow. . . .[14]

Of course, proper maintenance is constantly required for the safe and useful life of any building, particularly with respect to those features—such as parapets—that are most exposed to the weather. But pointing the mortar joints and keeping them in repair would not have sufficed in this case. The malignancy was too deep-seated to be overcome or corrected by a surface treatment; only demolition and rebuilding with proper mortar could have corrected the problem.

The same is true of jerry-built timber construction. If the wood has not been adequately cured and seasoned before its incorporation in a building, it is subject to warping, twisting, undue shrinkage, and/or splitting. No amount of subsequent treatment can restore the woodwork to its desired condition and proper form.

Unsafe building practices revealed in earthquake damage

Because destruction reveals conditions and features that might otherwise go undetected, probably the most comprehensive and detailed evidence of jerry-building is presented in on-the-spot reports of earthquake damage. A particularly revealing report of inadequate and shoddy building practices deals at length with the conditions and circumstances contributing to the seismic devastation that befell the port city of Palermo, Sicily during the night of September 1, 1726. This descriptive and analytic account covers the nature of the alluvial soils that irregularly overlie a soft and poorly weathering stone. These conditions made for very unstable foundations but were nonetheless widely and irresponsibly used to support even four- and five-story buildings.[15]

Another earthquake report—also from Italy—records the conditions and the damage sustained from a temblor that occurred some eighty-five years later. This account touches upon many of the points we have been discussing with respect to poor materials and practices in building construction.

The conditions which made the catastrophe so great were the geological features on the one hand, and the state of the buildings on the other. . . . With regard to the buildings, . . . the foundations were bad, and the construction of the worst kind. The houses were much too high, and the roofs so built as actually to press the walls away from them. After the great earthquake of 1783, it was duly recognized that *the buildings must be low, of one story if possible, and they were so constructed, but as the years went on and the population increased, stories were added one after another, even to five stories, while the retaining walls were not strengthened in proportion. . . . The materials were faulty, the smooth round pebbles from the alluvium being used, and these offered no grip to the plaster. The mortar was inferior and without cohesion. The façade walls were not tied to the lateral walls but merely leant against them, and so with the partitions. Nothing was securely riveted to anything else. All the characteristics of lazy, happy-go-lucky jerry-building are in evidence. Moreover the cracks made by old earthquakes were simply plastered over, and the walls built upon as if they were sound. One house there was, that of Prof. Camerari, which remained intact amidst the surrounding devastation. It was scientifically built of good materials. . . .*[16]*

The persistence of jerry-building

Jerry-building has been with us for a long, long time and, most likely, will be a fact of architectural life for a long time still to come. Its practice continues despite the modern proliferation of all kinds of building bylaws, zoning ordinances, and building codes at the local, municipal, state, regional, and national levels.[17] Added to which, builders must secure building permits before construction begins and, in many cases, submit to periodic building inspections thereafter. This proliferation of ordinances is undoubtedly inevitable as the components of building—layouts, construction, equipment, services, and the interdependence of buildings—become more highly complex and specialized.

Throughout the past, and continuing at an accelerating rate, a myriad of buildings have been constructed worldwide, during periods of slack activity as well as in eras of exceptionally creative building productivity. Normal mortality, "acts of God," or willful destruction by man aside, many of these buildings—particularly the ordinary or run-of-the mill ones—have collapsed or been torn down as hazardous and unfit for use. There is, of course, no telling how many jerry-built structures have perished due to poor construction, but their numbers must be legion. The wonder is, it would seem, that so many buildings were successfully achieved and served a useful life—that so many could survive as long as they did. Some, after many centuries, survive still. They are a heartening testimonial indeed—despite all the transient and exploitative jerry-building that has occurred—to the predominance and persistence of integrity in skill and craftsmanship down through the ages.[18]

5

Process and outcome are intimately related. The logic of the approach may be a greater challenge than the specific conclusion. And the exhilaration of deducing a well-conceived course of action may outweigh the satisfaction of completion.[1]

Prior Planning and the Order and Sequence of Building Operations

One generally thinks of building construction as comprising exclusively those activities of assemblage and erection that take place at the building site. To be sure, the realization of a building is the whole point of the undertaking. But the conspicuous and sometimes dramatic operations at the site are the culmination, the end product, of a great deal of prior planning. Moreover, much unapparent but indispensable activity continues to transpire during the fabrication of the building, both at the site and elsewhere.

The key words that apply to this complex total undertaking—at least for buildings of substantial size and importance—are preparation and logistics. As a term usually associated with the military, logistics has been defined as the procurement, distribution, maintenance, and replacement of material and personnel. In construction, for example, equipment, materials, and subassemblages must be brought to the site and incorporated into the building as the work progresses. Obviously, the coordination and timing of the several phases of building can be of major significance. In any case their superintendence requires effective administrative skills based on a thorough and comprehensive knowledge of the work.

Preparation before construction

Preliminary planning was of course essential whenever permanent buildings of large size and complexity were contemplated. But even quite modest buildings, as often as not, required organization prior to actual construction. Although not ordinarily within the province of the builder, the components of physical planning—surveys, site selection, and overall layouts—nonetheless constituted essential preparatory steps in the total process of building. So it seems appropriate to comment on one or two significant examples of each from previous eras.

The layout and grading of aqueducts in mountainous terrain, which required special instruments for very precise measurements up and over rugged territory, was throughout the past a large and important category of surveying.[2] It was the necessary prelude to tunneling operations through intervening peaks. It was also required for erecting transits across valleys, where the slightly sloping conduit was carried on long files of masonry arches, with pressure towers at strategic points to effect the flow of water through inverted syphons. Though such surveys were doubtless directed by an engineer, the actual field work was done by technicians under the supervision of a contractor, himself usually trained and experienced in engineering.

Surveying was also commonly practiced in long-settled, urban civilizations where property boundaries had to be established and recorded. It was one of the recurring official duties of the Egyptian pharaohs because the annual inundation of the Nile displaced or obliterated many of the previous year's markers.[3] For the Romans, in particular, land surveying was a concomitant of civilization and stability throughout their vast empire for both populated areas and the marvelous network of roads that linked every city and provincial prefecture to the capital.[4]

Site selection may have been determined by a number of quite disparate factors: defensibility for a medieval castle, the presence of a good harbor for a maritime community, the immunity from potential avalanches for an alpine village, or the proximity to an adequate and reliable well for a desert environment.

Early Christian churches followed a criterion thought to be absolutely vital to the choice of site. No longer confined to clandestine worship in such places as the catacombs, the early Christians built their churches on consecrated ground hallowed by the grave of a saint or martyr. The earliest churches were constructed exactly above the spot in the Roman catacombs where the bones of a martyr lay buried.[5] Later, because the catacombs were outside the city and hence at an inconvenient distance for daily attendance, the bones were reburied within the city and a church built on the newly consecrated ground. But as Christianity spread—north of the Alps into Gaul, for example, and westward into Spain—churches were needed in areas where no saint or martyr had yet died for the faith. So sometimes a group of monks set forth to scout the land. Selecting a desirable site for a church, they would secretly bury a sacred relic at the spot. When it was miraculously "discovered" some time later, a church had to be erected at the site. Because of this deep-seated veneration for relics, universal throughout the Christian world at the time, the famous shrine and pilgrimage church of Santiago de Compostela in far north-western Spain was built over the supposed grave of St. James. But, according to modern scholars, the widely traveled apostle never set foot in Spain.

A famous instance of an overall layout (the plot plan, in modern terminology) is the ninth-century plan for a monastery, preserved in the chapter library at St. Gall in Switzerland.[6] This unique manuscript-drawing, on vellum, is an annotated general scheme for an entire monastic complex. It encompasses around the monastic church—the heart of the community—all the essential offices and ancillary buildings and accommodations that made the religious community self-sufficient and self-contained: a chapter house and library, dormitories, a residence for the abbot, an infirmary, and a school for novices; an alms house and a hospice for travellers; a bake house, a brew house, kitchens, and storage cellars; workshops for a blacksmith, cutler, silversmith, cooper and other craftsmen; a fish pond, orchards, a vegetable and an herb garden; a grist mill; granges and accommodations for a variety of domesticated animals. Because the monks had to be isolated from the lay workers and the surrounding public—who were served by the establishment and who used some of its facilities—to plan the efficient location and interrelationship of these and other features took a good deal of careful thought. The St. Gall manuscript was an outcome of a council held near Aachen in A.D. 819. Worked out and proposed by a group of churchmen-administrators, it represents a specific project that was drawn up as an authorized standard or ideal plan for a large monastery, subject to modification as local needs might dictate.

Finance, materials, labor, and equipment

As we have noted, financing can be a critical factor in building. Consequently, very few of the great cathedrals of the Gothic era, for example, were achieved in one continuous campaign of building. Instead, the work often stretched out over a number of generations, with long pauses between periods of building activity occasioned by the need to raise money to continue. Canvassing of many sorts—local, regional, and even international—were resorted to, along with various indulgences granted by the ecclesiastical hierarchy.[7] The fees for one such indulgence, paid to the church for permission to eat butter during Lent, financed Rouen Cathedral's splendid northwestern tower, which was thereby nicknamed "The Butter Tower."

Determining what materials to use in a given building was a major step in planning its construction. The builder was concerned with not only the kind of stone, for example, that was chosen but also, in pragmatic terms, the location of its source, the reliability and sufficiency of its supply, the feasibility of its procurement, the methods and routes of its transportation to the building site, its quality, and its cost.

One of the most outstanding advantages of Roman concrete was the cheapness and abundant availability of its ingredients. Extensive beds of pozzuolana (a volcanic sand, superior as a natural cement to all others up to the manufactured Portland cement of the nineteenth century) lay just below the surface of the ground wherever volcanic action had occurred, including the site of the city of Rome itself. Moreover, great quantities of large aggregate were ready to hand in the form of sharp-edged stone fragments from ubiquitous stonecutters' yards as well as hard-burned brickbats and shards of broken, discarded pottery from the refuse heaps of communities large and small. Obviously, neither quarrying nor transporting these ingredients posed any significant difficulties.

In connection with the transportation of materials, it is worthy of note that many of the cathedrals in southern England were built largely of a fine-grained oolitic limestone. Desirable as a "freestone" (a stone that is virtually unstratified and can therefore be cut in any direction), it was quarried near Caen in Normandy and shipped across the Channel.[8] As for procurement, recall the pride and satisfaction with which Abbot Suger reported on his personal discovery of twelve huge oak trees that would provide the roof timbers of his enlarged church at St. Denis when his professional foresters could find none on their rounds.[9]

For major undertakings, an adequate and appropriate labor force had to be secured—from gangs of unskilled laborers to highly competent craftsmen, together with the foremen and overseers who coordinated and directed their activities. In ancient Egypt hordes of common workers (excavators, carriers, haulers) were impressed into the pharaoh's service from throughout the land when the annual inundation kept them from their normal pursuits. Captive peoples, such as the Jews in the time of Moses, were required to make bricks to build fortifications and to construct vast military storage depots on the country's eastern frontier.[10] The Romans often used troops stationed throughout their wide-flung empire for building projects. They sometimes undertook public works that were at once evidence of the Roman presence in the conquered provinces and confirmation of the substantial benefits of Roman rule. But most structures were of a military nature.[11] As for military victors, it is well known that, in the ruthless massacres he imposed upon the many cities he subdued in his widespread conquests, the Mogol Prince Tamberlaine gave strict orders to spare all craftsmen.[12]

The assemblage and coordination of equipment was an important and expensive aspect of the builder's preparation. Nonetheless, he could call upon a varied repertory of constructional aids and devices. For a particular job some of this equipment had to be specially constructed at the site: centering for a large arch, for example, or heavy shoring for a structure in imminent danger of collapse. Unwieldy assemblages such as these were usually discarded when they had fulfilled their purpose.[13]

But much of the builder's arsenal of essential equipment was salvaged and reused in subsequent situations. Capstans, windlasses, gins, and simple cranes as well as sledges, wagons, and boats of various sorts and capacities have all been employed throughout the past to move men and materials or to facilitate building construction in one way or another. Great wheels, for example, installed above the vaults in many lofty churches of the medieval period, were sometimes left in place after completion of the structure to facilitate repairs to the fabric.[14] Indeed, some of the builder's equipment (ropes and ladders in particular) outlived service on any one job. Thus scaffolding poles—both the upright standards and the horizontal ledgers—were customarily lashed together with ropes and could be readily disassembled for reuse elsewhere.

The order and sequence of construction operations

The many aspects of a major building project that had to be considered and planned for in advance were paralleled by the need for thorough coordination of the procedures adopted at the building site itself, once the work got under way. Clearly, the order and sequence of operations to be followed in the erection of a substantial building are often matters of the most critical significance. The more complex and sophisticated the building is, the more carefully the sequence of these building operations has to be worked out and adhered to.[15] Numerous considerations can be involved in arriving at the best—sometimes the only feasible—solution. Following are some of these considerations.

Often the envelope of the building (roof and walls) must be secured first so that the more delicate and perishable finish work within may go forward protected from delay and possible damage due to the weather. This is certainly true of buildings whose interior finishes would stand up to neither rain nor excessive heat and of those built in a cold climate where artificial heating is necessary and differentials of expansion and contraction in the finish materials have to be provided for. Obviously, the envelope must be immediately established for edifices of great size and elegance. But for buildings of modest size and much lower expectation of permanence, a simpler life style on the part of the inhabitants permits more rudimentary accommodation from the start, though the need for protection is still felt. Thus in parts of Africa, Southeast Asia, and many of the Pacific islands, the primary concern in house building is to provide a reliable roof as shelter and protection against torrential rains or excessive solar heat. Consequently, in certain areas of Africa when a family moves, a few friends and relatives carry the

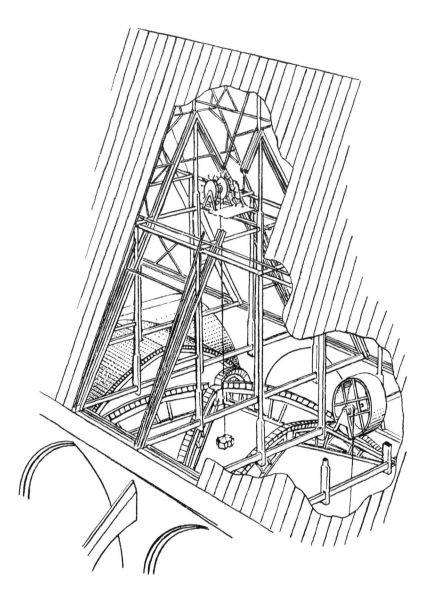

A great wheel device
for lifting heavy loads,
mounted on the tie
beams of a Gothic ca-
thedral roof. A heavy-
duty windlass appears
in the upper portion
of the roof structure.
(John Fitchen, *The
Construction of Gothic
Cathedrals,* 1961, fig.
51, p. 139.)

Lashed scaffolding in
rural Holland. (Photo-
graph by author.)

house roof, complete and intact, to another site where it is mounted
on a new series of posts quickly set up to receive it.[16] The walls—of
mud or matting or wattle-and-daub—can be fabricated independently, piecemeal, and in convenient installments by one or more
individuals. Here the roof is the dominant and most essential feature of the dwelling, and therefore its construction receives the first
and most careful attention.

    Unlike the classical Greeks whose finest temples (save for
the timber roof beams) were built exclusively of marble, the Romans customarily built in concrete, with only a veneer of costly
materials applied to the structural core.[17] In their complex, monumental edifices, the Romans' sequence of building operations was
affected by this clear-cut distinction between structural core and
decorative veneer, whether outside or in. Thus, the basic concrete
structure of the vast imperial baths, for example, was constructed
in a single continuous campaign of building; that is to say, the massive carcass was erected in its entirety before any decoration was
applied. This was not done just to isolate enclosed space from the
weather. By differentiating core from veneer, the materials could be
exploited to their maximum advantage and effectiveness, for the

Ressauts in central
concourse of Roman
thermae. (Eugène Em-
manuel Viollet-le-Duc,
Discourses on Ar-
chitecture, vol. 1,
trans. by Benjamin
Bucknall, 1959, fig. 4,
facing p. 128.)

structural bulk of the building on the one hand and for its surface treatment on the other. Any shrinkage or settlement in the former would have taken place before it could injure or fracture the latter. Thus, as is evident in the Basilica Nova of Maxentius or Constantine and in the ruins of the Baths of Caracalla, the cores of the entablature ressauts (the projecting architectural features at and just above the springs of the groin vaults) in the great central concourse were of concrete, built integrally with the rest of the structure.[18] Only much later were the huge marble columns eased into place beneath these deep structural corbels. As we can still see in the central concourse of the Baths of Diocletian—long since converted into a Christian church, the columns *appear* to support the vaults. But in reality they are non-load-bearing elements and so never in danger of fracture from the enormous weight of the concrete vaults they appear to carry.

Primarily, however, the distinction between core and veneer allowed the entire structure to be built without having any of the work contingent on fragile installations or delayed because of the uncertain shipment from afar of costly imported finish materials. Moreover, the building could be subsequently finished, outside and in, with the degree of opulence—whether a sheathing of exotic marble slabs, mosaic work, or marble-dust stucco—warranted by the condition of the imperial treasury at the time or the political stability and involvement of the state itself.

Adapting to specific conditions

Sometimes the order and sequence of building operations, particularly in major alterations or rebuildings, was a matter not of practical tactics or procedures in themselves but of occupancy requirements. In the erection of Glasgow Cathedral's double choir, for example, the first portion of the new work to be built was a shrine to house the bones of the local saint and to accommodate services in his honor, as set forth in this account.

When it was decided to pull down what had been built of Jocelin's church and to erect a new cathedral on the site, it was necessary, first of all, that a resting-place should be provided for the bones of Saint Kentigern—"a house of small magnitude" where might be "performed daily over his holy body, masses together with the other services." The plans of Walter's building having been drawn, it was arranged that a portion of the structure should be devoted to this purpose. A section of the south aisle of the new building having been selected, a corner of the old choir was pulled down, and the southwest compartment of the new crypt was constructed in its place. This small chapel, for such it was to be during the erection of the new choir, was designed as part of the south aisle of the lower church, and was vaulted and roofed over at the level of the choir floor. An altar was erected against the east wall, and beneath this altar the relics of the saint were reverently laid. When these had been conveyed with due ceremonial to their appointed temporary resting-place the remainder of Jocelin's choir could be pulled down, and the construction of the new edifice proceeded with as a whole. . . . On the completion of the vaulting of the middle compartment, about 1260, the relics of the saint would be removed to their permanent resting-place in the middle of the crypt, the wall at the back of the arched recess taken down, and the temporary altar cut through, so that the chapel became part of the south aisle of the lower church for which it had been designed. . . .[19]

The order and sequence of building operations relied, too, on the availability of the work force. Here is a partial explanation of how stringent this determinant could be in the case of a pioneer barn raising in colonial America.

Because his neighbors were often so far removed from his farmstead, and because they themselves were as busy as he in the struggle of agricultural pioneering, a farmer had to rely largely on himself; that is, on his own industry and that of his servant. Laborers were few and hard to come by. Moreover, one farmer could not expect the help of others who were quite as occupied and as hard working as he, except in special circumstances such as a barn raising. Even here, however, there was a stringent limitation on the amount of time he could ask his neighbors to give. So he had to have all in readiness before they arrived to help him. The trees would have been felled, the logs cured, and then snaked to the site; so much, he could have managed himself. But unless the farmer also happened to be a skilled carpenter, the shaping of the timbers and the cutting of the mortices in accordance with a carefully laid out plan would have been the work of a professional and experienced carpenter. . . . The preparation of the timbers and their test assembling would have been done by the carpenter, along with whatever assistance the farmer was competent to give. At the start of actual construction, too, the carpenter's direction, at least, would have been essential when the foundation stones were dragged in and set firmly in place. And this same professional direction would have been required during the heavy but precise work of assembling the framework of sills on top of these accurately leveled foundation stones. But at this point both the carpenter's direction and the toil of the farmer would have come to a standstill without the help of additional hands: a considerable number of men who were needed for the operation of raising the heavy

H-frames, and of setting the purlin-plates. In what took place there-
after, as we will see, the rest of the barn's erection—even including
the roof construction—could have been handled by the farmer and
his servant, plus either the carpenter or a competent hired man.

So it is clear that both the ordering of the work and, much
more significantly, the very structural system itself, were pervasively
affected (at least in pioneering situations) by the necessity to concen-
trate all group activity with respect to the barn's erection into the
shortest possible period of time: two days at most, and perhaps only
one long day, from dawn to dusk, in most cases. . . .[20]

Sometimes the need to prevent one part of the work from
interfering with the introduction or emplacement of another part
determined the order and sequence of building operations. In ancient Egypt a fifty-ton block of granite (ultimately used as a plug to
bar entrance to the pharaoh's tomb chamber) had to be propped up,
out of the way, until the pharaoh's body in its stone sarcophagus
had been brought in and all other work on the king's chamber had
been accomplished.[21]

Providing access for materials

One of the commonest considerations when planning the order and
sequence of operations was the need for convenient access of materials to the work in hand. The following account is a carefully rea-
soned reconstruction and detective-like disclosure of such problems
encountered in the erection of Glasgow Cathedral's double choir.

As the walls were almost always built from the inside, it was neces-
sary that the heavier stones should be wheeled into the building on
the level of the ground. The absence of heavy scaffolding and of far-
reaching cranes made it imperative that they should be brought as
nearly as possible under the position which they were to occupy on
the walls, and the appliances at the disposal of the builders required
that they should be hoisted vertically. The process implied a roadway
into the interior of the building; it required that the stones should be
wheeled in by this roadway on such hand-carts as that figured by
Viollet-le-Duc [vol. 5, p. 218, fig. 6], and that they should be hoisted
directly into their places on the walls. It is obvious that to do this in
the case of our Cathedral the middle vaulting had to be delayed until
after the clerestory walls were built. . . .

A glance at the plan of the lower building will show that no
opening of sufficient width could have been formed between the pil-
lars of the north and south aisles. Although only the major pillars of
the lower aisles are beneath the pillars of the choir, the smaller inter-
mediate pillars, and the arches which they carry, are necessary to the

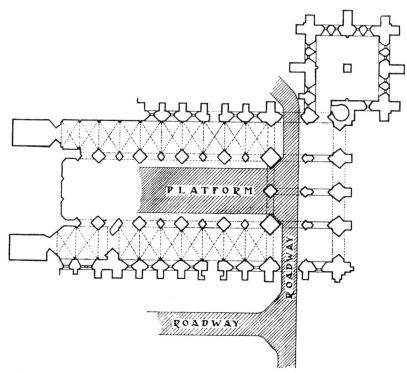

Plan of access road-
way during construc-
tion operations.
(Thomas Watson, *The
Double Choir of Glas-
gow Cathedral,* 1901,
fig. 46, p. 124.)

stability of the structure, and the whole range must have been built at one time. The width between the bases of the pillars at each side of the middle compartment is only 3' -6", and this is manifestly insufficient for the larger loads or even the ordinary traffic of the building. The openings between the eastern pillars, however, offer a clear width of 6' -6" between the bases, and form the only possible access for the hand-carts or other vehicles on which the heavier material had to be conveyed into the middle of the building. The chief part of the dressed stone for the clerestory walls must therefore have been brought in through the two large archways under the eastern gable and by way of the eastern aisle. It follows also that a roadway must have been formed from the exterior of the building into the eastern aisle, and for this purpose one or more wide openings must have been left in the outer walls. This could only have been done by leaving unbuilt the middle piers of the two-light windows of the eastern aisle or of the eastern chapels. . . .

It seems probable that the roadway was carried right through the eastern aisle of the lower church, branching off at right angles into the platform of construction of the middle compartment. By this route the heavier loads could be wheeled in from either side of the building and brought right under any part of the clerestory walls, the stones could be grappled by the lewis and hoisted vertically from the trolley by means of a windlass, and finally settled in their places with the assistance of a short crane or jib. . . .

The constructive problem which the builders of our Cathedral had to solve was altogether exceptional in respect that the choir consisted of an upper and a lower church, the latter being arched over with light vaulting and rising to a considerable height above the ground, and the former having a clerestory wholly within the aisle walls, in the construction of which comparatively large stones were employed. . . .[22]

Accommodating the exigencies of installation

Finally, the numerous and varied schemes imposed upon the order and sequence of building operations were sometimes due to considerations that involved the nature of the structural system and its connections. At other times, or even at the same time, they were the result of spatial requirements for installing or assembling building components—maneuvering and hoisting into place heavy blocks, for example. Thus for a New World Dutch barn (after the ground-floor platform was in place) the first step was to raise the central core; that is, to rear the bents of successive H-frames that defined the wide middle aisle of the threshing floor.[23] Greek tem-

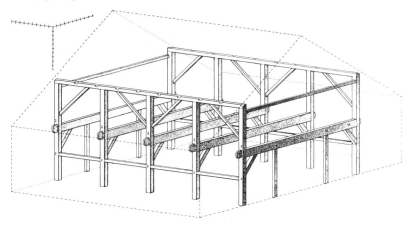

Central core of barn structure. (John Fitchen, *The New World Dutch Barn,* 1968, fig. 13, p. 130.)

ples, on the other hand, were built from the outside in. Once the temple platform had been established, the outer periphery of columns was undertaken before any other portion of the superstructure was executed.[24] These contrasting sequences evolved in response to the nature of the building materials, the methods followed in their assemblage, and the fact that the largest and heaviest units were assembled first because of the space required for maneuvering them into position. In the barns, the big, unwieldy H-frames had to be assembled at the site, tilted up into position one by one, and linked to each other before attaching the side walls and roof whose stability depended on the security of the central core. In the temples, the heavy column drums and lintels had to be eased close in to their destined location, then raised and positioned with the greatest care and nicety before undertaking the much less demanding erection of the cella walls.

The mark of outstanding practitioners

All the circumstances cited here that determined the order and sequence of building operations could be duplicated in innumerable examples, with respect to both general considerations and specific details. It is small wonder, then, that the master builders needed such a comprehensive grasp of the totality of building operations in all their ramifying complexities. Outstanding among the great master builders of the past were Imhotep and Ineni in ancient Egypt, Ictinus and Callicrates for the Parthenon, the anonymous architect of the Roman Pantheon, Anthemius of Tralles and Isodorus of Miletus for Hagia Sophia, William of Sens for Westminster Abbey, Eudes de Montreuil for Beauvais Cathedral, and Brunelleschi for the dome of Florence Cathedral. These were truly the geniuses of their eras, the all-time giants of the building fraternity. To have achieved such exceptional preeminence, men of this calibre obviously had to have the most complete knowledge and mastery possible of every phase of their work: the economic, political, financial, and aesthetic. And, of course, they had to understand the structural and constructional considerations, which included thorough prior planning and the most careful attention to the order and sequence to be followed, step by step, in realizing their undertakings.

6

Buildings, like people, are subject to many stresses. If not taken care of, the patient dies; that is, the building collapses. But it is possible to forestall congenital infirmities through proper diagnosis and treatment, and to mitigate hazardous attacks via the timely medication of maintenance.[1]

Stresses in Buildings and the Problems They Raise

Any building of consequence—that is, any structure intended as permanent rather than temporary or transient—is subject to a multiplicity of stresses that must be anticipated and provided for. Whether in the past or in the present, this is an immutable fact of nature.

But it raises difficulties for those trying to determine the conditions and circumstances under which a variety of stresses affected buildings in past eras and the steps that were taken then to deal with them. Until the modern era, no records were kept of these matters. Indeed, it appears that keeping records of building stresses was a concept foreign to builders everywhere. Throughout the long centuries before accurate data were compiled on the properties and behavior of building materials, before scientific investigations were made of their performance in the ensemble of the structure, before testing equipment was thought of and developed, formulas were at best "rule of thumb." There were, to be sure, many rules and prescriptions for determining proportions and other aesthetic considerations.[2] But these were mostly based on geometric, compass-evolved ratios (to which the ancient and medieval builders were so committed) rather than on the accumulation, testing, and assessment of structural data and on the need to contain or counteract the various stresses to assure stability. Apparently only one account prior to the Renaissance addresses itself to computing one of the stresses in a building—in this case, rib vault thrusts.[3] So in the end the builder relied on experience, empirical appraisal, and judgment based on perceptive observation. The buildings that survive from past ages are eloquent testimonials to the validity and effectiveness of these qualifications.

Today, in considering the matter of stresses in buildings of former times, perhaps we can merely pursue the following procedure: identify and comment on the kinds and the nature of the stresses that act upon or in buildings; briefly cite modern instances of the steps taken to deal with these stresses; and, having noted the circumstances and examined the results, speculate on the successful solutions to stress-imposed problems in buildings of the past.

Dead and live loads

In a bridge, for example, the primary stresses are due to gravitational loads. To meet these stresses the structure must be strong enough to support both itself and the traffic on it. The weight of the structure, which is constant, is called the dead load; the traffic across the bridge, which is intermittent, is one of the so-called live loads.

But there are other live loads, some of which are at times critical factors in the security and the very existence of the work. Chief among these additional stresses, particularly in lofty structures, are those due to wind action. Whether relatively steady or in gusts, winds create potentially destructive forces of two kinds. Unlike gravitational loads that act vertically downward, wind loads act laterally and at times even upward, lifting a structure such as a roof off its supports or getting under and forcing upward a far-over-sailing canopy that shelters a grandstand. Laterally, the wind may blow against the structure from any point of the compass, causing direct pressure on the windward side and negative pressure or suction on the lee side, now from one angle, now from another.[4] Moreover, the wind often causes racking or twisting forces, as when it blows against a tree with more branches on one side than another or when it blows diagonally instead of directly against one of the faces of a building. Whatever the direction of the wind, such stresses have to be met in an assured fashion. Sufficiently strong and advantageously placed members must be framed into the structure to secure the roofs against all anticipated threats of dislocation. In medieval England, for example, the timber roofs of parish churches, guild halls, priory granges, and great halls in manor houses incorporated framing systems that resisted more than simple gravitational loads. Whether serving as sway bracing or as wind bracing, the timberwork complexes in that era were at once structurally effective and decoratively noteworthy.[5]

Aerodynamic oscillation

Vibration, though a result of various causes, is the other potentially destructive consequence of wind. Very massive, thick-walled buildings, such as those erected by the ancient Egyptians and Romans, largely absorbed these vibrational stresses, which were consequently ignored. But the more lofty, skeletal, and attenuated a structure was (a Gothic church, for example), the more vulnerable it was to these destructive forces and the more it needed assured and positive counteraction throughout.

All buildings are subject to movement in some degree and

Wind-tilted farmhouse
in upstate New York
showing undeformed
triangle of the gable,
below which all the
rectangular forms
have been racked into
parallelograms be-
cause of the complete
absence of diagonal
members. (Photograph
by Lee Brown Coye.)

hence can be called flexible in their resistance to vibration. Aerodynamic oscillation, or flutter, is the condition of resonant vibration in
which quite minor but sustained wind action builds up oscillations
in light-weight structures. Only in recent decades has this stress
been recognized as a very serious problem. Its prevalence today is a
consequence of using tensile structures based primarily on steel
cables, where the ratio of dead load to span is unprecedented and
quite phenomenal.[6] With a few exceptions, the problem of flutter
could safely be ignored in the past. For in general buildings were
not light-weight tensile structures but either rigid frames in timber
or more-or-less massive masonry assemblages of stone, brick, or
concrete.

One exception in former times was primitive suspension
bridges whose cables consisted of vines, withes, or even twisted

Heavy timber roof framing of a small brick-walled farm building at Berville-sur-Mer, Normandy. (Photograph by author.)

grasses. These oscillated and undulated not only from the passing traffic but also from the variable currents of air around them.[7] But not until the Gothic period—with its extremely attenuated cathedrals and their tall, slender spires, some fashioned in open tracery—did permanent, sophisticated buildings of stone raise the problem of flutter.[8] Like other stresses though, it was neither precisely identified at the time nor given a specific name by the designers who had to deal with its effects.

Shear stresses

Shear stresses—stresses that tend to force one part of a unit or a material past an adjacent part—must also be recognized and guarded against. Types of shear are punching or impact shear, where, for example, columns tend to perforate a continuous foundation slab on which they rest; transverse shear, where, for example, a girder supporting a concentrated load close to one of its ends tends to be forced down past its support; and longitudinal shear, where, for example, the upper portion of a loaded beam tends to rip at its ends by sliding along the beam's lower portion.

Timberwork is particularly vulnerable to longitudinal shearing stresses because wood is generally less resistant along the grain than across it. The following account explains this circumstance as applied to timber framing in the past.

Most species of timber are highly resistant to shear across the grain, but are notably less able to withstand this kind of stress in the longitudinal direction. Consequently, the connections that are subject to tension, in a framework of timbers, constitute areas of critical weakness and have to be supplemented or taken care of in some equivalent fashion elsewhere. Yet this property of vulnerability along the grain bestows a welcome advantage at the time the timbers are first fashioned from logs, by allowing the trunk of the felled tree to be split with wedges, longitudinally. Such a method of fashioning big timbers from ponderous logs obviously requires far less expenditure of effort than would the process of sawing them by hand; and therefore weakness in resistance to longitudinal shear was a distinct advantage in the past in the reduction of big logs to squared timbers.

However, this particular weakness is the source of the most critical deficiency in timber framing. *The defect stems from the fact that, although wood in its natural state (that is, in the living tree) is almost equally effective in its resistance to both compression and tension, it is impossible to utilize its full tension-resisting potential in man-made joints. An instance of this is demonstrated in a typical mortice-and-tenon joint. Here the tensional stress is transmitted from the tenon (which is only about one-third of the timber's area in cross-section) via a wooden pin (which bears against perhaps one-quarter of the tenon's cross-section). Thus only about one-twelfth of the timber's substance, in section, is actively engaged in resistance to tension. In contrast to this deficiency under tension, it should be noted that the* entire *cross-sectional area can be involved in resistance to compression, as in the bearing of a column's base.*

When a wood joint fails under tension, it does so by ripping out along the grain. . . . This action, as we have seen, follows the line of least resistance; namely, its weakness in resistance to longitudinal shear. This weakness can be ameliorated, however, by lengthening the tenon. *Such an expedient provides a very much increased area of resistance to longitudinal shear, making it unlikely that the pin or wedge will rip its way out through the end of the tenon.*[9]

Salwin Valley suspension bridge of liana cane and saplings. Guy lines strung from two upper levels of the tall, slanting saplings, right and left, to points out along the 125-foot span of the main cables, somewhat lessen their undulations and swaying. (George Forrest, "The Land of the Crossbow," *National Geographic* 21(1910): 138.)

Long tenons in roof
framing of eighteenth-
century church near
Stone Arabia, north of
Mohawk River, New
York State. (Photo-
graph by author.)

Partial loads and kinetic stresses

Two kinds of stresses most strongly affect—and can be most clearly
detected in—modern railway bridges. They are due to partial loadings, as when a locomotive stands upon a quarter of the span, leaving the rest of the bridge free of cars, and kinetic loadings, as when
the locomotive puts the train in motion, creating strong longitudinal forces in the bridge.

In the past, partial loads and the stresses they occasion were
encountered primarily during the course of a building's erection;
that is, when temporary installations or provisional features were
used to meet structural situations until permanent features or portions of the building were completed. A fairly universal case was
that of masonry arches. The individual wedge-shaped blocks that
form the arch (the voussoirs) required temporary support until the
arch was built up on either side and the keystone added, completing
the arch ring (the curving ensemble of voussoirs) and making the
structure self-supporting. The temporary support (the centering)
was usually of timber. The chief problem in its design was not so

much to make it strong enough to support its load of voussoirs but to make it rigid enough to prevent any deformation in its curvature. In the incremental process of building up the voussoirs from either side, the haunches (the midportion of the arch ring, right and left) tended to become depressed with the weight of the voussoirs, while the as yet unweighted crown (the highest part of the arch) tended to rise in compensation. Numerous instances of failure have been recorded where the stresses due to partial loading were not sufficiently taken into account nor adequately provided for in the design of the centering.[10]

In native structures, the problem of partial loading was encountered—though seldom taken care of—in some of the handicrafted suspension bridges of Andean South America, Africa, and Southeast Asia. Tie-down ropes from below could have stabilized the curve of the main cables and kept it from deforming radically as a traveler started across the bridge. The usual practice of omitting tie-downs resulted in a pedestrian walkway that undulated, swayed, and trembled alarmingly, as described in a westerner's encounter with a native suspension bridge in 1863.[11]

In the past, undoubtedly the most critical cases of kinetic stresses were encountered in the bell towers of English churches, due to "the peculiarly British forms of bell music known as change and round ringing, in both of which each bell must swing bodily through more than 360° each time it speaks." When such a bell is rung, the fourfold increase in downward force can be easily met by adequately strong walls, but the lateral force is dangerous and difficult to counteract in terms of structural supports. If the supports are loose or springy instead of rigid, "a one-ton bell hung direct from two supporting girders . . . could produce punches amounting perhaps to as much as twelve tons, first in one direction and then in the other, and the supporting girders would be acting precisely as battering-rams against the tower walls." Even with absolute rigidity, "it is still necessary to diminish the three-ton pushes to be expected from a one-ton bell. This is done by deflecting them diagonally downwards so that part of the force can be absorbed in the vertical plane in which the tower is strongest. . . ."[12]

Lateral thrust in arches

A perennial stress in masonry construction is encountered in all arch structures. Every true arch consists of wedge-shaped blocks. Because it is the property of wedges under load to press apart, these wedge-shaped blocks combine to create lateral thrusts, to right and left, that must be resisted, neutralized, and/or grounded. The voussoir action is constant; thus the Arabs have a saying, "An arch never sleeps." So the arch thrusts must be met permanently by one or a combination of the following schemes: abutting the arch directly, as with a salient buttress; weighting the pier from which the arch springs so that the line of pressure is bent downward in a more vertical direction by superincumbent loads;[13] neutralizing the thrusts by opposing them in series, as in arcades formed by a row of similar arches; and employing exposed tie rods of wood or metal that act as tension members to restrain the sides of the arch from spreading apart at or near the level of their springing.[14] Of these, the last is probably the simplest and most direct. But it is also the least satisfactory, not only aesthetically but because the tie rods are subject to rust or rot and hence may give way without warning unless constantly monitored and maintained in good repair.

An arch fails in ways other than spreading apart at its supports. These are a consequence of the fact that the thrusts do not act in a straight line downward to right and left but operate in the form of a catenary curve (a contour dictated by gravity rather than derived from abstract geometry). A catenary curve, being a nature-imposed form, is never a semicircle nor a pointed profile. But, although other shapes have been used from time to time, pointed arches were the rule throughout the Gothic era. Otherwise, the commonest contour for masonry arches has always been a semicircle, for both aesthetic reasons and constructional convenience. Yet for any functional arch to be stable and safe from collapse, the catenary curve (which represents the line of pressure) must stay within the confines of the arch ring.[15] If it passes outside—beyond the extrados or below the intrados—the arch will collapse inward or burst outward respectively. Such deformation in the curving line of voussoirs can generally be prevented by building up masonry spandrels (areas of ordinary walling to right and left of the arch from spring to crown) against the haunches of the arch. This is often done, for example, to provide a more-or-less level roadway above a river crossing or to embellish architecturally a commemorative gateway into a city. But where an arch is freestanding and unsurcharged with superimposed masonry, deformation is largely determined by the thickness of the arch ring. The less the shape of the arch conforms to a catenary curve, the thicker the arch ring needs to be to keep the arch from bursting at the haunches and rising at the crown.

Although based on the arch principle and subject to many of the same stresses that occur in simple arches, masonry domes are nonetheless different because they are three-dimensional space-structures. To be sure, a dome creates centrifugal outward and downward thrusts that must be taken care of. But unlike a simple

Thin masonry dome of
brick under construc-
tion in northeastern
Spain, without benefit
of formwork, 1959.
(Photograph by au-
thor.)

arch spanning between opposite supports, a dome is stable and self-
sustaining at each successive horizontal level of construction. Thus
construction could be—and often was—terminated at some intermediate level. For the voussoirs in each horizontal course, in tending to slide downward and inward on their sloping bed, interlock
naturally to form a complete and stable circumferential arch ring of
their own. By the same token, ordinary schemes of centering—such
as heavy timberwork supports in the actual erection of the dome—
could be entirely dispensed with in domes of modest span.[16]

A number of the commoner stresses that occur in masonry
buildings and the problems arising from them are noted and analyzed in the following circumstantial account of a specific structure.

*Failure of the substructure of the tower is primarily traceable to two
causes . . . A) Imperfect Design: 1) Spreading of the arches at their
springing, 2) Flattening of arch curves, thus neutralizing the keying,
and rendering the arch insecure, by the liability of the voussoirs to
fall out, 3) Thrusting of the vertical supporting piers under the tower
arches out of the perpendicular, and 4) Transmission of the thrusting force to all adjoining piers, arches and walls, throwing them out*

of the normal, stable condition, verticality; B) Imperfect Construc-
tion: . . . 1) the crushing of the wrought stone facings which form the
casing of the piers, 2) the bursting asunder or drawing of the bond-
ers, of the various members of which the piers are composed, 3) rents
or fissures of the vaulting generally.

   The most prolific causes of failure in buildings are generally
two: unequally yielding of foundation trenches, and uncompensated
thrusts, whether from roofs or arches. . . .[17]

Seismic forces and lightning strokes

Many studies of the effect of earthquakes on buildings have shown
that the most destructive seismic forces act horizontally, generally
in a compass direction but sometimes in a rotational or even centrifugal manner.[18] Acting horizontally rather than vertically, these
forces produce the stresses that all buildings, as normally designed,
are least able to withstand.[19] Here is a brief explanation of the
characteristics of earthquake shocks.

If a glass of jelly be turned into a dish and the dish shaken lightly,
relatively great action of the jelly will ensue. This behavior is illus-
trative of the effect of earthquake vibrations in firm and soft ground.
The wave amplitude in firm material may be increased several-fold if
the overlying ground be soft, spongy or marshy. . . .

The writer goes on to summarize the behavior of structures of various building materials in Japan under the test of earthquake and
fire in 1924. Here, in part, he describes the response of wooden
structures:

In the fire-swept areas all evidence was destroyed. Elsewhere the per-
formance was generally good. In Japanese houses where heavy tile
roofs were carried by light wall posts with little bracing, more or less
racking with consequent cracking of plaster ensued and, of course,
there were numerous collapses of buildings inadequately braced and
stiffened. The Japanese are skillful carpenters and their houses are
framed with mortise and tenon joints and wooden pins, etc. The
combination of great strength with light weight that is the inherent
character of wood, is most advantageous in structures subjected to
earthquake shocks. At the same time the problem of efficient joints
and connections becomes increasingly important.[20]

   One kind of stress that builders in the past found bafflingly
impossible to deal with effectively was produced by lightning
strokes. Apparently neither the Egyptians' pyramids nor their tall
obelisks were subject to this kind of sudden destructiveness, for the
perennially sunny skies of Egypt (at least upstream from the delta)
were rarely obscured by rain clouds and thunderstorms were com-

pletely foreign to the area. Throughout most of the world, however, lightning has been a deadly force.

Particularly susceptible to damage by lightning were the towers and spires of Gothic churches. The great height that these structures attained vulnerably exposed them to powerful electric charges. The contemporary chronicles recorded innumerable instances of serious structural damage from the impact of thunderbolts and from fires ignited by the fireball (most often set high up in well-nigh inaccessible spots).[21]

The builders of the Gothic era had no means whatsoever to prevent strokes of lightning from occurring. When they did occur, provisions for handling them were totally inadequate. The master masons and master carpenters knew that covering spires and roofs with slates (especially with sheets of lead) was effective protection against rain, but not the slightest guarantee of insulation against lightning—tending, rather, to invite it. Without knowing the electrical property of lightning, the medieval builders had no realistic, pragmatic alternative but to go along with the prevailing ecclesiastical faith in the prophylactic power of relics. So they topped their spires with hollow gilded crosses that contained revered objects, hoping thus to interdict the catastrophic effects of lightning upon the sacred edifice. Not until Ben Franklin's experiments in the eighteenth century, resulting in his invention of the lightning rod, was an effective, scientific solution to the problem devised (if not always properly or adequately installed).

Fatigue

Fatigue is one phenomenon in the life of buildings that has only recently become critical, due to the widespread use of metals in modern structures.[22] Yet it is not a totally new phenomenon, as anyone knows who has seen or heard a great tree come crashing down unexpectedly on an utterly windless day after withstanding years of cold and heat, rain and buffeting storms. Fatigue in building materials is very difficult to monitor or assess with accuracy once they have been incorporated into the fabric of the structure. Of course, a constantly pursued program of maintenance helps to reduce the onset of fatigue (painting metals to prevent rust; keeping timberwork members exposed to air but protected from dampness to prevent rot or insect damage). To be sure, these precautions only keep the structure as healthy as possible, giving it stamina to resist failure of *any* kind. They do not in themselves alleviate fatigue. For it involves constant repetition of stress, alternating back and forth, which ultimately leads to rupture and collapse.

Actually, the problem seldom arises in timber construction because other causes of deterioration, such as the depredations of the deathwatch beetle or of the termite, usually precede destruction by fatigue. However, with modern use of steel framing members, steel suspension cables, and monocoque aluminum structures (as in airplane bodies), fatigue has become a worrisome because not completely ascertainable phenomenon. It is apparent that the life expectancy of these structures is greatly determined by the nature, alternating direction, frequency, and intensity of the loads on them. But we can only guess the extent to which fatigue—rather than other factors—caused a building's demise. Probably because metal was not formerly a major structural material, and perhaps because at least buildings of historic importance are being preserved and cared for today, we lack records of whether or not fatigue has been a significant problem in the buildings of previous centuries.

The factor of safety

Nowadays, when assumptions as to the magnitude of different kinds of stresses are reduced to mathematical formulas and the application of these formulas are figured for each major member or condition, it is standard practice to increase the computed allowable stress on the member by a ratio known as a factor of safety.[23] This fraction, or additional ratio of resistance, is intended to take care of extraordinary strains or unforeseen combinations of forces such as momentarily violent gusts of wind against an exposed structure or unprecedentedly heavy accumulations of snow on a roof. It also covers variations in the quality of the building material, whether loose knots and shakes in timber or fissures and pockets of weakness or disintegration in stone. Throughout the long centuries before scientific testing produced trustworthy data, experience and empirical judgment had to suffice. Extant buildings that have survived the vicissitudes of many centuries make clear that they did. Obviously, the practical experience and perceptive judgment of master builders were accumulated by and transmitted through successive generations of superior practitioners who met the challenge with astonishing skill, resourcefulness and, at times, bravura. Sometimes their well-honed instinct for providing a factor of safety led the builders to make the diameter of marble columns much greater than the normal loads on them required, as in the case of the Parthenon's peristyle. The builders of the vast Imperial Baths of Rome ingeniously countered the enormous weight and potential thrusts of the large-span vaults, not by the huge, freestanding marble columns that were such conspicuous features of the interior concourse but by massive abutments that tended to go unnoticed because of their incorporation within the simple rectangular outline of the building.

Most remarkable of all—because most complex and interacting—were the multiple stresses that had to be recognized and accommodated, along with a judicious factor of safety, by the master builders of the Middle Ages. In the case of the great French Gothic cathedrals two extreme conditions forced the structure to become ever leaner and more attenuated—the urge for both maximum height and maximum window area, to create incandescent tapestries of jeweled light within a building that soared heavenward. The result was a veritable skeleton of stone. Consequently, working within stringent structural tolerances, the builders had to be sensitive to every phase, every kind and degree of stress. Thrust had to be balanced by opposing thrust. Force had to be met by counter force. Pressures had to be directed and channeled to areas where they could most effectively and securely be received and eventually grounded. All this work took place within a spare framework of stone members whose leanness was adjusted with great nicety to their structural function in the ensemble.[24] Never before had such accuracy of structural judgment been required in building. Never before had such exacting perception and precise practical competence been tested. To be sure, in view of the unprecedented problems of height and attenuation imposed by the overweening ambition of the medieval clergy, time and again the building's structural design exceeded the limits of safety, and parts or all of the church collapsed. But it is astonishing that so many of these structures—often the loftiest, most attenuated, most splendid, in fact—have substantially survived centuries of rigorous climate and weather and even the ravages of modern warfare. Their survival is a signal tribute to the consummate expertise of the master builders in recognizing the precise location and degree of the stresses acting upon and within the structure and to the accuracy with which these builders assigned a factor of safety in forestalling the critical effects of all but the most extraordinary forces.

Stresses during construction

Certain stresses and stress-inducing situations were of special concern to the builder in charge of the process of construction. From a practical standpoint, for example, the builder responsible for the erection of stone buildings had to contend with various stresses in the handling of very large, heavy units. In ancient Egypt, although the temple columns were customarily built up in courses each com-

Powerful flying buttresses at Narbonne
Cathedral, France.
(Photograph by James
Dickinson.)

Slender flying but-
tresses at Beauvais
Cathedral, France.
(Photograph by Allen
Fitchen.)

posed of many carefully fitted stones, the lintels were invariably
huge monoliths. Eighteen feet or more in length and weighing approximately sixty tons, they had to be positioned as much as sixty
feet above the ground level, spanning from column-top to column-
top. The lintels were too heavy to raise by block and tackle. Instead,
having filled the temple with a gradual accumulation of earth as
the columns rose (so that the work on them could be carried on at
successive "ground" levels), the builders hauled the huge lintels up
to their level of installation on long ramps. Normally the process
did not involve the use of rollers to ease the effort expended. If rollers were used, the builders ran the risk of letting the ponderous
blocks get out of hand in case the towing ropes broke or the rollers
became skewed, as they so easily could.[25] The builders took no
chances in moving and installing the great stones. They guarded
against anything that might suddenly jerk or unintentionally let
slip the lintel in transit, for fear of fracturing the huge stone.

Similar but even greater precautions were taken in the case
of obelisks—enormous granite monoliths up to nearly a hundred
feet in length. To quarry an obelisk, transport it two hundred or
more miles (mostly by water), and erect it upright in front of some
major temple was an extreme achievement in engineering. The

enormous expenditure of labor and the fabrication of adjunct equipment such as transport barges were part of the extraordinary precautions that the Egyptians took to protect the gigantic monolith in every phase of the months-long operations.

Thermal variation and shrinkage

Another very different kind of stress-related problem, encountered in permanent structures everywhere, involves changes in dimensions due to thermal variation.[26] Generally a seasonal phenomenon in which building materials expand in warm weather and contract in cold, it is a condition that cannot be ignored. For thermal variation can create stresses so powerful that, if not adequately provided for, the structure may buckle and collapse. A familiar instance in modern times is steel-truss bridges of large span, where the bearings at either end of the structure (or more often at both ends) must be furnished with rollers to permit the truss to lengthen and shorten with temperature changes—to "breathe", as it were, right and left. Other examples that everyone is aware of today are the expansion joints in modern concrete highways and, at a smaller scale, those in cement sidewalks.

Thermal variation was of concern to the builder (at least in his handling of maintenance and repairs) of medieval vaults, even the healthiest of which were subject to cracks and fissures. Once opened up, the vaults never completely recovered their original crackless continuity because of dust and tiny fragments of stone or mortar that lodged in them.[27] Over the years of each widening and narrowing cycle, a fissure might enlarge sufficiently to create dangerous dislocations and hence set up new stresses. At the least, a crack would divert the stresses that had been adequately taken care of in the first instance into areas or directions that had previously not needed to be guarded against.

Closely related to, but distinct from, these thermal changes and the stresses they engender are those that come about due to the shrinkage of construction materials.[28] For example, the gradual shrinkage of the mortar had disastrous consequences in many medieval church piers, whenever the core masonry consisted of far more numerous and thicker joints than the carefully executed stonework of the casing blocks. Eventually the internal masonry was reduced to dust under the early effect of expansion in the freshly laid mortar, followed by its permanent shrinkage, leaving the load to be carried—if indeed it could be—exclusively by the outer ring of cut stones.[29]

In the case of timber construction, across-the-grain shrinkage could generate serious problems if the wood had not been thoroughly dried and seasoned. One of the more common dangers was that the wood pulled away from the brick nogging used to fill in the open panels of half-timber construction, allowing rain to penetrate the resulting cracks.[30] Another common danger was that shrinkage compromised the rigidity of a timber framework by loosening the joints and allowing undue movement in them (thereby setting up frictional wear in the joints and magnifying the stresses they were originally called upon to counter).

Heat in the curing of concrete

One aspect of the process of curing concrete is of special concern to the modern contractor because it occurs throughout the course of construction rather than after the concrete has set. Particularly in massive structures such as dams, not only does the drying out of the concrete result in shrinkage but also the process of hardening generates considerable heat.[31] This heat must be dissipated if the concrete is to cure properly. If not, either the concrete remains green indefinitely and fails to develop adequate strength or the thermal differential between the surface crust and the plastic interior produces seriously disruptive stresses. In the gigantic Hoover or Boulder Dam this critical problem was solved by embedding throughout the concrete mass an extensive system of pipes that circulated brine as a refrigerant to draw off the heat.[32] In less massive structures such as highway slabs, the freshly laid concrete is covered immediately but temporarily with tarpaulins and afterward spread for many days with a layer of straw kept damp by sprinkling. Such measures prevent the formation of a surface crust that would lock the water in the green interior indefinitely and arrest its consolidation.

It is interesting to speculate on how this problem was handled in some of the massive masonry structures of ancient times. The problem would not have arisen in the Great Pyramid because of the slow rate of building, course by course, and because the mortar was laid in such thin beds, serving primarily as a lubricant to facilitate the accurate placement and setting of the big stone blocks. But the Egyptians also built very thick, high walls of brick in which the mortar joints constituted a significant proportion of the ensemble. Perhaps both the shrinkage of the mortar and the heat engendered in the drying-out process were taken care of by their frequent practice of constructing massive walls in consecutive, alternating sections. In one section all the courses, top to bottom, were concave, in the next all were convex; or else all-concave courses alternated with all-horizontal courses.[33]

Undulating courses in a high, brick precinct wall, temple at Dier el Medina. (Auguste Choisy, *L'Art de bâtir chez les Égyptiens,* 1904, fig. 1 pl. 8.)

But we would most like to know how the problem was handled by the Romans, those supreme builders who were such masters of concrete construction. The Romans' usual method of laying concrete walls was to make shallow compartments bounded by a course of facing stones or a few courses of brickwork. Into these compartments chunks of stone were loosely deposited, then liquid cement poured over the chunks up to the level of the compartment walls. So much is generally accepted.[34] But apparently no one so far has come up with a satisfactory explanation for the so-called leveling courses that were an almost universal feature of Roman concrete work. These consisted of through-the-wall pavings of large bricks, each some two feet square, at intervals of one or two feet. As these thin brick layers were not keyed into the concrete above and below them, they created planes of weakness that would have been serious were it not for the great weight and massiveness of the solid concrete they interrupt. Could they have been put there as part of the curing process: to cover and protect the newly laid pour of concrete at each increment of construction and thus to insulate it from drying out too rapidly under the rays of a Mediterranean sun?

Rarely, if ever, were all of the above-mentioned stresses implicated in a single building at one time. But most buildings of any consequence had to deal with a majority of them in varying degrees, perhaps seasonally and intermittently or in emergency situations, but with the expectation of permanence. As we have seen, stresses on and in structures are endemic to the very nature of building. They can no more be ignored than can the heat of the sun or the cold of winter, the power of wind or the force of gravity—all of which, in their several ways, engender stress. To their everlasting credit, the all-too-often anonymous builders of past ages were able to create exceptional structures that in so many cases have withstood the ravages of centuries and a multitude of (once nameless) stresses.

7

The vitality of Architecture is constantly being manifested through the activity of erecting buildings, an activity that is public and unconcealed. . . . With a building in process of erection, all is energy and activity and planned coordination . . . in a cumulative sequence of physical operations. . . .[1]

Falsework and Lifting Devices

In building, the term falsework refers collectively to all temporary structures that are essential to the process of erecting (as well as decorating or repairing) a permanent structure. Both the nature and the extent of falsework are dependent on and intimately associated with the nature and the conditions of the permanent structure. In general, there are four categories of falsework: scaffolding, formwork, centering, and shoring.[2] Scaffolding consists of raised platforms from which masons or other building mechanics have convenient access to the work in hand. Formwork designates the continuous shell on or against which materials are temporarily supported during construction of a vault or a wall respectively. Centering is the frame or other structure that supports the individual units of an arch—giving the intended curvature to their ensemble—until all are in place and the arch becomes self-supporting. Shoring is the undergirding or bracing of parts of a structure when work goes on beneath it or when a portion needs to be straightened, reinforced, or replaced. The first three categories of falsework are prerequisite to a building's erection; shoring, however, is used more often for repairs and rebuildings.

Workmen's scaffolding

Scaffolding needs only to be strong enough to support the workmen and whatever they can handle or maneuver into position themselves; that is, their tools, a bucket or hodful of mortar, a few stones or bricks, but rarely a burden as cumbersome and heavy as a crane. There is great variety in scaffolds, but the commonest serve in the erection of straight walls of whatever height.[3] Sometimes these scaffolds have standards or uprights that rise from the ground, supporting ledgers at convenient intervals. Resting on the ledgers crosswise (at right angles to the face of the building) and secured to them are the putlogs. In the past these were short beams spaced frequently enough to prevent sag in the wattle-work hurdles (or, subsequently, in the planks) on which the workmen stood. For the so-called masons' scaffolds that used two rows of standards—one close to the wall, the other out about four feet—the putlogs rested on ledgers both front and rear. But the so-called bricklayers' scaf-

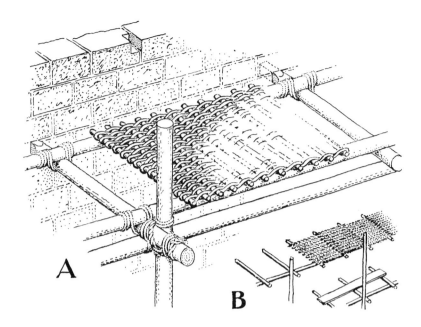

Putlog scaffolding.
(John Fitchen, *The
Construction of Gothic
Cathedrals,* 1961, fig. 4,
p. 16.)

folds had only one row of standards, and consequently the inner
end of each putlog was inserted into a void in the masonry left pur-
posely to receive it. In higher reaches of the wall, the platforms or
footpaths of the scaffolding were frequently supported exclusively
by the permanent structure of the wall itself, rather than relying on
standards based at ground level. Here the putlogs went all the way
through the wall and were subsequently drawn out and reused at a
higher level as the wall advanced and the scaffolding that served it
was reduplicated at the next level of construction.

The greatest advances in scaffolding practices—the evolution of the greatest economy of means, ingenuity, and daring in
scaffolding design and layout—occurred in the Middle Ages. Such
bold and skillful inventiveness was demanded by the loftiness and
attenuation of the buildings and by an envelope that was marked
by offsets, deep indentations, strong saliencies, and even conspicuously freestanding features such as flying buttresses. Medieval
builders profited from these ledges and offsets by hanging their
scaffoldings from the building itself—particularly from belfries and

openwork towers and, of course, the slender spires that jutted upward to such unprecedented heights.

As falsework of any sort—perhaps most often scaffolding—involves a significant expense in building construction, experienced builders give a good deal of thought to reducing its cost in terms of materials and labor. They rationalize the falsework's placement and extent, limit its use, design it so that it is reusable or at least salvageable, and reduce as much as possible the time required to position it in the first place and then to dismantle and remove it.

An extraordinary and atypical example of the magnitude of the costs that can be incurred involves the prodigal amount of massive timber falsework used for the all-stone Sacré Coeur in Paris, built at the end of the nineteenth century. Here, where the scaffolding was indeed called upon to support far-oversailing cranes and their loads of heavy stones, the architect himself informs us that "no wood or iron is used in the construction of the monument. The walls, the arches and the roof are in dressed stone." The stones were hoisted and positioned by means of a pincer-like device called a "Ram's head." According to the architect it "requires fewer men to put the stones in place, but necessitates the construction of solid timber scaffolding, at a heavy cost, to carry the cranes employed in lifting. On this account, up to the first of January, 1893, the amount expended for timber from the commencement of the work was 2,200,000 francs . . . while . . . to the same date the amount spent on masonry was 16,000,000 francs."[4]

If a permanent feature of a building under construction can provide convenient support for the workmen, it is sometimes possible to dispense with temporary scaffolding altogether. A striking case in point was the adoption of a permanent internal skeleton of timberwork above Salisbury Cathedral's crossing tower. It served not only as essential bracing for the extremely thin-shelled spire but also as a many-staged scaffolding for the workmen during the course of the stone spire's erection and during subsequent repairs.[5]

The New World Dutch barn was an all-wood building that acted in part as its own scaffolding. The structure required footing for the team of men who had to install the roof-supporting purlin-plate, a single longitudinal timber (sometimes as much as sixty feet long) set high across the tops of a row of columns. In this instance the columns themselves acted as scaffolding standards. A rod inserted transversely through a hole in each served on one side as an interim support for the purlin-plate and on the other side, laid across with saplings, as a footrest for the workmen.[6]

Scaffolding is required not only to erect or repair a building but also often to finish and decorate it. Sometimes decoration can

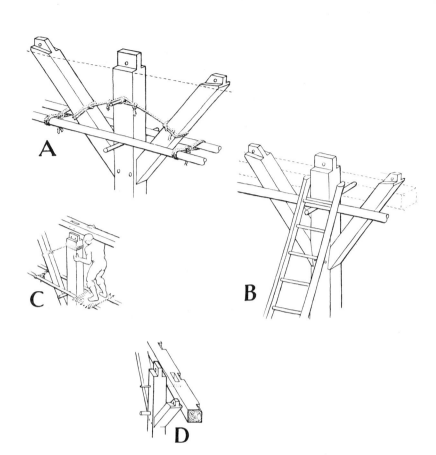

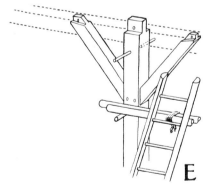

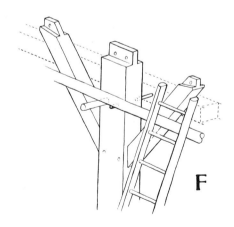

Raising holes used as
aids in barn construc-
tion. (John Fitchen,
*The New World Dutch
Barn,* 1968, fig. 14, p.
132.)

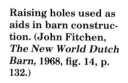

be handled from ladders alone. But ladders—narrow and steeply tilted—are designed primarily to provide means of vertical access. Unless used in pairs and fitted with brackets to support a plank spanning between them, ladders require frequent repositioning to forestall unsafe reaching. Hence they are inconvenient substitutes for customary types of scaffolding.

In multi-storied buildings today, the finishing work (such as pointing masonry joints, cleaning or sandblasting the surface, and painting it) is handled from suspended platforms hung from above and lowered as work progresses from the top downward. Such rope-hung platforms were also used in the medieval period, for example, in installing the glazing of stained-glass windows in Gothic churches.

A scheme utilized by the ancient Egyptians substituted earth for wooden scaffolding. In a land where wood had to be imported, this scheme was employed in both the construction and decoration of their temples. As the stones of the great hypostyle halls—columns, walls, and then the roof—were set in place, the rooms were gradually filled with earth or sand so that each block could be positioned at successive "ground" levels, as it were, with a ramp leading to them from outside, up which the blocks were hauled. Once the huge lintels and the roof slabs were installed, the process of removing the earth could begin. Thus, as the artificial ground level receded, it served as a working platform on which groups of skilled craftsmen undertook the delicate finish work of executing relief carving on ceiling, wall, and column.

Where the structure was complicated with projections and indentations, with returns and interruptions (as in the freestanding higher portions of Gothic cathedrals), the design of the scaffolding required special skill and knowledge of the work in hand from the man responsible for it and special care and aplomb from those assigned to erect it. In this connection Viollet-le-Duc illustrates and discusses in detail how he would have met the tricky problem of providing masons' scaffolding for the tops of tall towers and the bases of the lofty, slender spires that so often surmounted them.[7] His solutions are based in part on a very careful examination of the traces of former scaffolding—holes and points of bearing—in these areas of actual medieval churches. But they result, more particularly, from an analysis of the possibilities for seating and securing scaffolding members in relation to features in the masonry that was under construction. These features included tall, slender window voids in the outer walls, various offsets and ledges, holes left in the stonework (later to be plugged up), and stable though confined stages behind parapets or pinnacles where the square tops of towers change to the octagonal bases of spires.

Viollet-le-Duc's ingenious solutions are worth studying for their points of support, their scheme of bracing, and their hung, oversailing platforms designed for masons working in particularly exposed and hazardous locations. But it is unlikely that the medieval builders made their temporary assemblages exclusively of squared timbers connected with the carefully shaped, intricately devised clasps and keys, using the notched and symmetrically paired framing members depicted by Viollet-le-Duc in the nineteenth century. Rather, they would undoubtedly have fashioned scaffolding much less expensively of round poles that, lashed together by cords, needed no cutting or preparatory fitting, no time-consuming shaping of their intersections or connections. In the early twentieth century, when lashed pole scaffolding was still widely practiced, rope lashings consisted of many turns. They were made tight—and kept tight in all weathers—by driving long, slightly tapered wedges between the lashing and one of the sapling members it was wrapped around.[8]

Even today, where wooden members as opposed to metal units are still used for scaffolding installations, sapling poles secured with rope lashing enjoy very widespread currency. Wherever these long, straight, only slightly tapering sapling poles are readily available, their continuing use makes sense. They are cheaper than the metal units that have become so familiar, particularly in the high-rise installations of America. And they create a stronger ensemble, in terms of weight-strength ratio, than the sawn lumber with nailed attachments which preceded the appearance of metal units in the Western world and which have increasingly superseded the traditional pole scaffolding in Europe. For rope-bound pole scaffolding does not suffer penetration or interruption in the continuity of the grain of the wood, nor notching or mechanical injury in individual members. Hence, it is completely salvageable for reuse, and quickly and easily dismantled.

It is interesting to note that in the Far East, to this day, the highest paid carpenters are those whose exclusive job it is to set up and dismantle scaffolding assemblages. They work primarily with bamboo, which is eminently strong, slender, and light.[9] Even with relatively light sapling poles, however, erecting a scaffold is not an easy undertaking, but one that requires muscle, skill, and daring. It may very well be an important factor in the widespread preference for sawn scantlings (wherever wood is still used for scaffolding) that sawn members are generally shorter than those used in pole scaffolding. They are therefore easier to manipulate, set into place, and attach by nailing.

Lashed pole scaffold-
ing at Notre-Dame-de-
Mantes, France, 1953.
(Photograph by Allen
Fitchen.)

Gins, cranes, and other lifting devices

For masonry structures of some magnitude and major buildings of
any sort, lifting devices have invariably been required to raise and
position building materials at too great a height for men to carry
them repeatedly up ladders. They have also been needed for materials that were too heavy for men to handle unaided. We have
mentioned that, in the past, the platforms or footpaths of scaffolding were rarely used to support cranes or other devices for lifting
extremely heavy loads. Occasionally, when a hoisting apparatus
was required for raising big roof timbers or major keystones for the
vaulting, for example, the lifting devices were stationed on the tops
of walls—if bracing for them could be found. But much more frequently they were placed on major timbers in the permanent roof
framing, where they sometimes were allowed to remain in place to
serve in subsequent repairs.

Two considerations were involved in hoisting operations: the
lifting mechanism itself and the means by which the objects to be
raised were grappled or otherwise harnessed to the raising rope. It
seems appropriate to deal with the latter when covering the building practices adopted by specific civilizations. They are therefore
dealt with elsewhere in these pages.

As for the devices used for raising loads, one of the most ancient was the gin. Three poles some twelve to fifteen feet long were set with their feet apart and lashed together at their tops, forming a tripod assemblage from which a pulley was hung. A rope was passed over this pulley and brought down to a windlass secured between two of the poles at a convenient height to allow the workmen to operate handspikes let through the axle to right and left of a winding drum.

Although this device has been used from time immemorial, and continues in use today, it has some disadvantages that limit its adaptability in a number of situations. In common with most ancient lifting devices, movement is confined exclusively to direct vertical lifts. Moreover, normally the distance that an object can be raised is not very great because its starting position is at ground level and its upward limit defined by the encroachment of the three poles and the pulley they support. (Of course, where the starting position is not at grade but at an indeterminate distance below it—as when digging a well—the distance covered in the lift can be considerable.) Finally, the wide-straddling legs of the gin generally prevent its use at elevated locations, such as at the top of towers or on narrow lofty walls. But where these three limitations do not preclude its use, the gin is a simple and effective contrivance.

Somewhat related to the gin is the shear-legs device in which two spars with feet astraddle are lashed together near their tops and hung with a pulley. The spars tilt outward, held in postion by a guy line (or sometimes by another spar) that runs from their apex back to a secure anchorage. With shear legs, again, little more than a straight vertical lift is normally possible. But, with only two legs instead of the gin's three, this apparatus can be utilized in lofty locations such as the edge of a flat roof or even from a projecting cornice or behind a parapet at the eaves of a sloping roof.

Medieval builders used cranes, most of which were quite small and of uncomplicated design, for lifting buckets of mortar, bricks, stones that could be manipulated and set by hand, and similar light items. Such cranes consisted of a vertical standard of timber, fitted at the top with a short horizontal arm. One type, shaped like an inverted L, had a pulley at the free end of the arm, over which passed the hoisting rope. The other common type was T-shaped, with the rope passing over a pulley at one free end of the cross-arm and across to a pulley at the other free end.[10] In both types, the device was sometimes fashioned so that either the standard with its fixed cross-arm or the cross-arm alone could be rotated. Thus, once the load had been hauled up, it could be swung around a few feet to come to rest on a stable platform or on the part

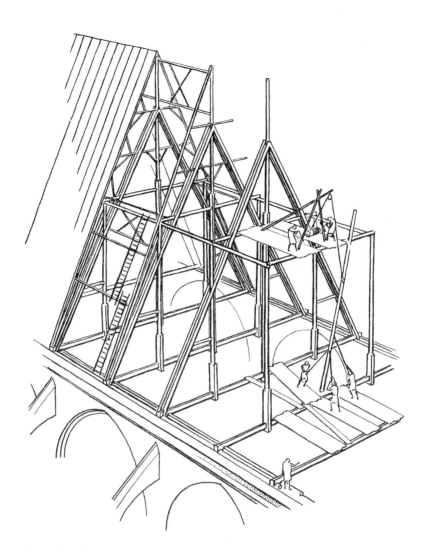

Shear-legs device with
windlass, used to erect
a cathedral roof. (John
Fitchen, *The Construc-
tion of Gothic Cathe-
drals,* 1961, fig. 9, p. 27.)

of the building where it would be incorporated. It is interesting to note that in many of the contemporary delineations of cranes, the standard is furnished with cleats by way of access to the cross-arm. This suggests that the hoisting rope must have frequently become fouled at or jumped off the pulleys.

Late in the medieval period much larger and more powerful cranes were developed and used, on the ground at wharfside or high aloft a building. As often as not they were built so that the whole contraption could be rotated (like huge Dutch windmills subsequently) to permit the desirable operation of displacing the load laterally in addition to the essential process of raising or lowering it.[11]

This ability to rotate such cranes is noteworthy. Again and again, historians have stated that the builders of the past had equipment necessary to raise heavy loads, but that they could do so only in a vertical direction. Although this assertion is true for a very large number of cases, we have seen that some lifting devices could indeed offset the strict verticality of their lift at its high point by swiveling the load a few feet. Real freedom of movement in this regard was not achieved until the steel cranes of modern times. But it is inaccurate to insist that no hoisting device in former times could manage lateral movement.

For example, by the late Middle Ages (and probably in ancient Greek and Roman times as well), the yardarms of sailing vessels were often used to load and unload ships' cargoes of moderate weight. The spars were ready-made for such work because the ropes and pulleys were already in place to raise and lower the sails and to tilt and trim the yards according to the wind direction when the vessel was at sea.

The great wheel was a hoisting device that provided the power for its own lifts.[12] Used by the Romans as well as throughout the medieval period, it worked on the principle of a revolving squirrel cage. A great wheel was in reality two wheels whose rims were united by planking to form a treadmill pavement within, on which one or more men tramped to rotate the wheel. A rope was wound around the axle at one side—the difference between the radius of the wheel and that of the axle drum giving great mechanical advantage. Thus the great wheel could raise loads of considerable weight—large bells, heavy timbers, massive keystones, and arch centerings. If this device was installed high up, as on the tie beams of the roof above a vault, no pulleys were involved; hence any friction that would have cut down somewhat on the efficiency of its performance was not a consideration. A number of great wheels are still in use, including a large one that is operational at Mont-Saint-Michel in northern France.

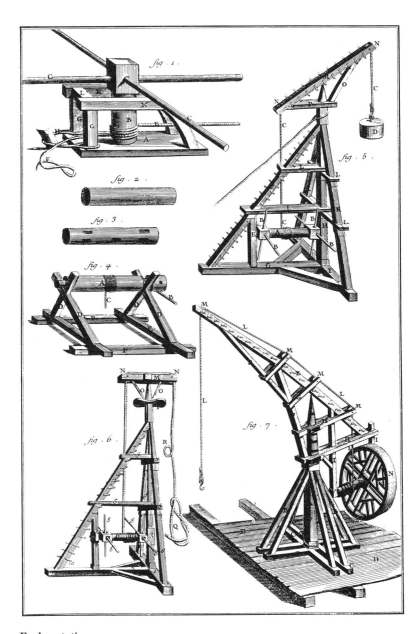

Early rotating cranes
and other devices for
raising or moving
loads. (From Diderot
and d'Alembert, re-
produced in Antoine
Moles, *Histoire des
charpentiers,* 1949, fig.
155, p. 146.)

95   Falsework and Lifting Devices

**Great wheel from a Ro-
man grave slab. (Josef
Durm,** *Die Baukunst
der Römer,* **1905, fig.
399, p. 365.)**

Shoring

As we have seen, the primary purpose of scaffolding is to furnish building mechanics with elevated platforms or footpaths in handy proximity to their work. Shoring, on the other hand, is not concerned with accommodating the *workmen,* but with providing some part of the *building itself* with the support of temporary bracing, lateral abutment, or underpinning. Two situations require such support. One is during the original erection of the building, when some portion of it needs to be temporarily braced or held in place pending the introduction of another part of the building that will secure it permanently. The other situation involves major repairs to, enlargements of, or replacements in, an existing building.

The first category encompasses various applications, none of which is very complicated. Nowadays, for example, carpenters commonly adopt the practice of propping up the outer edge of porch roofs in frame construction, thereby postponing the installation of permanent columns until all else has been completed. Another type of shoring is the practice of securing wall-assemblages by stay laths or similar means of tilt-up construction, whether of wooden frameworks or reinforced concrete slabs. The heavy sloping braces in deep excavations (such as subbasements and their foundations) and the horizontal struts that hold apart the walls of trenches are examples of shoring used to prevent earth or mud cave-ins. Similarly, stout timbers are usually provided in mine galleries to prevent the ceilings from collapsing. In the past, the ancient Egyptian pyramid builders propped up the huge granite plug at the entrance to the king's chamber until all work there had been completed. And the Romans constructed falsework towers to undergird massive centerings, as in the case of the great masonry arches of the Pont du Gard.

Shoring that involves existing buildings, however, calls for the special resourcefulness of the builder. In general, the problems are much more varied and difficult than for shoring during construction. Usually, too, they require much more extensive paraphernalia, much heavier and stronger means of support.

Sometimes it is a matter of straightening walls that have become dangerously tilted because their foundations have subsided. The following is part of an account that depicts the steps that were taken in 1908 to correct this situation in the case of Partrishow Church, Breconshire.

a) The wall was shored up both internally and externally, as shown diagramatically on the section.

b) The weight of the roof was taken off the wall.

Modern high-rise construction in Spain, using traditional sapling poles to support formwork for successive floors, March 1982. (Photograph by Nicholas Rezak.)

c) The windows were strutted up outside the tracery so that the whole wall might move together.

d) The wall was cut free from the return walls of the nave, which join it, and from the porch.

e) Grooves were cut below ground level in both the outer and inner faces of the wall.

f) The whole wall was then jacked over until it was brought up in a vertical position against the internal shoring.

g) The grooves were then made good, and the wall was underpinned and rebonded to the return walls and to the porch.

h) The roof was lowered into position, and shoring and strutting removed.[13]

Sometimes the root cause of a shoring problem stems from foundations that have settled, requiring underpinning and consolidation there, along with extensive repairs to the superstructure because of dislocations in the vaulting. Here is an account that describes this situation in some detail.

The rebuilding of the foundations of the retro-choir and lady chapel of Winchester Cathedral which was carried out in the autumn of 1906 necessitated the erection of a very elaborate and complicated arrangement of shoring to uphold the masonry while the work of underpinning the walls was being carried on. The foundations of the eastern portion of the cathedral were found to be dangerously insecure, being in fact laid upon a bed of soft marl only ten feet below the surface of the ground, in spite of the fact that at a depth of 16 ft. a hard solid stratum of gravel, at least 6 ft. thick, is arrived at. The medieval builders without doubt entertained suspicions as to the sustaining power of their proposed foundation, and so as to ensure stability, as they thought, strengthened it by placing below the masonry horizontal layers of beech trees, filling up the interstices with hard chalk and flints. These contrivances were not sufficient to prevent the gradual sinking, through succeeding centuries, of the heavy mass of masonry. This not only affected the footings of the building, but caused fissures of an alarming nature in the vaulting and walls. Under the direction of Mr. T. G. Jackson a carefully designed arrangement of shoring was applied, consisting of raking shores, flying shores and needling, for the purpose of the underpinning, with specially designed timbering to support the arches and vaulting while they were undergoing repair. The foundations were found to be much undermined by water, which filled the excavations made for the underpinning in such quantities that it was necessary to employ a diver to deposit cement concrete in bagfuls upon the gravel bed to which the new foundations are taken down.[14]

Centering

Centering, it will be recalled, is the temporary framework whose upper contour establishes the intended curvature of an arch and provides support for the individual stones or bricks of the arch during the course of its erection. Because centering sometimes involves very large spans, construction in lofty positions, or the need for unobstructed passage (as in the case of bridges over waterways where river traffic has to be maintained), it is the most difficult and demanding type of falsework. The problems of decentering and removal of the centering, too, always require particular care and knowledgeable experience.

Centering for arches that are of more than minimum span consists of many members framed or otherwise secured to each other in such a way as to prevent sagging or deformations that would affect the regularity and the accuracy of the arch's curvature during its construction. This is no small or easy requirement. For in the normal course of erecting an arch, the voussoirs are built up from the spring of the arch on either hand to converge on the final block (the keystone) at the crown. Thus the haunches of the arch weight the centering frame before the middle portion receives a load of arch stones. These partial loadings tend to endanger the curving contour of the centering frame by depressing it, right and left, which causes the central portion to rise in compensation.[15] To counteract such deformations the centering frame must be rigid. In addition, intermediate supports—many if the span of the arch is considerable—are provided between the two abutments at either end of the arch-to-be. These must be built with adequate foundations to forestall even the slightest settlement when they become loaded. Moreover, deformation due to subsidence in the intermediate piers is further guarded against with pairs of folding wedges. These can be adjusted with great accuracy at any time to level the centering frame and maintain its strict horizontal alignment across the tops of the supporting piers.[16]

The most critical operation involved in this category of falsework comes in the process of decentering; that is, the freeing of the timber frame from its supporting role to make the masonry arch independent and self-supporting. In arches of very small span this is sometimes done by forcing the keystone down into the less-than-sufficient space left for it between the top-most voussoirs to right and left of it.[17] But in most cases the lowering (by not more than a couple of inches) of the centering frame is managed by retracting the wedges on which the centering frame rests.[18] This procedure has to be done with the greatest precision and evenness, gradually, over a period of days. Most arch failures, in fact, occur when the centering is being eased away from contact with the arch.[19]

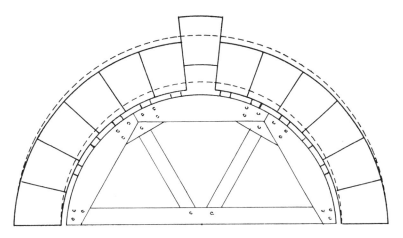

Centering scheme for
small-span arch in
Spain. (John Fitchen,
"Some Contemporary
Techniques of Arch
Construction in
Spain," *AIA Journal*
34(1960): 33.)

In addition to this most critical—and dangerous—operation,
removing the centerings altogether involves difficulties and complications.[20] The installation of a centering frame (including hoisting
it up into position and furnishing its upper surface with cleats or
battens) is managed from *above*. But once the arch has been completed, the centering is covered by the arch and must be dismantled—freed from the arch and disposed of—from *below*. In arches
of large span or in lofty positions (as over deep chasms or high
above the naves of Gothic cathedrals), this can involve engineering operations of considerable difficulty and delicacy so as not to in-
terfere with or damage work that has already taken place or is in
process of construction below it.

In most cases where the spans are large, the only feasible
way to remove the centering frame is by dismantling it piece by
piece. Often it is far too heavy and cumbersome to be lowered to the
ground as a single complex. Moreover, it is understandable that
when first installed the centering frame would have used projections—either permanent offsets or ledges in the building or temporary corbels—as stable supports, at either end, for the frame itself.
Obviously, these projections would impede lowering the centering
frame directly to the ground.

Occasionally the ingenuity of the builders, profiting by the
circumstances of a particular situation, could circumvent some of

the hazards and difficulties involved in lowering huge centering frames as complete ensembles. One such operation has been illustrated and described conjecturally for the eighty-foot central span of the Romans' huge Pont du Gard aqueduct in southern France.[21] The centering frame, which probably had intermediate support from three timberwork towers, could have been swiveled horizontally in order to clear its ends from their corbelled bearings. Thereupon, suspended from heavy beams while the falsework towers were removed, the entire centering ensemble could have been lowered by strong ropes.

Formwork

Formwork (usually referred to in England as shuttering) is required during construction to confine semiliquid or plastic concrete, to undergird a platform on which a floor is to be built, or to support and impart the intended curvature to the ensemble of stones or bricks in vaulted structures. One of the oldest building practices involving formwork still survives in pisé or rammed earth construction.[22] It is a worldwide practice, found in England, Europe (particularly in the arid region of France east of the lower Rhône River), South Africa, Tibet, and elsewhere.[23] The process consists of firmly securing boards between which properly prepared earth is strongly tamped in successive courses, or "lifts," to heights as great as three stories. The Romans employed somewhat similar but much higher units of this kind of formwork to fashion foundation walls of concrete below grade. Here the adjacent ground could sometimes be counted on to resist the considerable pressure of the concrete before it hardened.[24]

In their concrete works above grade, the Romans used effective kinds of formwork that were not discarded after use because they constituted an integral part of the permanent structure. One of the commonest of the various schemes they adopted was to make their lifts out of brickwork composed of triangular-shaped bricks. Using diagonally cut square units in thick beds of mortar, these triangular bricks were laid up with their hypotenuses as the face of the wall.[25] A number of courses of such brickwork created the lateral boundaries of a compartment. Once the mortar had dried, lumps of rock were placed therein and the semiliquid concrete poured over them. Thus during construction the brickwork acted as formwork, keeping the liquid concrete from leaking out and at the same time, with adequate bracing, maintaining the integrity and regularity of the wall's perimeter at successive increments in its height. The staggered points of the triangular bricks tailed back

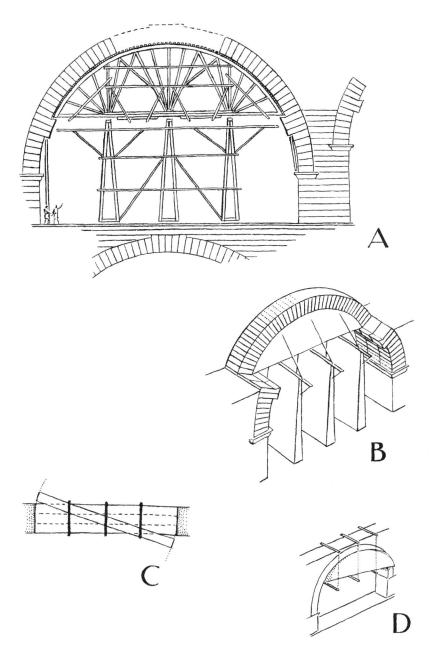

A

B

C

D

Decentering scheme
for Pont du Gard
arches. (John Fitchen,
*The Construction of
Gothic Cathedrals,*
1961, fig. 3, p. 12.)

Formwork used in
rebuilding war-
destroyed medieval
vaulting of Warsaw
Castle, Poland, 1973.
(Photograph by Miec-
zyslaw Samborski,
reproduced with his
kind permission.)

into the concrete core, making a secure, permanent bond between it and the brick facing. A very large number of Roman buildings, in a more or less ruinous state today, look as though they were built exclusively of brick. But one can be sure that they were invariably of concrete; what appears is their permanent constructional formwork.

In large-span barrel vaults of concrete, the Romans rationalized the formwork in a different but equally effective and economical way.[26] Spanning from one transverse centering frame of timbers to the next were heavy wooden planks laid parallel but a number of inches apart. These defined the curvature of the vault-to-be and provided support for a continuous pavement of square two-by-two-foot bricks. A second (sometimes a third) layer of bricks set flatwise and breaking joints with the first layer were laid in a thick mortar bed. Thus the drying mortar created a formwork crust that served as an impervious dam to prevent the subsequently poured semiliquid concrete from leaking through. But this was not all. Above each of the transverse centering frames, where they received maximum direct support, arches were built of the usual two-by-two-foot bricks, this time set radially. Partitions of two-by-two-foot bricks set on edge linked the brick arches at regular intervals around the curve of the vault, forming rectangular compartments two feet deep. These coffer-like compartments were thereupon filled with concrete in the usual manner, which made the whole complex strong enough to sustain a massive overburden of concrete of whatever thickness the builders deemed appropriate. Without these rationalized procedures, the cost of falsework to support the enormous weight of the high, wide-spanning concrete vault would have been staggering in terms of time, materials, and labor, both during construction and in the process of dismantling temporary supports.

One aspect of the Roman scheme of laying bricks flatwise has been utilized much more recently for light vaulting. During the latter part of the nineteenth century, a system was perfected that fundamentally changed the nature of vault action from a voussoir to a shear-resisting process. In the latter scheme (known as the timbrel vault system), three or more layers of tiles with corrugated surfaces for greater adhesion and resistance to shear were laid flatwise in thick beds of mortar.[27] After the triple layers of tiles were erected, their proper curvature was permanently maintained by means of a light fill above (as up to a level floor) or below by means of thin vertical diaphragms of tiling. Thus the layers of tile could—without deformation—perform their structural function of bridging space by resistance to shear.

The following example illustrates this principle. A pile of three unrestrained planks presents a single rectangle in side view,

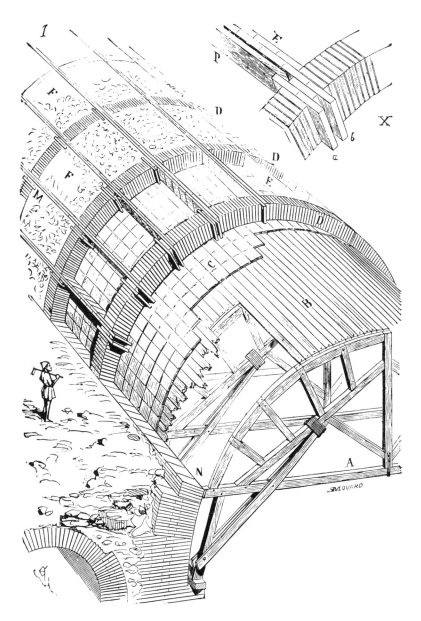

Construction of large-span Roman concrete barrel vault. (Eugène Emmanuel Viollet-le-Duc, "Voûte" in vol. 9 of *Dictionnaire raisonné*, 1858–68, fig. 1, p. 466.)

equal to a single beam of similar length and total depth. But on application of a heavy load, the planks sag (deflect); that is, their upper surfaces shorten (compress) and their lower surfaces lengthen (expand). Thus the bottom of an upper plank slides at its ends along the top of a lower plank. Nailing or gluing the trio of planks prevents this sliding and allows them to act as a rigid, undeflecting unit.

In the timbrel vaulting system, a similar restraint against sliding is imparted by the mortar's firm grip on the corrugated tiles. Vaults of considerable span but very slight rise are thus feasible. Often employed in Spain to support floors in multi-storied buildings, the light fill between them and the floor maintains the integrity of the vault's total curvature. One of the great economic advantages of this system, quite aside from the remarkable saving of headroom due to the slight rise of the vaults, is that the formwork for it can be minimal and extremely light or sometimes even dispensed with altogether.

The use of earth to support and shape masonry vaults is a very primitive device whose origin predates history. Often employed where wood was scarce, this kind of falsework in any event circumvented the need for sometimes complicated carpentry work and the skilled building mechanics who could fashion it. But, perhaps because the practice was considered commonplace and unremarkable, there appear to be no contemporary accounts (at least until the Renaissance) of mounded earth as formwork for vaults or domes.[28] Nor are there delineations of this practice in the miniatures or the stained-glass panels of the entire medieval period. Probably nothing about the scene lent itself to pictorial expression, illuminated the activities of the workmen, or identified their tools and equipment. Nonetheless, it seems that ground-story tower rooms in England during the early Middle Ages, for example, were customarily completely filled with earth and the top of the fill shaped to accommodate the construction of the room's vault. The walls of the tower were necessarily thick enough (with but one or two small openings) to withstand the lateral pressure of the earth fill.

Throughout much of the past, in fact, the practice of using mounded earth to support and give form to both flat stone roofs and single bays of masonry vaulting alike was such a universal and time-honored tradition that it was almost never recorded in the contemporary chronicles. But that it was and still remains a viable procedure is confirmed by its survival as a construction device even today. A recent example is that of a building in Anacapri, Italy, constructed in 1953. There, the rough platform of planking on which the earth was mounded took the form of five planes (half a

Vault erection at
Anacapri, Capri, Italy,
1953. Mounded earth
is used as formwork
on a platform that is
pentagonal in eleva-
tion. (John Fitchen,
*The Construction of
Gothic Cathedrals,*
1961, fig. 11, facing p.
30.)

Formwork, shoring, and removal of spoil in a tunneling operation. (Woodcut in F. W. Simms, *Practical Tunnelling,* 2d ed., 1860, p. 98.)

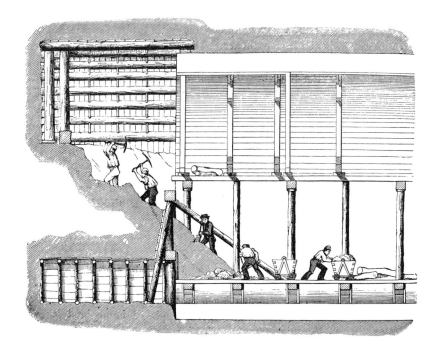

decagon in vertical section), thus greatly reducing the weight of the earth required and simplifying the process of removing it.[29]

Tunneling operations employed a special type of formwork. The actual excavation, as the work advanced, was shored up by heavy planking blocked up with unsquared timbering, called "poling." Soon after excavation, the thick permanent lining of the tunnel was executed in brickwork on lagging that stretched between the centering ribs and was keyed by so-called cross-lagging.[30]

In the mid-nineteenth century Viollet-le-Duc (distinguished architect, prolific restorer, and extremely knowledgeable architectural historian) proposed the cerce device as the most economical, handy, and adaptable means for constructing the stone courses in the webs of Gothic ribbed vaults. The cerce is an extensible pair of boards, cambered along their top edges to the desired curvature of the vault and slotted throughout most of their length so that they can be adjusted to stretch between two diverging ribs. The cerce's length, held in place between the ribs at either end and varying its span as the ribs' divergency increases, is said to have provided support for each successive course of web stones as the work progressed.

But this device, whose makeup and operation were described so confidently by Viollet-le-Duc, seems rarely to have been put in practice. For its operation involved serious and unresolved difficulties.[31] Moreover, the web courses in numerous existing vaults display breaks in their continuity, which proves that they could not have been erected by means of the cerce device. By contrast, the stone-weighted rope device was indeed a practical scheme for dispensing with continuous formwork in erecting the webs of quadripartite vaulting in the Middle Ages.[32] Here the web stones were buttered with mortar on two surfaces: their bed face and the side that made contact with a previously set stone. To prevent the stone from sliding down on its freshly laid mortar bed, a stone-weighted rope (secured behind and above the web stone) was looped over the stone to press and maintain it in position until the mortar adhered. This handicrafted scheme was completely in the control of the mason. It required no complicated formwork on the part of the carpenters, no time-consuming difficulties in setting it up, decentering it, and then dismantling or removing it. And, perhaps most advantageous to the experienced mason, it was completely adaptable to changes in the length and direction of the web courses.[33]

The remarkable resourcefulness and inventiveness displayed by the builders of former times is striking. They achieved great and complex works with mediocre facilities but maximum economy of means. How they tailored their equipment and procedures to the

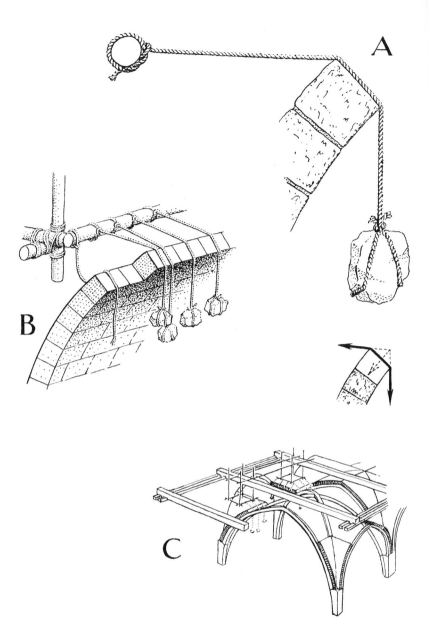

The stone-weighted
rope device for erect-
ing the webs of Gothic
vaults. (John Fitchen,
*The Construction of
Gothic Cathedrals,*
1961, fig. 69, p. 182.)

available materials and work force is instructive even today. Above all, we can be profoundly impressed by their skill and ingenuity in accommodating their falsework solutions to the particular nature and conditions of each job.

8

The last-named [fiber] as used in cloth and cordage, enters so largely into the economy of everyday life, that on the lake ficus-trees have become heritable property, while the 'njombo' and others, through their accommodating facilities, have so impressed the native mind with the idea of tying, that the verb build has no place in their language, no structure being built but tied.[1]

Of all the paraphernalia utilized in the operations of building construction, a Ladder is the item which is unfailingly and inevitably most intimately related to the physical stature of man.[2]

Ropes and Ladders:
The Builder's Habitual Implements

Various types of construction equipment are needed wherever building operations are in progress. Scaffolding and hoisting devices, for instance, are common and characteristic items. But the layman tends to ignore and overlook some essential equipment, perhaps because of its familiarity and its common use in so many other roles. Chief among these common utensils are rope and ladders, both of which make indispensable contributions to building construction, not only initially but also for many years thereafter during repairs or rebuilding.

It is astonishing—and hard to account for—that to date almost nothing whatsoever has been written, in either technical or more general terms, about the nature, the forms, and the uses of ladders.[3] As for rope, a number of articles were published during the nineteenth and the early years of the twentieth century that dealt with the fibers and their properties,[4] how they were prepared,[5] and occasionally the handicraft methods used in their fabrication into rope.[6] But it is remarkable, considering the universality of rope from earliest times, that its applications in buildings and building construction of former times have received no systematic historical coverage. The following pages address these two indispensable construction aids, in general and as they relate to building operations.

The particular virtue of rope is obviously its resistance to tension. In building, this attribute allows rope to be used constructionally (as a haul rope in towing operations or as a hoisting rope on a crane) or as a permanent feature of a structure (as in a suspension bridge). Or rope may serve both functions, constructional and structural. The nomadic Bedouin, for example, use ropes to erect their tents and to maintain their conformation and stability, once erected. This triple capability of rope is unusual enough to require explanation and substantiation.

Rope as an integral part of a building

Throughout the past the structural use of native rope has been represented worldwide in the handicrafted cables of suspension bridges. Some survive to modern times in undeveloped areas of South America, Africa, Southeast Asia, China, and elsewhere.[7] In

Axial view of a liana suspension bridge in Upper Burma showing in detail the crude but effective fastenings at one end. Here a pair of vertical posts are steadied and held upright against the pull of the main cables by tiebacks secured to anchorages, right and left, behind the viewer. The tiebacks may readily be kept taut by turning the rods, which are thrust through their twisted strands. (George Forrest, "The Land of the Crossbow," *National Geographic* 21(February 1910): 149.)

this application, stiffness outweighs pliancy as a virtue. For no terminal knots or sharp bends are required in the main cables, and the anchorages are fixed, resistant to axial stress alone on the part of the cables. As tensile strength is the overriding requirement, the composition of the cables can therefore be quite coarse and uneven, such as very roughly twisted cane or willow withes.[8]

Another instance of rope as a permanent part of a building can be seen in certain thatched roofs. A net or grid of cords, invariably tied down somehow or weighted with dangling stones at the eaves, is strung over the thatch to keep it smooth and regular and to prevent its displacement by high winds.[9] Inevitably smaller in diameter than those used as suspension cables in bridges, these ropes are not only evenly textured but also pliant. Thus sharp bends are possible and knots can be tied wherever separate lines cross and are secured to each other.

A considerable variety of knots have been devised over the centuries, each type fulfilling some particular purpose in a direct, appropriate, and basically uncomplicated way.[10] The principle on which all rope knots, hitches, and bends are based is, of course, that one or more places in the critical turns of the rope wedge together in a jamming juxtaposition, which prevents slipping or disentanglement as long as the knot is tightly tied and/or kept under stress. Consequently, in all but a few building-related situations, the criteria for knot tying include security from working loose and, equally important, ease of untying when the knot is no longer required. Consider the timber hitch—so quick and easy for the lumberjack to reeve around a log, so automatic to undo when he relaxes the stress—and the sheepshank—used to shorten a length of rope under tension, it virtually falls apart when the tension is released.

To be sure, there are instances—some of them building-related—where knots once tied are intended to remain tied: cargo-handling nets, fishnets, the tie-down grids over roof thatching, and the assemblages of native suspension bridges that often featured cable railings with protective lacings between them and the walkways. All of these examples occur out-of-doors, in exposed situations subject periodically to rain or immersion in water (producing mildew and rot) and to solar heat or dryness (producing brittleness and diminished resistance to wear).[11] For example, the properties that determine rope's effectiveness in salt or fresh water are critical in marine situations. Both the shrouds and the running gear on sailing vessels are subject to shrinkage and/or loss of strength when wet. The salt spray can be deleterious, and tarring the rope to prevent, or at least retard, the deterioration can somewhat diminish the rope's pliancy. Too, fishnets, weirs, and haul-ropes connecting cork floats must be periodically dried out to forestall mold and decay. Other marine situations that involve rope include the mooring of pontoon bridges and the lashing together of log rafts.

Rope in building-related operations

One whole category of rope fastenings associated with building that has prevailed throughout history is the practice of lashed connections.[12] The great majority of vernacular buildings erected during past centuries by non-European indigenous peoples of many cultures have used—and continue to use—lashing to secure the component members of the structural frame, whether of walls or roof. In the Western world, moreover, the practice of lashing wooden members together still survives in many areas in scaffolding assemblages. Hence both permanent and temporary installations have customarily employed lashing, whether of native lianas, rattans, and vines or of locally handicrafted rope. The predominant reasons for the universality of lashing among indigenous peoples are clearly economic (the saving of skilled carpentry work), practical (the use of readily available natural materials), and structural (no notching or mechanical injury to the continuity of the grain in the wooden members, which would impair their strength).

Among peoples of nonmechanized societies where human labor is cheap, many mechanical operations have been conducted by coordinated teams of men using ropes. Two examples from the Far East, photographed for *National Geographic*, are explained by these brief descriptions:

A Three-Man Shovel (Fusan, Korea): A tool peculiar to this country, being a long-handled scoop from which two ropes extended. While the one holding the handle guides the implement, the two others furnish the power by pulling the ropes from a distance of about twelve feet. . . .[13]

Annamese Farmers Have Devised a Novel Means of Irrigation. Manipulating woven bamboo baskets with ropes attached at top and bottom, they dip water from the stream and by deft, rhythmic movements empty it into irrigation channels. There is no loitering, for to make this method successful the workers must move in unison.[14]

Most devices for raising and lowering men or materials or both require ropes: gins, shear-legs, cranes, great wheels, and windlasses. An example of the makeup and use of handicrafted rope in such circumstances in China and of its life expectancy under constant use is given in an account that begins:

The rope used by the miners on their windlasses must needs be very strong, as it has to raise and lower coal and men. The rope is twisted

Time-honored, non-mechanized method of tamping layers of earth on levees and dikes. The Chinese use the same device (a heavy disc heaved aloft and allowed to drop on target with a resounding thud) for pile driving wherever space allows the operation of this highly coordinated activity. (Photograph by C. D. Jameson, in *National Geographic* 36(1919): 240.)

of three strands of bamboo strips. No doubt experience taught the Chinese that such ropes have a limit of usefulness, and they are accordingly used not longer than ten to fifteen days.[15]

This startlingly short lifespan of usefulness in ropes is worthy of special note. For it corroborates and helps to explain the circumstances under which ropes were, or were not, used by the ancient Egyptians (who, of course, arrived at their own practices and procedures entirely independently). To be sure, the Egyptians fabricated ropes and utilized them widely in construction operations. But they neither used ropes for hoisting huge blocks vertically nor, in general, employed them in situations where their sudden breaking would endanger either the workmen or the ponderous blocks they were moving, or indeed cause damage to a previously installed portion of a building.

Rope is also indispensable for capstans, which operate by winding a cable around a drum set on a fixed vertical axle. The power to make the drum revolve is provided by men pushing round and round on long poles inserted through holes in the top of the drum. Their most spectacular and extraordinary use is recorded in contemporary engravings of a scene in which both men and horses activate some forty-eight capstans to move and, notably, to erect the Vatican obelisk in Rome.[16] Instances such as this and those cited above make it clear that rope may be an essential element in the very structure of a building; but, much more important, they underscore its absolute indispensability in the *erection* of any building of consequence.

The versatility of ladders

In one form or another, ladders have been used since time immemorial. Their primary purpose, of course, has always been to provide the means by which people, one at a time, could get from a given stage or level to another, whenever natural or customary means of ascent and descent were inconvenient or unavailable. One of the earliest references to a ladder is found in the Bible (Gen. 28:12), where Jacob tells of a dream in which he saw a ladder stretching from earth to heaven, with angels of God ascending and descending upon it.[17] Probably the oldest pictorial representation of a ladder is in a Fifth-Dynasty tomb at Saqqara in Egypt.[18] This mural depicts a spirited scene of a number of men who appear to be engaged in dressing the surface of a large stone block from various positions on a ladder. The ladder has only eight rungs, but their wide-apart spacing is unusual—some two feet, assuming that the ladder is in scale with the workmen clinging to it. Undeniably exceptional, however, the ladder is fitted with wheels for rolling it into position.

The vast majority of ladders (though not provided with wheels) have always been movable. This portability accounts more than anything else for their perennial usefulness and versatility in both original construction operations and in connection with repairs and maintenance.[19] The standards of a ladder usually rest on the ground or on some other stable platform or base, with their tops leaning against the wall or the cornice of a building or lying up along the slope of a roof. But sometimes a ladder is fitted with hooks at the tops of the standards so that it can be hung from above, hooked over the ridge of a steeply pitched roof, or similarly secured to an offset or horizontal member of the framework higher up. In recognition of both types of support, a Canadian regulation of 1823 by the government of York, near Toronto, "required every home in the Town of York (because of the fire hazard) to provide a readily available ladder of sufficient length to reach the eaves as well as another one supplied with iron hooks to be hooked over the ridge, in order to reach the chimney top. . . ."[20]

The typical ladder

A typical ladder consists of two uprights or standards, linked at convenient regular intervals by horizontal rungs that serve as steps. Today, in the western world, ladders are manufactured almost exclusively of metal. But throughout the ages and well into the first half of the twentieth century, ladders were customarily made of wood; it is these with which we are concerned. Different species of wood have been employed in making ladders. For the rungs, the most satisfactory wood (in America) was ash. A tough but resilient wood that resists breakage, it stands up well against the abrasive wear of constant traffic. The standards, on the other hand, were usually of some variety of conifer. These species— lighter than oak and comparable hardwoods—can be obtained in long straight pieces that taper only slightly and are naturally free of all but the smallest, inconsequential knots. It was customary for the standards to consist of matching halves of long straight saplings that had been split longitudinally by wedges. These members, half-round in section, not only involved less preparation work than the rectangularly cross-sectioned standards of modern times, but also were stronger. This was because the split saplings preserved the continuity of the wood's longitudinal fibers throughout, along the edges, instead of interrupting the continuity, here and there, by conforming strictly to a saw-imposed rectangularity. Augur holes were bored through both halves of the sapling either before or after they had been split apart; and into these holes the ends of the rungs were snugly driven. The ladder's stability and security against lateral racking depended upon the tight fit of the rungs in their holes. A sufficient angle of slope prevented it from overturning in the direction of the user.[21]

An alternative method of securing the connections between rungs and standards was to lash flat slats to the faces of the standards instead of inserting the ends of round rungs into holes. This was an unsatisfactory substitute, resorted to either temporarily or when the ladder was expected to remain in one position. Changes in humidity constantly jeopardized the effectiveness of the rope lashings. Thus during long periods of hot, dry weather the lashings in-

Before the advent of machines powered by steam, gasoline, or electricity, tasks that required extraordinary amounts of force sometimes used batteries of capstans. Here men and horses are shown activating no less than forty-eight such contrivances to raise a gigantic obelisk upright in St. Peter's Square, Rome. (Engraving after Carlo Fontana, in Niccola Zabaglia, *Castelli e ponti. . . .* 1824, pl. 50.)

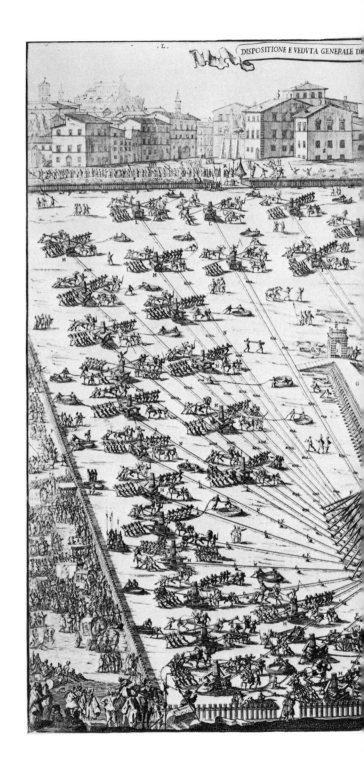

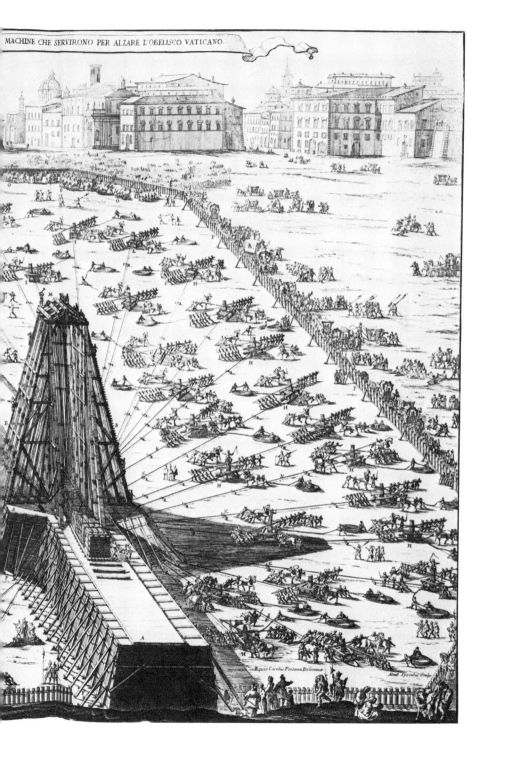

Eques Carolus Fontana Delineavit

Alext. Specularis Sculp.

evitably slackened, causing the slats to slip awry on the standards and offering insufficient resistance to racking on the part of the standards themselves. The lashings, on their part, not only were subject to abrasion but added to the total weight and clumsiness of the ladder, making it more difficult to move it about and set up. Furthermore, when exposed to the weather, the rope deteriorated more rapidly than the wooden rungs and standards.

Nowadays, for ordinary straight ladders, the spacing of the rungs has become generally standardized at twelve-inch intervals. But formerly the rungs were set closer together. Likewise, the interval that separated the standards was often less in the past than it is today. But too narrow a spacing of the standards contributes to the ladder's instability and makes it precarious to climb about on. To correct this instability somewhat, the standards were at times set nonparallel, wider apart at their feet than at their tops. The spacing of both rungs and standards was commented on some three-quarters of a century ago by A. G. H. Thatcher, a British building surveyor. He writes that the rungs are spaced 9″ apart, and that "the sides [or standards] which may be of sufficient length to receive 100 rungs are 9″ apart at the top and from 12 to 13″ apart at the bottom, according to the length of the ladder."[22] Even with less than half the number of rungs Thatcher says are possible, clearly the muscle of at least two strong men would be required to set up such a tall ladder.[23]

Extremely tall, regular ladders, often mounted on wheels or some kind of carriage and fixed in a vertical posture, are sometimes part of the housekeeping equipment of major churches and other large, constantly used auditoriums. (One such serves the interior of St. Peter's in Rome.) They afford the workmen ready access to scaffolds high overhead for major painting or refinishing; they facilitate inspection and minor repairs; and they are useful in hanging and removing special decorations.

Single-standard ladders

One type of ladder used in special situations throughout the past had a single standard with rungs that pierced it and projected on either side. Such ladders were either movable or fixed. But although single-pole ladders of the movable sort were used by firemen[24] and by besieging armies,[25] seldom indeed were they employed in building construction. On the other hand, fixed ladders of one standard were often part of building operations. Two medieval manuscripts depict this type of ladder as providing access to the pulley-supporting crossarm of T-shaped cranes.[26] In these and other examples, the ladder aspect of the contrivance was used far less frequently than ordinary ladders and hence did not need to be as convenient. The slanted one-pole ladders functioned primarily as struts to brace and stabilize the crane's vertical post and were only incidentally fitted with rungs passing through and projecting to right and left, by which a workman could climb up and disentangle the rig if the rope fouled or jumped its pulleys. Similarly pierced with rungs, one or more of the legs of high timberwork trestles or huge construction gantries have served in subsequent centuries as a means by which the workmen climbed to and from the upper part of a structure during its erection and afterwards for periodic inspection and maintenance.[27]

Single masts, guyed with cables to sustain their erect posture, were employed in building operations by the ancient Greeks. Sometimes they fitted the masts with rungs that projected on either side permitting ready access to both the hoisting tackle and the guy lines at the top of the masts. Apparently similar contrivances, dating from the third quarter of the eighteenth century, were used in a battery of nine single-pole units, each of 26 rungs, to raise the centerings for the Pont de Neuilly across the Seine on the northwestern outskirts of Paris.[28]

Even though they may have often assisted in periodic inspections and minor repairs, in general the various types of permanently fixed ladders do not concern this study (rope ladders, for example, provided by the ratlines and shrouds of large sailing vessels,[29] and the series of iron rungs—often without connecting standards—that are attached to tall chimney stacks). For in our examination of the ladder's role in building construction, mobility and ease of relocation are the major criteria of usefulness. A number of movable types of ladders have been developed in relatively modern times. But among these, probably only two have become of widespread and versatile use in building construction; namely, the familiar collapsible or folding stepladder and, more recently, the extension ladder.[30] A particularly convenient type of portable ladder, apparently dating from the late Renaissance, is based on the scheme of interlocking short sections.[31] The standards of these short-section ladders are not quite parallel and are notched, above and below, in order to lock into the rungs of adjacent units. (In function, then, they were forerunners of the modern extension ladder.) The shortness of the individual units makes such ladders easy to handle, easy to set up in confined spaces, and easy to transport, particularly where they must be carried on the backs of horses or burros along narrow trails in rough terrain.[32] But they are somewhat precarious in multiple assemblages and nowhere nearly as strong or trustworthy as ordinary ladders.

Ladders as tall as these, made up of so many short units, were probably never leaned against a building. For bending stresses at their levels of attachment subjected them to buckling out of alignment. But shorter, interlocking ladders were often adopted for their adaptable lengths and the convenience of positioning them. (Niccola Zabaglia, *Castelli e ponti.* . . . 1824, pl. 9.)

A device that preceded all other types of ladders consists of tilted logs with deep notches, serving as treads, cut into the smooth trunk in a straight line at regular intervals. Notched logs survive in isolated, primitive environments, for they are obviously easier to fashion than regular ladders, requiring but one tool, an axe. For instance, they have been employed for centuries in some of the *cenotes*, those deep underground grottoes that still provide the water supply for the Indian population of the Yucatan peninsula in Mexico.[33] Again, many native peoples living in the jungles of Southeast Asia, in New Guinea, in the islands of the Pacific, and elsewhere still customarily use tilted, notched logs for access to their elevated houses.[34] Among some tribes, even the dogs climb them. Although —if at all lengthy—most notched logs are difficult to move, their relative heaviness makes their fixed installation as permanent stairways both stable and assured. In some areas of the world, however, notched logs have been employed in actual building construction. A pictorial record of one instance of this practice shows a busy scene of house construction in southeastern Tibet. Three deeply notched logs, each of some thirteen treads, lean against the gangways of a workman's scaffold, from which earth is being rammed between wide boards held in place by numerous tall poles.[35]

Built-in ladders and ladders as scaffolding

Sometimes builders permanently incorporated into the structure the means by which the workmen could clamber about on it during the course of erection. In other words, they established the equivalent of built-in construction ladders. One such situation is encountered among the Musgun pagans in what was formerly German East Africa: "The houses of this tribe are curious fortlike structures: a compound consists of five or six round huts built close together usually in a circle, the huts being connected, but only the first and last have a door into the open. These latter are usually the largest, and their conically shaped surfaces are covered with *regular protuberances used as ladders in the construction of the building*. Some of them are twenty feet in height. Both walls and roof are made of mud. [italics added]."[36] Another writer speaks of the clay houses of a small Massas community in Central Africa: "On the outside a number of regular flutings give life and accent to these geometrical forms and afford a foothold by which the summit of the hut (often 20 to 25 feet high) can be reached; they enable it to be built without the aid of scaffolding. . . ."[37]

These and other examples provide evidence of ingenious economy in native building construction, following long-established tradition. Nowadays, for painting, refinishing, or repairing buildings of modest height, ladders themselves may become a significant part of a scaffolding apparatus. Pairs of ordinary ladders lean against a wall, spaced at convenient intervals. Projecting brackets are hooked over one of their rungs; planks are then laid across from one bracket to the other to form a platform from which carpenters or other building mechanics can work. Whenever applicable, this scheme dispenses with the standards and putlogs required in customary scaffoldings and capitalizes on the maneuverability of equipment (namely, ladders) that is necessary in any case to the prosecution of the work.

Ladders as agents of defense

As already noted, the maneuverability of ordinary ladders makes them highly flexible pieces of building equipment. But it has had important consequences beyond strictly constructional situations. Thus some ladders provided a means of protection. Consider, for instance, the defensible stone towers above the western porch of churches in early medieval England. From ground level to upper story, there were no permanent, built-in stairs, neither of stone nor of wood. Instead, access was gained by a ladder that could be hauled up through a trap door, after the garrison of defenders had assembled in the upper stages of their thick-walled stronghold. From there they overlooked anyone approaching on the outside of the building. Or, if the aggressors had succeeded in battering down the door and gaining entrance to the church, the defenders could shoot at them from above as they desecrated the sanctuary and looted it of its altar plate.[38]

In the Hopi and other Indian pueblos of the American southwest, the inhabitants used exterior ladders to pass from one level to another. But the ladders themselves were adapted for the inhabitants' protection. First, recall that a Hopi pueblo community consists of thick-walled adobe dwellings clustered into two- or often three-story complexes of geometrical, rectalinear units. Their flat roofs offer space for cooking, for children's play, for sleeping, all at a level above the surrounding terrain. The ladders leading from the ground to the terrace roof above the first floor are curious in one respect. Their uprights or standards are customarily fashioned (at least they always were until recently) from whole pine saplings that taper very slightly through a length often twice or even thrice the distance from ground to terrace. In other words, the total height of the standards is as much as three times that of their functional portion, which is furnished with rungs.

Quite apart from any psychological or symbolic reasons for the ladders' excessively tall, gradually tapering standards, there existed a very basic, practical consideration to account for the adoption of this feature. Namely, they served as protection from intruders, whether animal or human: a sort of equivalent to locking the door at night. Because of the counterbalance provided by the high standards, even a child could pivot one of these ladders against the edge of the roof, swing it up out of reach, and then swerve it onto the surface of the terrace, out of sight from below. Two further practical considerations were the additional weight of the high standards (which helped to stabilize their feet at ground level) and the convenience of having a newel post, as it were, to grasp on arriving at or descending from the upper level. Particularly in the larger pueblo complexes, where the second- and third-story units made irregularly shaped terraces, the extra length provided a further advantage. The access ladders were not always maintained at a familiar and unchanging place at the terrace's edge. Consequently, the tips of the ladders' standards, projecting above an intervening second-story unit of the building complex, served to identify the current location of the means of descent.

Clearly ladders have uses that far outlive their employment in the original construction of a building. Above all, however, as pieces of constructional equipment they have always been essential to the process of building man-made structures.

9

Were it not for Wood our whole civilization on this planet would probably not have evolved the way it did. Certainly our buildings throughout the ages would have turned out quite differently without wood's multiplicity of roles, both in the structures themselves and in the constructional means of executing them.[1]

The Role of Wood in Building Construction

Wood is a product of the natural growth of trees, whose life cycle is generally predictable. The timbers derived from the many species that grow tall and straight are ideally suited to use in man-made structures, either as supporting columns or as load-bearing beams that can span considerable space in one piece. What accounts for their effectiveness as horizontal beams is the timbers' resistance to both compressional and tensile stresses. In masonry, by contrast, these two properties do *not* combine equally, for brick and stone resist tensile stresses to only a limited and rather unreliable degree.

Wood members can be assembled by lashing them together with rope. But their distinct advantage in permanent structures is that they can be worked with hand tools and fashioned into rigidly jointed frames to create a skeletal structure that not only supports some kind of weather-resistant envelope but also offers a built-in scaffolding or gantry for the workmen during construction. In masonry, on the other hand, the workmen as well as the space-spanning structure itself must be provided with extraneous support while the building is going up. The need for such falsework assemblages—scaffolding for the masons, centering and formwork for the permanent structure of arch or vault—adds appreciably to the cost of building and makes the process of erection more difficult and complex. In a very real sense, the history of masonry building construction consists primarily of the development of these essential falsework applications and the planning and coordination of their installation and subsequent removal. In general, buildings that consist largely of wood require far less in the way of falsework or construction equipment than do those in which brickwork or, especially, stonework is the dominant material. Stonework under construction (vaulting, for example) requires extensive provisional support; whereas the framing of timberwork can largely be executed integrally, by making temporary use of permanent increments of the ensemble.

The problem of rot

Wood is subject to deterioration by rotting. Yet timber piles with fire-hardened points, driven into soggy ground, have been utilized from earliest times as foundation supports. They were also driven into lake bottoms to carry a superstructure of clusters of prehistoric dwellings. Provided they remain completely below the water table in the ground, wooden piles are virtually indestructible. For example, intact piles have been discovered dating from Roman times. In the latter part of the nineteenth century hundreds of piles were exhumed at such prehistoric sites as the terramare settlements of northern Italy and the lake dwellings of Switzerland. Of course, once these very ancient timber piles were exposed to the air they disintegrated rapidly; but it is astonishing that they survived some six or seven millennia, immersed and undisturbed in ground water.

Well digging in the recent past illustrates a use of wood that capitalizes on timber's virtual indestructibility when permanently immersed in ground water. One of the chief methods of digging water wells manually through sandy, gravelly, or clayey soil employed a stout, heavy but simple ring of timber. Its inner diameter equalled the intended size of the well hole and its conformation consisted of a flat upper surface and an outward-sloping surface underneath. When the timber ring was placed on the ground where the well was to be located, the digger set to work within its circumference, spading out the earth and undermining the ring itself so that it descended as the excavation proceeded. Meanwhile, from the outside, a mason went to work building on the ring of wood, course by course, a hollow cylinder of brick or stone. As the digger excavated the hole deeper and deeper, the mason continued to work outside the

Cutaway view of heavy timber ring used in handicrafted well digging. (Drawing by A. Meggett, after author.)

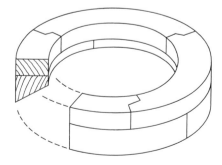

excavation at ground level. Thus the masonry lining followed the digger's downward progress, preventing cave-ins. Finally, when the depth of the well had surpassed a reliable groundwater level, the digging was halted in the confident assurance that the supporting timber footing would not rot away at the bottom of the well (nor the masonry lining collapse) because the wooden foundation ring remained constantly immersed in water. In this process the hollow cylinder of masonry, as it grew taller and increasingly heavier, made the work of excavating less arduous; it also dispensed with temporary shoring that would otherwise have added to the expense and interfered with the removal of the spoil.

It is the frequent and periodic changes from dampness to dryness that destroy wood. Thus the builders of the Gothic era submitted to considerable expense to cover their timber roofs with a surface of slate or, especially, sheets of lead. In masonry structures medieval builders generally encouraged air to circulate freely around the interior structural timberwork to prevent rot due to condensation. In exposed situations, as in the remarkable "mast" churches of Norway (some of which, still extant, are said to date from the twelfth century!), a thick coating of tar has protected the exterior wood surfaces from insect damage and from dry rot alike.

So-called dry rot, in fact, has always been one of the shortcomings of wooden structures, and much has been written about how to deal with it. The following is excerpted from an 1825 building guide:

The most effectual mode of preserving timber from decay is to char it; . . . charcoal being the greatest anti-putrescent known, and no moisture within the influence of its action will become putrid or decomposed. . . .

The seasoning of timber by fire is the best way of all for piles and other pieces that are to stand under the earth, or water. The Venetians [practice] this method, and the way by which they do it is this: they put the piece to be seasoned into a strong and violent flame; in this they continually turn it round by means of an engine, and take it out when it is every way covered with a thick coaly crust; by this means the internal part of the wood is so hardened, that neither earth nor water can damage it for a long time afterwards. . . . [2]

The author also provides specific information about a number of methods then in use for seasoning newly cut timber, along with prescriptions to be followed *at the time of installation* to forestall dry rot in floors, wall paneling, doors, and closets. He finishes by warning that "air that is stagnant is equally pernicious as stagnant moisture. . . . Ventilation, and the use of charcoal, are the best preventives." In an age when seafaring ships were universally of wood, the curing, preservation, and longevity of wooden structures were subjects of major concern and attention to the builders of ships and buildings alike.

Our merchant ships are at times troubled with [dry rot]. Our ships of war being built of live oak, cedar, and locust, are less exposed to this evil. The live oak appears to be almost indestructible, except perhaps by its contact with other species of wood, the juices of which, as in tree nails, may injure it . . . . The object of every process for the preservation of timber must be to extract the water of the sap, and to destroy the absorbent power of the wood, and chiefly of the sap vessels. . . . The first method is suggested by a very common usage of charring posts which are to be placed in the ground. This method is of very ancient date, it having been used by the Grecians and the Romans; and the piles so used, either for bridges or foundations of temples, are now frequently found in a state of complete preservation, after a lapse of 2000 years. . . . [3]

Advantages of wood

Two other shortcomings of wood as a building material are that it is combustible and that knots can weaken critical areas. These disadvantages, however, are overshadowed by wood's resistance to both tensile and compressive forces, its characteristic length in relation to cross section, and the relative ease with which it can be worked with hand tools. Ideally suited for tall masts and weight-bearing columns, wood is also eminently effective as beams of all sorts, including floor joists and roof rafters. Moreover, until the late-nineteenth-century development of structural steel members, wood was the only material that could achieve far-oversailing cantilever construction.

The great variety of trees and their distinctive characteristics and properties allow wood to be applied to vastly different building projects. Evergreens generally grow tall and straight, with very little taper and quite small branches. On the other hand, oaks and many other hardwoods have huge branches. In the past enormous hardwood branches or roots together with trunks furnished large, strong, curved or angular members whose shapes—useful in ship timbers and in some timber arch constructions—provided in a single piece a rigidity that was much more reliable than many a built-up assemblage of a jointed framework. Some woods are by nature heavy and dense, others light but stiff. Some resist abrasion, mechanical injury, and splitting; others are flexible. Some indurate on exposure to the air, becoming very difficult to saw and nail after they have thoroughly cured. Some species stand up particularly well in water; others swell by absorbing water. Still others possess a high degree of dimensional stability, resisting *both* expansion and contraction due to changes in temperature. Moreover, quite apart from their structural properties, different woods possess a wide range of textures, tones, and colors, as well as graining, patterns, and distinctive markings, all of which make wood highly desirable as a finish as well as a structural material.[4] But it is wood's role in building construction that has made the carpenter an indispensable member of society universally, wherever wood has been available.[5]

Cutting and rough-shaping the timber

For various reasons, trees were traditionally felled in the wintertime. In premechanized America, for instance, it was the season when workers (such as farmers) were largely free of their normal pursuits. With frozen ground, moreover, the logs could be transported out of the woods with less chance of wagons or skids becoming mired. Then, taking advantage of the spring flooding of the rivers, the logs could be cheaply floated in great numbers to the saw mills. (Such immersion in water diluted the sap, which assured a more even and gradual curing, free of warping, when the lumber was subsequently stacked in the drying yards.)[6] Aside from cheapness and convenience, another consideration was the effect of the time of cutting on the treatment or curing of timbers (the latter varied according to the species and the size of timbers).

Two factors of the time of cutting which may affect seasoning are 1) the amount of water in the tree and 2) the weather conditions after the cutting.

It is generally supposed that trees contain less water in winter than in summer, and it is a common expression to say the "sap is down in the winter." This is partly, if not wholly, wrong, as some trees contain as much water in winter as in summer, if not more. The first effect of the time of cutting is that there is more water to be evaporated from fall and winter cut timber than from spring and summer cut timber. . . .[7]

After the trees were felled, the logs brought out of the forest, cut, and cured (against too rapid or uneven drying that would produce splits, warping, or excessive shrinkage), the process of rough-shaping them began. Throughout much of the world this shaping was accomplished primarily by saws, broad axes, adzes, or hand hatchets, though many other tools were developed for specialized tasks.[8] Long, large logs were often split longitudinally by means of wedges, a practice that required less time and much less effort than sawing. Wedges were used notably in cruck construction, to obtain very large, curving, branch-plus-trunk members in matching pairs.[9] Unlike longitudinal sawing, which cut into the grain here and there, *wedge-splitting techniques* did not disturb the continuity of the wood's fibers. But where boards were required, the most universal means of fashioning them out of big timbers was the *pit-sawing method,* still used to this day in underdeveloped lands. In pit sawing the log is usually propped up at an angle over a saw horse, with two men operating the saw. The man above, standing on the log, guides the saw and retrieves it at every stroke; the man below does the major work of cutting by pulling the saw downward.[10]

The most primitive kind of timber construction is the log cabin and related types of whole-log structures. For the traditional peasant dwellings of northwestern Russia, for example, long, straight trees were felled and stripped of their branches in the nearby forest, hauled to the building site, and aligned ready for erection. They were then rolled or skidded up a pair of slanted logs to take their place on the walls of the large, sometimes two-and-a-half-story buildings.[11] In rural Bohemia and other central and eastern European countries as well as in Switzerland, wherever extensive upland forests furnish a ready supply of tall straight trees, a more sophisticated type of log construction exists, in which the logs are hewn square and erected with flat wall surfaces both inside and out. The greatest variety of indigenous types of log construction, however, are found in the Scandinavian countries, where evergreen forests are abundant and the vernacular tradition has prevailed for centuries. Particularly noteworthy are the notches cut into round or squared logs to make the corners of the building tightly interlocked and secure against any movement, vertical or horizontal.[12] Such interlocking notches were shaped by a saw and a hatchet, two hand-tools with which Norwegian and Swedish carpenters are uncommonly skilled and proficient to this very day.

Probably because log cabins in America were commonly built by pioneers who had neither the schooling nor the leisure that would permit them to write down a circumstantial account, few detailed contemporary descriptions of the erection of a primitive log cabin have survived. The following account was recorded by a German traveler in the mid-nineteenth century.

The erection of [a log cabin] proceeds with unbelievable speed; seldom are more than three or four days required. The procedure is as follows: First of all a suitable site is chosen (above all, it must not be damp), and then a day is fixed upon which, with the help of the neighbors, the building material is collected. With the exception of a few nails, this is furnished by the locality itself in the form of trees which the practically constructed American ax fells and properly smooths in about as many hours as the German ax would require days. A man with a team of horses or oxen drags them to the building site and places them ready at hand at the ends and sides of the rectangle upon which the structure is to be erected. The following morning the building men gather for the setting and raising. For this purpose four "corner men" are selected who notch and join together the logs while other men place them one upon the other. As soon as the first course is fixed, the carrying beams and floor planks are fit in. When the walls have reached the intended height, a three-foot-wide entrance is chopped or sawed, and on one short side of the rectangle an opening where the fireplace is to be attached. The latter is constructed below of fieldstones and mortar and above usually of pieces of wood cemented with clay; sometimes it appears quite slanting and unfirm. The roof, which generally slopes only very little, projects in the front on some of these cabins, forming a small porch; on others it projects toward the rear. With this the back-woodsman's home is finished, and the third day is used only for the laying of a ceiling over the room, for the caulking of cracks and joints (using lime), and for the finishing of the door (which seldom has a lock, but commonly only a wooden handle). Windows are considered superfluous. . . . Before the occupant moves into his new shell, however, the product of his skill and neighborly assistance must be dedicated; just as our carpenters and masons have their "lifting celebration," so the workmen in the backwoods have their housewarming, *at which there is much dancing and an abundant consumption of whiskey. . . .* [13]

A rather special and short-lived practice of wood construction (which required an inordinant number of nails) flourished for a brief period in rural northeastern America when the forests were still abundant sources of timber and water-powered saw mills were ubiquitous. In this scheme, house walls consisted of solid wood, made up of innumerable courses of full one-by-six-inch boards. Alternate layers of the boards were offset by an eighth to a quarter of an inch; these staggered indentations then served as keys for plastering. The plaster not only formed a smooth surface, outside and in, but sealed the continuous horizontal joints against penetration by wind and rain. In the severe winters of central New York State, the outside plaster was protected from injury and the walls further weatherproofed by clapboarding nailed to the exterior. But because of the lack of vertical and even diagonal members to consolidate and stiffen the structure, the walls were relatively unstable, and the scheme enjoyed but scant popularity.[14]

Solid wooden walls of
laminated boards laid
flat, 1956. (Photographs
by author.)

Timber framing

During the Middle Ages, in northwestern Europe and particularly
in England, the art of timber framing achieved its most impressive range and highest degree of expertise.[15] Its accomplishments
reached anonymous vernacular buildings as well as grand edifices. An
astonishing variety of complex joints were used in the timberwork
of multi-storied houses, church spires, granges, and tithe barns and,
preeminently, in roofs of all sorts. Complicated notchings were
coupled with splines, cogs, or internal keys, representing remarkable triumphs of stereotomy. Moreover, dovetail joints and angular
cuts were developed that prevented joined members from pulling
apart under stress in the framing of timbers.[16]

Medieval builders in England invented two widely used
structural schemes of roof framing in timber; one employed crucks,
the other hammer beams. Always used in pairs, cruck blades were
long, heavy, curved or angled timbers that combined the functions of

columns and principal rafters into one pointed-arch unit. Secondary members were framed into each pair of crucks so that the entire framework of walls and roof hung on them.[17] The hammer-beam roof was much more sophisticated and decorative, making resplendent numerous great halls and church interiors of the medieval period.[18] Structurally, a hammer beam is a horizontal timber—braced by a curved strut from below—that projects inward at the top of the masonry wall and, together with its mate on the opposite side, reduces the length of the timber required to span the void from wall to wall. It has other advantages. Braces curving up from the inner ends of each hammer beam meet, under the center of the tie beam they reinforce, in the form of a pointed arch that relates the timberwork to the masonry structure. All these curving braces—some linked to vertical posts rising from the salient ends of the hammer beams, some to wallposts set below—as well as the horizontal tie beams or collar beams and the hammer beams themselves, when secured to the principal rafters, create a truss that theoretically

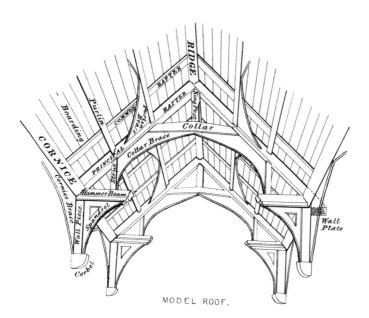

MODEL ROOF.

Hammer-beam roofs. Both drawings show wind bracing in the form of curving members in the planes of the roof. (Philip Freeman, "On Foliated Wooden Roofs," *Cambridge Camden Society Transactions* 1(1842): pl. 1 facing p. 106.)

S. MARY, BVRY S. EDMVNDS.

produces no lateral thrust. Instead, its wind-induced pressure against the masonry wall on the lee side acts many feet below the top of the wall. Thus the stability of timber roof and masonry walls alike is assured, and high winds can never slide the roof off the walls.

(One problem in timber *house* framing—because of the presence of floors—was that numerous structural members had to find secure bearing at the same level, such as at the top of a corner or wall post. To accommodate the convergence of timbers, many posts were installed upside down, as it were, hewn from the inverted trunk of trees.)

Timber joints

Joints are the critical factors in any wooden construction, and a great deal of ingenuity has gone into making them secure. One of the simplest—mainly confined to utilitarian, rural buildings—was a tying joint for transverse beams linking stout posts that stood opposite each other in the outer walls. From the top down some distance a slice of each post was removed, forming a deep slot into which the neck of the tying beam was lowered. The beam was then capped with a wood insert to fill the slot above it. A second simple and seldom noted joint was frequently found in symmetrically shaped roofs at midspan in the triangle's base. Today the central vertical member in a triangular roof frame is called the king post, which implies that it is in compression, supporting the ridge from a bearing on the tie beam below. As often as not in the past, however, this central member was in tension, hung from the apex of the triangle, with diagonal struts branching up from its lower end to brace and prevent deflection in the principal rafters half way up their slope. In this role, the king post did not carry down to the tie beam; indeed, there was usually a considerable void. But in many cases a metal strap was bolted to the bottom of the king post and passed down around the tie beam, acting as a stirrup to prevent the beam from sagging. In the Gothic era—particularly in France—the situation was different, largely because of the very steep pitch of the high roofs then in vogue. For to erect a Gothic roof required seating the vertical member(s) of the timberwork complex upon the base provided by the main tie beam. Subsequently, side pieces (and an insert below) were attached to the base of the vertical member(s) in order to clasp the tie beam and secure the conjunction of the major timbers there.

Many joints in medieval timber framing were lap joints—connections in which a (usually secondary) member was pressed

Knob and neck tying
joint. In the near view
a stout corner post has
been cut with a deep
vertical slot into which
the neck of a trans-
verse beam has been
lowered to form a snug
joint resistant to both
tension and compres-
sion. Instead of a fork
only deep enough to
accommodate the
transverse beam, a
lower position was
adopted here so that
the beam could sup-
port the floor of a
loft within, whose
headroom near the
wall would be incon-
venienced by an
eaves-level position.
(Photograph by au-
thor.)

into a matching sinkage in the side of another member and pinned there. This kind of joint greatly facilitated the assembling of a frame because all the lapping members could be installed after the other elements of the frame had been put together. But the vast majority of pinned joints in timber framing consisted of mortice-and-tenon connections. Some form of mortice-and-tenon joint has apparently been used from prehistoric times.[19] Preserved timbers recovered from peat bogs show that this technique was used for joining timbers in the Stone Age lake dwellings, dating from at least as far back as 4000 B.C. A mortice is a rectangular hole chiseled out of one timber in order to receive the tenon (a tongue constituting the reduced end) of another timber. The tenon is usually secured in the mortice by one or two "tree nails," that is, wooden pins or pegs driven into a hole bored through both members. At first, mortice-and-tenon joints were used exclusively for right-angle assemblages. But soon diagonal struts—introduced to prevent swaying—were mortice-and-tenoned, too. To ensure that each joint was properly cut and shaped, the entire framework was test assembled on the ground. Raising the bents, establishing their permanent positions, and linking them together could then proceed quickly and confidently.[20] The mortice-and-tenon joints affected the order and sequence of assemblage in a fundamental and inexorable way. This was because the tenons, usually one at each end of a member, made the member's overall length greater than the distance between the timbers that it spanned. Hence one of these timbers could not be positioned until after the tenon at the far end of the member had been secured in its mortice; only then could the second timber be brought into position to engage the tenon at the member's near end.

Subassemblages

The sequence of assembling the various members in a timber frame was a problem not only in the case of individual connections but, more important, with respect to subassemblages. Here it was a question of determining the most expedient and efficient practice of rearing the bents—the transverse frames—of a structure; that is, a question of how many and which members could conveniently be assembled on the ground and raised as a unit (or tilted up, in many cases) to their final position. Such assemblages varied in accordance with the spans involved, the size of the individual members, and the complexity of their connections as well as with the number and nature of the longitudinal links securing one bent to those adjacent to it, right and left. Hence the rearing of each framing system had to be worked out specifically for each situation.

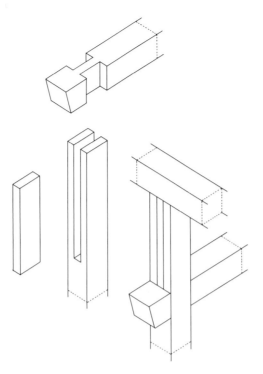

Scheme of knob and neck joint in timber framing. Clearly the beam cannot be withdrawn or replaced once the wall-top plate has been set in place. (Drawing by A. Meggett, after author.)

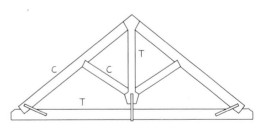

Framing of traditional triangular roof truss, typically Renaissance, where the king post is in tension. (Drawing by A. Meggett, after author.)

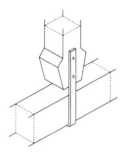

Detail at base of king post in Renaissance-type roof, showing metal stirrup. (Drawing by A. Meggett, after author.)

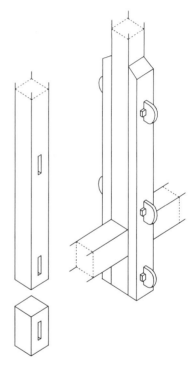

Detail at the base of one of the principal vertical members in a French Gothic cathedral's roof complex, showing the clasping arrangement where horizontal tie beam and vertical column are linked. (Drawing by A. Meggett, after author.)

In general, all conjectures as to how subassemblages were raised involve tilt-up procedures for at least the major part of a bent. Most, if not all, proposed solutions seem reasonable enough in the case of English tithe barns and manorial halls, where the individual members could be readily assembled on the ground and the ensemble pivoted into an upright position with the aid of raising frames and guy lines.[21] In a few tithe barns, however, the timber columns rested on masonry piers to prevent dampness at the ground level from rotting the wood. Assuming that the stone piers were part of the original construction and not a subsequent expedient to replace the deteriorated lower portion of the timber columns, the piers would have restricted the customary tilt-up operation (requiring a temporary leveling up of the earth to their height).

But a more significant situation puts in doubt the probability that a tilt-up procedure was invariably followed in erecting huge and cumbersome timber frames. This problem was encountered in the great timber roofs above the vaults of Gothic Cathedrals, particularly in France. For these roofs had to be reared, not at ground level but from the lofty top of relatively narrow clerestory walls, sometimes a hundred or more feet above the ground. It seems most unlikely that the bents could have been tilted up as major subassemblages. Instead, each of the timbers of the roof structure was probably hauled up to the level of the eaves, one by one, beginning with the great tie beams. As various observers have assumed (and this writer has demonstrated elsewhere), the roof would have been built before the high vaults. Thus the separate timbers of the roof could be raised aloft from the nave floor unobstructed, in direct vertical lifts.[22]

For a number of reasons, the main tie beams were not only long (spanning up to 45 feet or more across the void of the nave) but also thick in cross section. Structurally, they served primarily in tension to prevent the feet of the rafters from spreading apart. But they also acted in compression to transfer the wind load acting against one clerestory wall to the one opposite, where flying buttresses transmitted the load to the stable outer buttresses. Moreover, during construction—of both the roof structure and subsequently the vault—the tie beams supported powerful lifting devices, including great wheels, used to haul up timbers and later to raise and lower the vault centerings. And, of course, the tie beams provided support for a localized working platform from which the carpenters assembled the framework of the entire roof itself, bent by bent. Clearly, however, this platform could not have duplicated the conditions or the advantages provided by a ground-level scene of operations. The elevation of operations created the chief differences between the roof framing of granges and tithe barns, on the one hand, and of major churches, on the other. Consequently, the framework of a cathedral roof consisted of many more individual members. Except for the tie beams, the members were generally smaller in cross section and therefore lighter in weight and easier to handle. Moreover, their individual connections were simpler, less complicated to assemble.

The close cooperation between carpenter and mason in Gothic building

What is apparent in any discussion of the problems involved in the construction of Gothic cathedral roofs is the close relationship and interdependence between the work of the mason and that of the carpenter. During that era the master mason and the master carpenter were equal in status and authority; and it is clear that major undertakings required a close professional collaboration. This partnership inevitably came about as a result of the fundamentally different nature and properties of the two major building materials of the time: timber and stone. The structural contribution of stone was to resist compression; hence, when stone spanned more than two or three feet, it took the form of an arch, with the voussoirs pressing against each other in wedged sequence. On the other hand, timber was indispensable in resisting tensile forces, and thus could be used as tie beams as long as fifty feet. It is interesting to note that the steep pitch of the high central roofs of Gothic churches brought about the complete separation and independence of the *ceiling*—a stone vault—from the *roof*—a superstructure of timberwork that supported a weather surface of slates or, more often, sheets of lead. This characteristic feature is found particularly in France and central Europe north of the Alps.

In the order and sequence of construction it was both realistic and distinctly advantageous to construct the roof first. Covering in the building at the earliest possible moment protected the exposed work that had already been carried forward up to the level of the eaves and kept rain and snow from damaging further work in the interior. The multitudinous assemblage of timberwork constituting the roof structure also stabilized the high masonry walls, both by its great weight and by linking them into wind-resisting cooperation. And so the stage was set for building the high masonry vault. The timberwork ensemble now served as a high gantry where great wheels could be positioned to haul up centerings for the ribs and perhaps massive carved keystones, where cords of the stone-weighted rope device could be secured in the process of building the vaulting, block by block, and where stagings could be hung (on

Cutaway presentation of Église St. Urbain à Troyes, regarded by many as the most sophisticatedly engineered building of the Gothic era. Its ensemble rationale of a skeletal structure involves a complete separation of timber roof from thin stone-vaulted ceiling; a circulation system that includes integrally built-in spiral stairs with horizontal passageways both outside and in; maximum areas of glass; stone pinnacles to weight the abutments; and flying buttresses reduced to straight, extremely slender stone struts in compression, mounted on equally slender arches. (From a drawing by M. P. Lorain, *Le Moniteur des Architectes,* 1873, pls. 49–50.)

This vertical section through the thin-walled spire of Salisbury Cathedral reveals permanent but replaceable strutting of timberwork (used during construction as a many-tiered internal scaffolding) fashioned so that the entire spire is cross-braced as well as stabilized against overturning. (Francis Price, *Cathedral-Church of Salisbury,* 1753, pl. 6 facing p. 31.)

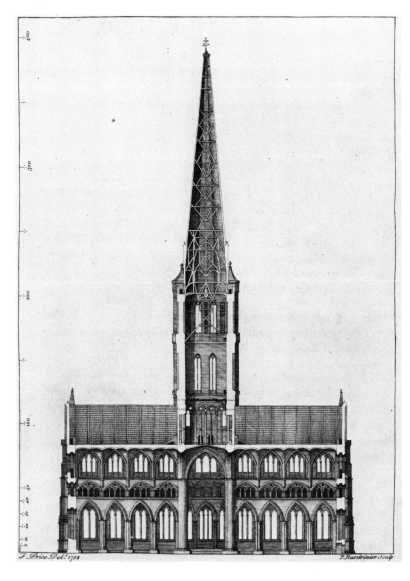

F. Price Del. 1738   P. Fourdrinier Sculp

Upper portion of Salisbury Cathedral's spire. Much of its weight is hung from the capstones at the apex by an iron hanger from which the central spine of the interior timberwork is suspended. (Francis Price, *Cathedral-Church of Salisbury,* 1753, pl. 9 facing p. 40.)

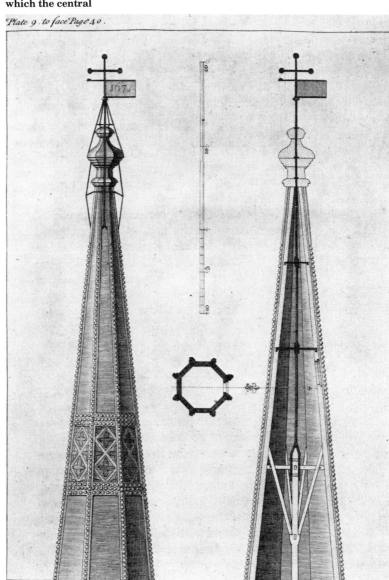

Plate 9. to face Page 40.

F. Price Del. 1746

P. Fourdrinier Sculp.

ropes let through voids in the vaulting) to serve the workmen as they painted or repaired the stone ceiling.

Probably the most remarkable instance of the intimate collaboration between master mason and master carpenter is the spire of Salisbury Cathedral, the tallest medieval structure in England. Considering its towering height the spire is extremely thin-shelled. Everything possible was done to reduce the weight of square tower and octagonal spire alike, for they stood on four unusually slender piers at the crossing, a central area that the clergy wished to keep as open and spacious as possible. The spire's 415-foot height exposed it to frost, driving rain, and buffeting wind. Were it not for preventive measures built into the design throughout, the spire would have faced overturning by every storm.

Chief among these preventive measures was the axial spine of the spire, a vertical chain of timbers that hung (when the stonework was carried up to the topmost block) from the standard of the weather vane. At regular intervals along this timber chain wooden struts were hooked into it, bracing the masonry shell laterally in four directions at each level. These attachments were secured in such fashion that they could be readily removed and repaired or replaced. This structural spine of timberwork, with its branching ribs, served during construction as an indispensable scaffolding, in convenient stages, from which the masons could lay the stonework of the spire's shell, course by course. But the primary function of the timber spine was to assure the stability of the entire spire complex. The tiers of wooden struts braced the shell from within and preserved its integrity as a total entity against buckling or deviation in vertical alignment. More significant, hanging the entire weight of the spire from its capstone effectively consolidated its ensemble and inhibited its tendency to sway or overturn in storms. In other words, instead of resorting to such extraneous means as masonry props or buttresses (which would have added considerably to the weight on the crossing piers and produced a much less elegant silhouette) stability was achieved within the boundaries of the spire itself.

Although the walls of the spire are thin, probably forced to it by the lightness of the arcade, and the accidents and fractures that attended the work, I cannot omit mentioning the architect's particular and curious invention, for adding artificial strength without overburthening the former work. He contrives, in the cavity of the spire, a timber frame, consisting of a central piece, with arms and braces, as may be seen in the general section . . . and in the section of the upper part of the spire. . . . This timber frame, though used as a scaffold while the spire was building, was always meant to hang up to the capstone of the spire, and by that means prevent its top from being injured in storms, and so add a mutual strength to the shell of stone. The central piece of timber is not mortised, to receive the arms which served as floors, but has an iron hoop round it with hooks riveted through; and upon these hooks a flat iron bar is fitted, with an hole in it, which is fastened on to the brace: The upper part of the brace is mortised, and the arms tenanted at the end, to slide into and through the mortise in the brace; so that by a key, or wedge on the outside of the brace, the connection is made compleat; the central piece, and the other end of the arm, being provided with iron, as before, renders it the most compleat piece of work imaginable; nor is its connection at the top inferior to it.

The said arms and braces may be taken out and put in at pleasure, consequently capable of an easy repair. It was before said, that this timber frame served as floors, or scaffolds, till the work by its tapering, or diminishing, became too small for the men to work in the inside; and therefore we must suppose, that they at last made a scaffold on the outside, by thrusting out timbers horizontally, which were tied down in the inside to the central piece. It is probable, that when the sides of the spire drew near together, so as not to admit of timber floors, then the artists began to think of tying all the timbers up to the capstone of the spire; and for this purpose cross bars of iron are yoted into the walls of the spire, so that the standard of the vane has hooks to hang them up by, and at the same time is fixed to the upper part of the central piece, in a most extraordinary manner.

It is therefore worthy of the strictest observation, to keep all these connections in good repair, and particularly with regard to the standard of the vane passing through the capstone, and being so ordered, that the whole was intended to hang up to the top. . . . [23]

The preceding pages seek to convey some impression of the extraordinary versatility of wood as a building material and to illustrate the relationship of timber work to construction procedures and equipment. During the innumerable centuries that men have worked with wood, they have come to appreciate its characteristics, to understand its properties, and to devise ways in which to diminish or circumvent its limitations, to exploit and enhance its advantages. We cannot but applaud their achievement.

10

All the primitive builders are chary of scaffolding; they do not like, and the Greeks least of all, to perform labour which is to all appearance useless, that is to say, which is to leave no trace. . . . Moreover, these builders take good care never to elevate large blocks when they can avoid it. Above the lintels or architraves there are no longer found any but stones of comparatively small dimensions; and it is evident that to avoid too great expense and difficulty, the Architecture itself cedes to the means of execution. . . .[1]

Oversized Blocks and Projecting Stones as Aids in Masonry Construction

As we have seen in wood construction, those in charge of building operations were remarkably adept at fashioning a structure so that it aided its own erection. This was particularly true of masonry structures. Sometimes, when no longer needed, these temporary features were covered up and ignored. Examples include unfilled putlog holes (as found in innumerable medieval and Renaissance buildings throughout western Europe) and slots or holes chiselled into blocks to accommodate lifting devices (as found in such configurations as lewis holes and the U-shaped sinkages of classical Greek buildings). Other features used in masonry construction—oversized blocks, and projecting stones—were removed and discarded. It is to these that we now turn our attention.

Oversized blocks

Today large or costly stones are customarily protected within a girdle of wooden battens or crated individually for transit from quarry or stonecutter's yard to building site. In the Middle Ages, because the stones were generally small enough to be handled by men rather than machines, it was standard practice to ship them from the quarry—sometimes even in finished form—protected by nothing more than layers of straw.[2] But in ancient times, to protect the stone from damage such as chipped edges or gouged surfaces, blocks were roughly hewn with two or more inches of material beyond what was required. Such oversized quarrying of blocks was invariably practiced by the Egyptians because of the superhuman size and weight of their stones and because of the long distance these blocks had to be transported. Providing the exposed surfaces of the blocks with extra stock also permitted the stonework to be dressed down after it was positioned and therefore without fear of injuring its smooth surfaces, sharply defined moldings, or detailed ornamentation.[3] Thus, once aligned, the oversized cylindrical column drums of Greek temples were dressed down into concave flutes separated by clean-cut arrises, all managed with the subtle entasis the Greeks were noted for. Thus, too, the extra stock of plain walling (later to be polished and painted) was dressed down to immaculate

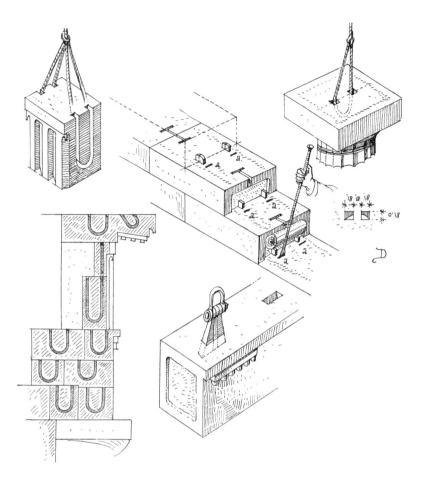

Greek lifting and positioning techniques. A prybar is used to nudge a block, an inch or two laterally, into snug juxtaposition with an adjacent block, after the loop of a hoisting sling has been flipped out of its U-shaped sinkage. (Josef Durm, *Die Baukunst der Griechen*, 1892, lower portion, fig. 63, p. 80.)

smoothness in the marble surfaces of the Athenian Parthenon[4] and in the limestone casing of the Great Pyramid at Gizeh.[5]

The practice of quarrying stones oversized continued to be followed in subsequent centuries. The following account dates from the mid-nineteenth century in England, where sawing had superseded the more ancient techniques of roughing out building stones with stone hammers.

Stone that is to be used at a distance from the quarry cannot be profitably applied to architectural works, unless capable of being sawed with facility; as experience teaches us that it is cheaper to have blocks larger than necessary, and run the risk of damage in loading and unloading, than to take more time and care to prevent such mischief; the value of the cubic contents of the stone that is thus wasted being less than that of the time which would be occupied in packing it with greater care. If the blocks can be reduced to the requisite dimensions by sawing at a moderate expense, the saving will be considerable, as the sawed faces are nearly fit to pass as finished for 'plain work,' and the surplus pieces serve for ashlar, paving, &c. But should the expense of sawing be so great as to render it unadvisable to proceed in this way, then the blocks must be roughed out at the quarry, and left a few inches larger than required, on account of the damage likely to occur on board ship, and in the various removals to their final destination. The plain surfaces must then be worked by manual labour, and the surplus stone which is chipped off will be merely rubbish, after having paid for its freight, cranage, cartage, and many other expenses. The sandstones are all expensive to saw, on account of the excessive wear and tear of the saw-plate. . . . The Craigleith stone, which deserves to be classed among the best of the sandstones, costs nearly four times as much to saw as Portland stone.[6]

The extra stock, then, was an essential and indispensable safeguard (both before and during the process of erection) against flaws, nicks, or any other blemishes that might mar the perfection of finish in the stonework.

Projecting features that aid construction

Much more strikingly apparent than this rough protective crust, projecting features were indispensable aids in the actual erection of masonry buildings. Today, when the stonework of buildings is almost invariably a mere veneer applied to or hung on the real structure (steel or concrete), we have all sorts of efficient cranes and derricks and machinery with which to raise and position each unit of a building's fabric with ease and precision. So it is difficult to

appreciate the extent to which builders once used the stones themselves to facilitate construction by installing permanent blocks that
temporarily featured large and strongly salient projections. Yet, at
the time, it must have seemed the most natural thing in the world
to form temporary corbels or ledges from projecting features in
stone buildings—to employ them as built-in scaffolding, as it were,
to accommodate the activities of the workmen, to facilitate the installation of sometimes large and cumbersome building units, or to
support or anchor construction equipment.

The difficulty of reporting these features should, however, be
noted. Such protuberances were intended to be removed once they
had fulfilled their constructional purpose. Obviously, their removal
destroyed the physical record of their participation in the erectional
process. Fortunately, a small but revealing number of partially finished buildings (especially those of the ancient Greeks) still retain
operational projections that the builders did not bother to remove.
These permit us to study and assess the extent of the various prac-

**Sketch of an oversized
granite facing block on
the unfinished Third
Pyramid at Gizeh.
(Flinders Petrie, *Ten
Years Digging in
Egypt,* 1891, fig. 4, p.
17.)**

Axial dowels for permanent alignment of column drums in classical Greek buildings. The sinkages for these dowels, top and bottom of each drum, also served in the process of rolling the big blocks from quarry to building site. (Josef Durm, *Die Baukunst der Griechen,* 1892, fig. 71, p. 94.)

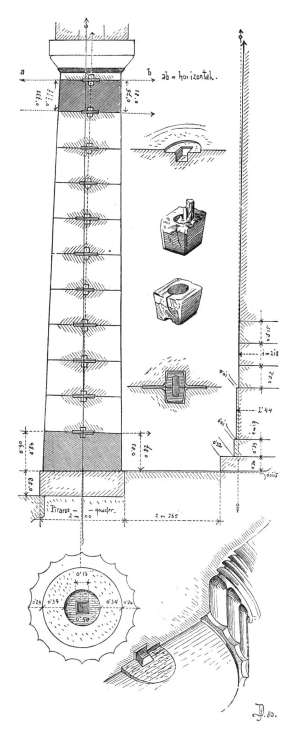

tices adopted by the ancients in achieving their masonry structures.[7] Following are representative instances from various periods of the past of projecting stones that assisted construction. With these as guides and clues, it is perhaps reasonable to speculate on analogous practices for which no solid evidence survives.

Bosses

Probably the commonest occurrences of temporary projections were the bosses left on blocks of stone as an aid in handling them at the building site. The most familiar bosses were the ancones on the column drums of Greek temples. Four of these ancones protruded at quadrant intervals around the cylindrical drums, accommodating pairs of rope slings by which each block could be suspended from a tackle and lowered onto similar blocks as the column rose course by course. The slings were looped over the bosses so that the heavy drums could be held precisely horizontal and eased down accurately into position without the slightest damage to their edges.

So much is well established and reported by many writers. But what has not been seriously considered is the mechanics of elevating and positioning the column drums. It has generally been assumed that the Greeks used a gin to raise and lower the blocks. The gin, however, is confined exclusively to vertical movement. Yet each successive column drum had to be shifted horizontally before being lowered vertically. It seems likely, therefore, that the Greeks fashioned some sort of gantry, involving a horizontal staging to which the drum was raised aloft, then carefully nudged sideways on timber rails or skids set temporarily beneath it, to a point directly above its destined position. Whereupon another block and tackle lifted the drum off the rails and (with the rails removed) lowered it onto a previously set drum.

On at least two counts, any of the tilted-boom or guyed-mast devices that the Greeks used as derricks would have been impractical in maneuvering the column drums of, for example, the Parthenon.[8] First, these marble blocks—over six feet in diameter and averaging two-and-a-half feet in thickness—were too large and heavy. Second, each block had to be eased into contact and aligned with the drum below with great precision. From the writings of the first centuries B.C. and A.D. (particularly from the textbook of Hero of Alexandria, our best source of knowledge about ancient mechanical technology) it seems clear that the devices then in use for raising loads and swinging them into position would not have been equal to the task. Alternatively, as the peristyle of columns was always erected before the cella walls were raised, it is conceivable that the Greeks followed the Egyptian example of constructing earthen ramps, as the columns rose, so that each successive drum could be positioned at a new "ground" level. Here, to be sure, a normal-sized gin could have been used to lift each drum off the sledge on which it had been hauled up the slope to a precise position above previously set drums, then to lower it into place. But this scheme appears quite foreign to the customary practices of the Greek builders who, unlike the Egyptians, had adequate, ready supplies of good timber for falsework. Moreover, Greek temple sites often made such a procedure unfeasible. In the case of the Parthenon, for example, the range of columns along the south flank of the temple is so close to the edge of the precipitous escarpment of the Acropolis that there would have been insufficient room for an earthen embankment high enough to furnish "ground-level" placement for the drums of the 34-foot-high columns.

The risers of the steps that invariably edge temple platforms, and indeed the very cella walls of a few unfinished Greek temples, still retain bosses on their exterior faces, usually a pair for each block. Occurring on relatively small and quite easily handled blocks, these bosses (like the ancones of column drums) would seem to have been useful primarily in connection with lifting slings. In other cultures, however, where large heavy stones were customarily employed, bosses were adopted exclusively to receive the points of levers by which they were tilted or jacked up in the process of positioning them. Ancient Egyptian examples of such "handling bosses" include the quartzite masonry of the "Osireion" of Seti I at Abydos and the granite casing blocks near the entrance to the Third Pyramid at Gizeh.[9] Half a world away, some of the superbly crafted megalithic walls of the Incas, as at Ollantayambo in Peru, have large, irregularly shaped but tightly fitted blocks with sharply protruding bosses, two to each stone, near their bottom edge.[10] Because of their position so close to the base of the block, these bosses could obviously serve only in levering, not in lifting operations from above.

Corbels

A well-established use of projecting stones (to be hewn off after construction, flush with the adjacent masonry) were the corbels employed as temporary supports for the ends of timber centerings in arched bridges. The best known of such structures—in which integral evidence of constructional procedures has survived—is the famous Pont du Gard, built by the Romans in what is now southern France. Here, pairs or triplets of the huge voussoirs just below the

**Projecting stones on
Pont du Gard struc-
ture. (Photograph by
Allen Fitchen.)**

angle of friction were fashioned oversized so that they projected inward beyond the curving line of the intrados, with the top of the corbelling portion of the uppermost voussoir in each group hewn to form a horizontal shelf on which an end of the timber falsework rested.[11] These provisional features reduced the amount of timberwork needed in the falsework, thereby bringing about substantial savings in both materials and the labor required to position and dismantle the massive timber centerings.

That the Romans never got around to hewing off the inward-projecting blocks is most fortunate for us. The lack of similarly unequivocal evidence in the great majority of masonry arch bridges that have been built throughout the world in the intervening centuries prevents us from knowing with certainty the pervasiveness of this use for temporary corbels. But a detailed specification for the execution of the oblique arch bridge over the King River in Cumberland County, England, suggests that the practice was well understood and continued to be followed up through the nineteenth century.

Dated May 6, 1893, the specification reads, in part:

The centres shall be supported in the following manner, that is to say, corbels shall be left in the abutment walls of sufficient substance and strength (to be neatly broken off after the centres are removed), these corbels shall be further strengthened by having stout wooden props placed underneath each corbel, each prop shall rest on a solid footing, and wedges shall be driven between the head of each prop and the underside of each corbel, and at a suitable distance below the springer line, to support a beam on which the ends of the centre shall rest, each centre on two hard-wood wedges. . . .[12]

The construction corbels of the King River bridge were set in the abutment walls "at a suitable distance below the springer line" instead of below the angle of friction in the curving arch ring, as in the Pont du Gard. The spring line position appears to have been the more customary one (at least in cases of medium or modest spans) but it did not involve as economical a use of timber for the centerings as did the Roman Pont du Gard scheme. It is worthy of note, moreover, that constructional corbels set at or near the springs of arch bridges were sometimes allowed to remain in place permanently for their aesthetic contribution, accenting the level at which a pier or abutment became the spring of an arch.

Other constructional corbels on the Pont du Gard pertain to this study; namely, the big header blocks that protrude in a seemingly random pattern from the piers and spandrels of the great arches on both the upstream and the downstream faces of the structure.[13] The intention was certainly to hew off these projections after they had served their constructional purposes. Such purposes are not entirely clear today, but were undoubtedly multiple and quite significant, considering the magnitude and height of the structure, the great size of the stones composing its dry-wall masonry, and the cumbersome shape and weight of the centering frames.

It is probable that these corbels were used as scaffolding attachments for the workmen as well as lodgements for secondary hoists of some sort. But some at least of these corbels undoubtedly served as anchorages around which ropes were secured in connection with shifting and repositioning the heavy timber centerings. Each arch of the lowest tier consists of four contiguous rings, each of the middle or main tier of three contiguous rings; the same centerings were used four and three times respectively, for each of these spans. Thus the Romans rationalized their erectional procedures by economizing on the required falsework, making it only a quarter or a third of the bridge's thickness between the upstream and the downstream faces. Each span's centering had to be shifted to successive positions as the contiguous arch rings were separately constructed. Then the entire centering frame had to be skewed to free its ends from the inward-projecting voussoirs in order to be lowered and dismantled. To accomplish these shifts and maneuverings of the ponderous centering frames, strong anchorages had to be provided at strategic and convenient places—a purpose fulfilled by the massive corbels left projecting on the faces of the structure.

Among numerous instances worldwide of projections of the sort just referred to may be cited some of the huge brick dagobas of Ceylon, which retain regular rows of corbels protruding round about the great circular mass of their lower, vertical form.[14] These projections consist of the square headers of large bricks and are spaced about four feet horizontally, three feet vertically. Undoubtedly they served as integral supports for scaffolding in the original construction and subsequently in connection with finishing, maintenance, and repair work.

The removal and occasional retention of constructional projections

As we have noted, the salient portions of most projecting blocks used in construction were eliminated when no longer needed. For example, in all probability the Egyptians employed constructional stairs in building the Great Pyramid. For the blocks of this pyramid to be raised by the rocker device, would have required constructing an access stairway that consisted of a central zone of casing blocks shaped as steps instead of the smooth continuous slope they would eventually become.[15] In other words, some of the casing blocks themselves were hewn oversized and installed as rectangular instead of trapezoidal shapes in longitudinal section. When all the blocks had been raised and positioned, the rectangular saliencies of these steps were dressed off, so that their weather surfaces constituted the even plane of the pyramid's sloping face.

A somewhat analogous procedure of hewing off projecting stock is said to have occurred in the tholos tombs of Greece in Mycenaean times. These tombs were built as circular structures in a pit on a hillside. In the case of the most famous and best preserved—the so-called Treasury of Atreus—a ring of hewn stones some 48'-6" in diameter in the clear, was set around a leveled area at the bottom of the pit. Then stones for successive concentric courses of the structure were slid down the sides of the pit (from the quarry farther up the hill) and shoved out into position at each additional increment of height so as to encroach more and more on the void, until finally a single thick slab could span the remaining void at the highest course. As the stones of each circle of inward-shelving courses were shoved into position on the horizontal tops of the previously set course, ballast was packed in behind them; thus the stones of each course were maneuvered from the exterior at a new "ground level." During the course of construction all the stones were rectangular in elevation as well as in plan, which made their setting easier and quicker. It is reported that

the blocks of stone were in plan square or rectangular, so that there were wide gaps at the back which were filled with small stones and clay, even in the upper courses where the stones approached more nearly the shape of voussoirs. The inner faces of the masonry appear to have been dressed down after the construction was complete.[16]

This dressing down was done to give a smooth beehive-shaped surface to the impressive interior of the rotunda, which was then painted and studded with gilded bronze rosettes.

To be sure, a few instances exist in which the projections worked on stone blocks as construction aids were allowed to remain in place as decoration. One such example—a famous and much photographed monument—is the sixth-century Tomb of Theoderic in Italy. This monumental structure, two tall stories high, is capped by a single block of Istrian limestone in the shape of a low dome 35 feet in diameter and quarried a long way from the building site. What is unique about the monolithic lid of this building is the row of pierced, rectangular projections ranged evenly about its otherwise undisturbed upper surface just slightly within the outer circumference. There are twelve of these projecting "ears," indisputably constructional in purpose. Absolutely essential in handling the

Theoderic's tomb at
Ravenna, Italy. (Wil-
liam Longfellow, ed., *A
Cyclopaedia of Works
of Architecture,* 1903,
fig. 161 p. 337.)

470-ton monolith, they served as handles to grapple the otherwise
smoothly contoured circular shape that had to be transported from
afar and then maneuvered into position atop the tomb. If the ears
had ever been intended to remain in place, there would surely have
been ten, not twelve of them, and they would have been made to
align with the blind arches or the angles of the decagonal first and
second stories or at least made to correspond with the location of
the doorway of the tomb. Apparently the raising and setting of the
huge block (doubtless by means of ramps and blocking) proved so
difficult that its orientation was misaligned during the process of
erection and could not be corrected when the great monolith had
reached its ultimate elevation, capping the masonry walls of the
tall, freestanding structure. In any event the integral stone handles
survive today as conspicuous, eye-catching decorations that relate
the *scale* of the otherwise featureless lid of the building to the architectural elements below it.

By the very nature of the ways in which oversized blocks
served, actual examples that remain intact today are not numerous.

But there is a sufficient variety in these examples that stretch over so many centuries to reasonably assume that such practices were far more common in the past than the surviving instances, alone, would lead us to believe. For what, one asks, would have served the builders' needs more naturally and economically (in their terms) than hewing the stone blocks oversized and making them contribute to the process of construction?

11

Whether in the form of individual travel or the migration of entire tribes, mobility has been practiced by man and bird and beast alike from remotest time. In its relation to building construction mobility as manifested in the transportation of both men and materials is an imperative which has taken on a great many different forms, means, and devices throughout history.[1]

Transportation in Building Construction

Transporting materials to and from the building site

Building materials for a particular structure have rarely been found at its site, whether the structure is large or small, vernacular or princely. Consequently, transportation was an inevitable factor in building construction throughout former times. For example, the quarries that supplied stone structures were usually at formidable distances from the building sites. Instance the famous granite quarries of ancient Egypt, located at the First Cataract some 225 miles upstream from Thebes, where so many huge blocks were brought to give the longtime capital such timeless and impressive monumentality. Instance the figured and richly veined marbles, quarried in Spain and North Africa, on the islands of the Aegean and elsewhere, that were shipped in such limitless quantities to adorn the Eternal City in Roman times.[2] Instance the monoliths of Stonehenge, many of which had to be hauled overland from their source some 70 miles distant.[3] Instance the oolitic limestone so extensively quarried in Normandy and barged across the Channel to build many of the cathedrals of southern England. Building materials other than stone were often transported from afar. It should be recalled, for example, that during and after the medieval era there was a brisk trade to England from the Baltic and across the North Sea in "Estrich" timber, usually fir or deal, which was used both structurally and decoratively as the availability of native oak diminished.[4] Even for quite unprepossessing buildings, abundant natural materials such as rattans,[5] palm fronds, grasses, or rushes for thatching had to be gathered and brought to the building site from a distance. Similarly, clay for the adobe structures of cliff dwellings and mesa-top communities in the American Southwest had to be brought from the river valleys and carried up steep, tortuous trails to the sites.

Transportation was also needed to remove excavated materials from the site, as in spoil from a tunnel or a mine, silt dredged from a harbor, or earth removed in making a canal, railway cutting, or even a cellar. Each of these operations had its special problems; and the ways of dealing with them have varied considerably. Following is part of an on-the-spot account of a large-scale operation of

Conjectural prehis-
toric scene of men
dragging overland,
erecting, and elevating
huge monoliths, aided
only with levers and
timber blocking. (Con-
stantin Uhde, "Er-
bauung der Dolmen"
in *Baudenkmaeler in
Spain und Portugal,*
1892, fig. 3, p. 3.)

removing earth, in which the workers employed only hand held
tools of the simplest and most traditional kinds:

*Where the ground was moist and the clay tenacious, the material in
the borrow pits was cut by spades into blocks each containing about a
quarter of a cubic foot. . . . On the low embankments it was usual to
place coolies in rows extending from the borrow pits to the embankments, and to toss the blocks of clay from hand to hand until placed
in the construction. Another method which proved economical was to
lay planks from the borrow pits, and by posting workmen along these
boards at short intervals the blocks of clay were slid on the wetted
planks until finally placed in position in the fill. Then, again, sleds,
drawn by coolies over roadways of wetted clay, were used to transfer
large loads of block to the embankment.*

*Where the clay contained a certain percentage of sand, the
blocks did not retain their form sufficiently to permit tossing or slid-*

*ing, and in these cases baskets suspended at the ends of bamboo
shoulder poles were in general use. . . .*

*In the rice fields and low ground the tools used were both
long-handled and short two-handed wooden metal-tipped spades
which blocked out the clay. In the dry earth and in the hill cuttings
the coolies used a heavy metal-tipped wooden hoe to cut out the earth
and drag it into the baskets. . . .*[6]

It must be remembered, too, that among nomadic or seasonally migratory peoples the relation of transportation to building
was a perpetual concern. For them it was not just a question of
moving materials to and from the site but of moving their structures from site to site. The need to move on to more favorable sites
determined the type of structure: thus, the yurts of the Central
Asian Kazaks; the tents of the Bedouins; the tepees of the American Plains Indians; and the thatched roofs, all in one piece, uncol-
lapsed and intact, of some African tribes.[7]

Human carriers

Universally, the transport of burdens has been by humans using
nothing more than a simple device to distribute or adjust the load to
the anatomy of the carrier.[8] American Indian women (among many
others) made use of a tumpline—a band across the forehead—to
hold a burden on their back.[9] Chinese coolies continue to employ, as
they have for untold centuries, the shoulder pole, from either end
of which half the load is suspended, making it possible for them to
transport many kinds of loads and even to proceed, at times, at a
dogtrot.[10] Sometimes the loads carried by human porters were spec-
tacularly bulky and/or heavy, like a long plank or even a squared
log carried by one man over a mountain trail[11] or a load of tea in
bricks—up to an incredible burden of 360 pounds—transported to
distant markets by one person in the mountainous hinterland of the
Sino-Tibetan border region.[12] According to the following account,
loads of extraordinary weight and cumbersomeness have at times
been actually *carried* by gangs of men in India (and elsewhere).

*The block (of stone) is detached by means of wedges introduced into
natural fissures and artificially drilled holes. Two or three stout logs
are placed under the slab at right angles to its axis and equidistant.
Under these are fastened four bamboo trunks, two on either side parallel to the axis of the stone, and beneath these bamboo series of
smaller bamboos like the rounds of a ladder. The whole forms a gigantic crib-work, or carrying frame. Three or four hundred men can
unite their efforts thus in picking up and carrying it to its destination. In two or three hours the stone may be transported a mile. It is*

set up by means of guy ropes and lifting, and planted in a hole previously prepared.[13]

Sometimes the nature of the terrain imposed conditions that were too rough, precipitous, or narrow to be negotiated by any other means than human carriers.[14] Men cannot individually, of course, carry as much as can a big cart or a wagon. But a wagon and the animals harnessed to it need a prepared trail or roadway sufficiently wide to accommodate them and free of disrupting encumbrances. Human carriers, on the other hand, are more adaptable. They can carry a hod of mortar on their shoulders up a ladder; working in very cramped quarters, they can extract and carry out ore from a mine; they can climb in and out of the hold of a ship to unload its cargo. Moreover, human carriers can (either themselves or for each other) mount the burden they carry on their backs and dismount it when they stop to rest. And because human porters are paid for their labor, they are accountable for the delivery, without undue delay, theft, or damage, of the goods they carry.

Beasts of burden and draft animals

For countless generations, where they are native to the region or acclimated to its conditions (such as high altitude, arctic weather, or waterless desert), domesticated animals have been used for transporting loads, either as carriers or as haulers. Horses, mules, burros, llamas, camels, and yaks have all been employed to carry loads strapped to their backs or roped to their sides. In the desert regions of Africa and Asia the camel has been the indispensable beast of burden because of its cushioned feet that prevent it from sinking into sand and its ability to travel long distances in hot arid climates without having to stop for water. But in the high mountainous terrain of central Asia it is the plodding, phlegmatic yak that has served as burden-bearer.

Yaks are of an independent nature and like to make a new trail whenever possible. For this reason roads in Tibet usually consist of many parallel paths. . . .

Light straw cases, which had served admirably for porter transport, were not adapted for use on the backs of less considerate yaks. These sturdy animals . . . have an unfortunate habit of brushing past each other, without making allowance for the loads strapped to their sides. Breakable loads are apt to be smashed; others scraped off. So we procured wooden cases, and had fresh hide sewed over them, with the hair side next the wood. In one day this had shrunk in the sun until it became almost as hard as steel, and the cases thus reinforced served us well. . . .

*At every halt the loads were removed, but the wooden pack
saddles were allowed to remain on the animals. The Tibetans have a
quick and easy method of fastening loads, which are placed one on
each side of the animal, not on top of his back. The man (or woman)
picks up a case and holds it against the side of the yak. A leather
strap, tied to the front of the saddle, is brought around the side of the
case and fastened to the back of the saddle. Then another strap, from
the center, is passed under the case, and its end tied, on the outside,
to the middle of the first strap. Often a third hand is required in the
process, and for this purpose the Tibetan uses his teeth, holding
the end of one strap tight with them while taking up another.*[15]

Draft animals were also employed in *hauling* burdens. Here the
loads were positioned in or on some sort of conveyance rather than
carried on the animals' backs. Countless instances of the use of
horses and mules come to mind, including the twenty-mule teams
that hauled wagons loaded with borax in America's arid Southwest
and the solitary mules that towed canal boats in the eastern part
of America. Elsewhere in the world such haulage has been done
by water buffalos, oxen, Eskimo huskies or other dogs.[16] In India
elephants have been used to sort and pile logs at lumberyards and,
in the forests of southeast Asia, to move logs in incredibly difficult
jungle terrain.[17] In Lapland reindeer serve as draft animals drawing sleighs.[18] Draft animals obviously arrived on the scene later
than pack animals. For their use required the design and construction of appropriate vehicles (wheeled or wheelless) on which to pile
loads and of harnesses, especially collars or yokes, to allow the animals to exert their full strength without danger of strangulation.[19]
Both of these considerations took many generations of trial and error before satisfactory solutions were arrived at. It is even a moot
question whether the spoked wheel or the padded, shoulder-applied
horse collar was more effective, at least for heavily laden horse- or
oxen-drawn vehicles.

Sometimes, the overland transport of roughed-out blocks
of stone was not entrusted to specially built, heavy-duty wagons
(which in any event might break down in transit over rough roads)
because of the expense of building them in the first place, the uncertainties of mounting great blocks on the wagons, and the many
hazards to which the load might be subject in transit.[20] Thus the
ancient Greeks devised an ingenious but basically simple means of
moving their column drums, using the drums themselves as solid
wheels. A banded circlet of boards served as protective tires and a
simple fork-shaped frame of metal acted as a hitch for pulling the
block it straddled, the ends of the tines turned for insertion into
previously cut axial sinkages in the center of the drum, to right and

Egyptian temple at Edfou. Stone pavements sometimes required exceptional treatment because of their exposed situation. Here, to secure permanent horizontal alignment in the coping blocks of a temple wall, the masons inserted two rows of double dove-tailed cramps set flush with the pavement's surface. (Auguste Choisy, *L'Art de bâtir chez les Égyptiens,* 1904, fig. 2, pl. 19.)

left. Other heavy blocks, such as lintels, the Greeks sometimes crated with wooden staves or boxed in cylindrical wooden frames in such fashion that they could be rolled from quarry to building site by a single team of oxen.[21]

Transport overland

Well-established trade routes existed in ancient times, with names that reflect their principal traffic: the Silk Roads out of China and the Amber Roads south from the Baltic are probably the best known, though there were various others in Asia, Africa, England, and on the continent of Europe. Chiefly for military and governmental purposes, the Romans established, maintained, and administered an extensive system of stone-paved roads, said to have covered some fifty thousand miles and to have included permanent stone bridges spanning at least the smaller rivers. Traversed primarily by groups of religious travelers, two pilgrimage ways celebrated during the Middle Ages were the Way of St. James, across the Pyrenees to Santiago de Compostela in northwestern Spain, and the road to the shrine of St. Thomas à Becket at Canterbury in southeastern England. By the year 2000 B.C., many centuries before the vast and extraordinary Roman achievement, a broad highway paved with bricks set in asphalt linked Babylon with Nineveh. On the other side of the world the Road of the Incas, a most astonishing engineering feat dating back to A.D. 900, was constructed for some three thousand miles along the western slopes of the Andes: it was stone-surfaced, with excellent bridges.

These and other exceptional achievements in road engineering were extraordinary projects established by a strong, central government or a powerful prince, with sufficient funding, a large work force, and all the best technical skill the times could command.[22] Much less generally appreciated in the annals of history were the largely anonymous, indigenous roads that evolved, sometimes slowly as economic and social conditions remained sufficiently stable, sometimes quite suddenly as changed conditions imposed a special and often transient need for them. Such roads were of two sorts: ordinary, local roads serving multiple uses within a limited area, and temporary or provisional tracks or trailways such as access roads, particularly those for conveying building materials or facilitating construction projects.[23]

Because ordinary Chinese roads demonstrate, even today, little change in makeup and in traffic over the generations—as compared with ordinary roads in the Western world—it seems appropriate and illuminating to cite examples that have been in constant use for centuries.

The ordinary road is a mere path, generally undefined by ditches or hedges, winding through the paddy fields or over the uplands, wherever the traveler can find the fewest obstacles to his progress. In the north, where carts are used, it is a common thing to see a new track cut right across a field of growing wheat, in spite of the efforts of the owner to prevent it. . . . Bridge building is regarded as a virtue in China, and there are some fine specimens in all parts of the country. . . . Where dykes are built along the banks of rivers or canals they become public thoroughfares, and as they must be kept in a fairly safe condition, they may be counted among the best roads in the country. . . .[24]

And so the narrow roads are crowded practically every day from daylight to dark with these patient, ambling burden bearers [the Chinese coolies]. Usually the roads are provided with a row of flat stones for pavement, end to end on the second class or less used roads, and side by side on the more used thoroughfares. Along the way every few miles, usually in little villages, are rest shelters, tea rooms, or lunch counters. At night their stops are usually at the Chinese inns in the towns or cities.[25]

Access roads were of more direct concern to the builder than were the ordinary roads. Often, in the past, they were even his specific responsibility, as in the case of lumbering and quarrying operations. Of course, the builder was always in charge of roads into and within the arena of the building site.[26] For example, where desirable timber once felled could not be immediately floated or rafted to sawmills on the spring floods of rivers, logging operations have had to cut access roads through to the trees, for removal overland.[27] One lively, circumstantial account of the early days of lumbering in the Adirondack forests of New York State realistically describes cutting through and maintaining the access roads, fabricating and handling the wheelless conveyances utilized, and dealing with the many hazards that were encountered.[28] For ancient Egypt, instance the surviving evidence of extensive supply ramps from quarry to river bank, from landing stage to pyramid site, and up onto at least the lower courses of the pyramid itself. Some service roads were not roads at all in the usual sense but temporary embankments, levelings, or skidways prepared for the movement of very heavy or bulky items. Of this sort were the steep exits from the quarries on Mount Pentelicus in ancient Greek times[29] and the huge embankments sometimes thrown up by besieging armies in both Roman and medieval times to bring catapults and other cumbersome engines of war into range against a beleaguered stronghold.[30]

Among the ancient Assyrians and, especially, the Egyptians enormous monoliths carved in the shape of winged bulls or a seated pharaoh and mounted on a timber sledge were moved by long, multiple files of human haulers tugging on cables attached to the sledge.[31] With or without longitudinal skids for the sledges to ride on, the Egyptians (unlike the Assyrians) never employed rollers to ease the overland movement of their enormous monoliths. There were compelling reasons for the Egyptians' steadfast refusal to use rollers. For one, they had an almost unlimited supply of unskilled laborers, many of whom served as human draft animals. The overriding consideration, however, was their lack of safeguards against accidents if they had used rollers. For example, the fibrous materials of the Egyptians' hauling cables and ropes, of uneven quality at best, dried out and became brittle in the unremitting heat of the sun. Breaking without warning, the ropes would have released the ponderous blocks from all control if rollers had been inserted under them. Moreover, constantly retrieved from behind and repositioned in front of the sledge as it moved along, the rollers could become skewed unpredictably despite the most careful attention to their placement and alignment. Again, unless the track under the rollers were kept absolutely and solidly level, without the slightest dip or rise, the great weight of the block could cause it to swerve and lunge about in response to gravity. Rollerless sledges prevented any of these mishaps and assured the haulers' constant control over the process of movement.[32]

The overland movement of obelisks was accomplished in quite a different fashion because of their long, relatively slender bulk. A great number of levers were set closely along either side of the recumbent obelisk. As these levers jacked up the monolith incrementally, higher at the butt end than at the pointed end, earth was packed under the tilted block at each lift until it was undergirded by a sloping mound of considerable height. Thereupon the block was forced to slide down the forward extension of this artificial ramp, and the process of jacking up, creating a new sloping mound, and shoving the block down it was repeated again and again.[33] This procedure for moving a gigantic obelisk overland was slow and laborious, but foolproof.

Transport by water

Since ancient and even prehistoric times and among peoples of remarkably diverse circumstances and varied stages of civilization and culture, transport by water has been astonishingly common. For one, most of the waterways that were traversed existed naturally; that is, little of their extent had to be constructed. Lakes, rivers, and the oceans themselves were there *ab origine* for those who made boats, canoes, or other craft and who had the daring (in many cases) and the skill to venture forth in them. Elsewhere—most notably in China from very early times—a man-made system of canals (that, nonetheless, exploited natural waterways) provided arteries of traffic over extensive areas of the country. For another, sometimes rivers or estuaries provided the only feasible routes for moving about in jungle or heavily forested lands, where impenetrable undergrowth crowded down to and even encroached on the water's edge, leaving no room for tracking along the banks.[34] In other situations, land travel for bulky and/or constant convoys of goods was largely thwarted by towering and precipitous cliffs and all the hazards and difficulties of mountainous terrain.[35] For this reason the Yangtse River gorges in central China have been much traveled; for generations heavily laden junks have been hauled upstream through the rapids by plodding gangs of men straining on tow ropes. A further advantage offered by water transport was its relative speed compared to overland transit, considering the general inadequacy or even lack of roads in the past.[36] Moreover, very heavy or bulky cargoes could be conveyed by water much more easily and relatively safe from injury—loads that, if consigned to all the difficulties and arduous labor of overland transit, would require an inordinant expenditure of manpower.

In this connection, the extreme case of an Egyptian obelisk is particularly revealing. Ideally, the roughed-out obelisk, freed from the parent rock of a cliff quarry bordering the Nile, was slid carefully down a man-made ramp of earth to a previously prepared depression in the floor of the valley. The bottom of the depression in which it came to rest, along with a wide trench leading toward the river, had previously been excavated to an even, horizontal depth well below the river's expected flood crest. When the annual inundation was developing, barges or large pontoons were floated in along this channel as it began to fill with water and into the basin where the obelisk lay. The pontoons then took up positions along either side of the great block. Strong ropes, previously passed under the obelisk and brought up on either side of it, were securely attached to the pontoons as the rising waters inundated the monolith. Soon thereafter, buoyed up by the flood waters, the pontoons freed the great stone from its resting place in the basin. It could now be floated out along the channel and onto the broad, watery highway of the river itself, where the current took the flotilla of two parallel rows of pontoons (with the submerged burden between them) downstream under attentive, constant piloting.[37] On arriving at its destination after a voyage of some 225 miles, the flotilla was guided out of the main stream and along a previously prepared channel to a basin similar to the one from which its voyage had begun. Here the flotilla was parked, close to the site where the obelisk was to be erected. As the waters receded, the pontoons were unhitched and removed. Finally, when the river level had returned to normal and the land in the basin had dried out, the obelisk was maneuvered out of the depression and erected to an upright position.

This transportation operation took full advantage of two conditions. One was regional—the predictable, annual phenomenon of the inundation. Probably the oldest masonry structure of the ancient Egyptians was a Nilometer, necessarily repaired and reconstructed during various dynasties but always kept operational. Each year, it measured the maximum flood crest, which averaged some fifty feet above normal river level at the First Cataract. But fully as significant, the Nilometer indicated the daily, incremental changes in the water level. This information was essential for the successful timing of many operations along the river, including the conveyance of obelisks from start to finish. The other condition is known to everyone who has dived into and swum about a lake with a rock-strewn bottom; namely, that while under water, he can easily lift a big rock out of water, he cannot budge. In layman's terms, the weight of the obelisk when submerged was reduced by the weight of the water it displaced. Thus, in effect, the transport of the obelisk was greatly facilitated through the radical reduction of its weight when floated in a submerged state.[38]

An incredible variety of marine craft for conveyance by water were developed to suit the particular ambience in which they operated. Their names alone suggest some of this variety: dingy, caique, coracle, shallop, dhow, felucca, proa, pirogue, sampan, dugout, kayak, catamaran, among the small craft; trireme, galleon, barque, brig, windjammer, trawler, junk, yawl, corvette, and many more among the larger cargo carriers. But the entire history of water transportation is not our concern. The remarkable achievements of timber shipbuilding—which burgeoned in the Western world with the Age of Discovery (with Marco Polo, Columbus, Magellan, Drake, Hudson, and a host of other oceanic adventurers and early seafaring traders)—is outside the scope of this work. In any event the vessels in which these intrepid navigators voyaged have already been studied and accurate accounts published. More pertinent are some of the primitive, traditional types of water transport and the land-based works needed to support the maritime traffic.

In the past, the small, handicrafted vessels that were propelled by paddles or oars (with or without sails) were of three basic kinds: the dugout,[39] the bark canoe,[40] and the built-up wooden hull.[41] In the normal course of events, none of these was called upon to—or could, in fact—transport large and/or heavy cargoes destined for building construction. But without the skills acquired in their fabrication and handling, the construction and mastery of much larger, commercial vessels would doubtless never have been achieved. One of the most primitive means of conveyance by water, which has persisted in some parts of the world well into this century, involves inflated skins. These vary in numbers from a single unit (employed as a sort of life buoy to sustain a lone swimmer guiding a small raft across a turbulent stream) to many score or even hundreds (to float large shipments of bulky products down a broad river).[42] More frequently, however, rafts conveying bulky cargoes have consisted of logs.[43] In any case cargo-bearing rafts are rarely propelled by either oars or sails. Rather, they move downstream in response to the current of the watercourse in which they operate, their oars or sweeps employed only in steering. Occasionally one encounters descriptions of unconventional, special-purpose rafts of the past. One such, developed of necessity by a tribe living in Madagascar, differs radically from ordinary rafts in that its activity is limited exclusively to vertical movement.

In the rainy season, when the water rises, it enters into the houses of these people, and they then put together several layers of Zozoro (sedge) to form a kind of raft, so that, as the water rises, this raft rises with it. Upon these zozoro they make their hearths and their beds; and there they live, rising and falling with the water, until the rainy season is over and they can live on the ground again.[44]

Harbors and their facilities

With some striking exceptions (such as the long voyages between distant islands in the Pacific from prehistoric times onward) most travel in small boats, whether on inland or coastal waters, was confined to daylight hours. Merchant vessels both large and small—notably in the Mediterranean region—customarily put into a harbor for the night.[45] Thus Bronze Age vessels carrying ingots of copper or bronze from Cyprus to European markets hugged the coasts in transit. Later, the steady shipments to Rome of grain from Egypt (as well as the occasional obelisk) and of costly marbles from the Sea of Marmara, the Aegean Islands, and North Africa were carried in merchantmen that seldom sailed out of sight of land, whatever their tonnage might be. (The point seems substantiated by the numbers of ancient shipwrecks that modern underwater archeologists have been excavating, particularly off the coast of Asia Minor.)

In any event, the marine traffic widespread throughout the eastern Mediterranean and into the Black Sea from earliest times—Minoan, Cretan, Phoenician, Greek, Roman, and Byzantine—required harbors and roadsteads, to protect ships during storms and in the winter months when they were repaired and refitted as well as to provide calm waters for loading and unloading their holds. Breakwaters or moles for protecting ships in basins of various sizes were, in fact, common throughout the Mediterranean. In the busiest ports such as Rome's Ostia and Egypt's Alexandria, as one would expect, the ample basins were lined with magazines, extensive warehouses, and facilities for transferring cargo of many sorts. But only a single, detailed description by an ancient writer of a dry dock constructed in Alexandria would suggest that the usual method of maintaining the hulls of small ships took place only when they were hauled up and careened on shore.[46] That the pharos of Alexandria was considered such a renowned structure in the ancient world would indicate the general lack of lighthouses and would further substantiate the belief that ships of that busy maritime era operated in the main only during daylight.[47] In any case, for ancient times, much more is known technically about the construction of commercial and naval vessels and how they were steered, rowed, and/or sailed than about the harbor facilities that served them.[48]

However, it is true that

the vast sea-borne trade of the Roman Empire made elaborate dock and harbor works inevitable. In these the Romans followed the lead of the Hellenistic world, repeating again and again on a smaller scale the general forms of the pharos *or lighthouse at Alexandria, but carrying even further than the Hellenistic designers the careful, practical, and yet monumental treatment of mole, pier, and dock building. At Portus, close to Ostia, first Claudius, then Trajan, built enormous enclosed artificial harbors, protected by ample break-waters, and lined with rows of well-designed warehouses, broken here and there by temples and administrative buildings. The skill of the engineers in so constructing these as to break the sea, and yet not permit gradual silting up or the formation of bars, was great, as is shown especially at Pozzuoli on the Bay of Naples, where the break-water, instead of being solid, is arched to allow the current to sweep through, and the harbor is lined by a mole with two set of arches—the piers of the inner set being set opposite the openings of the outer set, in order to break the force of beating waves . . . .*[49]

Somewhat related to harbor installations are the land recla-mations of peoples in marine-threatened environments. The he-roic, classic example is, of course, Holland, where for generations the national consciousness has of necessity focussed on reclaiming below-sea-level land and maintaining the viability of the poldars. Basically, an enormous dike has evolved along the whole northern boundary of the country, which has permitted more and more land to be reclaimed for communities and for crop growing. Through-out the past, the windmills of Holland have been ubiquitous visual reminders of the nation's perennial commitment against being flooded by the sea. (Fortunately, the greater the danger during storms, the more energetically the windmills pump). Today, the Dutch have updated the unrelenting battle against the sea with sluice gates and shipping locks—enormous engineering complexes that use huge amounts of steel and seemingly unlimited cubic yards of concrete. The vastly different nature of premechanized, exclusively handi-crafted practices of land reclamation is made clear by the following account.

At various places off the coast of Malaita (Solomon Islands), a series of small inhabited islets have been built up upon the fringing reef [some 12 sites are identified]. The islets appear to have had their origin in raised patches of coral upon the reef flats, which have been laboriously added to and gradually built up by their inhabitants un-til a solid foundation, well raised above the water, was produced. They are undoubtedly of very ancient origin. The islets are faced with a wall of coral stones about six to eight feet high, with here and there an opening like an embrasure with a sloping beach for the admission of canoes.

They vary from a little under a quarter of an acre to two or three acres in extent, and are densely populated by a seafaring population, who speak a different dialect from the bush natives of the mainland.

The inhabitants live by fishing. They sell the fish to the natives on the mainland in exchange for vegetables and manufactured articles. They are very skillful in their boats and see to it that the inhabitants of the mainland have no boats, so that their island homes are safe from attack.[50]

Canals

Man-made waterways have been constructed in China, Babylonia, Egypt and elsewhere from very early times. Apparently the first and primary reason for such undertakings was to create irrigation projects.[51] But early on, artificial waterways—recognized as highly useful means for traffic by water—were enlarged and proliferated in the regions mentioned. Sometimes they were constructed, from the start, exclusively for inland water transport, as in the case of China's Grand Canal. This vast undertaking, totaling some one thousand miles in extent, was constructed in three widely separated campaigns, the first (central) section as early as the sixth century B.C., the third (northern) section from A.D. 1280 to 1283.

In the northern part, owing to scarcity of water, frequent locks or dams are necessary and are passed with difficulty. The ordinary canal lock consists of heavy granite bastions, forming a gateway and carrying on their opposite faces deep grooves, in which are set heavy timbers to form a dam. These timbers are raised by means of heavy stone-set capstans.[52]

Accompanying this account is a photograph of one of the locks showing a houseboat floating through the gates: "The fall from one side to the other is some five feet, and the boats are pulled up the rise by many ropes carried by capstans on each bank." Another photograph shows the native inhabitants, male and female, young and old, manning the capstans as a boat is hauled through the gates of the lock. In the Western world inland transportation on canals became widespread, once efficient locks were devised (in the Renaissance) to handle frequent changes in level wherever natural watercourses were used as part of the route. Thus extensive canal systems were developed in France, Italy, and England.[53] Later, in eastern America, they were designed to accommodate a specific type of craft—the canal boat or barge—powered by neither sail nor oars but by a mule treading along a towpath on one of the canal's banks.[54]

To establish and maintain these inland waterways required much effort. Like the earlier and more universal irrigation systems, the canal transportation systems were always coordinated with nearby streams, rivers, and lakes. Such existing bodies of water constituted the major part of the inland waterways; in any case they were tapped as feeders to replenish the water in the canals, particularly along stretches that required locks. But on much of the route, even taking advantage of natural waterways, large portions of the canals had to be dug, with the excavated earth thrown up on either side. Adjacent streams had to be dammed to impound water for tapping in the dry season in order to regulate and maintain navigable depths in the canals. Hence sluice gates and lock mechanisms (or their predecessors) had to be constructed, operated, and maintained. Permanent bridges across the canals had to be erected at intervals to accommodate pedestrians and commercial traffic. Complete canal systems were naturally a tremendous boon to transportation.

Throughout many centuries in China, the efficacy of transport canals has been proven by the astonishing volume of daily traffic (including good-sized junks on the larger canals).[55] Moreover, this widespread and undiminished reliance on canal transport has influenced travel by land. For in general, the best roads in the Chinese countryside have inevitably come about by the tread of innumerable generations of burden bearers plodding along the tamped, level tops of the canal banks. Clearly, to assure the viability of the canals, their embankments had to be maintained and kept in good order. Breaks in these dikes would not only devastate the countryside with floods but would bring all traffic on the canals themselves to a standstill. Breaks have occurred occasionally, to be sure, in spite of reasonably attentive upkeep and preventive measures taken against leaks and other sources of weakness in the embankments. A major break occurred in 1902 when the Hwang-ho ruptured one of its embankments. Fortunately for us, as it turned out, an American engineer was subsequently on hand, not as a participant but to photograph some of the critical steps in the process of repairing the breach and to explain how the native engineers dealt with the stupendous problem. Here are the legends accompanying two of his photographs.

The last serious breach in the dikes, which in normal times control the waters of the Hwang-ho, occurred in September, 1902, near Liu-Wang-Chuang, and was 1500 yards wide. Through it most of the river flowed. It was repaired by building out from each side dams in the form of a series of pakwerks of kaoliang stalks and sacks of clay, each pakwerk or buttress being joined to the previous one by ropes and piles. By this means the breach was reduced to 55 feet, and this, after two destructive attempts in which the lives of many workmen were lost, was effectively closed on March 16, 1903 . . . when a huge mattress was successfully swung into position. This turned the turbulent waters back into their proper channel. The rush through the opening was previously reduced by the construction of a deflecting groin on the up-river side of the breach, constructed like the pakwerk, and projecting some 120 feet into the current. The width of the river channel abreast the breach had been 600 feet, but was reduced to 300 feet by the formation of a sand bank on the opposite side of the river.

Before being lowered into the gap, the last gigantic mattress was anchored to the side of the river by many 15-inch hawsers, in order to prevent canting due to impact of the current. More than one hundred 8-inch ropes spaced closely were stretched across the breach and made fast to anchor piles. On these were then placed alternate layers of kaoliang stalks and sacks of clay. When these materials reached the level of the sides of the dam, the ropes were manned and, at a given signal, were lowered foot by foot. The kaoliang of which the mattress was made is a kind of sorghum, probably identical with Barbados millet. The core of the stalk, except for a very thin and weak covering, is entirely pith, but it has a matted bunch of fairly hard and strong roots which form its chief virtue for construction work. The stalk is about 6 feet long, three-fourths of an inch in diameter, and the bunch of roots, 3 to 5 inches in diameter. The face of the pakwerk, including the sides, is composed of the roots which mat and make a splendid surface for keeping out water.[56]

The foregoing accounts and comments indicate something of the extent to which transportation was carried out in the past and the variety of means by which this traffic, whether overland or by water, was served. The needs of transportation and construction met in several ways. In the case of transport by water (with analogies to some extent in the case of land transit) two aspects of construction involved boats. The primary connection was the creation or fabrication of the vessels themselves, along with substantial undertakings that supported marine traffic, such as breakwaters, harbor and docking facilities, dikes, locks, and associated installations. The other connection was the use of watercraft to transport building materials—particularly stone—from their place of origin to the building site. In this respect, the contribution they made to many an important building throughout history was both outstanding and indispensable.

Native engineers directing Shantung coolies in curbing the yellow flood of "China's Great Sorrow." (C. K. Edmunds, "Shantung—China's Holy Land," *National Geographic* 36(July–December 1919): 236.)

Lowering into place the last mattress of koaliang stalks and sacks of clay, which finally forced the Yellow River back into its banks after the devastating flood in 1902. (C. K. Edmunds, "Shantung—China's Holy Land," *National Geographic* 36(July–December 1919): 237.)

12

Stationed just within the single orifice of the hive, the worker bees perform the office of ventilators. Two currents—one in-going, one out-going—are established in the hive by the fanning motion of the bees' wings, which produce a complete circulation of the air of the hive, and keep down the temperature to that point which is fitted to the nature of the animal. Thus the carbon acid, and other products of respiration, are got rid of by ventilation.[1]

The Problem of Ventilation

In man-made structures many kinds of situations, from the simple to the complex, required the design to address the problem of ventilation. To maintain the structural integrity of a building, susceptible areas (such as cellars) had to be protected against mildew; decay or rot also had to be inhibited in the actual building materials (such as the timbers of wooden structures or the point of contact between timber and masonry).[2] Sometimes the contents of the buildings had to be preserved (such as harvested crops stored in barn structures).[3] More often problems of ventilation were compounded by the need to illuminate dark interiors, to eliminate smoke from fires used for cooking and/or warming, to circulate and cool air in hot climates, and to control humidification—conditions that affected the *performance* of buildings with respect to the needs, comfort, and health of the inhabitants. Frequently, the necessities of ventilation, warmth, and illumination in indoor living spaces came into conflict. In addition to these concerns, problems of ventilation arose in connection with the safe and efficient execution of building operations, at the time of construction, in underground or dark interior places. The following pages elaborate on these problems and on the effective solutions that were arrived at in former times.

Illumination and its effect on ventilation

From earliest times throughout the world, men have dug deeply into the ground—often through rock—to build underground burial chambers and many-galleried subterranean cemeteries (the catacombs of Rome, for example); to establish extensive mining operations for extracting precious metals, removing coal or quarrying unweathered stone for building; or to excavate cisterns and tunnel long aqueducts for protecting water from evaporation in the sun.[4] Often, depending on the nature of the work and the geological conditions in which it took place deep below the surface of the ground, adequate provisions had to be worked out for furnishing illumination and, above all, ventilation.

For example, coal deposits are found worldwide in conjunction with various gases that are either toxic to the miners or inflammable, causing violent explosions especially when coal dust is in the air. Metalliferous mines, by contrast, are seldom plagued by noxious and/or explosive gases. But because the metal is usually found in association with very hard rock (such as quartz, in the case of gold), fire has often been used to break up the rock and make extraction of the ore somewhat less difficult. Consequently, ventilation was required to assure that the fires would not go out for lack of oxygen. In both cases, it was essential to provide the miners with light in the dark interiors of mine shafts and galleries. But if the illumination was produced by flame (as it customarily was, from candles or oil lamps), the presence of noxious or combustible gases jeopardized the activities and the very lives of the miners. Moreover, preindustrial man's method of excavating in rock was ordinarily to pulverize it with stone hammers, handheld balls of harder stone, or, later, metal picks. Naturally, a considerable amount of dust was generated in the process. Without positive ventilation, the air thus clouded both obscured the work in hand and endangered the workers' health (though the latter consideration was doubtless ignored at the time).[5]

Most building operations have required lighting wherever the workers have had to toil in dark interiors or underground areas. Today we take for granted the electrical lighting of these spaces. But this instantaneous and unpolluting benison dates only from the end of the nineteenth century as a light source. Previous methods of artificial illumination used fire, whether in torches, oil lamps, candles, or similar devices. The product of combustion, this light inevitably produced soot and discoloration along with disagreeable odors at times. And it depleted the air of oxygen. As late as the last quarter of the nineteenth century, such oxygen-exhausting illumination added to the hazards faced by workmen digging in the caissons under New York City's East River, in excavating for the Brooklyn Bridge's deep pier foundations. To combat this critical problem, Washington Roebling (who took charge of constructing the great bridge his father had designed) devised "flaming lights" for illuminating the Brooklyn caisson "from squat sperm candles that blazed like torches at the end of iron rods planted alongside the walkways. . . . At first the candles had burned with such vigor in the compressed air and sent up such clouds of smoke that the air had become intolerable. This had been overcome somewhat by reducing the size of the wick and of the candle and by mixing alum with the tallow and drenching the wick with vinegar. Even so Roebling worried about the quantities of floating carbon the men were breathing into their lungs."[6]

With respect to illumination alone in otherwise dark places where constructional or decorative work was taking place, a completely different scheme of lighting was used from the remotest times (one that totally circumvented the problem of smoke). Shiny reflective surfaces were set up in the open, outside the scene of operations. These were tilted by an attendant in such a way that the sunlight was directed through what at times might be quite a small opening into the interior. Perhaps burnished bronze panels were used in lieu of actual mirrors, but any highly reflective surface would have served to scoop the light of day far underground or into an interior. Particularly in ancient Egypt, where "the incessant splendor of the sun" was perennially unrelieved by overcast skies or rainy weather, the penetration deep into the interior of light from this source was assured throughout the day. In contrast to the unlighted darkness, the intensity of this scooped-in daylight would have been remarkable. It would certainly have been more than sufficient to illuminate any tasks going on deep inside, even in the case of complex layouts where the light had to be redirected into alcoves and side passageways by supplementary reflective panels.[7] Medieval builders—and doubtless many others as well—also employed light-directing reflectors to funnel the brightness of daylight into dark interior work areas.[8]

As a source to illuminate daytime work in progress in areas of the world where weather conditions permitted and the climate was temperate, this scheme was a great boon, inexpensive and dependable. But in spite of its smokeless performance, this reflected light scheme did not eliminate the need for ventilation. Air vitiation from the respiration of workmen operating in often confined quarters could be a serious and debilitating hazard. Moreover, like mining, such building operations often involved excavation in rock, with the concomitant production of choking dust.

The requirements for both illumination and ventilation in finished buildings involved features that had to be planned for and accommodated in the design of the building from the start. For example, in the huge dome of the Roman Pantheon, the twenty-eight-foot-diameter oculus at the apex of the structure provided a central source of natural light—like an enormous chandelier, as it were—by which the great rotunda and its alcoves were dramatically illuminated during daylight. But this opening at the top of the dome also served as an escape for the air within the rotunda, vitiated by the breathing of crowds of people and by the combustion of candles and lamps at the numerous altars.

Later, during the Renaissance, the provision of natural illumination from a central source in a domed building was perfected in the striking feature—architectural and highly decorative as well as functional—of a so-called lantern that crowned the oculus. Furnished with vertical windows, the lantern assured light throughout the day, in all kinds of weather, and even in climates subject to snow accumulation. These lanterns were later provided with louvers that allowed the close air within to escape, thus meeting the ventilation problem.[9] An analogous situation on a more modest scale was that of the louvered timber canopies (these, too, were called lanterns) that crowned the roof ridge above the great hall of medieval castles and early manor houses. As these habitations were windowed in at least one of their walls, the lantern served primarily as an escape hatch for the smoke from a central hearth.[10]

Ventilating smoke-filled interiors

Some form of heating for indoor living has been a necessity of mankind from remotest times. The cave dwellings of the earliest prehistoric ages certainly counted on a fire at the mouth of the cave as protection against predatory animals; this same fire was undoubtedly used for warmth and cooking. But the fire, indispensable for its warmth throughout the winter season, made the interior almost intolerable when adverse winds drove its smoke into the cave. Smoke, in fact, continued to be a serious problem throughout the ensuing centuries well into modern times; and it is still troublesome in both urban and rural slums.

In the latter half of the nineteenth century, when great advances were made in residential and large-scale heating systems, the public showed little knowledge and concern about the need for proper ventilation of interior areas for living, sleeping, or working. This was true even though popular magazines and technical journals kept publishing articles and discussions on the evils of inadequate ventilation, particularly as they reduced the productivity of the workers in industrial societies.[11]

During the nineteenth century, the ill effects of factory and tenement on the health of the proletariat were notoriously magnified and exacerbated by overcrowding. Yet comparable ill effects based on similar causes, though operating on a smaller scale, had prevailed in other societies for a long, long time. Thus Charles Tomlinson wrote at mid-century:

The Laplander, during eight months of the year, inhabits a little hut with a small hole in the center of the roof for the admission of light and the escape of smoke, and obtains heat from a smoky lamp of putrid oil, as the Esquimaux does in his hut of snow. The effect of this arrangement is, that the whole nation of Laplanders are afflicted with blear eyes. The Greenlander, indeed, builds a larger hut, and contrives it better, but it is often occupied by half a dozen families, each having a lamp for warming and cooking, and the effect of this arrangement, says Egede, 'is to create such a smell that it strikes one not accustomed to it to the very heart.'[12]

It is understandable that the smells in the interior of a snow igloo are overpowering and offensive—at least to the uninitiated. But Tomlinson omits to mention the remarkably effective ventilation system of the Eskimo igloo, which the natives have so perfectly adapted to the stringent and uncompromising conditions of their winter climate. With only snow and animal skins as building materials, and in spite of tempestuous winds and extreme cold, the interiors maintain a pleasurable degree of largely smokeless warmth. For fresh air from without is constantly replacing the vitiated air within, all subject to controlled adjustment in relation to the weather conditions outdoors. One factor in this system involves elevating the floor within the igloo to a level just above the top of the entrance tunnel, through which the inhabitants enter and exit by crawling on their hands and knees. With polar bear skins spread out on the floor and a couple of oil lamps constantly burning, the occupants of the rather confined interior can comfortably wear very little clothing, whatever the temperature may be outside.[13]

Nonetheless, smoky, smelly, inadequately ventilated habitations have been the norm elsewhere for centuries, as in the case of the transportable yurts of central Asia and the peasant huts of Ireland, Scotland, and various parts of Europe.[14] Among more sophisticated peoples—those less close to the exigencies of mere survival—the stench of illuminating oil and of candles was mitigated somewhat by perfumes. But eliminating the smoke could not be handled by mere cosmetic expediencies; a positive means of ventilation was required to assure its escape to the exterior. Thus in the tepee (or tipi) of the American Plains Indians, adjustable smoke flaps secured a healthy, comfortable, and smokeless interior environment for the inhabitants throughout the year and in all kinds of weather.[15]

There have been instances, to be sure, in which the smoke was actually induced to remain in the interior of domestic habitations instead of encouraged to escape to the exterior. A striking case is reported for the so-called Black Houses of Lewis in the Hebrides Islands:

The "Black House" is a product of long labour and sacrifice; it is part of the price that a people of immense ability and high character have to pay for their civilization. It is a fundamental part of the only system of agriculture formerly found possible in this island of gneiss rock, clay, and peat moss. . . . The peat smoke in the house without chimneys is tolerated and encouraged day and night throughout all the winter that the straw on the roof may be saturated with the dis-

*tilled products of the peat, and thereby converted into a specific ma-
nure for the soil. Similarly the 'cattle-housing' where the cows live
practically with the people, may be deplorable and disastrous, but
the point is that it has a perfectly intelligible purpose. Fodder is very
scarce, so the animals must be kept in a warm house to save expense.
If they are so weak at the spring 'lifting' that they need to be helped
into the open, they gather force again on the moors, where the children live with them at the shielings for all the summer.*[16]

The Hebrides islanders' toleration of smoke from continual
fires for warming and cooking—because of the accumulation of
soot in the thatch to fertilize the soil of their rocky, nearly barren
farms—is obviously an exceptional situation.

One of the most familiar means of exhausting the smoke
from hearth fires was the wall fireplace. Appearing initially in the
castles of the wealthy during the medieval period, wall fireplaces
eventually spread to the houses of Everyman. Thanks to clay-lined
or brick chimneys of adequate height and to such features as dam-
pers that prevented cold air from entering the room when not in
use, these built-in wall fireplaces were adopted throughout the
northern temperate zone of the Western hemisphere. They could be
found in the log cabins of the American pioneers as well as in the
cottages and tenements of rural and urban England (as the chim-
ney-dominated skylines still bear witness). Wall fireplaces have
undergone a long development toward increased efficiency and improvement in securing a dependable draft and in creating smokeless
interiors.[17]

Throughout the ancient Mediterranean world, the oil lamp
was probably the most common light source during the hours of
darkness. In the Bible for example, lamps are referred to some
three-and-a-half times more than are candles.[18] Following is a commentary on the nature and the performance of ancient lamps.

*While it is true that the Egyptians and Greeks used lamps, yet there
is evidence to show that they were not in general use among the Romans until about 300–250 B.C. . . . Before their introduction, candles made of wax and tallow; torches (taedae or faces), bits of pine
wood or a sort of cornucopia filled with flax, or tow, and covered with
resin, oil, pitch, or wax, were used for illuminating purposes. . . . The
great majority of lamps had but one wick, and the light must have
been rather feeble. Even when there were several wicks the illumination could not have been brilliant. The necessity for many lamps is
then apparent. That the odor and smoke from these might be very
annoying is evident, and probably frequent attention had to be given
to keep them trimmed. The reservoirs were never large, rarely measuring over 3" or 4" in diameter and 1" high. The oil would have to*

be replenished often, which could easily be poured in by the use of a guttus *or small terra-cotta pitcher designed for this purpose. Juvenal speaks of the number of lamps at a school, the odor and the smoke, in a familiar passage in his seventh satire. He is speaking of the school-master, and says, 'Lose not your whole reward for having smelt as many lamps as there were boys round you; while Horace was altogether discolored, and the foul smut clave to the well-thumbed Maro.' To avoid the odor of the oil, perfumes were sometimes used. To prevent smoking the wicks would have to be snuffed and occasionally drawn out. In the case of bronze lamps we know that trimmers and sharp needles were used, for they have often been found. Some such device must have been used in the case of terra-cotta lamps also.*[19]

Obviously, such lamps would have been a poor and unsatisfactory means of lighting dark interiors without some sort of refinements to ameliorate the situation. One expedient that may have been arrived at was the discovery of a smokeless wick, an example of which is described in the following account. "M. Ringelmann has been carrying on experiments in the use of ancient lamps. Three Punic lamps from the VII, VI, and IV centuries B.C. were used with olive oil. Wicks of pith, goat, sheep, and dromedary hair, as well as linen, were tried. The linen wicks were the only satisfactory ones. They must be small, however, to avoid smoke. With a wick 3 mm. in diameter composed of 12 linen threads, he obtained a flame 30 to 35 mm. high and 6 to 8 mm. thick, provided salt was added to the oil. There was no smoke, but there was some odor."[20]

Smoke was not the only source of foul air connected with the warming of interiors. Actually a much greater health hazard was posed by the charcoal braziers used so widely in Greek and in Roman times and, indeed, among many peoples in the ensuing centuries right up to the late nineteenth century. Although the brazier was a portable, convenient device and the charcoal an apparently clean fuel, the effects of this method of warming interior spaces were insidious and thoroughly unwholesome. In the process of respiration, any depletion of oxygen creates an increase in carbon dioxide. In the following account, "carbonic acid" is an obsolete term for carbon dioxide, which produces headaches in people and makes them gasp for breath. What can kill by asphyxiation, however, is carbon *monoxide,* generated by burning carbon in air from which much of the oxygen has been removed, as when charcoal braziers are used in a closed room. Here is how the situation was explained in the mid-nineteenth century, before today's accurate admeasurements had been ascertained and before precise scientific knowledge and its terminology had been formulated.

A single pound weight of charcoal consumes in burning 2⁶/₁₀ lbs weight of oxygen, which is the quantity contained in between 13 and 14 lbs weight of atmospheric air. Now, a good-sized room, 20 ft. by 13 ft., and 10 ft. high, does not contain more than about 200 pounds weight of air, and as the combustion of one pound of charcoal produces 3⁶/₁₀ lbs of carbonic acid, which, by mingling with the rest of the air in the apartment, renders, at the least, 36 lbs weight of air unfit for respiration, making in all about 50 lbs weight of air, it follows that, in such a room, the air will require, for healthy respiration, to be renewed many times an hour.[21]

Throughout the ages, the concurrent warming and proper ventilation of interior spaces posed a perennial difficulty. The warm air tended to rise immediately and to escape through the apertures provided for ventilation, whether the open hole in the roof of the Laplander's hut, the louvered lantern astride the ridge over the manor house's great hall, or the smoke flue penetrating the wall at a steep angle above the early fireplaces of the medieval period. Even the ordinary fireplace, so common and familiar throughout the first two hundred or so years of American life, was troubled by this dilemma. According to estimates assessing the performance of domestic fireplaces (built without special features), even today some eighty-six percent of the heat generated by the fire escapes up the chimney. So, although a properly designed fireplace and its chimney draw off the smoke, they also draw off most of the desirable warmth. Thus the ordinary hearth fire warms primarily, by direct radiation, those objects or persons close to the fire. As a source of light, such a fire is neither very effective nor steady and dependable.

What a boon, then, when Franklin invented his iron stove! Set more or less centrally in a room and topped by a long, black, sheet-iron stovepipe, it was undoubtedly ugly. But functionally the iron stove did an efficient job of warming interiors without contaminating the room with smoke and soot, and was widely adopted throughout North America.

Isolating the fire's smoke and gases from the breathable air of a room was a long step in resolving the conflicting needs of warming and ventilation. But except for the use of manufactured iron products, the Franklin stove was not the first solution to the problem. Long before, in Roman times, separation of the noxious products of combustion from the air within a warmed room had been successfully worked out and applied to such disparate establishments as the great imperial baths of Rome itself, on the one hand, and the dwellings of prosperous Roman citizens in the far-off province of Britannia, on the other hand. This scheme is known as a hypocaust.[22]

The Roman hypocaust functioned by circulating the smoke and hot gases from a furnace located to one side and lower down, through a plenum chamber underneath the floor of the room. The plenum chamber was covered by a *suspensura,* a masonry structure either supported at frequent intervals by rows of low brick piers or, in rooms of modest floor area, spanning from one boundary wall to another without intermediate supports as a single, thick slab of concrete.[23] In either case, the upper surface was paved with tiles, mosaic, or marble flagging to serve as the floor of the room—a floor whose heat from the hollow space below it warmed the entire room. Sometimes the wall at the far end of the room had a battery of vertical flues set just behind the finished marble or stucco surface. These flues carried off the smoke and gases from the plenum chamber to the exterior and warmed the interior on their side of the room in the process. Incidentally, the plenum chamber had enough headroom to permit workmen in the off-season to crawl into it from the furnace end, in order to clean out its deposits of soot.

For centuries the Koreans and the Chinese have used heating systems similar in scheme to the Roman hypocaust.[24] Resting on blocks of stone or brick between which the flues deliver heat from the furnace, the floors are carefully laid in cement to prevent any leaking of smoke and gases into the room. But once they have been thoroughly warmed, these floors, being of masonry, retain sufficient heat for domestic comfort throughout many hours. All these hypocaust systems require major structural modifications and adjustments, from the start, in the building's design and layout. But in those regions subject to harsh or severely cold weather, given a sufficient supply of inexpensive fuel, the hypocaust systems met the problem of providing smokeless warming with admirable efficiency.

The supply and circulation of fresh air

Far removed from both Roman Italy and the Orient, the Indians of northern Mexico and the American Southwest developed a ventilation system adapted to their underground ceremonial chambers, the Kivas.[25] The subterranean aspect of the Kiva required integral planning, from the start, in the arrangements for its ventilation system. Rather than separate the smoke from the warmed air within the Kiva, the ventilating system introduced fresh air to serve not only the inhabitants but also the fire—located at the bottom of the underground chamber—in order to keep it from going out for lack of oxygen. The roofs of the Kivas were level with, and constituted the floor of, an outdoor plaza or courtyard from which a vertical shaft had been constructed to one side of the circular wall of the Kiva, down to its own floor level. Here the shaft turned horizon-

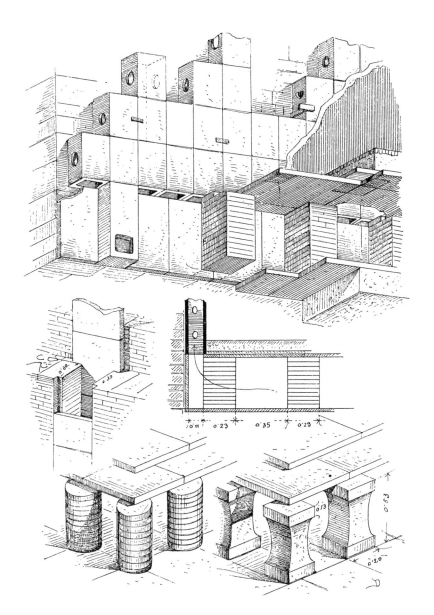

Details of the layout
and arrangements of a
Roman hypocaust.
(Josef Durm, *Die
Baukunst der Römer,*
1905, fig. 395, p. 358.)

tally in order to enter the Kiva by a tall, narrow aperture. An upright slab of stone, set across the opening a short distance in front, deflected the incoming air away from the nearby fireplace. Smoke from the fire eventually found its way out through the trapdoor in the roof. But the fire was prevented from dying, and the incoming air from the ventilating shaft kept the smoky atmosphere in the dark interior of the Kiva from becoming intolerable. The layman tends to think of ventilating shafts as exhaust conduits carrying contaminated air to the exterior. In the Kivas the opposite took place, with fresh air supplied to the fire, instead of smoke and gases of combustion drawn away from it. Yet this intake of fresh air operated quite naturally and automatically because the outdoor air, heavier than the warmed air within the Kiva, came down the ventilating shaft of its own accord.

The problem of fresh air and its circulation often presented itself when certain constructional operations were in progress. Throughout the past, widespread instances of noxious air have been encountered all over the world, not only in natural caves but in deep excavations and tunneling operations.[26] In such situations, stifling air—dizzying and enfeebling, at times incapacitating— occurred naturally and required positive ventilation to sustain the presence, let alone the activities, of human beings. Any building operations below ground, then, made ventilation a most critical problem, sometimes compounded by the complications of having to deal with lighting.

The digging of water wells by hand is a case in point. This kind of operation has been a worldwide necessity since time immemorial—in our own country, persisting even into the twentieth century. Many centuries-old wells throughout the Middle East, in England,[27] in southern France, and elsewhere are known to be at least one hundred feet deep. Yet even in digging quite shallow wells, close air, debilitating fatigue, and sometimes outright prostration may affect the excavating workmen. Following is an early nineteenth century account of the rather inadequate steps then taken to alleviate these hazards. Note that air quality rather than illumination was the primary concern in such instances.

Well-diggers experience sometimes great difficulty from a noxious air which fills the well, and suffocates them if they breathe it. . . . The usual mode of clearing wells of noxious air, is by means of a large pair of bellows and a long leathern pipe, which is hung down into the well to the bottom and fresh air is forced down to the bottom by working the bellows. This is intended to displace the damp air or gas, but is not very efficacious, because the damp air is of a greater specific gravity than pure air; so that ten gallons of fresh air is per-

haps blown into the well, before two gallons of noxious air is dis-placed; and this probably happens because the atmospheric air is specifically lighter than the noxious air, and ascends through the lat-ter to the top of the well, displacing but a small quantity of it. Such bellows, etc., are seldom to be procured on the spot when wanted, and are too weighty and cumbersome to carry about. If water is thrown down in a shower, it will sometimes clear the air; but this is labori-ous, in a deep well, to draw it up again.[28]

Above ground, a surprisingly efficient and well-designed system of air circulation—involving fresh air intake and smoke exhaustion—was worked out for the kitchen in a large four-story-plus-loft building that was part of the medieval Abbey of Ste. Marie de Breteuil in France. Here the fireplace occupied the entire space of the last bay of the ground-floor room, with the flue rising between two arches, thence offsetting diagonally below the main floor and continuing straight up all the way to the chimneytop at the peak of the gable. Down below, at the ground-floor level, were "exterior openings communicating by a throat with the air inlets intended to give a vigorous draft to the fire built on an elevated grate and to establish a sufficient current of air to carry away the smoke into the central flue."[29] This ventilation system was specifi-cally designed for a large-scale kitchen, able to handle the cooking for an entire monastic community. It was a dependable system that provided an adequate air supply, where it was needed, to keep a brisk fire going, and that, at the same time, took care of the smoke and fumes of a large and more or less continuously burning fire.

Ventilation in terms of air circulation was not confined ex-clusively to individual rooms in the interiors of buildings. A seldom noted and little appreciated but significant system of air circula-tion—one not involving the maintenance of a fire or the elimination of smoke but which served effectively on a very large scale in a complex building—was that of the Flavian Amphitheater in Rome. This huge structure has been variously estimated by scholars as having seated from 45,000 to 95,000 spectators. The efficient and expeditious handling of crowds of this magnitude presented the Ro-man engineers with planning problems on a grand scale.[30]

There were eighty portals around the periphery of this oval, fireproof building, whose perimeter was a wall some 157 feet high, pierced by open arches at three levels. The three tiers of these large arches lighted and ventilated the wide promenades just within the perimeter, as well as the innumerable banks of vaulted stairways occupying the greater part of the building's mass. An interior distri-bution corridor, deep within the structure, was vaulted high up im-mediately below a circumferential aisle between the lower and the middle banks of seats, so that metal gratings in the pavement of this aisle could furnish natural light and ventilation to the corridor below. At the ground-story level, the pavements of the radial passageways that gave access to this interior corridor were pitched slightly to the building's exterior, thereby carrying off the rainwater that fell through the gratings above and making it possible, after the crowds had dispersed, to flush their litter out of the building. Another series of interior chambers, higher up within the building's mass, were low-vaulted and otherwise dark, but they received natural illumination and ventilation from large light shafts cut obliquely through their vaulting to allow for flights of stairs which descended at intervals from an upper promenade.

In fact, everywhere within the vast mass of this structure, passageways and stairs were ventilated and lighted by natural means to accommodate the excited and emotionally charged spectators crowding the exits before and after the bloody performances. Even when the people were in their seats, a *velarium* (a tarpaulin-like sunshade hauled about on an overhead platform consisting of 240 tightly stretched radial ropes) was employed to shade the spectators on that side of the arena directly in the sun.[31]

As the Roman *velarium* illustrates, ventilation was not a requirement of indoor heating alone. Hot climates called for the circulation of fresh and constantly replenished air. Indeed, ventilating entire cities was a concern of Roman engineers and town planners, as we learn from Vitruvius's treatise on architecture, written in the reign of Augustus Caesar. Orientation of the streets with respect to wind direction was one consideration.[32] Moreover, the narrowness of all but the two main thoroughfares of Roman towns and cities, along with the prohibition against most vehicular traffic on them during the daytime, made these lanes reasonably healthy and agreeable for pedestrians through the hot months of the year.

After the Roman era, in hot climates such as those of North Africa and Spain, the very narrow streets were frequently canopied by sunshades of various sorts: trellises, mats, nets, or vines were "turned to good account for distilling the raw sunlight into a sort of optical liqueur."[33] With three- or four-story buildings on either hand, streets that were often too narrow for carts kept the direct rays of the sun from penetrating to the ground level. Thus the buildings themselves produced shade for the pedestrians; shuttered windows facing on these narrow streets ventilated the interiors in subdued light that made the air seem cooler. In Italy, at least, an additional story was sometimes built atop the palaces of the wealthy as a belvedere—a covered gallery open on all sides to the breezes—which insulated the rooms of the regular top story from

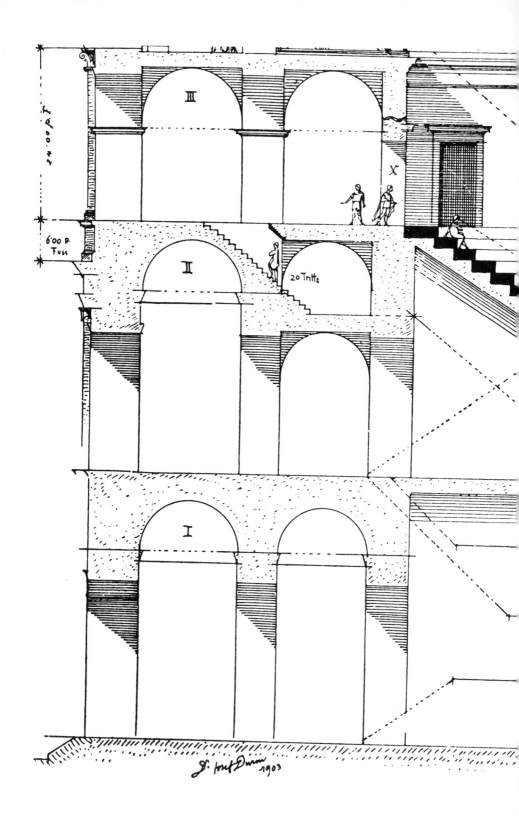

III

X

6'00 p.
Fuss

II

20 Tnttz

I

G. Josf Durm
1903

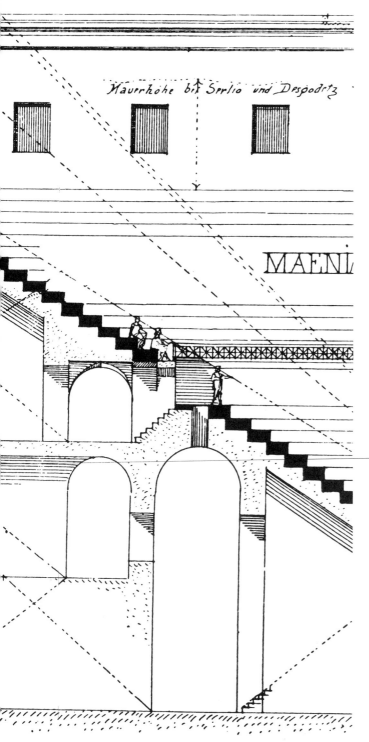

Section through part of the Roman Coliseum showing passageways and how they received natural light. (Josef Durm, *Die Baukunst der Römer*, 1905, fig. 747, p. 676.)

Axiometric drawing of Roman Coliseum at height just below second-floor level. (Drawing by Gaudet, *Le Moniteur des architects,* 1875, pls. 11–12.)

direct solar heat and provided a constant change of air high above the smells of the often foul and litter-strewn streets.

In the hot climate of West Pakistan, where the temperature soars well above one-hundred degrees Fahrenheit from April to June, the steady wind that always blows from one direction has been utilized for centuries to assure fresh air and cooling circulation. Fixed wind deflectors on the rooftops, one for each room even in multistoried buildings, direct the wind through built-in air shafts into the apartments below, air-conditioning them and furnishing welcome ventilation, with a constant supply of fresh air, to the inhabitants as far below as street level.[34]

As far back as the Minoan period, the layout of the domestic apartments in the Royal Palace at Knossos in Crete was designed to promote the health and comfort of the inhabitants. Built into the complex were numerous light wells, galleries, and porticos with many doors and windows for cross ventilation.[35] Later, light wells and open-air courts and patios were common in both Greek and Roman houses; most rooms featured windows and/or doors that opened onto the courtyard for light, fresh air, and ventilation. In addition, in the urban dwellings of well-to-do Romans, this patio contained a pool of water, the *impluvium,* which was often graced with a little fountain that splashed or pattered into it. The *impluvium* gave a sense of coolness along with visual and aural delight; and it actually humidified and hence reduced the temperature of the hot, dry air of the Mediterranean summers.[36]

Probably the most refined form of humidification occurred in the Parthenon.[37] There stood Phidias's huge statue of Athena— thirty-nine feet high including its pedestal. The statue was chryselephantine, that is, the flesh (face and bare arms) were of ivory, the drapery of gold. Of course, no tusks were ever large enough for the arms or face of the statue to have been carved from a single unit of this valuable material. Instead, individual segments of ivory had to be meticulously pieced together with such exactitude that their ensemble would *appear* seamless. Once the pieces were assembled, the slightest movement between them—occurring from expansion and contraction due to atmospheric changes—had to be zealously guarded against. Any such movement would tend to separate the individual pieces, chip their edges of contact, or perhaps discolor them at the joints. The segments of ivory were secured to a strong wooden armature within, which was kept dimensionally stable with respect to expansion and contraction by means of the following scheme.

When the floor of the cella was constructed, a depression perhaps a foot deep was fashioned in the pavement to receive the pedestal of the statue. Its dimensions were considerably larger than the area of the pedestal's base; hence, when that block was set in the depression, a trench was formed approximately a foot-and-a-half wide around the pedestal. The pedestal block itself was unique in not being of marble (the stone otherwise used exclusively throughout this building for architectural features and for sculptural decorations alike). Instead, it was of a very porous stone. With the trench at its base constantly filled with water, the pedestal block acted like a sponge through capillary attraction. It was glisteningly wet at all times, and its rising vapors created a sort of invisible cocoon of humidity around the statue above. Thus the armature was kept in an unchanging dimensional status and the flesh parts of the statue were maintained without crack or blemish, appearing as though sculptured from a single piece of ivory.

Ventilation problems in building the Great Pyramid

A number of the problems noted here in connection with operations carried on in dark and confined areas were encountered at a very early date; namely, during the construction of the Great Pyramid in Egypt. To achieve this stupendous project, certain unusual features had to be worked out and incorporated into the fabric as its burial accommodations were being met. It was only *while the work was in progress* that these special arrangements were required; for, once completed, the structure was intended to be irrevocably sealed against intrusion of any kind, for all eternity. Thus it was not the finished building but certain stages in its erection which mandated that the workers within it be able to go about their tasks without suffering either asphyxiation or entrapment.

For example, sectional drawings of the Great Pyramid of Cheops reveal long, straight six-by-eight-inch air shafts cutting diagonally through the interior mass of stonework to the south and to the north exterior faces, from the king's chamber and from the vestibule of the king's chamber, respectively.[38] Whatever mystical attribution these air shafts may be thought to have had, they certainly served two practical purposes at the time of the pyramid's erection. First, because of its size, the great granite sarcophagus of the deceased pharaoh had to be installed in the king's chamber before the walls of the room were built. As work on the pyramid progressed, the huge structure rose around and above the king's chamber and left it as a cavity within the solid mass of stonework. Thus, the tomb chamber was deprived of all natural light and, save for the air shafts, of all air circulation, both of which were needed by the craftsmen who still had to execute delicate finishing work of various sorts on the interior. Second, the ventilation shafts were

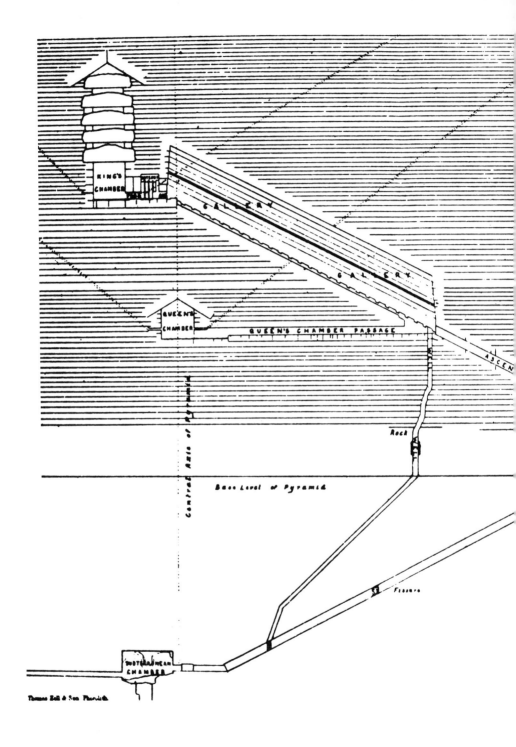

KING'S CHAMBER

GALLERY

GALLERY

QUEEN'S CHAMBER

QUEEN'S CHAMBER PASSAGE

ASCEN

Central Axis of Pyramid

Rock

Base Level of Pyramid

Fissure

SUBTERRANEAN CHAMBER

Thomas Bell & Son Plymouth

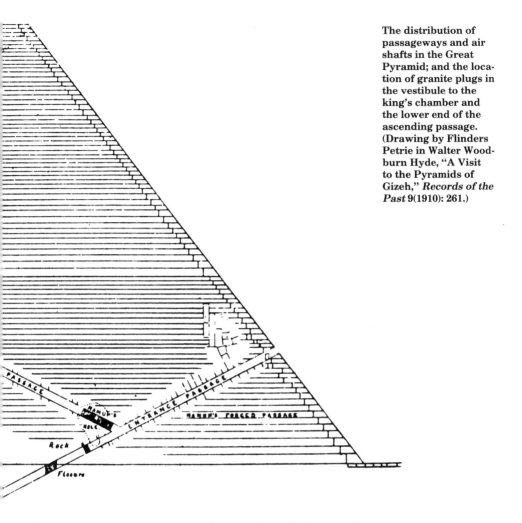

The distribution of passageways and air shafts in the Great Pyramid; and the location of granite plugs in the vestibule to the king's chamber and the lower end of the ascending passage. (Drawing by Flinders Petrie in Walter Woodburn Hyde, "A Visit to the Pyramids of Gizeh," *Records of the Past* 9(1910): 261.)

PASSAGE

MAMUN'S HALL

ENTRANCE PASSAGE

MAMUN'S FORCED PASSAGE

Rock

Fissure

SECTION OF THE PASSAGES OF THE GREAT PYRAMID.

SCALE ₁/₄₈₀

The actual faces of the steps were measured for ten courses near the entrance, and at the base; the rest are filled in uniformly. Only the vertical joints in the ascending passage are put in, so as to shew these more plainly indispensable for the procedure of sealing off the tomb chamber. This operation involved the lowering of a fifty-ton block of granite engineered to slide diagonally downward, somewhat like a portcullis, in such a way as to plug the entrance to the king's chamber permanently. The massive plug had previously been propped up, above and to one side, out of the way, by a single stout timber.[39] When all was ready for the definitive sealing of the tomb chamber, the workmen set fire to the timber prop. When it had burned sufficiently to be too weak to support the stone portcullis, that huge granite mass slid thunderingly down, crushing what embers remained, to fit snugly into the recesses designed to receive it. Obviously there had to be positive assurance that the fire would not go out prematurely, leaving the entrance unplugged. The air shafts (one on each side of the plug) provided the oxygen required to sustain the fire's combustion. The smallness of their areas in section did not hinder the effectiveness of these shafts, for the draft produced by a flue depends primarily on the length of the flue in relation to its cross-sectional area. The north and south shafts are reported to be 234 and 174 feet long, respectively; so clearly the flue action was more than adequate for maintaining the fire, particularly as that purpose involved a single, nonrecurring event and hence no appreciable accumulation of soot.[40]

A steeper, crooked, and much larger shaft in this pyramid, undoubtedly for ventilation during the course of construction, was in the end used for a quite different purpose. This shaft runs up, at times vertically but quite irregularly, from a point near the bottom of the downward-sloping passage (three feet four inches high by three feet eleven inches wide) leading to the subterranean chamber, to a point where the upward-sloping grand gallery intersects with the horizontal passage to the queen's chamber. There, at its mouth, the shaft measures twenty-one-by-forty-eight inches. The subterranean chamber and much of its approach is not a part of the pyramid proper but excavated out of the underlying rock 101½ feet beneath the man-made structure. To aid the men collecting and removing the accumulation of pulverized rock at this depth, attendants would have been stationed at various points to fan the air with cloths, facilitating its circulation through the shafts and passageways to cut down on the incidence of heat prostration and choking incapacity to work.[41]

One of the overriding preoccupations of the Egyptian pharaohs was to provide for the inviolable security of their mummified entombments (hence the misleading passageways, the false doors, the sealed entrances, and all the other elaborate precautions their architects devised). So a file of three granite portcullis blocks—originally propped in the space between the narrow ramps on either side of the grand gallery at the time of its construction—were eventually allowed to slide carefully down into position at the lower end of the ascending passageway. Here they became a permanent triple plug against entry, at a point just above a limestone slab that was made a part of the smooth continuous ceiling of the descending passage to the subterranean chamber. Once in place, however, these immovable plugs left no outlet for the workmen who had lowered the massive blocks into place. The larger shaft, first used to ventilate the subterranean tunneling operations, then served as the workmen's means of escape.[42]

Ventilation problems encountered during the construction of buildings were sometimes of a most difficult and critical nature. But much less attention was given to them formerly (when in general no laws or regulations protected the health and safety of the workmen) than was given to those that provided for the performance of completed buildings. Solutions to these latter problems had to be worked out on a permanent basis and incorporated into the design of the building from the start. From a practical standpoint, ventilation has always been a critical factor in the well-being and in the very lives of people. Consequently, a study of the various solutions to ventilation problems adopted throughout the past can give us time-tested criteria for assessing our own performances in the field.

13

ARCHITECTURE *is one of thofe Arts which Neceffity has made univerfal: From the Time that Man firft felt the Inclemencies of the Seafons, it had its Beginning; and accordingly it has fpread wherefoever the Severities of the Climate demanded Shelter or Shade: It is to be traced in the Indian's Hut and the Icelander's Cave; it ftill fhews, in thofe barbarous Parts of the Globe, from what mean Original it rofe to its prefent Glory.*[1]

Native House Building

Throughout the past, native buildings have reflected the ways in which the climate of a given region has affected, directly or indirectly, the nature and source of a community's food supply and, therefore, the activities and life-style of the inhabitants. For example, hunting cultures tended to live in either transportable dwellings (Indian tepees) or seasonal habitations (Eskimo igloos). Somewhat the same seminomadism obtained for peoples whose livelihood depended on their herds, as summer and winter pasture lands were often separated by treks of many scores of miles (thus the transportable yurts of central Asia). Jungle dwellers have had to relocate almost every other year because of the rapid exhaustion of the soil's fertility in the clearings hacked out of the lush-seeming rain forests. Desert peoples living in fixed communities have been totally dependent on a reliable (often man-made) water supply by which they could make the desert bloom.

Concomitant attributes of the natural environment related more specifically to man's dwellings, namely, the materials at hand: snow for igloos; wool felt for the desert Bedouins' tent; bamboo and similar pole-like vegetation with rushes, grasses, and palm fronds for thatched dwellings throughout the world; mud for a variety of structures in Mesopotamia and parts of Africa; bark for roofiing and exterior walls in North and South America. Another sometimes vital consideration that linked nature (the characteristics of the site) with design (the skills and ingenuity of man) was the need to protect the inhabitants from hostile neighbors or marauding bands.

Worldwide, natural, readily available materials have furnished the essential ingredients for assembling quickly constructed human habitations and their ancillary buildings. Almost any native adult raised in the traditions of the tribe would have been taught the customary methods from childhood. In such circumstances the art of building was familiar and a fairly uncomplicated skill to acquire. Depending on the mores of the particular society, execution was assigned now to the women of the tribe, now to the men, sometimes to both in cooperation.[2] Where construction involved building canoes as well as houses (as in many of the islands of the Pacific, notably Samoa), the work was customarily done by a professional class of carpenters.[3]

The limited range of materials and the restrictions these materials imposed on the spanning of space, stability, resistance to wind and to the elements generally—as well as their impermanence compared to stone or brick masonry—would seem to allow for few variations in the shape and conformation of structures made from them. Yet the diversity of house types constructed out of these simple natural materials is incredible. Differences spring from the lifestyle of the inhabitants, whether communal or solitary, sedentary or seasonally nomadic. Sometimes the variety stems from the particular nature and composition of the materials themselves in their locally available forms, sometimes from the sites chosen for building, whether beside rivers, on hilltops, in forest clearings, or in open country. Obviously, a basic factor is the climatic differences due to heavy or light rainfall, periodic flooding, dense or sparse forest cover, the prevalence of strong winds, or location at high or low altitudes.

Native houses constructed from abundant, organic materials growing locally exist on the islands of the Pacific, in the jungles of Southeast Asia, in both the swampy reaches of the Amazon and the highlands of Andean South America, as well as many other regions. Probably the most remarkable variety of such house forms is found in Africa, where each tribe, each clan, even each subclan has had its own distinctive type of habitation.[4] The forms are quite as varied as the languages, as numerous as are the dialects. A given house type, like the speech of the natives who inhabit it, is a persistent reality, highly resistant to change. In fact, some anthropologists have noted that, in most native cultures, house forms are undoubtedly less subject to foreign influence or contamination by adjacent cultures than any other artifacts, crafts, or practices, including language itself.

Selecting the site and preparing the building materials

In a long and highly detailed account of native building practices among the Dyaks of Borneo, Edwin H. Gomes describes the selection of what might be called the building committee, as well as the kinds of preliminary surveys they conduct and the reports they make. He notes the care with which a site is selected. The committee considers such factors as the proximity of a good water supply, of a jungle to provide firewood, and of large tracts of land for rice cultivation. (Not mentioned as necessary in this particular instance, though ordinarily of paramount concern in most native cultures, are considerations of defensibility of the site, access to trade, and proximity of game animals.) Ritual plays a large and constant part in the process of constructing a Dyak communal dwelling, and includes the consultation of omens and the propitiation of spirits at every step in the undertaking. Analogous invocations, exorcisms, or ceremonies of various sorts that aim to assure an auspicious outcome have, of course, been practiced by most peoples elsewhere in the world, usually before, sometimes during, and often at the conclusion of the undertaking.[5]

Gomes describes the preparation of the site and the removal of encumbrances from it. Constituting the first steps in the actual construction, stout posts are set out and installed for the communal dwelling itself, which may house as many as thirty to forty families under one roof.

The posts, of which there are a great number, are about 12″ or less in diameter, and are of bilian or other hard wood, so as not to rot in the earth. A hole four feet deep is made to receive each post.

All the men combine to labour collectively until the skeleton of the house is complete, and then every family turns its attention to its own apartments. During the building of the house, there is a great deal of striking of gongs and other noisy instruments to prevent any birds of ill omen being heard. . . .[6]

An account of native habitations built largely of poles and grasses, with or without some mud plastering, discusses the constructional practices employed by the Hottentots of Southern Africa. The materials described include: poles, usually of willow; sinews and thongs, principally derived from game animals; small twigs and grass for interweaving between the poles of the structural frame; long, tough grass for thatching; a mixture of sand and fresh cow manure for plastering the interior; pipe clay and wood ashes diluted with sour milk as a size to wash over this plaster; finely pulverized earth from the ant hills for "a smooth durable floor which becomes as hard as a brick." In addition to the materials utilized and their preparation, the account discusses some of the social mores governing the hut's ownership and occupancy and who takes part in its building.

Two types of Hottentot huts, or kraals, are described. The second type, being unplastered, is transportable.

It consists of small poles tied together at the smallest ends, which, when secured, can be folded up like an umbrella; when needed for use opened out and covered with mats of grass and sometimes skins of animals. This hut or kraal is the property of the wife, and in its erection, removal, and repair, she receives no assistance from her husband. A young woman no sooner entertains a matrimonial proposal than she sets about the making of mats, accompanied by a friend or two. She trudges off to the river or other locality where the particular kind of reed is to be found, and after many days, returns with a sufficient quantity. The cord or twine which she also needs in the construction of the mats to cover the kraal [requires] another journey to obtain the fine inner bark of the white thorn tree, which she strips off and carries home for manipulation. . . . The lady now summons a number of children to assist in manducation. It is with this view that the long strings of bark are first steeped in milk or mutton broth, before they are handed to the hungry brats, whose juvenile jaws never cease to grind while a drop of liquid remains to be extracted. A little further preparation fits the fiber for being twisted by the hand into a strong and even twine, by means of which the reeds are threaded together with a stiletto formed out of the shank bone of the ostrich. . . .[7]

In another part of Africa—the Congo River area—the grasses used for thatching are sometimes of quite different species, with different properties. Consequently, the methods used in constructing grass roofs can involve one sort of grass for the purlins, another for the thatching proper.

There is a kind of grass which grows only on land which has been recently under cultivation; it is called nianga; *it is a capital material for thatching, for its broad blades all spring up from its root, not from the stalk. It is cut level with the ground, and when dry is brought up to the town, and cleaned by a process of combing, which removes the short, dry spathes, and any withered grass. . . . To the rafters of the roof were tied horizontally the thick stems of the giant* madiadia *grass, and on this the thatch was laid. . . . Twisted strips of the skin of split papyrus stems were used as the "string." A number of little bundles of thatching grass were laid along the eaves, the cut ends downwards. Rows (six or seven) of stout grass stems are tied over these bundles, right through to the framework of the roof underneath, and the thatch neatly spread. Then another row of thatch is tied on that, its ends about nine inches higher up; then another and another until the top is reached. The roof must be at a high pitch, to throw the rain off well.*[8]

There are frequent but scattered references to bark as a building material for habitations in many areas of the world. Various species of bark have been used in native houses as roofing surfaces, exterior walling, and even flooring (as well as for canoes) in both North and South America, Africa, and elsewhere. The waterproof attribute of bark, quite as much as its availability in long and/or large pieces, accounts for its widespread use in these circumstances.

The "long house," the characteristic Iroquois dwelling, is a substantial rectangular building 20 to 30 feet in breadth, approximately the

same in height, and from 50 to 150 . . . feet in length. A framework of
upright poles, beams, and rafters supports a rounded or arched roof
with holes for the escape of smoke. Flattened slabs of dried bark [in
this case, from elm trees] are laid like clapboards on the side and end
walls, and like shingles on the roof. . . . A platform of bark, about
twelve feet long by six feet in width, raised a foot or two from the
ground, and covered with mats and skins, serves [each] family as a
seat by day and a bed by night. . . .[9]

In one of the most completely detailed accounts of native
house construction, Charles Wilkes describes the Samoan council-
house at a time when the traditional materials, methods, and procedures were quite undisturbed by foreign modifications or European
innovations. He details the indigenous materials (species, size, and
makeup) as well as the nailless methods of attachment. The skillful
character of the house's structure and assemblage, quite as much as
its large size, required the services of a specialized group of men—
local carpenters and their apprentices. Undoubtedly the two most
interesting and unexpected aspects of the structure involve the construction of the roof: first, "a staging or scaffolding is erected, nearly
in the form of the roof, which serves for ladders and to support the
roof temporarily"; second, "the roof is commenced at the ridge-pole
and is worked downwards." Neither of these practices would be evident once the structure was completed.

In the process of erection, center posts—twenty-five to thirty
feet high—were raised first, supporting the ridgepole. Below this,
a somewhat complex system of crossbeams at different heights
and rafters made of short pieces to form the curve of the roof were
lashed together from the top down to the wallpiece. The whole was
thatched with sugarcane or pandanus leaves, which lasted for four
or five years.

After the whole is finished, the interior has the appearance of an
extensive framework, from the number of cross-beams, which are
used as depositories for their property, tapas, mats, &c., and in some
cases the favorite canoe of the chiefs is placed on them. . . . On one,
and sometimes on both sides of the centre-post of the houses, is a
small circular hearth, enclosed by stones of larger size; this is the
place for burning the dried leaves of the cocoa-nut, which serves
them for light at night.[10]

Transportable habitations

Because of the exigencies of their climate and its imposition of a
nomadic rather than a sedentary mode of life, many desert dwellers
and pastoral peoples have had to devise transportable habitations.

Notably successful solutions to the problem of transportability are the tents of the Bedouins, the yurts of the central Asians, and the tepees of the American Plains Indians. The structure of the Bedouins' tent is typically composed of nine poles in sets of three over which ropes are stretched and pegged firmly in the ground at either end.[11] Because the height of the poles diminishes somewhat from the center outwards, these ropes create ridges in the covering (which consists of a thick felt of black goat hair). The slopes thus formed carry off rainwater, however infrequent an occurrence. But much more important, the low, ground-hugging spread of the Bedouin's tent provides security against violent windstorms that might otherwise overturn or carry off higher structures presenting more of an obstruction to the wind.

The Kazaks of central Asia are nomadic in the summertime, dwelling in felt-covered tents called yurts.

The yurt, a light framework of wood over which strips of felt are stretched and secured by ropes, can be erected or dismantled in half an hour. The frame consists of three parts firmly bound together by thongs or cords—a circular and approximately vertical external wall [of laths, which expand and contract in lozenges, on the principle of lazy tongs] four or five feet high, a ring of wood at the center supported by a pole, and roof slats inserted into holes in the periphery of the central ring and sloping gently downward to the framework of the wall, to which they are tied. . . . The central ring is left free for smoke to escape and light and air to enter; in inclement weather it is closed by a felt. The yurt is well adapted to both warm and cool weather as well as to a nomadic existence; it can be opened up to the breezes, closed against the sun's rays, and its felt covers doubled for protection against the cold. . . .[12]

The felt of the Kazak yurt is particularly effective as an all-weather covering. It sheds water, yet "breathes" in the prevailing dry weather; it blocks the, at times, tempestuous winds; and it insulates against both heat and cold. Moreover, it can be rolled into bundles for transport by beasts of burden. In fact, in their constant peregrinations in search of adequate pasturage for their herds and flocks, the Kazaks stow all the elements of their yurts, including the collapsible sections of the lattice-work walls, onto the backs of camel, donkey, or yak.[13]

Various factors differentiated the mobile life of the American Plains Indians from that of the central Asian Kazaks. Most of these distinctions stemmed from the fact that the Kazaks were a pastoral people keeping watch over their flocks, whereas the Plains Indians were hunters dependent to a very large extent on the roamings and migrations of the wild buffalos. Along with meat and clothing,

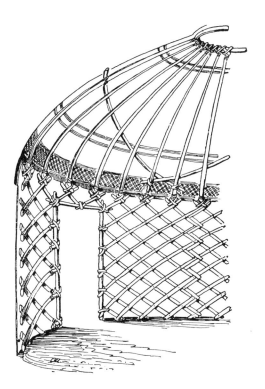

Detail sketch of the
structural components
of a Kirgiz yurt show-
ing where and how
these elements are tied
together. (Constantin
Uhde, *Baudenkmaeler
in Spain und Portugal,*
1892, fig. 67, p. 27.)

these animals provided the integument of their dwellings. The Indian tepee developed into one of the most beautiful, comfortable, and healthful habitations man has ever evolved, serving throughout the year, summer and winter, rain or shine, in blinding snowstorm as well as in broiling heat, yet ready on short notice to be quickly dismantled and reassembled at a different site.

The frame of a typical Sioux tepee consisted of fifteen to twenty slender, slightly tapered poles, twenty-one to twenty-five feet in length, which had been debarked and made completely smooth. Erection began with a tripod of poles firmly lashed together four to six feet below their tips, with their pointed butts stuck in the ground equidistant along a circular line that defined the circumference of the tepee. The other poles of the frame, rising from the circular outline in a carefully specified order and leaning against the crotches formed by the original tripod of poles, were bound together by a long length of rope. Twelve to fourteen buffalo hides that had been thoroughly scraped and tanned were cut and sewn together to form the cover, including the smoke flaps. When a cover was first installed, a smudge fire was lit inside the tepee [tipi], the smoke flaps crossed over and the door closed tightly, thereby making "the smoke permeate the entire hide cover. This helped to make the tipi waterproof and also kept it from getting hard and stiff following a wetting. Smoked skin retains its softness even after a complete soaking. Unsmoked skin does not, and water will ruin it."[14]

With a lining a tipi is almost as dry as a house—dryer than most summer cottages. The lining keeps the dew from condensing inside, and so is often spoken of as a dew cloth. . . . The lining, besides keeping away drafts and dampness, prevented rain from dripping off the poles and served a number of other purposes. It gave increased ventilation, helping to clear the atmosphere of smoke. The warm air rising inside the tipi drew in the cold air from the outside, which came in under the cover and went up behind the lining, creating a perfect draft for the fire and taking the smoke out with it. . . . The air space behind the lining also served as insulation, which helped to keep the tipi warm in winter and cool in summer.[15]

Pile-supported habitations over water

Some of the oldest communities of which evidence remains are those of the lake dwellers, said to date from around 4000 B.C. Prehistoric complexes of lake dwellings have been discovered throughout much of Europe, including Bosnia,[16] Belgium,[17] England, Italy and elsewhere, but notably and most extensively in Switzerland.[18] The vestiges of many of these habitations, constructed on piles above the surface of the water, are similar to those of the Paeonians, described by Herodotus:

Their dwellings are contrived after this manner: planks fitted on lofty piles are placed in the middle of the lake, with a narrow entrance from the main-land by a single bridge. These piles, that support the planks, all the citizens anciently placed there at the public charge; but afterward they established a law to the following effect: whenever a man marries, for each wife he sinks three piles, . . . but every man has several wives. They live in the following manner: on the planks every man has his hut, in which he dwells, with a trapdoor closely fitted in the planks, and leading down to the lake. . . .[19]

Dwellings on piles over water are still constructed and used today by various native peoples in Venezuela and in much of the southwest Pacific. In West Irian, formerly Dutch New Guinea (a land characterized as a "living museum of the primitive world"), these structures proliferate. For example, on the Waropan coast in an arm of the river almost completely circled with mangrove, some three hundred water-dwelling Papuans have built houses of palm slats, grass, and sticks set loosely on pilings out in the middle of the stream. The people spend most of their time sitting on or fishing from the bamboo floors of their houses or paddling about in their praus; for when they leave their house these Papuans must either go by prau or swim, as there is no dry land to walk on and the mangroves impose an impossible barrier.[20] Their dwellings, however, are generally well made.

In the northwest the Malay type prevails. We find each family with its own house. This is placed on poles out in the water with sides of 'attap,' or pandanus mat, and roof of thatch. This thatch is made by taking sagopalm leaves and braiding the blades all on one side of the midrib. These are then laid on as clapboards would be, and make an excellent watertight roof.

In Geelvink Bay . . . the regular house is a long communal structure. These great turtle-back houses shelter from 80 to 100 people. . . . The women work on the back piazza nearest the forest-covered shore—convenient agents to spread the alarm should an attack be made by some marauding tribe. . . .[21]

In Humbolt Bay, on the frontier of New Guinea . . . the bay runs back from a wide mouth, its sides closing in after a mile and a half. In this constricted part the view into the inner bay is almost completely cut off by [a wooded islet]. On the innermost sheet of water . . . are several villages which are set on poles, and the houses are arranged to form irregular streets.[22]

Various articles and books on prehistoric lake dwellings and terramare settlements describe this very ancient type of community built on piles over water. But data on how they were actually constructed are lacking. Specifically, there is no circumstantial account, no precise information to indicate the manner in which the piles were first reared upright and held in position, then driven into the lagoon or lake bottom.[23] Ascertaining the necessary length of the piles requires knowing the height of the platform above waterlevel, the depth of the water, and the degree to which the piles penetrated the bottom of the bay.[24] The longer the piles—that is, the larger the sum of these three factors—the heavier and more unwieldy they would have been to handle, position, and drive into the submarine soil. The Papuans, Moros, Fiji Islanders, and other peoples of the adjacent Pacific areas who built structures on piles over water also built land dwellings that were set high on posts planted in the ground.[25] But the problem of erecting stilt structures is quite different on land, where the holes to receive the posts can be excavated before their insertion and where there is adequate, stable footing for any number of men to help rear the tall, often heavy posts. In the case of pile-supported structures over water, some sort of raft—anchored by poles or "spuds" thrust into the bottom of the bay or lake—must have been employed in lieu of solid ground. Herodotus notes "a narrow entrance from the mainland by a single bridge." Such a gangway, however rickety or unstable the footing on "poles that roll about," would have provided not only an essential pedestrian link to land but also, at the time of construction, an incremental means of erecting the entire complex of piles, for bridge and houses alike, from the land outward.

Floating habitations

The floating structures examined here were neither commercial nor military in nature, but domestic. On rivers subject to recurring floods, in estuaries affected by tidal variations, and in canal basins and lakes where population growth outstrips the availability of land for more conventional dwellings, floating habitations have been used for a long, long time. For instance, from the beginnings of traffic via canals, boats plying them have customarily served as the residence for the family who owned and/or operated one. Houseboats that were more or less permanently moored in one place, and whose seaworthiness required little more than an ability to float, had a certain vogue in the eastern and southern United States during the late nineteenth century. The practice continues today in many of the urban canals of Holland. Throughout the Far East, sampans still serve as homes for great numbers of Chinese families; their teeming ranks in the harbors of Hong Kong and Shanghai, for example, are familiar sights. For the poor, sampans are perhaps the only possible alternative to domestic dislocation from the periodic floods that have devastated the major river valleys of the region for untold centuries. One type of floating habitation resorted to during periodic inundations involves placing individual huts on rafts that can be maneuvered into positions according to the varying depth of the flood waters.

In Cochin China and Cambodia, a further phenomenon is encountered in the existence of immense tracts of country lying below the river level, which in times of high water are converted into enormous swamps or lakes, whence only the upper branches of the trees emerge. The great lake of Tale Sap, i.e., the Inland Sea of Cambodia, which is a depression in the soil of this character, and is fed by the Mekong, experiences transformations so violent that in the rainy season its length increases from 70 to 120 miles, its area is tripled; and while in the low waters the fish with which it abounds, can almost be ladled from its shallow trough, then from 2 to 4 feet deep, it is swollen by the floods between June and September to a depth of 30 to 50 feet. In Cambodia the abodes of men adapt themselves to these fluctuant conditions, for they consist of palm-leaf and bamboo huts, which, if belonging to a stationary village, are raised upon wooden piles from 5 to 15 feet in height above the ground, or are placed upon floating rafts moored by long poles to the bed of the stream, and capable of being shifted from site to site according to the height of the waters.[26]

The snow igloo of the polar Eskimos

The first, and probably most critical, procedure in building an igloo is to find a deposit of snow of the proper consistency. In order to determine the compactness, depth, and general availability of the snowdrifts, a snow-tester is standard equipment in making a camp on a sledge journey. This is an Eskimo tool some three feet long and about the diameter of a little finger; one end is sharpened and the other, formed as a button, is held in the palm of the hand.

Having halted on some lake that they know by certain signs has not yet frozen to the bottom (this is generally done by lying flat on the ice, and placing their eyes as close to it as the nose will allow, when some varying peculiarities of the ice-colors decide their conjectures), the men scatter out like skirmishers along the deep snow-drifts near the shore, and commence prodding with their testers. . . .

It takes considerable experience, coupled with good judgment, to pick out the best building-site; and, while the constant prodding with testers oftentimes looks foolish to a spectator, it is no inconsiderable part of the performance. Snow which looks perfect on the crust may be friable beyond use a few inches deeper, and this the tester will reveal. Soft drifting snow may cover a bank of splendid building material. Again, the drift may be freely interspersed with hidden stones and boulders, which the testers will bring to light if freely used.[27]

It usually takes from ten to fifteen minutes to test for good snow. But sometimes the process drags on for an hour (the time it takes to construct the igloo itself). Sometimes, in fact, the lake that appears most favorable has to be abandoned after its whole perimeter has been scouted.

The actual layout and building of Eskimo igloos has been described in great detail by Frederick Schwatka, who has watched the process many times, recorded every step in their construction, and lived in them throughout two long seasons. His account covers such items as the shape and handling of the wide-bladed, two-handed snow knife; the stance and the body-action involved in cutting out the snow blocks (from one to one-and-a-half feet wide, one-and-a-half to two or three feet long, and eight to ten inches thick) and in trimming them to conform to the hemispherical shape of the structure. He delineates the order and sequence followed in placing the blocks, starting on the right of the entrance and work-ing counterclockwise in a spiral of ever more inward-tilting and trapezoidal (and ultimately triangularly shaped) blocks. Finally, he describes how the blocks are thrust into position, supported below on their tilted beds and kept from falling inward by their snug con-tact with the adjacent, previously laid block.

The blocks all laid, the igloo is now complete, except the "chinking" of the joints to render it air-tight, there being many large crevices. The chinking of an igloo is a very ingenious affair, the materials being cut diagonally from the lower edge of the upper block on the horizontal joints, and from the left edge of the right block on the vertical ones, if the person be right-handed. As the knife in the right hand thus trims the edges, the left fist, tightly clinched, follows the knife, and rams the cut portion tightly into the crevice, rendering it as perfectly air-tight as the body of the snow-block itself. An active Innuit will go completely around the igloo on a single joint in about a minute, and it seldom takes over ten to do all the chinking in a large hut. . . .

Meanwhile the boys and women have been busy throwing the loose snow from the trenches, and piling it on the house, often follow-ing closely upon the work of block-laying, covering the whole to a depth of from six inches to half as many feet. The depth to which this is carried depends on the length of time they expect to use the hut, and on the temperature. . . .

14

When we try to reconstruct some forgotten building practice of former times, it is sobering and more than a little daunting to realize that very perceptive and inventive men were on the scene long before us, actually achieving a solution which we can do no more than guess at today. [1]

I have spoken of the snow-walls, when chinked, as being
fectly air-tight. This is not strictly correct; the snow being mor
less porous, and allowing a slow but ample current of air to pa
through. In fact, at night the door is sealed, and the only mear
ventilation is through the body of the snow.

The various structures presented above exemplify tim
honored practices of indigenous house building in a number
intersecting categories: semipermanent, seasonal, and transj
able. What is apparent in this brief survey of representative
ples of generally quickly built native habitations is how rem
well they have evolved to meet the conditions of their specifi
vironments; that is, adjusted to the multiple risks and hazai
along with the benefits—imposed by geography and climate
a tribute indeed to "unsophisticated" man's sophisticated in
tiveness and adaptability to nature.

Building Cheops' Pyramid

The Pyramids of Egypt, one of the Seven Wonders of the ancient world, continue to awe and fascinate everyone who has stood in their enormous, timeless presence. Confronting them, one inevitably asks, "How were they built?" The answer is not as constructionally simple as their geometrically stark shape. Professional Egyptologists and engineers alike have wrestled with this problem off and on since the eighteenth century without devising definitive or even generally accepted solutions. Investigations and speculations continue, with a new theory proposed every few years to explain how the thousands upon thousands of blocks were raised to their destined positions in the artificial mountain of stone.

Before evaluating any previously proposed solutions or presenting new considerations of construction methods, it is necessary to review and comment on the traditional operations of the ancient builders and what is known about their equipment, tools, and customary procedures.

Jacking apparatuses

It can be stated categorically that, except for a very few stones of relatively small size (and even these, only in special circumstances), the ancient Egyptians never lifted blocks by means of tackle and pulleys nor suspended them by ropes from above.[2] Their massive, sometimes colossal monoliths precluded the possibility of suspending their dead weight from ropes. Instead, blocks of stone were raised—whether by wedge, lever, or rocker—by jacking operations. A jack is a device for exerting great pressure in moving an object within a short interval of space. Its advantages are not only the great pressure it can apply but, above all, the precision of control over the application of that pressure, largely because it is exerted within such limited and prescribed boundaries.

For example, the water-soaked wedges used to sever an obelisk from the parent rock acted like jacks, in that they created even, gradually applied but intense pressure, yet only within the very small bounds of their own expansion: obviously, none of the force remained in effect once the rock had been split off along the line of the wedges. Similarly, levers used for raising blocks produce action analogous to that of jacks, in that great pressure is exerted when fulcrums are placed close to the block. Each lever arm may be long and counterbalanced with a rock for additional weight at its outer end. Action is confined within prescribed limits determined by the arc of the lever arm's sweep from the tilt-up, "ready" position to the point where the arm is forced all the way down to the ground. Not until the block is secured can the levering action be repeated.

Levers were also used in a vertical position, that is, for moving a block laterally. They were often employed, too, for tilting, as in the rocker device.[3] The rocker (for raising medium-sized blocks of a few tons in weight) was a strongly built assemblage of wooden pieces consisting of two runners (flat above and curved to a large radius below) that were linked by a number of stout rods. The pattern thus formed allowed wooden levers to be inserted between two rods at either end in order to rock the device and its load, first one way then the other. As the device was rocked back and forth, slabs of wood (the shims) were positioned under the raised runners alternately to left and right. In this way a practiced team could raise blocks quickly and with the minimum of danger to any of the work—or the workmen—below. The great weight and massiveness of the stones they quarried, transported, and set up in their tombs and temples, restricted the Egyptians to raising all but the smallest blocks from below, by one of the jacking operations just described.

Parts of this process may have employed a constructional device that is occasionally used in Egypt today, the balance beam. Although no examples have been recovered from the dynastic period, its simplicity and purpose suggest that it was utilized by the ancient Egyptian builders. Its cumbersome bulk can account, in part, for no example having survived. More particularly, as the balance beam has probably been in continuous use from ancient times to the present, each device serving to a point beyond repair and then discarded, no individual trace remains.

The balance beam works on the principle of the steelyard.[4] It involves a raised horizontal beam free to rock on a fulcrum set beneath the beam near one end. Loading the end of the long arm of the beam with rocks gives the short arm great mechanical advantage to lift within a limited distance. One or more of these balance beams may have been employed to suspend some of the less ponderous stones (such as the core blocks of the pyramids) sufficiently to permit the insertion of a sled or runners beneath them. This use of ropes to lift blocks momentarily is essentially a jacking operation, acting within quite small limits and subject to close control throughout.

With sufficiently numerous and sufficiently long, strong levers (counterbalanced at their outer ends if need be by one or more stones, once the inner end of each lever had been inserted under the block and the fulcrum firmly positioned) the Egyptians could jack up their largest monoliths as well. This essential process permitted heavy timberwork sleds to be slid under colossal statues preparatory to overland transit.[5] Doubtless a number of bosses were left protruding at either side of the huge stone statues for the levers to act against. Perhaps because of their temporary nature and because the Egyptians would have regarded such bosses as distractions from the conceptual reality of the statue, they are never indicated in the contemporary representations.[6] Nonetheless, from a practical standpoint, the bosses would have been necessary to allow enough clearance for the sled to be hauled lengthwise between the two rows of levers and positioned under the block. At the destined site, conversely, to remove the sled from beneath the statue would have required a reversal of this process, or something similar. Once no longer needed the projecting bosses, along with any other temporary constructional features, would have been eliminated and the finished surfaces smoothed and polished.

Invariably, the pictorial reconstructions that illustrate modern suppositions as to how the pyramids of Egypt were built show them at a stage of construction where they have achieved no more than a third or less of their final height. It is perhaps to be expected, as this is near the maximum level reached by the long, paved ramp from the landing stage at the riverbank, from where teams of laborers dragged the blocks three quarters of a mile up to the building site. Parts of this massive ramp for the Great Pyramid at Giseh are still traceable.[7] A few writers claim that in addition to this supply road, ramps were used at the pyramid itself so that blocks could be hauled up an ever-lengthening slope to their places at successive levels, all the way to the apex.[8] Most serious writers, however, agree that ramps would not have been constructed to the higher portions of this pyramid. So, beyond occasional speculations that are either vague or patently improbable, little if any attention has been focused on the problem of how the upper portions were built.[9]

On two counts, the access ramp was essential to work on the lower level. First, it was needed to handle the constant traffic involved in supplying the enormous numbers of blocks used in both the core and the casing of the pyramid up to this stage of the work. Second, it facilitated the transport and maneuvering of the oversized blocks for the king's chamber, including the fifty-ton granite plug at its entrance, the tiers of great ceiling beams, and the pairs of tilted relieving stones above them.

From this stage on up, the diminishing mass of the pyramid required far fewer stones, all but one of which were of a size that permitted them to be rocked up, in stepped sequences, from a staging area at the top of the wide access ramp. The one exception was the massive pyramidal capstone; and this, as we will see, could have been levered up vertically in regular stages, as each successive level was achieved, to its final position at the apex.

The rocker device

To lift the normal-sized stones—both core and casing blocks— above the staging area at the top of the access ramp, rockers could have been used, such as the one discovered in a foundation deposit at Queen Hatshepsut's temple at Deir el-Bahari.[10] Using this simple device, a team of perhaps as few as four men—one working a lever to the right and one to the left, plus a couple of men to hand up and insert the shims—could raise a relatively heavy stone surprisingly quickly, skew it around on arrival at each stepped stage, and repeat the process from each new higher level. A central strip of the pyramid's slope above the access ramp would have had its casing blocks shaped rectangularly as steps, to be hewn off to a sloping plane when no longer required for construction.[11]

If the rocker device was indeed employed to raise blocks to the higher levels of this pyramid, a central zone of casing stones— where these operations would have taken place—must have been formed as a series of steps instead of as the continuous sloping plane it would eventually become. But due to the steepness of the slope of the pyramid faces (some 51°52′), each single row of casing stones, cut rectangularly as a step, would not have been deep enough to accommodate the process of raising stones with the rocker device. The bases of the casing blocks—particularly the corner blocks—were substantially wider than the single step's tread. In addition, the width of this tread would not have furnished room enough to permit a ninety degree horizontal rotation of one of these blocks, as each lift was made, in order to shift it inward and start the operation of the next lift. Therefore a central stairway of two-course steps flanked by stairways of one-course steps would have been necessary to raise blocks by the rocker device. These one-course steps would have provided stairs for the labor force to climb to and from the level at which the work was progressing, carrying whatever gear—ropes, timber blocking, levers, prybars, and other tools—they required for their tasks.

That these lifts by means of rockers could be executed with surprising rapidity can be suggested by recalling a clown act in the circus a generation or two ago. In it, a clown sat in a rocking chair, rocking vigorously back and forth while his companions inserted shims front and back. A height of eight or ten feet was achieved in a few moments; then, with no break in the continuity of his rocking,

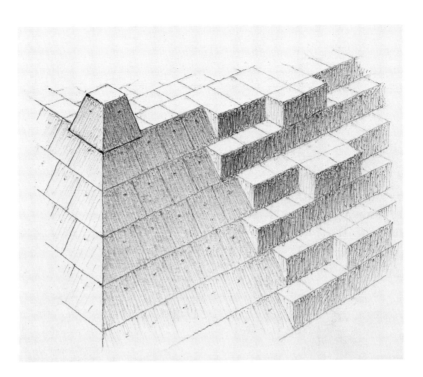

Constructional stair-
way formed of casing
blocks hewn rectangu-
larly, reduced later to
a smooth slope. (Draw-
ing by author.)

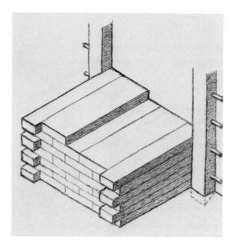

Wooden standards
(left), fixed to a double-
course riser, bracket a
column of shims. Their
narrower, longer end-
pieces, laced together
alternately right and
left, prevent the shims
from spreading. The
same or other cords
looped around pegs in
the standards would
hold the column steady
against the masonry. A
frontal view (right) of
the column of shims
shows a loaded rocker
in successive positions.
(Drawing by author.)

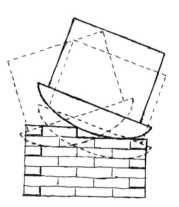

the clown returned to ground level in an equally short time as his companions removed the shims in reverse sequence.

In the ancient Egyptian operation, a skilled team of two men, each working a lever to right and left among the stout rods that linked the runners of the rocker, could use the weight of the block itself to reduce substantially the amount of effort they had to expend in the process of tilting the block. Other adept members of the team could position the shims in the proper place and at the proper instant, securing them as the alternate tilting of the block progressed.

The actual installation of the shims and the pattern in which they were placed are not self-evident because of uncertainty about the height to which the column of shims had to be carried and about how steadiness was maintained in the column as successive layers were added. First of all, the column required internal stability. This could have been achieved by overlapping the shims in alternate layers. A length of rope that zigzagged back and forth from each projecting endpiece would have held the shims secure against creep or shucking about laterally (as they were merely laid upon the previous layer without positive attachments as the column rose). Two or three turns around each of the projections, right and left, as these endpieces were set in place would have consolidated the intervening shims at successive levels as the pile rose. Such a quick and simple linkage could have been done so that the subsequent dismantling of the column was neither tedious nor time-consuming.

Securing the entire column against tilting away from the masonry behind it, as well as preventing it from swaying laterally, might have been handled as follows. Two sturdy timber standards would have been fixed securely to the face of the masonry riser so as to bracket the column of shims. Layer by layer, the shims would have been inserted between these standards with their far ends thrust against the masonry riser. To prevent the column of shims from tilting away from the masonry, at intervals ropes would have been passed back and forth out around the pile of shims from pegs let into the far side of each standard.

These expedients would have secured a column of shims higher than any required to raise stones in stepped sequences of two-course lifts by the rocker device. In addition, assemblage would be less subject to error because this scheme uses a minimum number of different elements in a simple alternating sequence. The men who handled the shims would have done so from the front and consequently would have been at all times out of the way of the men activating the levers at either side. Once the boundary standards had been secured in their upright positions, all the other operations involved in rocking up the stone blocks could have been performed quickly and without wasted motion or duplicated efforts. This would be true for both building up a column of shims and dismantling it preparatory to elevating another block. All the required paraphernalia would be reusable again and again, showing no undue strain or abrasion. Moreover, as the shims of a just completed column were taken down, one by one, they could have been inserted, one by one, into a column being erected at the next higher level.[12]

For core and casing blocks alike, each lift probably involved somewhat more height in the column of shims than in the riser of a two-course step. This was because the block had to be moved inward from the pile of wooden shims to the stone platform of the next step, where the ensuing lift would take place. Arriving at the top of a lift (somewhat over two courses in height), the casing block would have needed to be skewed around by the levers at right angles to its rocking position and then tilted inward so as to be levered down onto a different rocker at the level of the upper step. To transfer a casing block from one rocker to the other, one pair of levers would have been thrust through the rods of *both* rockers to keep their sloped tops in perfect slanted alignment, while the other pair of levers was used to ease the block down the slope from one rocker to the other. From there, with the second rocker now loaded with the block and skewed around ninety degrees to its rocking position, the lift operation would have been repeated at this higher level.[13]

It seems likely that the men of each rocker team were responsible for, and performed their tasks at, a single lift operation instead of following a given block all the way up from the ramp to where the block was set permanently in place.[14] Such an organization of manpower, with a different team at each step, would undoubtedly have been more efficient and saved time. Moreover, it would have been consistent with the Egyptian deployment and utilization of a labor force at specific tasks and in prescribed areas of activity.[15]

The order and sequence of placing the blocks

A considerable amount of published speculation has proposed that the casing blocks were installed as a veneer from the top down after the core mass had been constructed. There can be no doubt, however, that the casing blocks were put in place as the structure rose. More than that, they were undoubtedly the first stones to be positioned as each new level was attained. The confusion all started with a misreading of Herodotus's statement that the pyramids were "finished" from the top down. His proper use of the term was not constructional but technical and meant arriving at a finished surface by removing all excess stock, along with smoothing and polish-

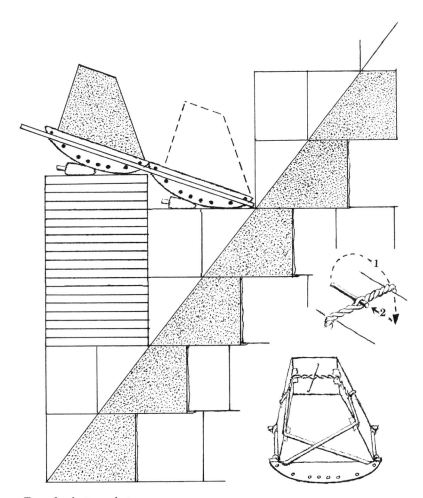

Transferring a casing
block from one rocker
to another. The main
portion of this draw-
ing shows the extreme
case of a corner casing
block being shifted,
which accounts for
what would appear to
be a 180° turn of the
block from its rocking
position but is, in real-
ity, the usual 90° turn.
(Drawing by author.)

ing the final surfaces. It is axiomatic and inevitable that such a process takes place from the top down, just as it is equally obvious and inevitable that the construction of an all-masonry structure proceeds from the bottom up.

The outer surface of the casing blocks (destined to become the smooth face of the pyramid) was unfinished at the time they were positioned, with two inches or so of extra stock left on the weather face as protection from damage, both in transit and during the final finishing of the pyramid's even, polished planes.[16] At each level, these casing blocks would have been set first, all around the periphery, so that their accurate emplacement (with one exception, as we will see) might be handled at each level from *within* the area of the working platform. Thus each casing block could be positioned quickly but with great nicety by nudging it out to its destined site at the edge of the platform, using prybars or levers that found a purchase in one or another of the joints between the core blocks.

The procedure would have begun with the double-sloped corner casing blocks, the largest of all the "regular" stones of the pyramid. These would temporarily be set farther out along the diagonal of the square platform than their subsequent final position. This provisional position would permit the casing blocks in each of the straight runs along the sides of the platform to be positioned snugly against each other. Some can still be seen, in fact, in the extant masonry of the casing's lowest courses, where the joints are so hairline as to be scarcely noticable.[17] When the four straight runs were in tight alignment, the corner casing blocks would be drawn inward diagonally to their final position. To accomplish this maneuver, ropes would be looped over the corner block around wooden plugs driven into and projecting from shallow holes that had previously been cut into the extra stock of this block's two outer faces.[18] Then, with the loop at the other end of the rope secured to a fixed anchorage among the core blocks, the rope strands would be twisted together around a heavy stick (a method shown in some bas-reliefs for tightening the ropes that secured colossal monoliths to their sled). This simple device, known as a Spanish windlass, shortened the rope as it became more twisted, inching the block inward in a controlled jacking action toward the fixed end of the rope.

Another practical reason for this procedure was to align the salient, sloping edge of each corner block accurately, according to sight lines established from below for the diagonals of the pyramid, in order to forestall any twisting in these edges. Each of the four faces of the Great Pyramid represented, when completed, an area of approximately five acres; and it was important that the intersection of each pair of these sloping surfaces be absolutely straight. Hence the accurate alignment of the corner casing blocks along the

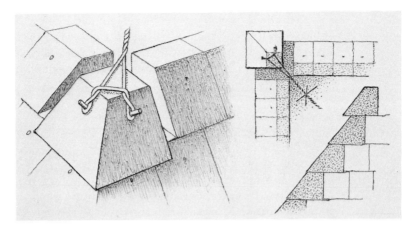

Spanish windlass device. Drawing by author.

diagonal was a first priority and one that, having been painstakingly ascertained at the start of each new level of construction, was undeviatingly maintained in the final positioning of the corner blocks by the Spanish windlass.[19]

The exception referred to above in positioning the casing blocks was the break that occurred at the middle of the access side. For here it would have been most inconvenient and troublesome, if not impossible, to move all the core blocks over the rim of the casing blocks and to lower them into snug alignment within the established confines of this outer cordon of stones. Instead, a breach was probably left in this outer cordon, perhaps three or four blocks in width. The core stones would be maneuvered through the breach to their destined compact juxtapositions, directly from the top of the access stairway. The jambs of this embrasure would have been slightly splayed, that is, a bit wider apart on the outside than on the inside.[20] When all the core blocks were positioned and it came time to fill the embrasure with the three or four remaining casing blocks, these could be eased into place from without (somewhat like inserting the keystone of an arch, as it were). These casing blocks could be maneuvered from the outside because of the shelf or ledge provided at the spot for raising each block to this level. The blocks that finally closed the breach became part of the stairway used to move both the core and casing stones for subsequent courses up to higher levels of the pyramid. As the casing blocks that closed the breach did not have sloping faces but were rectangular in section, they could be nudged inward by prybars without damaging their outer, lower edges.

In the tight and careful placement of the many thousands of blocks in this enormous structure, the nature and the function of the mortar used in the Great Pyramid is important. It consisted of sand and gypsum (rather than lime) with a considerable admixture of impurities. Consequently it had practically no adhesive power. None was needed, however, for friction and dead weight secured permanent stability for each of the ponderous blocks. The mortar, squeezed into extremely thin beds by the stones' weight, had two other functions. One was to insure that each stone rested evenly and completely on the blocks beneath it, with no voids or hollow areas that could crack the stonework because of uneven weight distribution. Its other function was to facilitate the laying of the stones.[21] Both were essential in the Great Pyramid's construction.

Raising the capstone

Meanwhile, the ponderous capstone would have been levered up, a course at a time, from its position in the center of one platform to the center of the next, so that the core blocks could be consolidated beneath it. By tilting the capstone first in one direction, the timber blocking could be withdrawn from below its raised side and core blocks permanently inserted; levering it in the opposite direction, the rest of the timber blocking could be replaced by core blocks. Then the capstone would be raised to a new course level on timber blocking and a similar operation repeated.

The placing of the stones of the pyramid's two highest courses was complicated by the presence of the massive capstone around and under which the "ordinary" blocks had to be maneuvered. The interference of the temporary timber blocking required that the stones of these uppermost courses be nudged into place from the outside instead of from within the periphery of the structure. But hewing the casing stones in these uppermost courses (except for the corner blocks) rectangularly, rather than with sloping outer faces, produced horizontal ledges all the way around; these ledges provided additional space to fit the blocks of the next higher course around the capstone's blocking. It was from these ledges, too, that prybars could inch the blocks accurately into position from the outside inward, substituting for the Spanish windlass device. Slots chiseled in the floor of the ledges—as purchase for the prybars—would of course disappear completely when they were hewn off and the pyramid's stepped faces reduced to smooth slopes. In the meantime, however, the ledges functioned as a solid scaffolding, as it were, to accommodate setting the uppermost stones in the crowded and constricted scene of operations at the top of the pyramid.

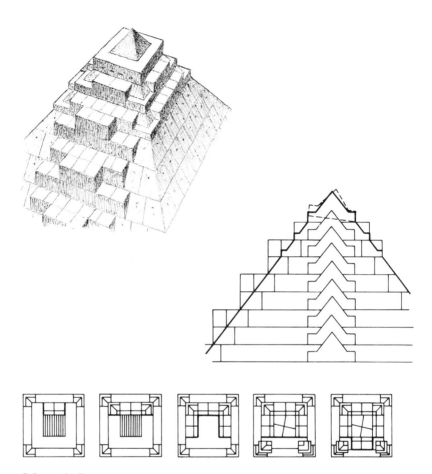

Schematic diagram (right) of incremental lifts of the capstone block. Bird's-eye view (left) of top of pyramid, showing access stairway and constructional ledges at the two uppermost courses. Series of plan views (below) indicating the order of installation for all the blocks in the highest course, just below the capstone. Core blocks beneath the capstone would have had slightly skewed joints (exaggerated in the drawing) to permit their snug installation. (Drawing by author.)

Here, particularly at the penultimate course immediately below the capstone, the order in which the blocks were delivered up the two-course steps of the supply stairway was especially critical. The first blocks to be positioned in the topmost course were the central casing stones on the far side from the stairway. They, and then the corner blocks flanking them, would have been maneuvered out around the blocking under the capstone and nudged into their destined location. Previously, the blocking would have been limited— in plan—to its minimum feasible area, which was somewhat less than the space left between opposite pairs of the casing blocks when they were all in final position. Next in order came the setting of the casing stones to right and left of the blocking, in accurate and closest alignment. With the casing blocks established on three sides, the temporary timberwork blocking could be removed, as the weight of the capstone could now be transferred to shims resting on these permanently positioned casing blocks. Then core blocks would be packed in solidly, filling the area that had just been occupied by the timber blocking. Next to be brought up were the two front corner blocks, which were temporarily positioned half a foot or so to the right and left of their final positions, out of alignment with the casing blocks behind them. This temporary location allowed sufficient room to set the front casing blocks—those at the top of the access stairway—accurately in place, close against the core blocks behind them. Then the flanking corner blocks were eased into their permanent locations with the aid of prybars. All that remained was to lower the capstone itself onto the completed stone platform furnished by the topmost course of blocks. This would have been accomplished by inserting levers into sinkages near the base of the capstone (or under bosses there), tilting up this terminal block sufficiently for the workmen to draw out the shims and ease the block down to its final resting place as the apex crowning the gigantic stone mountain.

Removing all projections and finishing

With core and casing blocks and capstone finally in place, the four faces of the pyramid needed to be stripped down to their intended smooth planes and polished. The stripping—technically known as "dressing"—would have involved removing the constructional steps, hewing off the capstone's bosses, and smoothing away the extra inches of stock left on the weather faces of all the casing blocks.

Scaffolding for the stripping operation could have been minimal and of the simplest kind, despite the enormous areas to be worked. Previously, holes would have been cut at intervals into the protective extra stock of the casing blocks, the axes of the holes being made normal to the slope of the pyramid's face. Into these holes short wooden rods would be driven at a given level to serve as supports for a narrow ledger or footrest for the workmen. As the blocks of one level were made smooth, eliminating all trace of the row of holes above, the rods would be driven into existing holes in the next lower tier, the footrests shifted to that level, and the stripping process repeated there. Meanwhile the detritus of rock chips and fragments would cascade down the slope to the base of the pyramid where it was collected and removed to a very extensive dump nearby, (still extant today as an artificial plateau of discarded masonry scraps).[22]

The foregoing explanation of Egyptian building practices cannot be unequivocally documented today. It is doubtful that we will ever know with certainty how this gigantic structure was actually built, stone by stone. Based on the thorough and comprehensive data presented in 1930 by Somers Clarke and R. Engelbach, this study has examined the building of Cheops' Pyramid from the practical approach of the general contractor. Perhaps the builders of the Great Pyramid did not, in fact, employ the rocker device. But here is an analysis of how it might have operated, had it indeed been used as the primary erectional technique.

In any event the procedures discussed here may provide a fresh look at the difficulties encountered, along with the ramifying secondary problems that had to be recognized and dealt with. Only by taking into account and pursuing the consequences of a particular scheme can the feasibility of that scheme be assessed. Only by making a comprehensive effort to assess in realistic detail the complete picture involved in the erectional techniques of the ancient builders can the practicality of their methods and procedures as originally adopted be appraised. They have fascinated and baffled travelers and professional engineers alike for centuries. Yet today we are still less than certain about every aspect of how it was done.

Epilogue

Throughout this book we have come to recognize some of the constant characteristics of the builder in former times: his awareness of the conditions imposed by nature and his recognition of the possibilities they offered; his accuracy of diagnosis; his pragmatic economy of means.

This builder of the past often operated in a quite different fashion and made his judgments on quite different evidence, in the main, from the builder of our own day. Today, the activities and decisions of those who undertake building operations of any scope and complexity are largely dependent on an ever-expanding machine technology. This is doubtless inevitable and necessary in view of the machines available to the modern builder: all the way from mobile cement mixers, far-oversailing tower cranes, and ponderous earthmovers, to the computer with its superhuman memory and its ability—almost instantaneously—to digest complex data and to present specialized charts, tables, graphs, and the answers to intricate mathematical formulas.

The accomplishments of the builder of the past, by contrast, were the fruits of direct and perceptive observation of the world and the workings of nature, at the human, visually verifiable level. Repeatedly, when confronted by constructional problems of a relatively simple or an extraordinarily complex nature, the builder of former times devised solutions that still astonish us with their unerring aptness, their classic avoidance of redundancy, and their ingenious economy of means.

We have seen, for example, that this builder studied and effectively capitalized on the *properties of materials* in such cases as the inexorable swelling of wooden wedges immersed in water to free an Egyptian obelisk from the parent rock of a quarry and the tenacious matting of roots in the formation of huge mattresses used to plug the breach in the embankment of a rampaging Chinese river. In the Eternal City the builder's understanding and exploitation of the extraordinary virtues of pozzuolana allowed the Romans to produce large, well-lighted interior spaces, free of intermediate supports, to accommodate large numbers of people for specific purposes —becoming, in a sense, the first to develop a social architecture.

It was the actual builder, too, who contrived to circumvent or at least greatly reduce the expense of *temporary falsework* for masonry structures by initiating the stone-weighted rope device for building the webs of quadripartite vaulting in the Gothic era and by resorting to spiraling courses in the erection of thin Spanish domes of brick and Eskimo igloos of snow blocks, both without any supporting formwork. And it was the builder who, in America, worked out an ingenious scheme for hand-digging water wells and simultaneously lining them with masonry, thereby totalling eliminating the expense and inconvenience of shoring against cave-ins. On a grand scale, in medieval England, the builder organized and coordinated all the interrelated steps in the incremental erection of a lofty, thin-walled stone spire whose internal timberwork served as temporary scaffolding during the course of erection, and thereafter, permanently, as both reinforcement and suspended stabilization for the entire superstructure.

Especially throughout Europe, the builder designed and built *constructional machinery* such as great wheels for raising loads aloft and capstans for moving heavy objects both horizontally and vertically. As far as possible he shunned using very large, very heavy blocks of stone in elevated positions. But when the need arose, he could supply the appropriate means for moving huge monoliths overland, for shipping them by water, and even for raising them up to span a wide opening or to crown a building.

These and other instances of the builder's achievements in past eras demonstrate how thoroughly thought out and thriftily implemented were many of the handicrafted methods he devised. It is to be hoped that we are not yet so far removed from the human perceptions and direct observational criteria of yesteryear—not yet so unquestioningly committed to the impersonal computations of the present—that we cannot still cast a nostalgic eye (or at least turn an appreciative, even a wondering glance) at the achievements of the past. In the case of building construction it is quite possible, in fact, that we can learn much of value and benefit to our own undertakings, from studying the methods and procedures adopted worldwide by the builders of former times.

Notes

Chapter 1

1. George Martin Huss, *Rational Building* (1895), p. 2.

2. An informative, well-researched article (according to its longtime editor, "perhaps as important as any ever published by the Royal Institute of British Architects") is Wyatt Papworth, "Notes on the Superintendents of English Buildings in the Middle Ages" (1887).

3. During the Middle Ages, the stonecutters could pursue their labors in the shelter of their workshops throughout the winter season, but actual progress outdoors on the building's fabric came to a standstill. So, as we know from many miniatures and illuminations of the time, all partially built walls and columns had to be protected from the weather until work could be resumed. This protection was usually provided by mounding a thatch of straw and stable litter on the exposed tops of incomplete portions of the masonry.

4. For techniques of loading wagons, see engravings XV and XVI in Niccola Zabaglia, *Castelli e ponti* (1824).

5. For an annotated listing of building stones, see E. G. Warland, *Modern Practical Masonry* (1929) chap 6., pp. 112–30.

6. Wherever sophisticated stone buildings call for accurately cut, closely-fitting and usually unmortared blocks, the stonecutters resorted to chiseling masons' marks on one of the exposed surfaces of each stone (later to be dressed down to a smooth finish). These cyphers constituted a record of work done, establishing the identity of the stonecutter who had executed the shaping of the block so that he could be credited with its execution and held accountable for its craftsmanship. Moreover, when another team, the *stonesetters*, began to assemble and lay the blocks that had been individually hewn to shape, the cyphers made it possible for them to proceed without delays, ambiguities, or errors of placement. This primary function of the cyphers was adopted universally for *timber frame* structures, though these cyphers consisted of Roman numerals alone.)

7. Many workmen's manuals have been published about the common burnt bricks and tiles of the Western world. An early one, dealing with walling, simple arches, chimney work, and paving, is the section on "The Bricklayer's Complete Guide" in C. F. Partington, *Builder's Complete Guide* (1985) pp. 353–400. For sophisticated practices of bricklaying in thin-shelled vaults and domes, see Fernando Cassinello, *Bóvedas y cúpulas de ladrillo,* 2d ed., (1964).

8. Lead, for example, was used in various ways in buildings of the past. For instance, in the dry-wall construction of ancient Greek temples, metal clamps that secured adjacent blocks of marble to each other were set in lead. In the Parthenon, it was used to inhibit deterioration in the hardwood dowels set axially between each successive pair of column drums to assure their permanent vertical alignment. Gaskets were formed by pouring molten lead through a small drill hole into a wide but shallow sinkage previously drafted into the upper surface of each drum. The area of contact with the drum above it was thereby reduced to a very precisely chiseled outer ring of stone. The Romans also used this metal to make pipes, some of which were as much as a foot in diameter.
    Medieval builders principally used lead in sheets, as impervious roof coverings for cathedrals and other important buildings, and in *cames*, as the structural armature in assembling—and as an impervious consolidation of—the individual pieces of glass in stained-glass windows. Informing accounts of lead as applied to buildings of former times are found in Partington, pp. 580–88; C.F. Innocent, *Development of English Building Construction* (1916), pp. 275–77; and [Eugène Emmanuel] Viollet-le-Duc, "Plomberie," in vol. 7 of *Dictionnaire raisonné de l'architecture française* (1858–68), pp. 209–20.

9.   The Egyptians invariably painted their stone temples with bright colors—pylon walls, cornices, and portals outside; walls, ceilings, and columns within—as extensive, grandiose billboards for the permanent display of hieratic, pharaoh-glorifying subjects. Important masonry structures elsewhere in the world have been painted, too, usually over a smooth, prepared surface of gesso, plaster, or marble-dust stucco, as in Pompeiian villas, Romanesque churches, and Mayan temples. The major purpose of painting in these and many other examples was *decorative*. The classical Greeks, however, had an important concomitant purpose: to *protect* the surfaces of their marble buildings against discoloration and other deleterious effects from the salt-laden air of the sea (never very far away). These majestic buildings, almost invariably of fine-grained, gleamingly white marble, were painted by a transparent vehicle—the encaustic method. Like the staining of wood (which allows the wood's graining to show through), the encaustic method allowed the fine crystaline aspect of the marble to reveal itself. For the pigment was mixed into a colorless wax that was applied hot (i.e., in a liquid state) to the surface of the marble, thereby creating a tenacious glaze of color, at once decorative and protective.

10.   Much about the duties and responsibilities of the builder as well as of the architect was recorded a century ago in Robert Kerr, "Observations on the Architect's Functions in Relation to Building Contracts" (1887).

11.   Only in the last two decades or so have the multiplicity and complexity of the contractor's services and responsibilities been reflected in the new title of construction manager. This title, though not explicitly used in the past, has always been implicit (at least in large undertakings) with respect to the contractor's involvement in the production of a building.

Chapter 2

1.   William Eton, *Survey of the Turkish Empire,* 2d ed. (1799), p. 224.

2.   For example: Helen E. Fitzrandolph and M. Dorial Hay (vols. 1, 2, 3) and Anna M. Jones (vol. 4), *Rural Industries of England and Wales* (1926–27); Rudolph P. Hommel, *China at Work* (1937); and Christopher Williams, with photographs by Charlotte Williams, *Craftsmen of Necessity* (1974) (coverage includes Austria and Eastern Europe, Egypt, Finland, Italy, Morocco and North Africa, Scandinavia, Spain, Syria, and Turkey).

3.   This interest started in Scandinavia long before it took hold in America. As early as the middle of the nineteenth century the concept of the folk art center in conjunction with the open-air museum was inaugurated in Sweden. It gradually spread to various (mainly northern) European countries, decades before America became interested in its own preindustrial heritage. For the inception and progress of this trend see Dr. Hans Huth, chap. 4, "Open Air Museums and Folk Art Centers," in *Observations Concerning the Conservation of Monuments* (1940), pp. 54–63, with extensive bibliographies and wide-ranging commentary and assessments.

4.   See Joseph Needham, with Wang Ling, *Science and Civilization in China,* vol. 4, pt. 2. (1965).

5.   Jean Gimpel, *Medieval Machine* (1976), p. 142. Echoing this attitude, *A Practical Abstract of the Arts of Fortification and Assailing* (possibly the earliest book printed in English that deals with the art or science of engineering) makes a plea for the authority, validity, and independent jurisdiction of the engineer versus the interference or quibblings of lawyers, directors or business men "who can see in engineering only a superior sort of craftsmanship. . . ." The book begins with a chapter that discourses "On the True Character of a Complete Engineer." After listing five essential qualifications and commenting on them, the author expatiates at greater length on a sixth point: "He is to be of solid judgement and quick of apprehension to judge

aright of the defects and advantages of places. . . . He is not to give account of his actions to any, but to the Generall, or to the lieutenant Generall of the Ordinance; if he be in an army, or in a Garison, only to the grand Committee, and to the Governour; and as for all other kinds of men, inhabitants, souldiers or officers; he is not bound to expostulate the case, if they demand of him reasons for anything he directs or commands to be done; neither ought he if he regards his reputation, and makes conscience of his ways, to comply . . . with the humour of the greatest in authority, or be led to assent to any resolution, that is against the maxims of his Art, by the Logical and Sophisticall reasons and arguments of Scholars or Churchmen; for some of them are now a days over-busie in things that go beyond their element, and endeavor to oversway Artists by rhetorike, considering not that their reasons are no reasons at all to the reasons of art. And this last quality is the essential part of a good Engineer; for all the others are but to small purpose without this." Condensed from an editorial, "The Complete Engineer of Three Hundred Years Ago" (1910), p. 17, the argument might well apply with equal force and validity to the building contractor.

6.   Among the large number of publications dealing with stone, for example, as a building material, see Warland, *Masonry*, pp. 112–30, for the characteristics and properties of building stones (mainly those of the British Isles); Charles H. Richardson, *Building Stones and Clays* (1917), with over three hundred photographs of building stones quarried in America; and C. H. Porter, *Paper on Building Stones* (1868), for considerations with respect to the selection of building stones.

7.   Different aspects or approaches are followed today in published accounts that deal with the structural systems used in buildings; namely, design, inspection, and testing. However, prior to the scientific computations currently in use (for which the literature is legion), such appraisals employed scale models of proposed buildings and/or precise visual observations and assessment of failures in existing buildings, or parts of them, that had collapsed or appeared in imminent danger of collapse.

8.   For the full range of these contemporary accounts in medieval England, see L. F. Salzman's remarkable book, *Building in England Down to 1540* (1952). For a single building, contemporary procurement and expense accounts are excerpted in Rev. R. B. Rackham, "The Nave of Westminster" Oxford (1910) pp. 33–96. Also an appendix in George Gilbert Scott, *Gleanings from Westminster Abbey* 2d ed. (1863), pp. 231–61, lists and translates pertinent passages from the Fabric Rolls of Westminster, as well as reproducing and interpreting the Fabric Roll of 1253.

9.   Three of the best known special synods of master builders in the Middle Ages concerned the following cathedrals: Chartres Cathedral, to assess the fractures and determine the steps to take in strengthening the vault abutments (see Victor Mortet, "L'Expertise de la cathédrale de Chartres en 1316" (1900) pp. 308–29); Milan Cathedral, to determine whether the *trivium* or the *quadrivium* would be used as the basis of design (see James S. Ackerman, "Ars sine scientia nihil est" (1949) pp. 85–111); and Gerona Cathedral, to consider the feasibility of vaulting the western portion of the church in one all-embracing span (see George Edmund Street, *Some Account of Gothic Architecture in Spain* (1865), in which an English translation of the report of the 1417 junta of twelve architects appears as appendix H, pp. 501–13).

10.   For example, in 1486 Mathias Roriczer published a small pamphlet "On the Ordination of Pinnacles," explaining, with drawings, how to design this architectural feature. For a translation with commentary, see Elizabeth G. Holt, ed., *Documentary History of Art,* vol. 1 (1957), pp. 95–101.

11.   John Fitchen, Review of *Development of Carpentry, 1200–1700* (1969), pp. 8-9.

12.   Among many examples of traditional methods and procedures of construction still practiced in the twentieth century by native builders, the following references

offer particularly clear visual documentation: A native house under construction on the island of Mouli in the Ouvea atoll of the Loyalty Islands, in Bernard Gorsky, *Island at the End of the World* (1966), with five color plates, pp. 72–73, and description and commentary, pp. 88–89; "Natives Constructing Grass Houses: Many tribes of the Congo construct round or oblong huts of grass stems over a framework of forked posts. Both the walls and roof of bamboo poles are thatched with banana leaves. . . . There is only one door for entrance and ventilation. . . ," illustrated in *National Geographic* 42 (October 1922): 348; roof and its thatching under construction for a Tambu house, Solomon Islands, illustrated in *National Geographic* 40 (December 1921): 549; and closeup view of house wall of reeds and bamboo and Masai women making village huts in Africa, illustrated in *World Outlook* 6 (September–October 1920): 24, 27.

13.   The presence, for example, of unfilled putlog holes, in masonry buildings can provide information about the nature and extent of the falsework used in the construction or repair of walls and towers. See John Fitchen, "The Occurrence of Put-log Holes and the Location and Extent of the Scaffolding They Reveal," appendix B of *Construction of Gothic Cathedrals* (1961), pp. 248–52.

14.   There is an extensive literature on *what* was done in connection with repairs and reconstructions of damaged and ruinous buildings, particularly in England, beginning with the late 1830s. As for *how* these undertakings were accomplished, significant coverage was not generally reported until nearly a hundred years later. Following are illustrated accounts of some of the procedures adopted in the mid-twentieth century: Alban D. R. Caroe, *Old Churches and Modern Craftsmanship* (1949), particularly chap. 4, pp. 54–93; Paul Leon, *La Vie des monuments français*, particularly chap. 10, "La Restauration des monuments" (1951) pp. 359–538; and J. Trouve-lot, "De la restauration des monuments historiques" (1950) pp. 38–50.

15.   Today, each major cathedral of the Middle Ages has a master mason in charge of the execution of repairs and structural maintenance as well as alterations, additions and rebuilding operations. One, an Englishman, has been indispensable in realizing the fabric of the National Cathedral in Washington, D.C., whose main vaulting system (constructed throughout in stone masonry without recourse to support from structural steelwork) is modeled on that of Exeter Cathedral in southwestern England.
    In France a well-funded program has been in effect since 1941 for the instruction and certification of an elite corps of superior young building craftsmen whose training includes (as in the Middle Ages) fashioning a *chef-d'oeuvre* in the form of a scale model of some demanding project (a timberwork spire, iron grille-work, a monumental, curving stairway in masonry) often based on centuries-old historical precedents. For a copiously illustrated account of this nationwide organization, with impressive establishments in eleven of the major cities of France, see *L'Oeuvre des Compagnons du Devoir* (1961).

16.   For example: Frederick Starr *Indians of Southern Mexico* (1899), with 141 plates, over a quarter of which pertain to this study, and James Wilkinson Breeks, *Primitive Tribes and Monuments of the Nilagiris* (1873), see pls. 8–9, 13, 15, 21–22, 26, 28–29 and, for native implements, 77–79. Such albums of photographs should not be confused with the much earlier accounts of Western European explorers and intrepid travelers to faraway realms. These accounts were often accompanied by many *drawings* that illustrated the manners, customs, and activities, the artifacts, costumes, and habitations encountered in strange and foreign regions of the world. But the text of the notebooks and diaries of the earliest travelers tends to be more reliable than the accompanying sketches, because the oral accounts may have omitted to mention the environment, which the illustrator, however, felt constrained to display. Sometimes the scenes depicted were entirely fanciful and untrustworthy, based solely on travelers' tales and/or drawn in Europe by artists who had never set foot outside their own communities. So one needs to evaluate with a degree of skepticism and interpretation many of the graphic representations in such works as de Bry's *Grands Voyages* (with editions published in Paris, Frankfort, and London between 1590 and 1632) and, much earlier, *The Book of Marco Polo,* first published in French in 1298.

In the third quarter of the eighteenth century, however, the articles and the innumerable carefully drawn plates in the multi-volumed *Encyclopédie* of Diderot and d'Alembert reflected and helped to usher in the age of scientific discovery. This great work gave status and very wide dissemination to the accurate reporting of medical doctors, geographers, botanists, anthropologists and other professionals. Consequently, the accounts of men like William Eton, Peter Kalm, Baron von Humboldt, Baron Tavernier, and Charles Wilkes, who followed this lead in the late eighteenth and early nineteenth centuries, reflect close observation and knowledge of what they observed—including building practices.

17.   Some modern writers have endorsed the one-log-one-board process; i.e., where opposite sides of a whole log were hewn down to the board's intended thickness, using not a saw but an axe. This wasteful procedure was undoubtedly adopted at times. But there is plenty of contemporary pictorial evidence that saws were used, even by the ancient Egyptians, to fashion boards. In any case, traditional pit sawing methods are still practiced today. For documentation, see below, page 274 n.10.

18.   The problem in any work of excavation is not only one of digging but of removing what has been dug. For a remarkably full and detailed account, in both text and photographs, of this process as a handicraft undertaking (including the tools employed and the procedures followed), see Justin Burns, "The Actual Building of a Chinese Railway" (1904) pp. 380–401, with 30 photographs.

19.   The process of mud plastering or mud walling is clearly depicted, with accompanying commentary, in such scenes as: "Hopi Women Building a House," in George Wharton James, "Primitive Inventions" (1903–1904), fig. 8 p. 134; wattle-and-daub house under construction, in T. Lynn Smith and Alexander Marchant, eds., *Brazil: Portrait of Half a Continent* (New York: Dryden Press, 1951), pl. 17a, p. 174; two photographs in "A Beehive Village of the Massas" [in French Equatorial Africa], *Travel* 53(October 1929): 39; and photographs in G. M. Greenwell, "The Strange Beehive Village of Talbeseh" (1936): 20–21, 58. The brief account reads in part: "The houses were built of unbaked mud-brick covered with white clay. . . . With roofs built in oval shapes, domed in beehive fashion, the rain would not enter the house and would run off easily. Exposure to sun and rain smoothed the mud down, automatically filling the cracks. . . ."

20.   See Harry Tschopik, Jr, "At Home in the High Andes" (1955), p. 143. The illustration depicts a busy scene of "thatching a roof at an Aymara housing bee, where the roofers lay down rolls of Titicaca rushes across the rafters (a latticework of poles), while clumps of *ichu* grass, dipped in mud, shingle the top." Among countless scenes of thatching, the following give some idea of its geographical distribution: Formosa in *National Geographic* 37(March 1920): 280; Tonga Tabu, S. Pacific in *National Geographic* 39 (January 1921): 52. Costa Rica in *National Geographic* 41(February 1922): 215, 218; Seminole Indians, Florida in *Travel* 51(August 1928): 36; and India (Toda hut) in *Travel* 67(August 1936): 35.

21.   Two profusely illustrated books devoted to scaffolding are A. G. H. Thatcher, *Scaffolding* (1904) and Karl Schmidt, *Die Baugerüste* (1949). Schmidt's section, pp. 202–18, on *Auslegergerüste* (outrigger scaffolding) is of particular interest. This type of scaffolding, hung from the building rather than supported on standards from the ground probably corresponds closely to medieval practices where scaffolding was limited to as little as possible and often erected in small units that leapfrogged to serve progressively higher levels as the work advanced.

22.   Twentieth-century photographs of buildings on piles driven by primitive means over water are found in the following: *National Geographic* 24(February 1913):

234, pile dwellings on Lake Maracaibo, Venezuela; *Travel* 57(October 1931): 24, bamboo huts on piles, built over the water, with connecting tressle walkways; p. 46, "On the outside, the Chinese Pier looks like an endless row of single wooden shacks far out in the water, with a long bamboo pier in front of them. . . ."; *Travel* 60(November 1932): 9. "At a Moro Water Village: Oftentimes the Moros build their thatched cottages on piling driven into the mud of lagoons. The rising tide brings the sea to their doors."; p. 10, "We anchored among a cluster of native houses built, after the Malay fashion, upon pilings driven into the mud. . . . During the night the tide had run out, leaving us high and dry on the [odiously smelling] accumulation of refuse that had been falling through the house floors for centuries"; p. 11, "The Wedding Guests Assemble via a high two-plank-wide tressle leading from the jungle shore to the pile dwellings."

23.   For example, for the position and function of so-called raising holes in eighteenth-century New World Dutch barns, see John Fitchen, *New World Dutch Barn* (1968), pp. 57–58, fig. 14 p. 132.

24.   In connection with the widespread rebuildings and reconstructions of medieval buildings in Poland badly damaged in World War II, Dr. Hélène C. Kaplan has been collecting a photographic record of the state-financed undertakings. A native of Poland now living in America, Mrs. Kaplan has made recent trips there to interview both the mason practitioners and the architects in charge of extensive repairs—of virtual rebuilding, in fact, in the case of collapsed vaults—for edifices of national significance. Of special importance, she has taken and/or assembled hundreds of on-the-spot progress photographs of the techniques followed and the falsework employed in reconstructing many late-medieval vaults. Likewise, Mr. Robert Van Nice—the indefatigable examiner and meticulous recorder of Hagia Sophia in Istambul—has had detailed photographs taken, step by step, of the procedures followed in the erection of the rib vaulting of the National Cathedral in Washington, D.C. Thus he has created a unique visual record of how the ribs, bosses, and web courses were assembled in this great modern church whose vaults are fashioned of stone throughout, without benefit of metal reinforcement.

25.   James Weir, Jr., M.D, "Animal Intelligence" (1893) p. 14997. For another astonishing eye witness account from the world of nature, reporting in thorough detail the actual construction operations by eels of a tidewater dam, see John M. Batchelder, "The Lamprey as a Builder" (1884), 469–70.

26.   "A Spider's Device in Lifting" (1884) pp. 432–33.

27.   For accurate drawings of large numbers of all-wood joints of various categories, see Cecil Alec Hewett, *Development of Carpentry, 1200-1700* (1969).

Chapter 3

1.   Quoted from a review by W. K. Brooks, "A New Law of Organic Evolution," *Science* 4(12 December 1884): 532–34.

2.   Arthur L. Day (Director, Geophysical Laboratory, Washington, D. C.), "Earthquakes and Their Effect on Buildings" (1926), p. 75.

3.   See Caroe, chap. 8, "Belfries, Bell-Frames, and Bells," in *Old Churches,* pp. 163–73, for valuable technical and practical information.

4.   Jos. 6:3–20.

5.   "After the great earthquake of 1783, it was duly recognized that the buildings must be low, of one story if possible . . . , but as the years went on and the population increased, stories were added one after another even to five stories while the retaining walls were not strengthened in proportion. . . ." "The Messina Earthquake" (1910), p. 95.

6.   "Part of this edifice fell down less than a century after the completion of the choir; and yet it was designed in such a way as to enable it to stand for centuries. This disaster, which has completely altered its character, was due to the indifferent execution, the lack of rigid support, or their too slight resistance and especially to the nature of the materials, which were neither large nor solid enough. . . ." Huss, *Rational Building*, p. 231.

7.   See "Checklist: Items of Simple Maintenance" in Caroe, p. 6.

8.   See "Traditional Methods for Treating Surface Decay" in A. R. Powys, *Repair of Ancient Buildings* (1929), p. 72.

9.   For a single important building, there is much information about both the kinds and the seriousness of structural cracks in masonry, illustrated by revealing drawings as well as photographs, in William Harvey, *Preservation of St. Paul's Cathedral* (1925).

10.   "One of the most fruitful causes of cracks is the alternate expansion and contraction of construction materials because of temperature changes, especially in climates with wide variations of temperature. . . . These temperature cracks also occur from the natural change of winter to summer weather, and sometimes even from the change of noon to midnight temperatures in the summer time. . . . Further, very cold weather opens up cracks and joints by freezing water contained in them." Edmund Astley Prentis and Lazarus White, *Underpinning*, 2d. ed. (1950), p. 11.

11.   This situation probably did not occur in ancient times because of the relatively slow, incremental rate of progress in handicrafted building operations. During the 20th century, however, the sometimes spectacular and devastating failures in high-rise structures and concrete dams, for example, can be accounted for by the use of major mechanical equipment and machines that have allowed extensive building operations to be dangerously accelerated.

12.   For the depredations of the deathwatch beetle, and the recommended steps for controlling it, see Caroe, pp. 133–36.

13.   "The effort to sustain, or rather renew, this architecture is necessarily as formidable as that which created it. Once every twenty years, since the reign of Emperor Temmu (673–686) every fence and building is completely rebuilt on an identical adjoining site. The present buildings are the fifty-ninth reconstruction. . . . For over twelve hundred years the symbolic youth and purity of Shinto architecture has been periodically retrieved. . . . The new home is identical in every respect to the old one, except for its polished, golden freshness." Arthur Drexler, *Architecture of Japan* (1955), p. 35.

14.   In 1954 the steeple of Boston's Old North Church was destroyed by high winds. A photograph taken at the moment of its overturning (for the second time since 1804) is given in Robert Irving, *Hurricanes and Twisters* (1961), p. 42. Throughout *Building in England,* Salzman documents numerous buildings or parts of buildings that collapsed because of storms during the Middle Ages. Beginning his list on page 25, he states that "[In 1091] there was a tremendous gale and hurricane in London, which shattered more than 600 houses, unroofed the church of St. Mary at Bow, and reduced other churches to ruin."

15.   "Lightning, besides causing the collapse of steeples and the outbreak of fires, can have incalculable results in its efforts to pass to or from the earth by the easiest route and to raise all conducting materials to the same potential on the way . . . ." In a

section on lightning conductors, the author notes that "the very difficult problems which can be involved when taking down a spire stone by stone after it has been struck, without causing the rest of the structure to collapse in the process, will be appreciated by reference to the illustration of Croscombe; see Frontispiece." Caroe, pp. 8, 194 n.1.

16.　For example, the pier foundations for the Pont Neuf in Paris were supported on timber grillages "composed of heavy planks 6″ thick, laid close together, resting on stringers or sleepers 15″ thick." A few years after these wooden platforms had been constructed in the bed of the Seine (ca. 1588), the piles and cofferdams were found to be in bad condition. "Investigations disclosed the alarming fact that at some of the piers the river scouring had dug out the bed to a depth of five or six pieds below the wooden platform." William Barclay Parsons, *Engineers and Engineering in the Renaissance* (1939) pp. 567, 569.

17.　An early (for America) instance of damage from ice is recorded in a letter written by R. Livingston, dated 2 April 1712, about repairing the sluice of the corn mill on his manor, which had been broken by the ice and required the services of six carpenters to restore it to use. E. B. O'Callaghan, *Documentary History of New York,* vol. 3 (1850), pp. 679–81.

18.　A familiar and widely reported catastrophe of this double sort was the San Francisco earthquake and fire of 1906.

19.　Mexico City, for example, has been plagued by settlement of its buildings for centuries. Its site is a former lake; and the various schemes that have been introduced for drainage and to prevent periodic flooding have lowered the level of the ground water, causing some of the older buildings to settle a number of feet.
　　D. H. S. Cranage provides specific information as well as a sectional drawing (fig. 1) and a photograph (pl. 1) on the condition at Winchester ("where this great cathedral was built over a running stream"), and what had to be done in 1909 to repair and strengthen the foundations of the presbytery. (For a detailed description of the foundation settlements at Winchester and the extensive measures that were taken to correct this alarming problem, see page 99). Cranage also comments on the foundations of St. Paul's, Norwich, Amiens, and Paris cathedrals. Cranage, *Cathedrals and How They Were Built* (1948), p. 3.
　　Throughout the past (as indeed today), below-grade foundations for substantial structures—from substructures for tall Gothic towers to piers for stone arch bridges—ordinarily consist of timber piles driven into the soil or the river-bottom mud. It should be noted, however, that piles are never driven down to solid rock. Instead, they are driven to "refusal"; that is, to a point at which repeated blows of the pile-driving mechanism produce no appreciable increment of further penetration. Thus their bearing capacity is dependent entirely on the friction between the surface of the pile and the material surrounding it. If this material has, and maintains, a constant ingredient of ground water, the pile will be immune from deterioration, and no settlement will occur. Of course, where a group of many piles is required, their individual refusal points seldom agree; so they have to be cut off at an even height well below the ground-water level.
　　Although not due to change in the level of the water table, a very serious cause of settlement in buildings, particularly in parts of England, has been the subsidence of ground above extensive mining operations, which has brought about major dislocations and damage to many buildings. For an excellent summary of this problem, see "Mining Subsidence" in Caroe, pp. 35–42.

20.　Catherwood's drawings in J. L. Stephens, *Incidents of Travel* (1841), are on-the-spot records of the degree to which great trees had disrupted and sometimes almost obliterated many of the masonry structures of the former central American civilizations.

21. Caroe, p. 10, lists vegetation as one of the principal destructive agents in buildings: "This can be very harmful, both through collecting dampness in undesirable places and also through the disruptive powers of growing roots."

22. Long before the exhaust fumes from automobiles had become a major problem in cities, and before worldwide public awareness and dismay over environmental pollution, a considerable amount of research and scientific investigation had been undertaken to determine the causes and assess the deleterious effects of these conditions on both human health and the decay of building stone. A comprehensive report on the latter is R. J. Schaffer, *Weathering of Natural Building Stones* (1933). This report was very thorough for its day (its bibliography lists 265 references), covering such factors in stone decay as moisture changes, sea salt, bacteria and microorganisms, gaseous nitrogen, the quality of mortar, air and rain, crystallization, volume changes, rock-boring Mollusca in concrete, efflorescence, sulfuric acid, vitricolous lichens, frost, sunburn, staining, parasitic ivy, and, of course, coal smoke and its accompanying ills. The hazards of the latter are not new, as the following excerpt indicates: "In the later mediaeval period buildings were often decorated with colour wash, and their disfiguration by soot was the cause of great concern. In 1273 the burning of 'sea cole' in London was prohibited, and in 1306 a citizen was executed for contravention of the law. A similar proclamation was issued in Elizabeth's reign, and in 1648 a petition was presented to Parliament praying that the importation of coal from Newcastle into London should be prohibited. . . ." Schaffer, p. 106.

23. "Paul of Caen . . . was appointed in 1077 to preside over this Monastery. He constructed the Church entirely anew of Stones and Tiles from the ancient City of Verulam, and of the Timber which he found collected and reserved by his predecessors. Eleven years were occupied in building. The present Tower and Transepts, and eastern part of Nave, are the remains of this structure." Rev. H. J. B. Nicholson, *Abbey of Saint Alban,* 3d. ed. (1876), p. 11.

24. The Great Pyramid "became a copious and convenient quarry, providing the stone required for bridges over irrigation canals, houses, walls, and other buildings in the neighbourhood of Giza and Cairo." I. E. S. Edwards, *Pyramids of Egypt,* rev. ed. (1972), p. 119.

25. For example, see "The Harvard Expedition to Samaria" (1909); and Dr. W. M. Ramsay, "The Early Christian Art of Nova Isaura" (1904).

26. "For a place whose importance as a religious and trade center lasted for over 2500 years, Sopara has few remains. Sopara was the capital of Konkon in the district of Thana in Bombay Presidency from about 1500 B.C. to 1300 A.D. . . . Of stone temples and stone-lined lakes and reservoirs many are said to have been destroyed by the Mohammedans in the beginning of the XIV century. Still enough were spared or repaired to excite the admiration and wonder of the first Portuguese (1530–1540). But during the XVI and XVII centuries the lake banks were stripped and the temples pulled down and the stones used in building Portuguese churches, forts and houses, the bulk of them probably finding their way to the great walls and religious and state buildings whose ruins still adorn the city of Bassein, which lies about four miles southeast of Sopara." S. Ghosal, "The Buddhist Relic Mound at Sopara" (1903), pp. 297–98.

27. With respect to the Forum Romanorum in the Middle Ages it is remarked that "its monuments were used as quarries and its precious marbles burned in lime kilns." Findlay Muirhead, ed., *Southern Italy* (1925), p. 113. "Rome's fortunes were at their lowest ebb during the period when the Popes removed their Court to Avignon in the south of France. . . . Countless fragments of antiquity were sold by the citizens, or cast into the lime kilns. 'Statues', writes a contemporary, 'lie buried in the dust, are ground to make cement, or used as building materials' . . . ." Rev. Albert Kuhn, *Roma* (1916), p. 76.

28.   "The fortification both of the town and of the harbour . . . was taken in hand with special vigour. Men, women, and children all lent their aid; and traces of the haste with which the work was carried on may be seen to this day in the curious mixture of materials brought to light in the most recent excavations. To ensure the permanent union of the town and harbour, the 'Long Walls' were erected (460–456 B.C.), stretching from the Pireus and from Phaliron to Athens itself." Karl Baedeker, *Greece*, 2d ed. (1894), p. 41.

29.   Part of a condensed summary of Prof. Pignorini's exhaustive report on the structure of the ditch, dyke, platforms, hearths of the station at Castione appearing in Robert Munro, *Palaeolithic Man and the Terramara Settlements in Europe* (1912), p. 309. See particularly pl. XXXII: photographs of many rows of piles set at about 45 degrees from the vertical and of exposed timbering of the block-houses; pl. XXXIV: a photograph of long, thickly set piles *in situ* in the Terramara of Parma and one of piles in a street of Castellazzo di Fontanellato.

30.   Llewellyn L. Henson, "Researches in Palestine" (1906), p. 42, including n.1.

31.   The persistence of tradition at the grassroots level is illustrated in a number of ways in an early-nineteenth-century article by J. H. Gibbon, "A Visit to the Salt Works of Zipaquera, near Bogota, in New Grenada" (1837). The author reports on three instances in considerable detail. He describes how "the salt works are managed upon the same general plan pursued by the natives before the conquest." This is a calcining process in which large earthenware pots are gradually filled with water from neighboring salt springs and strengthened by lumps of rock salt. The pots are then assembled in the shape of a barrel vault beneath which a fire of faggots is kept burning for many hours. The Indians who make the pots carry in wood from a consid-erable distance for stoking the furnace, in long bundles of faggots sustained on their backs by a bandage passed over the forehead. Despite the ready availability of coal that could be advantageously used to a greater extent, "it is thought judicious to en-courage the industry of the people in their own way, for it can with difficulty be drawn into other channels than those they have been long accustomed to." Gibbon also points out the undeviating, irrational preference on the part of one portion of the populace for grained salt in its impure native state, the other portion insisting on having salt that has been purified and hardened by calcination, though the price (but not the cost) is the same for both.

32.   In "The Beginnings of Stained Glass," chap. 8 of *Stained Glass of the Middle Ages* [1913], Hugh Arnold chronicles the early history of colored glass, including the small wooden and bronze lattices, used as window inserts, that were found in Pompeii.

33.   See the photographs of a number of substantially built cantilevered timber bridges in John Claude White, "Castles in the Air" (1914), pp. 366, 385, 387, 393, and 404.

Chapter 4

1.   *Building Code Recommended by the National Board of Fire Underwriters, New York,* 4th ed., rev. (1922). The quotation is from the foreword to the original 1905 edition.

2.   For Egypt and Rome, such regulations seem not to have been assembled and published in any systematic, comprehensive, and readily available form. References to them are encountered individually and only incidentally, if at all, in a variety of books and articles—not necessarily devoted to architecture. One reason for the lack of coverage, today, of Roman building regulations is that they were not codified by the Romans themselves. Instead, most seem to have been promulgated in the form of imperial edicts or decrees, some of which (like the height limitation, in number of stories, of multiple-dwelling buildings) were circumvented or ignored and had to be reaffirmed by successive emperors. Salzman, *Building in England* cites but does not index numerous medieval building regulations. Not until many centuries after Roman times were building regulations systematically organized into well-established codes, as in Antoine Desgodets, *Les Lois des bâtimens suivant la coutume de Paris* (1768), which comprises some seven hundred pages of text on building laws and regulations in eighteenth-century France.

3.   It is somewhat outside the scope of this study to comment on guild organization and the ways in which various building-related guilds policed the quality of their member's workmanship.

4.   Translated in "The Laws of Hammurabi, King of Babylonia" (1903).

5.   Such prescriptions are formulated in the "Visnudhermottara" and the "Mayamata." The latter specifies (15: 114–20) how to make good bricks, as quoted here from Stella Kramrisch, *Hindu Temple,* vol. 1 (1946), p. 102.

6.   E. Baldwin Smith, *Egyptian Architecture as Cultural Expression* (1938), p. 231.

7.   Specific instances of a community's unwritten but nonetheless binding insistence on accepted standards are frequently encountered. For a persuasive comment on the unchanging psychological power of tribal mores and taboos (even when—and undoubtedly because—they involve self-sacrifice and subordination to the group), see Andrew Oldquist, "On Belonging to Tribes" (1982), p. 9.

8.   Mimmo Castellano, *La Valle dei Trulli* (1968), with many photographs plus technical drawings.

9.   Fitchen, *Barn.*

10.   See Williams. This is one of the best—certainly the most observant, thoughtful, and sensitive—studies of the impact of nature (the materials available, the climate, and the imperatives of the environment) on the products of man's craftsmanship, including buildings.

11.   John B. Orr, "Artistic Stucco" (1917), p. 262.

12.   For an account of the Israelites' strife with the pharaoh over their gathering straw for bricks, see M. G. Kyle, "Bricks Without Straw at Pithom" (1909).

13.   Salzman, p. 230.

14.   Samuel Wyllys Pomeroy, "Remarks on the Coal Region between Cumberland & Pittsburgh" (1831), p. 345.

15.   Abate Ferrare, "An Account of the Earthquake which occurred in Sicily, in March, 1823" (1825).

16.   "Messina Earthquake," p. 96. This is a condensed summary of Signor Baratta's account (in the August and September 1910 numbers of the *Bullettino della Societa Geografia Italiana)* of the condition of Messina after the earthquake of 28 December 1908 and of the causes that produced the great devastation.

17.   For a brief but comprehensive review of modern building regulations and codes in America up through 1946, see Frank G. Lopez, "Building Regulations," in *The Encyclopedia Americana* (1949).

18.   See John Fitchen, "Architecture, the Optimistic Art" (1964).

Chapter 5

1.   Personal correspondence, letter of 3 December 1981 from John Hardy Fitchen.

2.   A specific and detailed account, including drawings of the instruments employed and explanations of their use, is given at length in Kenneth D. Matthews, "Roman Aqueducts" (1970), pp. 2–16.

3.   See Somers Clarke and R. Engelbach, *Ancient Egyptian Masonry* (1930), pp. 63–65, figs. 62 (field surveying scene from an eighteenth-dynasty tomb) and 63.

4.   Among the extensive literature on the subject of land surveying, see particularly Hunter Dupree, "The Pace of Measurement from Rome to America" (1968), pp. 19–40. Much of the coverage deals with the proportionate distribution of the components and the overall layout of the entire monastic establishment presented in the plan of St. Gall.

5.   "An early manifestation of a feeling which had a large influence on later architecture [was] the feeling that a church and an altar are hallowed by contact with the body or relic of a saint. . . . Churches erected in the place of the original memorial *cellae* derived their importance from the fact that they guarded the relics of the martyr, and there are numerous instances of the extreme care taken by architects in the reconstruction and enlargement of churches, to avoid changing the situation of the altar in relation to the sacred tomb. When the actual visits to the burial-places without the walls fell into disuse there ensued a curious change. The Church, no longer able to go out to honour the martyrs, brought the martyrs in to herself within the walls, and instead of building churches above the tombs, dug tombs under the churches in which the precious treasures were deposited. This was the origin, first of the *confessio* of the basilicas, and at a later period of the crypt which answers the same purpose in the Church of the early Middle Ages. In this way the Romanesque crypt is the direct descendant of the *hypogaeum* or excavation of the early Christian Catacomb." G. Baldwin Brown, *From Schola to Cathedral* (1886), pp. 65–66.

6.   Walter Horn and Ernest Born, *The Plan of St. Gall* (1979).

7.   For these and other means of financing churches and abbeys in the Middle Ages, see Camille Enlart, "Ressources des constructeurs: les donations," in pt. 1 of *Manual d'archéologie française* (1902), pp. 73–77, with extensive footnotes.

8.   For methods and routes of transportation for building materials in the Middle Ages, see "Transport de matériaux" in Enlart, pp. 77–80, with numerous footnotes; for transport by water in ancient Egypt, see chap. 4, "Transport Barges" in Clarke and Engelbach, pp. 34–45.

9.   Erwin Panofsky, *Abbot Suger on the Abbey Church of St-Denis and Its Treasures* (1946), p. 95.

10.   Kyle, "Bricks Without Straw" (1909), pp. 304–7.

11.   "When Servilius marched up from Cilicia with a Roman army about 78 B.C., he captured Isaura by turning aside the river, on which the city depended for water. This operation was easily within the power of a Roman army used to spade work; the river could readily be made to flow on the opposite side of the glen, behind and west of the isolated hill." Ramsay, "Nova Isaura," p. 320. "Shortly after the fall of Jerusalem the Romans sent an army under Silvia to besiege and take Masada. . . . Knowing that it would be impossible to starve the garrison into submission Silvia decided to storm the fortress. In order to do this it was necessary to throw up an enormous embankment on the west side of the fortress over which his enormous engines of war could be brought within striking distance of the walls. . . . This gigantic undertaking [involved]

the whole ridge [being] artificially thrown up by the opposing army. According to Josephus the Romans built a tower sixty cubits high which was covered with iron and from which they could throw darts and stones into the fortifications. They also used a battering ram with which they broke down the outer stone wall. . . ." Frederick Bennett Wright, "The Fortress of Masada" (1906), p. 370. In his *Commentarii de Bello Gallico* (iv:17) Julius Caesar describes the bridge his military engineers built over the Rhine in such detail that many drawings of its supposed appearance have been made in modern times.

12. "Whenever a city was taken by assault, orders were given to spare architects, painters and qualified workmen whom Timur [Tamberlaine] subsequently employed in the execution of his projects. . . ." (author's translation) *Mosquées de Samarcande* (1905) p. v.

13. It is on record that the timberwork gantry for one of the vaulting bays of King's College Chapel, Cambridge, was turned over as part of his fee—a bonus recompense—to the poet Geoffrey Chaucer in his capacity as Clerk of the Works.

14. For examples of and references to great wheels as lifting devices see Fitchen, *Gothic Cathedrals*, pp. 207, 208, n. 73.

15. A remarkably thorough investigation and analysis of the order and sequence of operations in a masterpiece of the Gothic era—including a discussion of the geometry of complicated stereotomies in the details of doorway corbels and window embrasures and of the setting out of the work generally—has recently appeared as John James, *Contractors of Chartres*, 2d ed. (1981). James has examined, stone by stone, the entire fabric of this noble building and has painstakingly recorded his findings in both text and innumerable drawings and photographs. He documents, from the evidence of the building itself, the extent of the work executed by a succession of master masons throughout the progress of the centuries-long undertaking. This is a major example of on-the-site research, impressive by reason of its scope, its attention to details, and its knowledgeable professionalism.

16. See annotated photographs in Bernard Rudofsky, *Architecture without Architects* (1965), n. pag., figs. 138, 142.

17. See Auguste Choisy, *L'Art de bâtir chez les Romains* (1873); John H. Middleton, "On the Chief Methods of Construction Used in Ancient Rome" (1888), pp. 41–60; and William J. Anderson, R. Phené Spiers, and Thomas Ashby, "Materials and Modes of Construction," chap. 3 of *Architecture of Ancient Rome* (1927), pp. 26–42.

18. For a photograph of the concrete core above the ressauts of the Basilica of Constantine, see Anderson, Spiers, and Ashby, pl. XLX facing p. 87; for textual comment on this situation, see H. Heathcote Statham, *Architecture for General Readers*, (1896), p. 77 fig. 70, p. 248, fig. 226.

19. Thomas Lennox Watson, *Double Choir of Glasgow Cathedral* (1901), p. 35.

20. Fitchen, *Barn*, p. 59.

21. See "The Bent Pyramid—Portcullis in open position" in Edwards, *Pyramids of Egypt*, p. 102, fig. 22.

22. Watson, pp. 118, 122–25.

23. See Fitchen, *Barn*, pp. 53–61, pp. 130–31, fig. 13.

24. For the sequence of construction operations in a Greek temple, see the account taken from Penrose's *Athenian Architecture* in F. M. Simpson, *History of Architectural Development*, vol. 1 (1921), p. 90.

Chapter 6

1.　　　Personal correspondence with JTT, letter of 20 January 1982.

2.　　　The best known of these is Roriczer, "On the Ordination of Pinnacles." Translated in Holt, *Documentary History of Art,* Vol 1, pp. 95–101.

3.　　　George Kubler, "A Late Gothic Computation of Rib Vault Thrusts" (1944), pp. 135–48.

4.　　　Modern scientific advancements in aerodynamics are, of course, well known to designers of aircrafts and of racing sailboats. In sailing, this knowledge has resulted in larger jibs and narrower mainsails to exploit the fact that some two-thirds of the driving force of the wind comes from the negative pressure on the lee side. The designers of the lofty, very steep roofs of many Gothic cathedrals undoubtedly had no scientific data for figuring the wind load on the roofs. But they were certainly well aware of the problem and successfully prevented these vulnerable superstructures from overturning or being blown off the clerestory walls. See John Fitchen, "A Comment on the Function of the Upper Flying Buttress in French Gothic Architecture" (1955), pp. 69–90.

5.　　　Drawings and photographs of medieval wind braces (in the plane of the roof) appear throughout F. W. B. Charles, *Medieval Cruck-Building and Its Derivatives* (1967) and in Thomas Morris, *British Carpentry* (1871), with woodcut illustrations of wind braces on p. 32 and facing pp. 48, 54, 72. The universal practice of employing *sway* braces (diagonal struts and braces in the vertical plane of both longitudinal and transverse frames) is depicted in innumerable publications beginning with Raphael Brandon and J. Arthur Brandon, *Open Timber Roofs of the Middle Ages* (1849), illustrated with perspective and working drawings of some of the best varieties of church roofs.

6.　　　Modern examples of structures subject to flutter are the Tacoma Narrows Bridge (which collapsed after spectacular writhings and undulations from flutter induced by only slight but sustained wind action); Nowicki's Stock-Judging Arena at the Raleigh, N.C. State Fair Grounds; Zetlin's Utica, N.Y. War Memorial Auditorium (a "bicycle-wheel" structure); and Saarinen's Ice Hockey Rink at Yale University.

7.　　　Thornton Wilder's 1928 Pulitzer Prize-winning novel, *The Bridge of San Luis Rey,* traces the lives of those who perished in consequence of the sudden collapse of an actual handicrafted suspension bridge in South America. Continuing well into the present century, primitive cable bridges spanned the deep gorges of the Salween River in Southeast Asia. As often as not they hardly deserved to be called bridges, consisting of nothing more than a single cable that swayed and undulated uncontrollably above the torrent.

8.　　　For an explicitly detailed and illustrated account of the remarkably lofty, thin-shelled stone spire of Salisbury Cathedral in England, see Francis Price, *Observations . . . upon . . . the Cathedral-Church of Salisbury* (1753).

9.　　　Fitchen, *Barn,* p. 33.

10.　　　For the consequences of partial loadings on arch centerings, see Fitchen, *Gothic Cathedrals,* pp. 14, 202, 296–298, including references to, and quotations from, other writers.

11.　　　Albert S. Bickmore (a naturalist and shell, bird, and butterfly collector), *Travels in the East Indian Archipelago* (1868), p. 427, facing page, woodcut of the bridge.

12. Caroe, *Old Churches,* chap. 8, "Belfries, Bell-Frames, and Bells," pp. 163, 168–69 and pl. X. In his clear and circumstantial account, Caroe covers the problem of and solutions to the ringing of bells in English towers (where the difficulties are so much greater than those encountered in carillons and in chiming bells that involve no heavy swinging parts).

13. This weighting of the pier from above is seen in countless instances. In Reims Cathedral, for example, the tall pinnacles surmounting the deeply salient buttresses and, much more powerfully, the higher portions of the clerestory walls together with the very considerable weight of the lofty lead-covered roof that bears upon them, contribute substantially to stabilizing the lateral thrusts from the high vaults.

14. For comments on metal and wooden tie rods, see appendix J, "Arch and Vault Ties in Medieval Construction" in Fitchen, *Gothic Cathedrals,* pp. 275–79.

15. For a discussion of deformation in an arch, resulting from the catenary curve of pressure passing outside the arch ring, see Fitchen, *Gothic Cathedrals,* p. 81.

16. For illustrated accounts of centerless dome construction, see Ir. H. J. W. Thunnissen, *Gewelven* (1950), p. 43, fig 3; and John Fitchen, "Some Contemporary Techniques of Arch Construction in Spain" (1960), pp. 32–34. See also Eton, *Turkish Empire,* p. 236: "In some parts of Asia, I have seen cupolas of a considerable size, built without any kind of timber support. They fix firmly in the middle a post of about the height of the perpendicular wall, more or less, as the cupola is to be a larger or smaller portion of a sphere; to the top of this is fastened a strong pole, so as to move in all directions, and the end of it describes the inner portion of the cupola; lower down is fixed to the post another pole, which reaches to the top of the outer part of the perpendicular wall, and describes the outside of the cupola, giving the difference of thickness of the masonry at the top and bottom, and every intermediate part, with the greatest possible exactness. Where they build their cupolas with bricks, and instead of lime use gypsum, finishing one layer all round before they begin another, only scaffolding for the workmen is required to close the cupola at top."

17. J. P. Seddon, "On the Shoring of Grosmont Tower" (1873), pp. 103–4.

18. Various nineteenth-century writers have recorded accurate observations and perceptive comments on earthquake devastation in various places in the world. Among these are Lt. J. M. Gilliss, "On the Earthquake of April 2, 1851, in Chile" (1856), 388–99; "City of San Salvator Destroyed by an Earthquake" (1854), pp. 277–84; and W. J. McGee, "Some Features of the Recent Earthquake in and around Charleston, S.C." (1886), pp. 271–75.

19. Occasionally one runs across photographs of native attempts at earthquake-resistant structures. For example, see Manuel Gamio, "Cultural Evolution in Guatemala and Its Geographic and Historic Handicaps," pt. 2 (1927), pp. 17–21. The captions of two of the illustrations on page 20 read as follows: "The 'bird-cage' construction of 'woven' wooden strips, with clay or adobe filling partly flaked away by earth-shocks" and "Native hut on which 'cinches' or wooden binding strips are employed to hold the adobe blocks in place during the weaving motion given the building by earthquakes. Neither this nor the 'bird cage' construction has solved the problem for the fearful native." The author also comments on the character and distribution of Guatemalan architecture with respect to areas affected by different degrees of geodynamic action. Gamio, pt. 3, pp. 72, 73. Probably the only technical analysis of native antiseismic construction is Demetrius Porphyrios, "Traditional Earthquake Resistant Construction on a Greek Island" (1971), pp. 31–39.

20. H. M. Hadley, "How Structures Withstood the Japanese Earthquake and Fire" (1924), p. 191.

21.   For an excellent, succinct account of the action of lightning strokes and the steps that can be taken today to minimize their damage (based largely on the U.S. Bureau of Standards, *Code for Protection against Lightning* [1932]), see Caroe, pp. 193–95. "The liability of any building to be struck by lightning depends partly on its surroundings. High ground is more dangerous than a sheltered position, and a building in a town is less likely to be struck than one in a lonely countryside. Shape is important; a building with a tower or large chimney is much more vulnerable than a low building. But the most important thing to remember is that, if an electrical charge does occur, the damage done is most likely to be serious in brick or stone-built buildings containing large metal objects. Thus many country churches, with their towers, their stone walls, their bells, and their lead roofs, fall into the most dangerous category. . . ." See Caroe's frontispiece: a photograph of Croscombe's stone spire after having been struck by lightning.

22.   W. K. Hatt, "Note on Fatigue in Mortar" (1922), pp. 167–73. As early as 1922 the author could state: "It is well known that metals will rupture under repeated application of loads below the ultimate strength, and that there is a percentage of the ultimate stress which may be applied indefinitely without rupture." Page 168. Today one of the clearest presentations of the insidious nature, the undetectable dispersion, and the deadly seriousness of metalic fatigue is Henry Petroski, "When Cracks Become Breakthroughs" (1982), pp. 18–30. Petroski describes and analyzes recent spectacular failures from this cause.

23.   "The working stress is the greatest stress to which a member of a structure or a machine is subjected during use or operation. If it exceeds the elastic limit there may occur permanent deformations not allowed for in the design, change of properties of the material, and when the stresses alternate or vary, ultimate failure. Indeed, the working or safe stress must be taken considerably below the elastic limit to allow for deterioration due to wear, unavoidable imperfections in workmanship and manufacture, lack of uniformity of material, accidental overloading, but *not for poor design.* As it is difficult under commercial conditions to determine the rather ill defined elastic limit it is customary to state the safe stress as a certain fraction, $1/n$, of the breaking stress; n is called the *factor of safety* and is determined by experience. . . ." Richard F. Deimel, "Strength of Materials," *Encyclopedia Americana* (1949), p.733.

24.   See W. R. Lethaby, *Architecture* (1912). In his inspired chap. 12, "Gothic Building in France—The Architecture of Energy," p. 201, Lethaby writes that "the ideals of the time of energy and order produced a manner of building of high intensity, all waste tissue was thrown off, and the stonework was gathered up into energetic functional members. These ribs and bars and shafts are all at bow-string tension. A mason will tap a pillar to make its stress audible; we may think of a cathedral as so 'high strung' that if struck it would give a musical note. . . ."

25.   "The Assyrians knew the value of the roller as a lessener of friction at least as early as the eighth century B.C. . . . It must be determined, however, why rollers were not invariably used by the Egyptians. In the case of moderate sized blocks, and with sufficient men on the spot, the running of the sled over transversely laid sleepers is a considerably quicker process than the use of rollers, which need a good deal of attention to avoid jamming or running sideways [particularly because] they are slightly thicker in the middle than at the ends. . . ." Clarke and Engelbach, *Egyptian Masonry,* chap. 8, "Handling the Blocks," p. 90. See also facing p. 224 fig. 267, roller probably of the Fifth dynasty.

26.   "But when subject to expansion and contraction caused by temperature changes, this ductility [of lead] is the chief cause of faults which develop so often in lead roofs and result in such frequent dilapidations; for lead will expand whenever the temperature rises and, while doing so, will try to tear away from anything which holds it back, but the slightest obstacle will prevent it returning to its original size when the temperature falls again. This is particularly the case on steep roofs, where the factor of gravity is important. Lead will expand downwards, but will not contract upwards, with the result that there is a constant tendency for it to 'creep' down. Good workmanship must give the lead freedom to expand, while at the same time providing sufficient checks to stop it creeping. . . ." Caroe, p. 141. This remarkably well-informed and thorough writer's valuable book has much to say about cracks of many sorts in old buildings: what causes them and what can and should (or should not) be done about them.

27.   Not all cracks in masonry are unsafe or unwelcome. "A prominent crack is often visible between the vault and a lateral wall, the crack running up the line of the wall-rib (where the vault is apparently resting on the wall . . .) and usually getting widest at the apex where the transverse ridge-rib meets the wall; and such a crack is sometimes thought to indicate that the vault is in a dangerous condition. In reality just the reverese is the case, and a crack in this position may be a healthy sign. Not only does the vault in no way depend on the adjacent wall for support at this point, but any attempt to mend this crack and attach vault and wall rigidly together is likely to lead to disintegration in a structure which may otherwise be in perfect condition. The thick wall remains relatively stationary throughout the seasons. The vault, however, is an exceedingly thin structure which reacts rapidly to changes in temperature. . . ." Caroe, p. 22.

28.   For a modern example, see J. C. Pearson, "Shrinkage of Portland Cement Mortars and Its Importance in Stucco Construction" (1921), pp. 133–49. "[I]t has been shown that the control of suction or absorption is the most vital factor in the control of shrinkage, both in the plastic and hardened mortars." Page 147. For a comprehensive and detailed coverage of many kinds of conditions and practices in modern concrete construction from the standpoint of a knowledgeable and experienced contractor, see Arthur R. Lord, "Notes on Concrete—Wacker Drive, Chicago" (1927), pp. 28–78.

29.   "The crushing of the dressed stonework in the pier facings . . . has taken place from the undue concentration of the weight on this facing; the backing being composed of rubble walling, with a greater number of mortar joints than in the facing, has settled down, leaving the casing to do the work of carrying the tower, and thus reducing the working area of each pier from 18 ft. to 8.34 ft. . . ." Seddon, p. 104.

30.   "Settlers also heartily disliked the tendency of log houses to dry and shrink over the years, with the consequent warping and twisting of all openings to windward. . . . A Settler's house was usually up and occupied within a month of the trees that composed it being cut down. . . . Rot in the bottom logs, caused by constant exposure to alternate wetting and drying, commonly resulted in settling. . . ." John I. Rempel, *Building With Wood* (1967), p. 31.

31.   "Concrete is essentially artificial stone. Its manufacture involves a chemical process, requiring a length of time which affords opportunity for handling and depositing it in molds or such other positions as may be desirable. It is necessary to complete any necessary manipulation of the concrete prior to the time that the hardening begins and hence before the chemical action has materially advanced. It follows that practically all of that chemical action occurs after the concrete is in place. This chemical action generates an appreciable amount of heat, which in turn increases the volume of the concrete while it is still in a condition to adapt its shape and volume to its environment. As the hardening proceeds under the increased temperature, its shape becomes permanent, and when the chemical action is completed the temperature subsides, and the volume is reduced accordingly. As the concrete contracts on cooling there is a tendency for long structures, such as pavements, walls, etc., to crack at intervals, which vary with climatic and many other conditions, but which must be reckoned with, if such cracks are detrimental, or for any reason undesirable. If such cracks are left to chance, they are ragged and irregular, and as changes of temperature occur, incipient disintegration is encouraged, and hence it is desirable to control the form and position of such cracks, by the provision of contraction joints, which can take care of small movements induced by temperature, and which are of many kinds, varying with the conditions that must be met." Arthur P. Davis, "Use of Concrete for Dams, Tunnels, Culverts and Canals" (1924), pp. 91–92.

32. For a thorough and highly technical treatise on the heat generated during the curing of massive blocks of concrete, accompanied by numerous illustrations, charts, and tables, see U.S. Department of the Interior, Bureau of Reclamation, *Thermal Properties of Concrete* (1949).

33. These walls of undulating courses—now in convex, now in concave segments—are treated thoroughly, with many examples in Auguste Choisy, *L'Art de bâtir chez les Égyptiens* (1904), section, "Murs de brique à lits ondules," pp. 21–42, figs. 13–32, and pls. I–IX.

34. See D. S. Robertson, *A Handbook of Greek and Roman Architecture*, 2d ed. (1943), pp. 232–34. At least one writer has claimed that the Romans sometimes partially filled the compartments with cement mortar and then pressed chunks of rock into this plastic mass. Such a scheme however, seems doubtful in the extreme because a puddling technique of this sort would have caused jarring and put an inordinant amount of pressure on the formwork (whatever its makeup).

Chapter 7

1. John Fitchen, "Architecture," p. 47.

2. An annotated bibliography of falsework literature pertaining to the past is given in Fitchen, *Gothic Cathedrals,* appendix A, pp. 241–47.

3. Always highly visible and often quite spectacular, scaffoldings are often pictured. Pieter Brueghel the Elder depicted scaffolding in his minutely detailed paintings of the Tower of Babel. A number of late medieval and Renaissance illuminations and drawings that show contemporary scaffoldings are reproduced in Pierre du Colombier, *Les Chantiers des cathédrals* (1953). Striking photographs of modern scaffoldings are shown from time to time in general-interest and travel publications and, notably, such technical books as Schmidt, *Die Baugerüste* and Antoine Moles, *Histoire des charpentiers* (1949). For commentary on scaffolding along with drawings and a photograph, see Fitchen, *Gothic Cathedrals,* pp. 14–19, 202–3 nn. 36–47.

4. Henri Rauline, "The Church of the Sacred Heart at Monmartre" (1893), p. 23.

5. A thorough treatment of this remarkable structure is found in Price, *Church of Salisbury,* pls. 6, 9.

6. For a description of raising holes see Fitchen, *Barn,* p. 58, p. 132, fig. 14.

7. See particularly Viollet-le-Duc, "Échafaud," in vol. 5 of *Dictionnaire*, pp. 103–14, figs 6, 8.

8. See Thatcher, *Scaffolding*. This handbook "for the use of contractors, builders, clerks of works, etc." is thorough and comprehensive, detailed and copiously illustrated. It was written at a time when lashed pole scaffolding was still widely practiced; hence much of it is pertinent to our present study. For example: "The members of pole scaffolds are connected by cordage. . . . The arranging of the various timbers used in erecting scaffolds in a dangerous occupation, and one requiring skill and considerable nerve on the part of the workmen. . . .(p. 20); "Scaffold cords are from 15 to 18 feet in length. Moisture will cause a shrinkage of 6 inches in an 18-foot cord." (p. 77, followed by diagrams of some 41 kinds of knots used by scaffolders); "For tightening cordage wedges should be about 12 inches in length and, as far as possible, split to shape. In cross section they should be semicircular. Their taper should be gradual and not too sudden, as otherwise they might work out. . . ." (p. 113).

---

9.   A capsulated account of this traditional *matsheds* system of bamboo scaffolding, lashed together with cane and rattan, occurs in connection with a photograph captioned "Hong Kong: Scaffolding, Chinese Style" in *Construction Methods and Equipment* 52(July 1970): 137–38.

10.   Illustrations of T- and inverted L-shaped cranes abound in medieval manuscripts and miniatures. In du Colombier, for example, L's in operation are depicted in fig. 11 p. 40 (sixteenth century); fig. 22 pl. XIII (1447); fig. 33 pl. XIX (1420); and fig. 55 pl. XXXI (ca. 1550); while T's are shown in fig. 15 p. 78 (sixteenth century); fig. 18, pl. X (15th century); and fig. 20, pl. XII (ca. 1430).

11.   For a large, annotated drawing of one such swiveling crane (often used on major projects before modern cranes came into being), see Moles, p. 146 fig. 7 (along with an earlier prototype, fig. 5. The drawing is reproduced from C. Perrault, trans. *Marcus Vitruvius Pollio: Les dix livres d'architecture* (1673). Three examples of the swiveling crane are shown in action in an eighteenth-century engraving of the colonnade of the Louvre, Paris, reproduced as fig. 133, p. 123 in Moles; others, seen more distantly, appear as fig. 148, p. 141. A huge crane of this type appears atop a tower in a late-fifteenth-century miniature, reproduced in du Colombier as fig. 38, pl. XXII.

12.   For detailed and illustrated data concerning the construction, location, and secure bracing of great wheels, see Charles Czarnowsky, "Engins de levage dans les combles d'églises en Alsace" (1949), pp. 11–27, fasc. 1–2. Various views of great wheels, reproduced from medieval manuscripts, are depicted in du Colombier, pl. VIII, XV, XVII, XXI, showing them on the ground as well as high up on a building. Some of the same illustrations are reproduced, along with additional examples, in Salzman, *Building in England,* pls. 6a, 17a, 17b.

13.   Caroe, *Old Churches,* pp. 57–58, fig. 8.

14.   James Bartlett, "Shoring," *Encyclopaedia Britannica,* 11th ed., p. 1006.

15.   "The subsidence of the haunches took place on the ribs of the centerings, which were subject to distortion throughout their ensemble from the start of the loading. In proportion as the voussoirs were laid down, a heaving up at the summit was produced near the key in spite of the provisional loads that could be placed there. At the bridge of Nantes, the settlement of the centering frames (spaced at 2.19 meters, each composed of four principal ribs 0.38 by 0.40 meters square) was 0.320 meters in the main arch. As for the centering frames of the bridge at Neuilly (fig. 484), whose arches were similar, and in spite of the frames being set closer together, the subsidence of the haunches and the heaving up of the crown were so considerable that, in order to restore them to their theoretical shape and to preserve it during construction of the arches, it was necessary to weight their summits successively by 122, 426, and 455 thousand kilograms. Yet the settlement of the haunches continued. When it came to the moment of closing in the vault by the emplacement of the keys, the subsidence of the centerings was generally of the order of 7 to 8 centimeters in twenty-four hours." Moles, p. 340. Translated by J. Fitchen.

16.   "When used in pairs as for shoring purposes, they are rectangular in cross section, and are termed folding wedges." Thatcher, p. 113. A more detailed account of folding wedges and their use is found in George Joseph Bell, *Segmental and Elliptical Oblique or Skew Arches,* 2d ed. (1906), p. 102.

17.   The illustration with accompanying commentary is from Fitchen, "Arch Construction in Spain" (1960), p. 33.

18.   The following quotation is part of the specification for a skew bridge of stone over the King River in Cumberlandshire, northwest England. "At least four rows of support shall be provided in the bed of the stream between the abutment walls the full width of the Bridge, either of stone or wooden piles as the case may require, and

on each of these four rows of stone pillars or wooden piles the Contractor shall place a beam of approved strength and quality on which the above 13 centres shall rest on hardwood wedges, as broad on the bed as the beams, and smeared with soft soap as above described. After the arch has been closed and properly keyed, each set of wedges shall, on the seventh day after the arch has been keyed, be driven back an inch daily, till the arch sustains itself and the whole of the weight is removed from the centres, when the spandrel walls may be commenced." Bell, p. 102.

19.   "Undoubtedly the most dangerous operation connected with the use of bridge centres is the process of striking them. No matter with how much care the arch may have been constructed, the drying and squeezing of the mortar will cause it to settle in some degree when the centres are removed, and this degree of settlement seems to be very largely affected by the time the centres are allowed to stand. By some it has been urged that the centering should never be removed until the mortar in the joints of the last course has had ample time to harden; others going to the other extreme have advocated striking the ribs as soon as the arch is keyed, claiming, not without reason, that the settlement of a *well-built* arch will never be so great as to become dangerous even though the supporting frames be removed when the mortar is green. But possibly the best practice lies not far from either of these extremes. It has, indeed, time and again, been amply demonstrated that to leave the centering standing till the mortar has hardened, and then take away all support, the mortar having become unyielding, is to cause the courses to open along their joints. To strike the centre, on the other hand, when the arch is still green will, seven cases out of ten, be followed by the fall of the bridge; but by easing the centering as soon as the arch is keyed in, and continuing this gradual easing till the framing is quite free from the arch, the latter has time to set slowly as the mortar hardens, and the settlement will be found to be very small." John B. McMaster, *Bridge and Tunnel Centres* (1875), pp. 69–71.

20.   There is at least one instance from the medieval period in which centering frames were not removed at all, but are still in place to this day. This happened only because the frames are hidden from view; for they would never have been allowed to remain *in situ* in the normal course of events. See Sigurd Curman and Johnny Roosval, *Sveriges Kyrkor* (1935), p. 95, fig. 150, p. 97, fig. 152, p. 100, p. 114 nn. vii, x; and Fitchen, *Gothic Cathedrals,* pp. 299–300.

21.   These drawings, along with accompanying analysis, are from Fitchen, *Gothic Cathedrals,* pp. 9–13.

22.   For a thorough description of this very ancient method of building, including the formwork required, the preparation and consistency of the earth, and the tools and procedures involved, drawing chiefly on French authorities, see Abraham Rees, "Pisé" in vol. 27 of *The Cyclopaedia* [1810–24], n. pag. An entire book on the subject—with numerous drawings and photographs of pisé and related handicrafted practices (such as stabilized earth and clay lumps or cob)—that concentrates mainly on England but covers other areas such as Germany, Russia, and Africa, is Clough William-Ellis, John Eastwick-Field, and Elizabeth Eastwick-Field, *Building in Cob, Pisé, and Stabilized Earth,* 3d ed. (1950). On page 12 the authors quote Pliny's *Natural History,* book xxv, chap. 48: "Have we not in Africa and in Spain walls of earth, known as 'formocean' walls? From the fact that they are moulded, rather than built, by enclosing earth within a frame of boards, constructed on either side. These walls will last for centuries, are proof against rain, wind, and fire, and are superior in solidity to any cement. Even at this day Spain still holds watch-towers that were erected by Hannibal." See also Choisy, *Romains,* p. 23 fig. 5. This drawing shows a conjectural shuttering mechanism for a Roman wall of rammed earth, in which square beams pass through the wall and have to be drawn out subsequently, leaving voids.

23.   Dr. A. L. Shelton (for seventeen years medical missionary at Batang, near the Chino-Tibetan Border), "Life among the People of Eastern Tibet" (1921), 295–326. See the revealing photograph of "A Tibetan House in Course of Construction," with

the legend "Poles are used to hold together parallel boards, between which mud is puddled. Then the forms are raised and another layer of closely packed earth added. Similar methods are used from Shanghai to Russian Turkestan." Page 307. Shelton states that "the mud is beaten into the forms until it is puddled, and when dry it is very hard." Page 299. See also William Simpson, "Mud Architecture" (1887) pp. 57–80. Simpson quotes the description of the process as given by the great Rabbi Maimonides [1135–1204]: "The builders take two boards, about 6 cubits long and 2 cubits high, and place them parallel to each other on their edges, as far apart as the thickness of the wall they wish to build; then they steady these boards with pieces of wood, fastened with cords. The space between the boards is then filled up with earth, which is beaten down firmly with hammers or stampers. . . ." Page 79.

24.   Choisy, *Romains*, p. 16 fig 2, depicts an unfaced Roman wall of concrete in which vertical chases are left as impressions of the posts used to resist the bursting pressure of the concrete during the course of construction. "Upright posts 10 to 15 feet high were stuck in the ground along the line of both faces of the future wall at intervals of about 3 feet, and against these posts wooden boards 10 to 11 inches wide were nailed horizontally, overlapping each other. . . . The hydraulic pressure against the wooden boarding must have been heavy, and in some cases we find a regular series of holes going through the concrete wall, showing where cross-timbers were fixed as ties to keep the boarding in its place till the concrete had set. . . . In most cases the holes through the wall are absent, and the boarding must have been supported by a series of raking shores or props. The upright grooves on the face of the concrete wall caused by the print of the posts were often filled up, after the woodwork was removed, by the insertion of square bricks thickly set in mortar." Middleton, "Construction in Ancient Rome," pp. 49–50, pl. I, figs. 1, 2.

25.   Drawings have often pictured these triangular brick facings for concrete walls, encountered in buildings great and small throughout Rome. Still, it is astonishing to come across a partition wall built by the Romans in this fashion that measures only 7 inches in thickness (using smaller bricks, of course). See Middleton, "Construction in Ancient Rome," pl. I, fig. 4.

26.   Drawings of Roman concrete barrel vaults—details and ensembles alike— are found in Choisy, *les Romains*. For example, ribs of brickwork with fins are illustrated in figs. 8, p. 34; 13, p. 40; 18, p. 47; 19, p. 48; 20, p. 50; 21, p. 51. Moreover, the following drawings show two layers of brick set flatwise around the curve of the vault, with smaller bricks laid on top of the two-by-two-foot bricks and breaking joints with them: figs. 28, p. 61; 30, p. 63; 31, p. 64; 32, p. 65; 33, p. 66; 34, p. 67. All but fig. 28 show formwork of widely spaced planks and are varieties of the same general scheme, with or without small upstanding bricks that functioned as randomly spaced keys locking into the concrete matrix.

27.   For a discussion of centering requirements, see R. Guastavino, *Cohesive Construction Applied to the Timbrel Vault* (1892), p. 134; for a brief explanation of the timbrel vault system, see Fitchen, *Gothic Cathedrals*, p. 66; a comprehensive but succinct treatment of the system (customarily built today in Spain with very light—or sometimes no—formwork), illustrated with detail drawings of masons at work, is found in Cassinello, *Bóvedas,* chap. 6, "Bóvedas Tabicadas," pp. 101–20 and chap. 7, "Escaleras Tabicadas," pp. 121–28.

28.   One of the most bizarre schemes proposed for supporting, during its construction, the enormous dome of Santa Maria del Fiore (Florence, Italy), was to fill the entire area with earth from the ground up. The chief argument promoting this scheme was that, if coins were embedded in the earth fill, its removal would be assured by the townspeople scavaging for the coins! See Parsons, *Engineers,* p. 588.

29.   A discussion of the mounded earth scheme of formwork is found in Fitchen, *Gothic Cathedrals,* pp. 30–31.

30. This process is described in detail and illustrated in McMaster, pp. 94–97. A more complete and wide-ranging account (of the construction of two railroad tunnels between London and Dover) is given throughout Frederick Walter Simms, *Practical Tunnelling*, 2d ed. (1860).

31. See Viollet-le-Duc, "Construction" in vol. 4 of *Dictionnaire,* p. 106 fig. 58, p. 107 fig. 59. The cerce's operation and its difficulties and shortcomings are discussed in Fitchen, *Gothic Cathedrals*, pp. 99–105.

32. See Fitchen, *Gothic Cathedrals*, pp. 178–88, for a description of the stone-weighted rope device, its operation and its advantages. Though undoubtedly employed for centuries, this device was first described in print by Johann Claudius Lassaulx in 1831. See Rev. William Whewell, *Architectural Notes on German Churches,* 3d ed. (1842).

33. Kenneth John Conant (in a 1964 review of *The Construction of Gothic Cathedrals,* p. 50) comments in detail, and with wonder, on having observed a mason at work repairing—actually rebuilding without benefit of any formwork—the terra-cotta vault of Munich's Feldherrenhalle. See also, Hassan Fathy, *Architecture for the Poor* (1973), figs. 7–18. These clear photographs record step by step an ages-old procedure of building masonry vaults out of mud brick as practiced today in rural Egypt.

Chapter 8

1. John Buchanan, "The Industrial Development of Nyasaland" (1893), p. 251. Rope made of twisted metal wires was known in antiquity. For example, a four-strand rope of bronze wire some fifteen feet long has been unearthed in the ruins of Pompeii. But no evidence exists of the widespread use of wire rope for building purposes until the latter half of the nineteenth century, when technological manufacturing processes and the use of mild (and especially high-carbon, open-hearth) steel revolutionized production and made available wires of extremely high tensile strength. So our present study excludes considerations of wire rope and deals only with the handicrafted products of vegetable fibers (and to a much lesser extent, of animal products) as found throughout the world and throughout history.

2. Personal correspondence with JTT, letter of 25 November 1981.

3. Perhaps understandably enough, Henry C. Mercer, *Ancient Carpenters' Tools* 3d ed. (1960) makes no reference to ladders; nor does Hans E. Wulff, *Traditional Crafts of Persia* (1966). In spite of its remarkably inclusive and comprehensive coverage, there are but two one-sentence references to ladders in Hommel, *China at Work* (pp. 262, 284). Viollet-le-Duc's *Dictionnaire* contains an eleven-page article on "Échelle," but only in terms of scale in architecture; he specifically states in the first sentence of this article that he will not discuss the term in its meaning of serving "les ouvriers pour monter les échaufauds" (5:143). Even definitions of ladders are infrequent and brief. The *Encyclopedia Americana* has none at all; the entire coverage of the term in the scholarly 11th edition of the *Encyclopaedia Britannica* is confined to one brief paragraph (16:59). Daniel Ramée, *Dictionnaire général des termes d'architecture,* (1868), p. 137, gives the following definition: "ÉCHELLE, s.f. (all. *Leiter;* angl. *Ladder;* ital. *Scala).* Escalier formé de deux montants, dans lesquels sont fixées de petites traverses carrées ou cylindriques; sert aux ouvriers pendant la construction d'un bâtiment, quand l'escalier n'en point encore posé."

4. An early but comprehensive account of the occurrence and properties of natural fibers growing abundantly in many areas of the world is James Mease, "On some of the Vegetable materials from which Cordage, Twine and Thread are Made" (1832), pp. 27–38. Mease's informed coverage includes fibers native to India, the Phillippines, Java, the Molucca Archipelago, Amboyna, Sumatra, Yucatan and elsewhere in Mexico, the West Indies, Columbia and other areas of South America, New Zealand, and even New Jersey in the United States.

5. A very detailed early account of the handicrafted methods formerly followed in extracting and preparing for use the native fiber known as Manilla hemp is found in Joseph S. Travelli, "Manilla Hemp" (1841), 200–203, with one small woodcut. Two accounts that concentrate on plants native to Mexico (a country abounding in useful examples) discuss the handicrafted methods by which fibers such as sisal or henequen were customarily separated from the plants' skin, pulp, and spines, and readied for use in cordage, mattings, and bags. See William B. Marshall, "Useful Products of the Century Plant" (1902), p. 9; and *National Geographic* 25(December 1914): 577.

6. Eyewitness descriptions of primitive handicrafted methods of fabricating rope are found (for Cedros, Mexico) in *National Geographic* 25(December 1914): 579, 584, with photographs on pp. 574, 575; and (for Puigcorda, Spain) in *National Geographic* 33(April 1918): 293, with a photograph on p. 298.

7. Photographs of native handicrafted rope bridges appear in the *National Geographic* as follows. 19(April 1908): 233, woven willow footbridge on the road to Cuzco, Peru, consisting of a main cable and two railing ropes; 21(February 1910): 138, bridge of liana cane and saplings, some 125 feet in span; p. 140, single-rope bridge of roughly twisted cane; p. 144, bridge of cane and lianas in Upper Burma; p. 150, a single-rope bridge fully 300 feet in span; 40(November 1921): 521, two bridges in Himalayan India of birch-twig ropes spread apart by V-shaped wooden cross-pieces; 42(October 1922): 422, a frail-looking bridge in the hinterland of Liberia, with a multitude of suspending ropes fanning down from tree branches above the narrow V-shaped walkway; 144(December 1973): 782–85, four color photographs of a newly built bridge across a deep gorge high in the Peruvean Andes. The 100-foot span involves six main cables of coarsely braided straw. This handicrafted bridge is replaced anew every year, as it has been for centuries, by the cooperative efforts of local farmers. See also Moles, *Histoire des charpentiers,* p. 182, fig. 221, a long-span three-cable bridge in French Equatorial Africa.

8. An on-the-spot account of one of the single-rope suspension bridges over the Salwin River, including the ordeal of crossing it, is found in George Forrest, "The Land of the Cross-bow" (1910), p. 140.

9. One of the most complete, circumstantial, and well-documented accounts of thatching, including the materials employed as well as the tools and methods used, is found in Innocent, *English Building Construction,* chap. 13, "Thatching," pp. 188–222. P. 203 fig. 58 shows thatch held down by closely set crossed ropes at Kirk Maughold, Isle of Man. Other photographs of stone-weighted or other forms of tie-downs appear in: *National Geographic* 25(December 1915): 552 (East Coast of Ireland); 36(July 1919): 38, 39 (Korea); 42(October 1922): 445 (Zulu huts, South Africa); and in *Travel* 51(May 1928): 17 (Ireland, of grass rope, good for 2 years); 51(September 1928): 12 (closeup view of Zulu hut); 58(December 1931): 30(Africa, grass rope in great circles). And note that, especially in Normandy, irises were customarily planted along the ridge of thatched roofs. Their ensiform leaves made a decorative crest in season and their intertwining roots capped and held the thatch securely in place where it was most vulnerable to weathering and dislocation.

10. Illustrations of all the common varieties of rope knots are today displayed and identified universally in publications such as dictionaries, seamanship manuals, and Boy Scout handbooks. One of the earliest European publications to delineate knots with precision and clarity was Diderot et d'Alembert, *La Grande encyclopedie.* 1751–80. More than a century later A. R. Emy, *Traite de l'art de la charpenterie* (1878) carried a plate illustrating a large number of knot types, which is reproduced at reduced scale in Moles, p. 145 fig. 153, "Noeud utilsés en charpenterie." Zabaglia, *Castelli:* pl. 2, illustrates 22 kinds of knots as well as instances of rope lashing.

11. For an instance of rope's stationary immersion in water, see Harry A. McBride, "The Land of the Free in Africa" (1922), p. 425. He documents a river crossing constructed by natives in northern Liberia that consists of logs roped together, corduroy fashion, and floated on the water's surface.

12. For descriptions of, and references to, lashing practices in both Europe and Asia, see Fitchen, *Gothic Cathedrals,* p. 132.

13. *National Geographic* 21(November 1910): 897.

14. *National Geographic* 60(August 1931): 185.

15. Quoted from the section on "Miners Rope Making" in Hommel, pp. 5–8, with figs. 16, 17; see also the section on "Hemp Spinning Wheels," pp. 167–73 with figs. 248, 249.

16. Engravings of this stupendous operation and of other installations of heavy-duty capstans are shown in Zabaglia, pls. VI, XXXIX, XLII, XLIII, LIV. Many dramatic, highly detailed engravings that are concerned with moving and erecting the gigantic Vatican obelisk are reproduced throughout Bern Dibner, *Moving the Obelisks* (1970). Photographs of twentieth-century capstans in action appear in the *National Geographic* as follows: 28(November 1915): 396, a long-poled capstan for hauling boats onto the beach at Entretat, 15 miles north of LeHavre, France; 36(September 1919): 250, groups of stone-set capstans used to pull boats up a five-foot rise in the sixth- through thirteenth-century Grand Canal, China; 42(December 1922): 614, the interior of the wheelhouse where the hoisting rope is activated by means of a crude capstan for raising and lowering the monks who dwell in one of the convents of Meteora. For a general view of the site of one of these monasteries in Thessaly, showing the full length of the rope by which access to the 300-foot-high rock top is attained, and for a view of the rope bag, suspended at close range, with a monk being carried in it, see *National Geographic* 20(December 1910): 800, 803.

17. This dream is recalled in the tall ladders carved in stone that decorate the late-Gothic façade of Bath Abbey in western England.

18. Clarke and Engelbach, *Ancient Egyptian Masonry,* fig. 83, facing p. 87. The legend reads: "Scaling ladder fitted with wheels and kept from slipping by a hand-spike, from the fifth-dynasty tomb of Kaemhesit at Saqqara. This is the only representation of a wheel known in the Old Kingdom."

19. Early representations of ladders are found in manuscript illuminations, miniatures, mosaics, frescos, stained-glass panels, and other media. Brueghel's meticulously painted 1563 "Tower of Babel," for example, depicts ladders among many pieces of construction equipment. Various reproductions can be found in Salzman, *Building in England.* His frontispiece (c. 1450) shows two long ladders from the ground to near the ridge of church roofs that are under construction, while shorter ladders are discernable in the scaffolding surrounding two church spires; pl. IV includes two representations (c. 1250) of somewhat incongruously placed ladders; pl. X (fourteenth century) reveals a six-rung ladder; pl. XIII (fifteenth century, with oversized people) shows an interior ladder stretching through all three floors of a three-story timber-framed building; and both pl. XVII (a fourteenth-century illumination) and pl. XVIII (a 1519 drawing) include short ladders.

A considerable number of medieval examples of ladders appearing in scenes of construction are included in du Colombier, *Les Chantiers.* A sixteenth-century pen drawing depicts a long ladder set at an unconvincingly flat angle in the course of building a German monastery p. 40; a miniature of 1023 features an oversized ladder of widely spaced rungs, pl. I; a mid-fourteenth- and a thirteenth-century miniature both show ladders in use, pl. IV figs. 5, 7; a twelfth-century mosaic from Monreale Cathedral depicts a ladder being set into position against a two-story Tower of Babel, pl. V fig. 9; a fresco in the Campo Santa, Pisa (c. 1470) shows, in convincing perspective and realistic detail, a ladder giving access to two stagings of a scaffolding for another Tower of Babel, pl. IX; miniatures from the fourteenth and fifteenth centuries include ladders in use, though the perspective makes their angle seem quite unstable, pl. X figs. 17, 18; a miniature (c. 1430) shows three ladders with widely spaced rungs employed on still another Tower of Babel, pl. XII fig 20; and a miniature portrays multiple building activities, pl. XIII (reproduced as Salzman's frontispiece, see above). Other reproductions in du Colombier's plates of miniatures, frescoes, or oil paintings that depict ladders in the construction of buildings, include figs. 23 and 24 (both c. 1480), fig. 29 (late fifteenth century), fig. 37 (1478–89), fig. 39 (late fifteenth century), fig. 55 (1550), and fig. 56 (1505–6). Finally, du Colombier's fig. 43 (c. 1540) delineates in clear detail both kinds of ladder formerly used in building construction: one supported from below (with standards made from two halves of a long straight sapling) and one hung above from the ridge, its standards rectangular in section. Curiously, the lowest and highest rungs of both ladders are rectangular in section, not round.

The dates of the examples cited here make clear that, with the exception of ladders, throughout the ancient world and indeed well into medieval times construction operations and equipment were rarely recorded graphically. In any case pictorial representations of construction equipment customarily lagged far—even centuries—behind their actual use in building construction. The devices and procedures known to the builders of the time, because they served only transiently (albeit indispensably), were not considered appropriate subjects for a permanent pictorial record.

20.   Rempel, *Building with Wood,* p. 9.

21.   The etymology of the term "ladder," according to some authorities, is from a Greek word meaning "to lean." It is certainly true that the great majority of straight ladders are positioned, when in use, so as to lean against a wall or a cornice or some other offset. Today there are even prescriptions for the home handyman and painter that designate the proper angle for the tilt of a ladder.

22.   Thatcher, *Scaffolding,* pp. 90–91.

23.   A ladder of about 28 rungs appears as fig. 27, "West Walton Church from the South During Repair, 1907," in Powys, *Repair of Ancient Buildings.* A combination of two overlapping ladders in the same roof plane, one set on the ground, the other hung from the ridge, the lower one accounting for perhaps 36 or 37 rungs, is pictured in two views on pl. XXV, "Morton Church, Cheshire," in Josef Strzygowski, *Early Church Art in Northern Europe* (1928). Another instance of overlapping ladders, in this case from ridge of church roof to apex of spire, at Barnstaple, Devon, the lower ladder having some 45 or so rungs, is illustrated in Fred H. Crossley, *Timber Building in England* (1951), fig. 46, facing p. 52.

24.   See a description, accompanied by a drawing, in *Century Dictionary* (1889–95), s.v. "ladder."

25.   The military use of ladders to storm stongholds or the walls of besieged cities has been resorted to from very early times. Sometimes the ladders were single-standard units, but much more often they had two standards. In either case, scaling ladders were provided with hooks at the top that grappled a battlement or some other projection and were hard for the defenders to pry loose when weighted by the ascending, armed attackers. To circumvent the possibility of dislodgement, however, and to minimize casualties from missiles hurled down from above, a scheme was devised by which the scaling ladders were independent of the ramparts and could be positioned very rapidly. Following is a brief account: "A ladder used for the escalade of an enemy's fortress. Besides an ordinary ladder with hooks at the upper end and similar fittings, which is the common kind, scaling-ladders have been made with braces to support them at the proper angle and wheels by which the whole structure was run close to the walls. . . ." *Century Dictionary,* s.v. "scaling-ladder."

26.   Reproduced in du Colombier, p. 78, a line drawing of a fourteenth-century miniature; pl. XII fig. 20, a miniature of c. 1430.

27.   Such fixed one-standard ladders used in major construction work of the past are illustrated in Moles, p. 130, a drawing showing about 60 rungs on each of four corner legs of a huge timber gantry used to raise a gigantic column in the Champ de Mars, Rome in 1750; p. 136, drawings (from Rondelet) showing about 47 rungs on two corner legs of a massive timber gantry used in the erection of a monolithic obelisk in Rome; p. 330, a photograph showing over 61 (probably 73) rungs on each of two tall units of shear-legs used in raising a pair of laminated wooden members for a low-rise, three-hinged arch spanning a hangar in Basel, Switzerland.

28.   An illustration of this operation, reproduced from an old engraving, appears in Moles, p. 340.

29.   Similarly, building construction on land did not make use of large-scale rope meshes that are sometimes draped over the sides of ships today as means for those in the water to climb aboard.

30.   The familiar extension ladder did not come into general use until the twentieth-century. It consists of two straight ladders of equal length and parallel standards, set face to face. The standards of one ladder are fitted with two pairs of projecting strap-irons that are returned at their free ends so as to contain the standards of the other ladder and permit it to slide up and down along the former's standards. A rope attached to the lowest rung of this movable (upper) unit passes between the two ladders and feeds through a pulley hung to the top rung of the ground-based (lower) unit, and thence, behind both ladders, to the ground. By pulling on the rope the upper ladder is raised, and a pair of pivoted, retractable mechanisms attached to the lowest rung of this upper ladder hook over one or another of the ground-based ladder's rungs, depending upon how much extension is required.

31.   Probably the earliest representations of sectional or interlocking ladders are those by Zabaglia, an illiterate but extraordinarily resourceful and inventive mechanic who nonetheless produced a sumptuous volume, first published in 1743, of large engraved plates that delineate various building devices and techniques. See especially pl. 9.

32.   An example of six such units, each only five rungs in length, as used by a surveying party in the U.S. Southwest is shown in the photograph facing p. 288 in *National Geographic,* 8 (October 1897).

33.   "One of the largest Cenotes is found in the village of Bolonchen. . . . To make the descent into this cavern possible, the Indians constructed a very crude ladder by tying the trunks of big trees together, utilizing their whole length, to make this ingenious structure as wide as possible. It is arranged in such a manner, that only half is used for the descent and the other for the ascent of the 'aquadores' (water carriers). The extremes of the trunks rest on the rocks or are sustained by big rafters. From the entrance of the Cenote down to the nine springs is a distance of 1400 feet, although the perpendicular depth is said to be only 500 feet. . . ." Natalie von Schenck. "The 'Cenotes' of Yucatan" (1906), p. 91.

34.   For example, see H. A. Lorentz, "An Expedition to the Snow Mountains of New Guinea" (1911), pp. 337–59. A photograph (p. 357) shows a Papuan house near the North (Lorentz) River whose walls and roof, supported on numerous quite closely set poles, are thatched at third-story height. The access ladders are very long, straight, strongly sloping saplings, small in diameter and with very little taper, regularly notched for steps.

35.   Three notched logs used as ladders are shown in a photograph entitled "A Tibetan House in the Course of Construction" in Shelton, "Life among the People of

Eastern Tibet," p. 307. The legend reads "Poles are used to hold together parallel boards, between which mud is puddled. Then the forms are raised and another layer of closely packed earth added. Similar methods are used from Shanghai to Russian Turkestan."

36.   Dr. Karl W. Kumm, "From Hausaland to Egypt" (1911), p. 232.

37.   See Casper Hunt, "The Empire of Darkness" (1929), p. 39. Two photographs show "A Beehive Village of the Massas," with a large number of different-sized units, and "Building a New Home," with two men daubing mud by hand at head-height.

38.   A somewhat analogous situation is pictured in Shelton, p. 306. The legend reads "Tibetan houses in the robber-infested bad lands: these houses are built primarily for protection. With the exception of the main entrance, there is no opening until the third story is reached. This style of architecture greatly simplifies the problem of defense against marauders." With the main entrance securely blocked, the interior can be entered only by ladders reaching to the roofs or to the upper windows. As for the flat roofs, much used for various activities, the author states that they consist "of mud, beaten onto a carpet of small poles supported by larger poles. . . . Along the edges raised rims are built. The beating or puddling makes the mud surfaces practically impervious to water. Women carry kegs of salt water on their backs to the roofs, *climbing up notched poles that serve as ladders.* The water is poured on the flat surfaces and evaporated by the wind." (italics added.) Shelton, p. 305.

Chapter 9

1.   Personal correspondence with JTT, letter of 28 February 1982.

2.   Partington, *Builder's Guide,* pp. 529–30. Other early-nineteenth-century accounts and speculations include Phineas Rainey, "On the Dry Rot" (1838), pp. 169–79 and John T. Plummer, "Brief Strictures on Rainey's Article" (1842), pp. 197–200. Both writers address themselves to such matters as where the sap goes, summer and winter; the nature of the alburnum and its amount relative to the darker heartwood; specific instances of resistence to rot; and the proper season for felling trees.

3.   G. Gibbs, "Observations on the Dry Rot" (1820); pp. 115–16.

4.   For an account of native American species of trees that is comprehensive, knowledgeable, and historically oriented to their properties (so well understood and exploited at the time) and their characteristics (so appropriately and effectively put to use), see Charles van Ravenswaay, "America's Age of Wood" (1970), pp. 49–66.

5.   It is interesting to note that in the Near East carpenters work as much as possible in a seated position. This practice and its consequences are discussed in the following accounts, the first of which states that "the Turks work *sitting* at every art or handicraft where there is a possibility of it; carpenters, for instance, perform the greatest part of their labour sitting. . . ." Eton, *Turkish Empire,* p. 223; John M. Hartman, "Syenite Quarries at Assouan" (1893), p. 14754; for a more general and wide-ranging account of man's versatile use of his foot see Dr. F. Regnault, "The Prehensile Function of the Foot" (1893), pp. 14868–69.

6.   See William F. Fox, "History of the Lumber Industry in the State of New York" (1901), pp. 237–305. The article includes a double-page map of "First Settlements in the State of New York" and a list of the first sawmills and their builders, by place and date, throughout the state. "It was claimed by many of the old-time lumbermen that rafted lumber was better than any other, because the soaking of the boards diluted the sap and resinous matter so that when piled again in the yards it would season quicker." Fox, p. 254.

7.   J. C. Williams, "Effect of the Time of Cutting Timber" (1910), p. 121.

8.   Large assortments of traditional timber-working tools are illustrated in Mercer, *Ancient Carpenters' Tools;* Hommel, *China at Work;* and Moles, *Histoire des charpentiers.*

9.   For considerations involving the timbers, jointing, and construction of medieval crucks, see Charles, *Medieval Cruck-Building,* pp. 16–24; Innocent, *English Building Construction,* chap. 4, "Curved Tree Principals," pp. 23–61; and Crossley, *Timber Building,* pp. 109–12, figs. 117–26.

10.   Photographs of pit sawing, worldwide, are found in the following issues of *National Geographic:* 15(March 1904): 130–32, two photographs of pit sawing in Manchuria; 16(April 1905): 173, pit sawing logs some eighteen feet long, Philippines; 36(November 1919): 415, small logs set horizontally, Armenia; 39(February 1921): 193, two-man pit sawing, Constantinople; 40(July 1921): 58, a battery of Japanese sawyers; 40(October 1921): 368, "A dozen boards ten feet long, a foot wide, and not more than half an inch thick will be produced from the log pictured," subtropical zone of the central Andes; 41(January 1922): 107, two fourteen-inch-square logs being cut into very thin boards, China; in *Travel* 54(1929): 13, rip sawing in Kabul, tilt-up position; and in *Camera* 34 (September 1955): cover, full-page, color photograph of three pit sawyers (one above, two below) in a Turkish lumber yard working on a long tilt-up log some fourteen inches in diameter.

11.   Numerous log buildings are figured in R. M. Gabe, *Karel'skoe derevyannoe Zodchestro* (Wooden architecture of Karelia) (1941). See particularly chap. 6, "Roof Construction" and chap. 15, "Methods of Raising New Buildings."

12.   The copiously illustrated volume by Gerda Boëthius, *Den Nordiska Timmerbyggnadskonsten* (1927) shows a large number of these ingenious notchings in clear detail, both as drawings and as photographs of actual buildings.

13.   Moritz Busch, "A Visit to the Backwoodsmen of East Kentucky," chap. 6 of *Travels between the Hudson and the Mississippi 1851–1852* (1971), p. 194.

14.   For details and comment on this scheme of horizontally laid boards, see John Fitchen, "A House of Laminated Walls" (1957), pp. 27–28.

15.   This expertise even included a number of instances in which the forms of complicated *stone* vaults, with all their curvatures of ribs and webs, were exactly duplicated in *wood*. Although it was a distinctly English phenomenon, one of the first to draw attention to this anomalous practice was Jean Hippolyte Raymond Bordeaux, "Des voûtes en bois et leur réparation" (1862), 35–70.

16.   A large selection of this bewildering variety of pegged timber joints, along with many clear drawings of the ensemble structural skeleton of timberwork buildings, can be seen in Hewett, *Development of Carpentry.* Hewett presents in chronological sequence explicit, detailed drawings—many of them exploded views—of different categories of joints. These categories include scarfs, tying joints, floor-joist joints, corner joints, and decorative treatment. Moreover, Hewett recognizes that different categories reached their peak development at different times.

17.   See Charles.

18.   A considerable number of visually impressive timber roofs (even involving two tiers of hammer beams, in two instances) are presented in measured drawings as well as in ensemble perspectives among the clear and informing drawings of Brandon and Brandon, *Open Timber Roofs.* Hammer beam and other notable types of timber roofs are also covered in Reginald A. Cordingley, "British Historical Roof-Types and Their Members" (1961), pp. 73–117; F. E. Howard, "On the Construction of Mediaeval Roofs" (1914), pp. 293–352; and J. T. Smith "Medieval Roofs: A Classification"

(1960), pp. 111–49. In the most remarkable hammer beam roof—at Westminster Hall in London, dating from 1399—a timber arch is incorporated into the design and the clear span is an unprecedented 67'-6". See F. Baines, *Westminster Hall* (1914).

19. There are no written records of the methods used in ancient times to cut out mortices and shape tenons so that they would fit snugly together. But the early nineteenth century saw the publication of carpenters' manuals that described and illustrated the jointing procedures in all-wood timber framing. Their practical usefulness resulted from the completeness and accuracy of their instructions, which gave in minutest detail every step in the process of shaping joints. The popularity of these manuals is indicated by the reprints and new editions that continued to appear over many decades (in some cases well into the twentieth century). Two of these manuals are Thomas Tredgold, *Carpentry and Joinery* (1892), which was originally published in 1820, but republished in many reprints and new editions that carried somewhat different titles and rewritings with later collaborators, and Edward Shaw, *Civil Architecture*, 6th ed. (1852). For highly detailed, circumstantial instructions on the scribe rule and the square rule methods of timber framing, see p. 116.

20. For an account of the numbering and test-assemblage procedures for New World Dutch barns of the eighteenth century, see Fitchen, *Barn*, pp. 35–37.

21. For many drawings of assumed tilt-up operations in the raising, positioning and linking together of timber bents in medieval times, see Hewett, p. 169.

22. See Fitchen, *Gothic Cathedrals*, pp. 28, 192, 206 n. 67, 227 n. 194, 292 appendix L; Fitchen, "Upper Flying Buttress" (1955), pp. 69–90.

23. Price, *Church of Salisbury*, pp. 39–41.

Chapter 10

1. Eugène Emmanuel Viollet-le-Duc, *Discourses on Architecture*, vol. 1 (1959), p. 49.

2. Except for some blocks "too big for carts," the great majority of building stones in the Middle Ages were transported overland either by wheeled carts or by packsaddles slung on horses; those conveyed by water were transported by ship or barge. Salzman, *Building in England,* p. 119, documents the fact that "a large part of the cost of masonry lay in the expense of carriage of the stone." In order to minimize this expense as much as possible, "large parts of the stonework were actually prepared in the Caen quarries (patterns being sent over) and, as custom was, practically finished ready to be put into the building before it was sent to England" for the rebuilding of Canterbury Cathedral after the devastating fire of 1174. Frances B. Andrews, *Mediaeval Builder and His Methods* (1925), p. 21.

3. "In the granite temple the same method of quarrying and transporting oversized blocks was followed, but there the wall was dressed and hence each stone at the corners of the chambers turns a little way round the adjacent walls, so that the corner is cut out of solid stone all the way up." W. M. Flinders Petrie, *Ten Years' Digging in Egypt, 1881–1891* (n.d.), p. 17.

4. "The unworked surfaces with a few exceptions were confined to the platform and columns and walls, these being the portions most liable to injury during the process of erection. On the completion of the temple the fluting of the columns was worked from top to bottom with that delicate entasis which gives such beauty to its outline; the faces of the walls were dressed and rubbed so that the bevels at the joints, and almost the joints themselves, disappeared; and the treads and risers of the steps were worked down to their smooth surfaces." William J. Anderson, R. Phené Spiers, and William Bell Dinsmoor, *Architecture of Ancient Greece* (1927), p. 124.

5.   "The practice of the Egyptians of laying their blocks with the minimum number of dressed sides had the result of leaving the face of a building, when the blocks had all been laid, quite rough. . . . The great unfinished pylon at Karnak furnishes several interesting hints on the manner in which the dressing was to have been carried out." Clarke and Engelbach, *Ancient Egyptian Masonry,* chap. 18, "Facing, Sculpturing, and Painting," pp. 192, 195. There follows numerous detailed illustrations accompanied by technical commentary on the practices followed by the Egyptians in establishing so-called facing surfaces and draft lines as aids in both setting the stones and dressing off their excess stock.

6.   C. H. Smith, "Lithology; or, Observations on Stone used for Building" (1842), p. 139. See plate designated "Map of that part of the Island of Portland in which the principal Stone Quarries are situated" and plate entitled "Portland Quarries: Sections of Strata in Different Parts of the Island."

7.   On page 121 of Anderson, Spiers, Dinsmoor, the authors list a number of Greek buildings "which for various reasons have never been terminated. . . . In all these temples the columns are still unfluted, and the treads and risers of the steps retain their rough unworked surfaces, being drafted at their junction so as to obtain fine joints; often they retain also the ancones or ears, projecting bosses by which the stones were lowered into their positions. . . ."

8.   For documentation (including contemporaneous drawings) of these ancient apparatuses for raising blocks, see A. G. Drachman, *Mechanical Technology of Greek and Roman Antiquity* (1963); A. K. Orlandos, *Matériaux de construction et la technique architecturale des anciens Grecs* (1966–68); and "Taille et mis en place," chap. 2 of Roland Martin, *Manuel d'architecture grecque* (1965), pp. 201–19.

9.   These handling bosses are illustrated in Clarke and Engelbach, fig. 81 facing p. 86, and figs. 99, 100 facing p. 99, along with commentary, p. 86.

10.   A clear, close up photograph of part of the Ollantayambo wall appears in H. W. Janson, *History of Art* (n.d. [ca. 1962]), p. 552, fig. 849.

11.   See Fitchen, *Gothic Cathedrals,* pp. 9–13; p. 10, fig. 2; p. 12, fig. 3.

12.   The complete specification from which this quotation is excerpted appears in Bell, *Oblique or Skew Arches,* pp. 98–104.

13.   Large elevation and section drawings to scale of the Pont du Gard, showing the position of these corbels, appear in the *Architectural Association Sketch Book* (1913), pl. 53. The drawings err only in designating the top surface of the inward-projecting portion of the voussoirs at the angle of friction as radial instead of horizontal.

14.   See the photograph in Dudley Stuart Corlett, "The Sacred Cities of Ceylon" (1922), p. 153.

15.   See chapter fourteen, "Building Cheop's pyramid."

16.   Anderson, Spiers, and Dinsmoor, p. 50, p. 49, fig. 11, plan and section drawings.

Chapter 11

1.   Personal correspondence with JTT, letter of February 1983.

2.   See William Brindley, "Marble: Its Uses as suggested by the Past" (1887), pp. 45–55, with a table (p. 56) of "The Principal Quarries Worked in the Time of the

Romans" and a double-page "Map of the Roman Empire, Showing the Sites of the Principal Quarries in Use"; also the same author's "Ancient Quarries in Egypt, with an Account of a Recent Journey across the Eastern Desert" (1887–8) pp. 5–26, with six plates.

3.   A much less well known instance of great stones (and huge timbers) being dragged from afar and up steep mountainsides is a site half a world away from Stonehenge, described in circumstantial detail in William C. Borgera, "Nias—The Island of Gold" (1936), pp. 23–25, 48.

4.   For information on the importation of Baltic timber, see Innocent, *English Building Construction,* pp. 102–5.

5.   "The country around is flat, with dense jungle, abounding with rattans. . . . It is in this locality that the agents of the various traders of Claudetown, both Chinese and Malay, congregate to barter with the tribes from the interior. Many of these traders build houses upon rafts, which are moored along the banks of the river at every landing stage. In these floating houses they live for months, and even years, until the raft is stacked with produce. They then float down river to Claudetown, sometimes bringing as many as 250,000 canes on one raft. . . ." Charles Hose, "A Journey up the Baram River to Mount Dulit and the Highlands of Borneo" (1893), p. 195.

6.   Burns, "Building of a Chinese Railway," p. 385; see photographs, "Chinese method of multiple levers in carrying heavy loads," p. 400.

7.   See Alice C. Fletcher, "An Average Day in Camp among the Sioux" (1885), pp. 285–87, for a detailed account of breaking camp and moving on, then setting up camp at a new location. All the household effects—carefully folded tepee cloths, gala dress, panniers filled with meat and corn, and the young children and puppies—were transported travois-fashion; that is, on a skin or blanket fastened between long poles that trail behind, a pair on each side of a pony.

8.   "The porter's knot is a device roughly made like a huge horsecollar, and fitted down over the head and shoulders and upper back of a man, to enable him to do his very best in carrying. . . . In addition to distributing the load over several parts of the body, they are padded so as to enable the carrier to take on hard boxes, furniture, and such things without bruising his flesh." Otis T. Mason, *Origins of Invention* (1895), p. 346.

9.   Even where travel by inland waterways was the customary means of transportation, portages were often inevitable, and the human carrier had either to surmount falls and impassable rapids or to get from one river system to another. Thus, on the Columbia River in the nineteenth century, the intrepid voyageurs of the Hudson's Bay Company had to turn from rowing their many-oared boats to unloading them and carrying both the cargoes and the boats themselves on their own backs, sometimes a matter of miles. With respect to the cargoes: "The load is secured on the back of the voyageur by a band which passes round the forehead and under and over the bale; he squats down, adjusts the load, and rises with the 90 lbs on his back; another places 90 lbs more on the top, and off he trots, half bent, to the end of the portage. . . ." Charles Wilkes, *Narrative of the U.S. Exploring Expedition,* vol. 4 (1845), p. 380.

10.   A comprehensive account of this traffic, detailing the astonishing variety of the loads transported by coolies, is found in the closely observed and remarkably thorough article by George D. Hubbard, "The Geographical Setting of Chengtu" (1923), pp. 109–32.

11.   "A very curious account is given of the trade with China in coffin planks over the Burmese frontier. The tree furnishing the planks is a juniper, much prized for its scented wood, which grows in the mountain valleys, between 6000 and 8000 feet

above sea-level. The planks are said to weigh 100 to 140 pounds when freshly cut, and 60 to 80 pounds when dry. They are cut by Chinese carpenters, who come over from Yunnan for the purpose, and floated down-stream in groups of ten, to be stocked for the winter. In early summer they are carried over the pass by coolies, each man taking one plank, which seems an extraordinary feat of endurance, as the journey lasts about ten days. . . ." From a review of *In Furthest Burma* by F. Kingdon Ward, in *Scottish Geographical Magazine* (November 1921), pp. 277–78. A full-page photograph of a similar operation appears in Ernest M. Wilson, "The Kingdom of Flowers—China" (1911), p. 1021. The caption reads: "A log of *Tsuga yunnanensis Mast* (a species of hemlock), 18'-6" long by 9" by 7" thick, carried by one man over mountains."

12. Photographs of these excessively laden porters appear in Richard L. Burdsall, Arthur B. Emmons 3d, Terris Moore, and Jack Theodore Young, *Men Against the Clouds* (1935), fig. 8 facing p. 162; and in Wilson, "The Kingdom of Flowers," p. 1028, where the caption reads "One man's load weighs 317 pounds averdupois, the other's 298. . . . Men carry this tea for hundreds of miles, accomplishing about six miles per day over vile roads." See p. 1029 for another picture and p. 1035 for text.

13. Mason, p. 82 (translated from A. L. Lewis, *Matériaux pour l'histoire de l'homme,* Toulouse, 2d ser. 7(1876): 185). This time-honored scheme of conveyance by complexes of carrying poles was used in Europe, too, as illustrated in Zabaglia, *Castelli e ponti* pl. XVII, which depicts scenes involving four, six, eight, sixteen, and thirty-two carriers.

14. On page 346 in Otis T. Mason, *The Origins of Invention,* 1895, "In some places, where vehicles are used, the bridges are so narrow that the mules are unhitched and led singly, while the carts are carried over on men's shoulders." Mason, p. 346 (quoted from Minister Denby, *Journal of the Society of Arts,* London, 40(1892): 166).

15. Burdsall, Emmons, Moore, and Young, pt. 1, pp. 58, 50, 54.

16. For a detailed description of the Eskimo sled, the thongs and simple harness of the dog teams—arranged so as to prevent snarling of the lines (especially when the dogs stop from time to time even when under full headway to engage in a general fight)—and the amount of load carried on the sleds, see H. M. Bannister, "The Esquimaux Dog" (1869), p. 526.

17. "So difficult is the task of removing the timber that five to ten years are required from the time a tree is felled until it is drifted downstream to Bangkok. . . ." Truman Bailey, "Trained Tuskers of the Teak Forests" (1942), p. 230.

18. See translation of part of a letter from E. F. de Furnfijelm, one of the officers of a scientific expedition sent out by the Emperor of Russia to the northern part of Finnland and Lapland, dated Kurfamo, Kappmark, 67° North Latitude, 28 July 1850.

19. For an overall account of these developments, including contemporary illustrations along the way, see E. M. Jope, "Vehicles and Harness," chap. 15 of pt. 4, "Transport" in C. Singer, E. J. Holmyard, A. R. Hall, and T. I. Williams, *A History of Technology,* vol. 2 (1956), pp. 537–62.

20. Zabaglia's engraved plate XV illustrates eighteenth-century views of loading big blocks on two-wheeled carts fitted with windlasses.

21. See Martin, *Manuel d'architecture grecque,* p. 171 fig. 68, "Transport de blocs (d'après Hittorf. Sicile)" and fig. 69, "Système de transport de blocs à Ephèse (d'après Vitruve)." The two drawings (from earlier publications) illustrate the way in which the Greeks rolled large lintels from quarry to building site by constructing timberwork wheels that encased and clasped the rectangular marble blocks at or near either end, the blocks themselves serving as fixed axles.

22. A great deal of information about early roads, culled from manuscripts and other obscure sources, is given in Parsons, "Roads and Road Transport," pt. 4, chap. 19 of *Engineering in the Renaissance,* pp. 290–319. Much of Parson's coverage deals with legal, jurisdictional, and financial matters in connection with the establishment, maintenance, ownership, and use of roads, chiefly in France. Most pertinent to this study are his quotations from and comments on the remarkably perceptive treatise by Guido Baldo Toglietta on the laying and care of pavements (pp. 292–93). Toglietta's manuscript dates from 1585–90 but was not published until 1878. See also R. J. Forbes, *History of Ancient Roads and Their Construction* (1934).

23. A considerable body of information about roads and bridges in eighteenth- and early-nineteenth-century England and, particularly, in America subsequent to the Revolutionary War and about the early establishment of canals prior to the advent of railroads, is found in Dirk J. Struik, "Turnpikes and Towpaths," chap. 4 of *Yankee Science in the Making,* rev. ed. (1968), pp. 135–74.

24. "Travel and Traffic in China" (1903), p. 31.

25. Hubbard, p. 131.

26. For a succinct but inclusive statement about the installation of access roads to and within a *modern* construction site see Clarke A. Torell, "Development of the Project Site to Support the Construction Activity," in chap. 12 of *Electric Power Generation Facilities* (1980), p. 467.

27. A specific and detailed circumstantial account of rafting in connection with transporting the timber of the forest to saw mills and to market on the eastern seaboard of America is found in Fox, "Lumber Industry in the State of New York," p. 251, "Rafting on the Upper Hudson" (excerpted from Mrs. Anne Grant, *Memoirs of an American Lady. . . . 1876);* pp. 252–53, "Construction of Rafts" (length, thickness, and detailed description of composition, including security of consolidation and means of steering); pp. 253–55, "Rafting on the Allegany"; pp. 255–56, "Log Driving"; pp. 258–60, "Log Drivers and their Work"; and pp. 274–75.

28. Henry Kreuger, "The Tote Road and the Pung" (1970), pp. 29–31.

29. See Martin, p. 167, fig. 66, "Système de descente des blocs (Pentelique)." The drawing shows a large, squared block of marble on a sledge being eased down a stone-paved trackway, where the descent is controlled by ropes snubbed around stone bollards, right and left, which are set at intervals in square pits at either side of the track.

30. See Wright, "Fortress of Masada," p. 370.

31. See the descriptive account, accompanied by a drawing of one of the hauling scenes, in Theophilus G. Pinches, "Assur and Ninevah" (1913), p. 40. The text reads in part: "The sculptures from Sennacherib's palace exist to confirm his records. We see the winged bulls, of colossal size, lying down in the sledges on which they were transferred from the quarries to the site of the palace, sometimes placed uprightly, and carefully propped up to prevent damage by breakage. The sledges . . . are being dragged and forced forward by means of enormous levers upon rollers by armies of workmen. . . . In the background, behind the slaves toiling at the great cables and the levers, we see the soldiers of the guard. . . . The ropes attached to the boat-like sledges or rafts are excessively long, and even in the incomplete state of the slabs as Layard saw them, 36 men to each may be counted. . . ."

32. Much lighter sledges are in use to this day in Kurdistan, Turkey, the Madeira Islands, and elsewhere. In Madeira they are drawn over the steep cobblestone streets, lanes, and mountainous byways without benefit of rollers. See illustrations in David Fairchild, "Madeira on the Way to Italy" (1907), pp. 753–55, 765; other information about wheelless vehicles is found in Gösta Berg, *Sledges and Wheel-less Vehicles* (1935).

33.　See Choisy, *L'Art de bâtir chez les Égyptiens*. A succinct description of this prehistoric method of maneuvering large blocks overland is accompanied by nine sketches on p. 76. Specifically in regard to Egyptian obelisks, the procedure is diagrammed in four progress views on p. 123 and in section on p. 124. Moreover, in the same author's *Histoire de l'architecture,* vol. 1 (1929), the prehistoric method is similarly diagrammed on pp. 4–5; that of obelisks is illustrated in six sketches on p. 36. These drawings are all plausible in principle but contain various errors of delineation: the apex-upward orientation of the recumbent obelisk; the ineffectively wide interval between the fulcrums and the lower edges of the monolith; the impossible verticality of the sides and upper end of its built-up supporting mound; and the unlikelihood of its riding on a great timber sledge of *single-length* runners.

34.　See particularly William Curtis Farabee, "A Pioneer in Amazonia" (1917), p. 72.

35.　For a vividly described account of the exhausting *ascent* of hazardous rapids in native dugouts, as negotiated with paddles, poles, and ropes, see Hose, p. 195.

36.　For some of the hazards, delays, and incredible hardships of land travel in wilderness situations, see (for the American Northwest) Wilkes, "Puget Sound and Okonagan," chap. 4 of vol. 2, p. 420; and (for the western Sahara) Henri Lhote, *The Search for the Tassili Frescoes* (1959), pp. 36–38.

37.　There is, to be sure, a well-known bas-relief from Queen Hapshetsut's eighteenth-dynasty temple at Deir-el-Bahari across the river from Thebes (reproduced in Clarke and Engelbach, *Ancient Egyptian Masonry*, p. 37 fig. 39). The scene ostensibly represents the shipment by water of two obelisks. Shown in great detail is a typical Egyptian sailing vessel (but one that is excessively large in comparison to its escorting craft) on whose deck, far above the waterline, are two great obelisks disposed in tandem. Without a doubt, obelisks were never transported in this way. For, perched high on deck as here indicated instead of in the vessel's hold below the waterline, they would have immediately capsized the vessel, once afloat. Moreover, such huge and heavy monoliths could never have been maneuvered on deck in the first place. Like the reliefs generally in Egyptian tombs and temples, such a representation should not be taken too literally. For example, mural representations of Egyptian watercraft (whether of skiffs from which a pharaoh is shown hunting waterfowl in a marsh or merchant ships plying the River Nile laden with local goods or foreign tribute) are invariably depicted in side view showing their complete hulls, as though they were floating entirely *above* the surface of the water instead of partially immersed by their own weight and that of their cargo. The purpose of all such permanent scenes in stone was never to give precise photographic information but rather to express an idea. In the case of the queen's obelisks there was no unequivocal pictorial language available to the Egyptian artists by which they could convincingly represent an obelisk out of sight in the hold of a ship or suspended under water from pontoons. So, to convey unmistakably the idea of shipment by water, the artists resorted to familiar images and concepts—perching the obelisks on deck, conspicuously in sight (as though presented to view on a display counter in a bazaar) but with everything greatly exaggerated to suggest the enormously oversized nature of the cargo.

38.　For a modern (and much less exceptional) instance of conveying bulky non-bouyant loads by suspending them in a submerged state, see Thomas Barbour, "Notes on Burma" (1909), pp. 841–66. The lower photograph on p. 857 identifies an Irrawaddy River scene in which "teak logs are so heavy that they will sink in water. For this reason they are rafted slung under bundles of bamboo."

39. A prehistoric dugout, fashioned from a solid oak tree and measuring 48' long, 4'4" wide, 2'9" deep was found in Brigg, Lincolnshire in 1886 (*Records of the Past* 8(1909): 317). Harry Lake, "Jahore" (1894), p. 285, reports that dugouts (native term, *jalors*) used on all rivers of the interior "are constructed from a single tree cut longitudinally, hollowed out by fire, and finished with the 'bliong' or Malay adse." Some of these canoes will carry 20 to 30 men. Rev. W. Holman Bentley, *Pioneering on the Congo*, vol. I (1900), p. 392, describes how dugouts are hollowed out (at the site where the trees are felled) and then dragged over wooden rollers to the river (sometimes an hour or two distant), as well as the ways in which these canoes deteriorate. For a specifically detailed account of the care with which exceedingly thin dugouts were prepared, maintained in their proper shape, and repaired when accidentally punctured or cracked, see Wilkes, vol. 4, p. 300, with a woodcut showing side view of "Canoe of Oregon Indians."

40. A thorough description of an Amazonian woodskin is found in Farabee, p. 79. This account includes the stripping and careful removal from a standing tree of a section of heavy bark some 20 feet long, all in one undamaged piece; the cutting of grooves through the outer bark around the sides but not across the tough inner bark of the bottom; the building of a fire inside to soften the bark at the grooves so that, with the ends lifted up until they are level with the sides, the pliable bark may be folded inside to make a waterproof joint; the tying of long poles along the sides from end to end, to serve as stays and to hold up the ends, and of short poles crosswise, to prevent the sides from folding in, with the addition of heavy bark bent across the bottom to prevent it from folding up in the middle; the handling of the cranky, heavy but fragile craft when in use; and the immersion of the woodskin to prevent it from drying out and cracking in the sun, whenever not in use. A brief but comparably informing account of the much lighter and more easily maneuverable birchbark canoe of the Algonquian and Iroquoian Indians of North America appears in John W. Harshberger, "Phytogeographic Influences in the Arts and Industries of the American Aborigines" (January 1904–October 1906), p. 140.

41. In the past, handicrafted boats whose hulls were built up of boards varied considerably in both size and purpose as well as in the techniques of assemblage and the apparatus for propulsion. The Greek historian Herodotus (II, 6) comments on those of ancient Egypt (see Clarke and Englebach, p. 36). For a closely observed and specifically detailed account of Samoan outrigger canoes, see Wilkes, vol. 2, p. 143. Two drawings accompany the text: one showing the side view of a Samoan canoe with outrigger, paddle, mast, fore and aft decks, and hull of irregular but closely fitted planks; the other, a detail section through the planking, showing how the planks are fashioned and secured to each other; for mid-eighteenth-century Hudson River "Battoes," see Adolph B. Benson, *The America of 1750* (1937).

42. Scenes of this means of conveyance are recorded in the ancient Assyrian sculptures at Nineveh. For the makeup, size, loads carried, superstructure (if present), and means of steering in the case of sizable rafts of this sort in underdeveloped countries in modern times, see F. R. Maunsell, "Kurdistan" (1894), pp. 88–89. Other accounts of rafts involving inflated bullock-, goat-, or sheepskins deal with this practice in various parts of China, in India, in central Asia as well as in the Tigris-Euphrates region.

43. For an account of the composition of a 50-by-18-foot log raft and the difficulties of navigating it in both turbulent and shoal waters on the upper Hwang Ho River in China's Kansu Province, see St. George R. Littledale, "A Journey Across Central Asia" (January–June 1894), pp. 467–68.

44. Review of *A Naturalist in Madagascar*, by James Sibree, *Scottish Geographical Magazine* 32(1916): 255.

45.　　The remains of one of the tiny man-made harbors used by the ancient Greeks are shown on a detailed map and in photographs in Joseph T. Clarke, Francis H. Bacon, and Robert Koldewey, *Investigations at Assos* (1902–21), p. 13, p. 15, figs. 1, 2; p. 19, fig. 2; p. 70, figs. 1, 2. We have a rather meager account of Cyzicus, a Greek port city that flourished in ancient times on the southern coast of the Sea of Marmara. Situated at the nexus of trade between East and West, at the European end of the long-established overland caravan traffic route from the Far East, its geographical position was excellent for commerce. For many years its roadstead—established in the strait separating the Island of Cyzicus from the Asiatic mainland—enjoyed wealth and power. But eventually it lost business and withered, superseded by Byzantium on the sea's opposite shore. Its demise, in spite of extensive harbor works, was nature-imposed: prevailing winds produced a gradual silting up of the roadstead and there was no adjacent river to wash the sand and silt back into the sea.

46.　　Probably the most extreme case of this ancient practice of beaching the relatively small ships of the time—hauling them up on shore, particularly in the wintertime, either in lieu of harbors or for repairs—was the Greek fleet throughout the ten-year siege of Troy.

47.　　See F. Adler, "Der Pharos von Alexandria" (1901), pp. 169–98. Atlas.

48.　　See L. G. Landels, "Ships and Sea Transport," chap. 6 of *Engineering in the Ancient World* (1978) pp. 133–69. A considerable amount of specific information is given about Greek and Roman ships: their construction (including protection of the hulls from marine borers); means of propulsion (generally, banks of oars for naval vessels, sails for merchantmen); speeds of motion and length of voyages; types of cargo and how stowed; size of ships and cargo capacity; loading; maintenance practices; wharfs and harbor regulations. As for Egyptian sailing vessels, information is given about hull construction, sails and rigging, steering devices, etc., but nothing whatsoever about harbor and docking facilities, in Clarke and Engelback, chap. 4, "Transport Barges," pages 34–35, with 17 illustrations.

49.　　Talbot Hamlin, *Architecture through the Ages* (1944), p. 161.

50.　　*Records of the Past* 7(1908): 215.

51.　　See Edgar L. Hewett, "Prehistoric Irrigation in the Navaho Desert" (1905): 322–29. This account presents the problems—and the ways in which they were worked out—in a specific region, illuminating conditions encountered elsewhere in the world and demonstrating some of the features that were common to and had to be dealt with in *both* irrigation and transportation waterways.

52.　　Charles K. Edmunds, "Shantung—China's Holy Land" (1919), pp. 249–51. A comprehensive and detailed account of irrigation canals used for commerce in an extensive area of western China—including types of boats utilized and the remarkable variety of cargoes they carry—is given throughout Hubbard.

53.　　To date, the most thoroughly researched and comprehensively documented coverage of early river and canal engineering in the Western world is found in Parsons, pt. 5, chap. 22–27, pp. 323–477 and appendix C (4), pp. 647–51. Chapter 23 (pp. 372–398, including figs. 132–143) deals specifically with Canal Locks; 20 and 21 treat river engineering on the Arno; chap 25 is on French river and small canal engineering; chap. 27 addresses French river transport; chaps. 22 and 24, on canal engineering at Milan, cover individual canals, including the Naviglio Grande, the Bereguardo Canal, the Martesana Canal, and the Pavia Canal; chap. 26, on French canal engineering, covers the Languedoc Canal, the Charollais Canal, the Bourgogne Canal, the Briare Canal, and the Craponne Canal. Finally, chap. 28 is devoted to "Normandy Ports and Harbors," pp. 460–77.

54.   For example, the Erie Canal was 363 miles from Buffalo on Lake Erie to Albany on the Hudson River. Forty feet wide at the surface and four feet deep when first built in 1817–25, it was enlarged several times. Finally, with work begun in 1909, it became a main waterway (340 miles long, 150 feet wide, and 12 feet deep) of the New York State Barge Canal. Before the final expansion took place, an interim description and assessment of the canal was published abroad in Hess, "Die Canale des Staates New York, nebst Bemenhaugen den Wasserverbrauch auf Schifffahrt-scanälen" (1867), pp. 513–44.

55.   Cheng Sih-Gung, "China's Geography: Historical and Social" (1918), pp. 290–91.

56.   Edmunds, pp. 236–37; see also pp. 232–35, 238.

Chapter 12

1.   From a long and specifically detailed account of worker bees operating in half-hour relays round the clock in all kinds of weather throughout the summer months, in Charles Tomlinson, *Rudimentary Treatise on Warming and Ventilation* (1850), pp. 157–61. For another astonishing achievement from the world of insects, see the account of the efficient, built-in ventilation system of termite structures on the Ivory Coast of Africa, in Karl von Frisch, *Animal Architecture* (1974), pp. 139–43. This chapter, "The Problem of Ventilation Through the Ages," appeared separately as an article of the same title in *Technology and Culture* 22(July 1981): 485–511.

2.   "It is difficult to exaggerate the dangers of dry-rot, which is more infectious to timber than any disease is to human beings. . . . Outbreaks of dry-rot start in timber which is not properly ventilated and is moderately damp. . . . Once started, the fungus can spread not only over timber, but also through cavities or fissures in any substance, growing up behind plaster and being able to penetrate even a thick but friable wall. . . ." Caroe, *Old Churches*, p. 132. To protect beam ends of timber built into masonry walls from the deleterious effects of lime in the masonry, the timbers were charred, encased in lead, or placed in minimal contact with the masonry. In *Repair of Ancient Buildings*, Powys states that, following medieval precedent, "they should never be built in closely with mortar or masonry. Always there should be space about the ends for ventilation, and this may be provided by forming clean pockets of concrete or masonry at least two inches wider and deeper and higher than the timber to be placed there: . . . no mortar should be allowed to come in contact with the timber" (p. 119).

3.   In New World Dutch barns, the hay was piled on a scaffold of sapling poles above the threshing floor so that air could circulate through it from below. See Fitchen, *Barn*, p. 9, pls. 23, 24, 26, and 29. In more temperate climates, where snow is not a problem, crops are customarily dried out in various types of farm buildings constructed with vented walls of brick or tile grillwork. See G. E. Kidder Smith, *Italy Builds* (1955), pp. 36–39, with eleven photographs. He states, in part, that "one of the most widely employed means of climate control in Italy can be found in the wonderful vented walls which are a handsome and integral part of so many barns, particularly those in the hay raising districts."

4.   From very early times, particularly in the Near East, countless excavations were made through rock as conduits for an assured water supply and for its convenient storage. Such water channels and aqueducts, along with cisterns and reservoirs, are noted on practically every page devoted to the areas east of the Jordan River and the Hauran farther northeast, in Karl Baedeker, *Palestine and Syria*, 3d ed. (1898), pp. 165–95. See also the account of extensive rock-hewn aqueducts in Syria, dating back through biblical times to much earlier Phoenician centuries in Benjamin W. Bacon, "Among the Sun-Temples of Coele-Syria" (1906), pp. 66–83, especially, p. 80.

5.   See Parsons, *Engineers,* pt. 3, pp. 177–220 (on mining engineering). In spite of its comprehensive historical coverage of early mines and mining operations, this remarkable book presents but scant information on the ventilation practices that were followed. Parsons does reproduce a plate from Agricola's 1556 treatise *De re metallica,* "A machine for ventilating mines" (p. 199 fig 91), and provides some brief commentary, beginning with the statement: "Artificial ventilation of mines was of course recognized as essential as soon as a mine passed beyond the pit, or shallow excavation, stage. Pliny records that in his day a change of air in underground workings was secured by shaking cloths which acted like fans to set the air in motion" (p. 190).

6.   David G. McCullough, *Great Bridge* (1972), p. 198.

7.   This very scheme, in fact, is used today in lieu of electric light bulbs to illuminate the murals and to light the passageways in some Egyptian monuments. Tourists are amazed at the unexpected brilliance of the light from this source.

8.   William Golding, *Spire* (1964), p. 148.

9.   *Glossary of Terms Used in Grecian, Roman, Italian and Gothic Architecture,* 5th ed. (1850). "Femerell: a lantern, louvre, or cover placed on the roof of a kitchen, hall, &c., for the purpose of ventilation, or to allow the escape of smoke without admitting rain" (p. 203, including a text illus.); "Lantern: in Italian or modern architecture a small structure on the top of a dome, or in other similar situations, for the purpose of admitting light, promoting ventilation, or for ornament. . . . In Gothic architecture, the term is sometimes applied to louvres on the roof of halls, &c." (p. 281); "Louvre: a turret or small lantern, (sometimes termed a *fomerel,*) placed on the roof of ancient halls, kitchens, &c., to allow of the escape of smoke, or to promote ventilation; originally they were entirely open at the sides, or closed only with narrow boards, placed horizontally and aslope, and at a little distance apart, so as to exclude rain and snow without impeding the passage of the smoke. When, as was formerly by no means uncommon, fires were made on open hearths, without flues for the conveyance of the smoke, louvres were indispensable, and when not required for use they were frequently erected for ornament, but in the latter case were usually glazed, and many which once were open have been glazed in later times" (pp. 293–94, including a text illus., p. 293).

10.   See Innocent, *English Building Construction,* pp. 248–64. The portion of this excellent book that deals with windows widely documents English, Scottish, and Welsh examples, which started out as mere peepholes perforated through wood or stone. Innocent presents much information on what windows consisted of before the general adoption of glazing and on the extent to which they provided both light and ventilation.

11.   For some of the environmental evils and health hazards that resulted from the high concentration of people in industrial cities of the nineteenth century, see Reyner Banham, "A Dark Satanic Century," chap. 3 of *Architecture of the Well-tempered Environment* (1969). This account makes abundantly clear that the crippling and calamitous blight of the cities and their inhabitants was largely attributable to inadequate or nonexistent ventilation.

12.   Tomlinson, p. 49.

13.   For a detailed account, with diagrams and a chart of temperature variations within the igloo, see James Marston Fitch and Daniel P. Branch, "Primitive Architecture and Climate" (1960), pp. 134–44.

14.   See George Peter Murdock, "The Kazaks of Central Asia," chap. 6 of *Our Primitive Contemporaries* (1934), pp. 140–41, including fig. 34.

15.   Specific data about the smoke hole and its adjustable flaps are given in Reginald and Gladys Laubin, *Indian Tipi* (1971), pp. 21, 38–40 (see especially fig. 2), 53, and 110–15 (especially figs. 18, 19). Camping one time in their Indian tepee, on a winter weekend after a snowstorm, the authors cleared away the drift at the doorway enough to enter and build a fire, which quickly made the interior warm and cheery. But in a few moments they had "burned up most of the oxygen in the tipi, which resulted in a stuffiness worse than smoke. The snow was packed so tightly around the outside of the lodge that no fresh air could get in. . . . After that, we always cleared away a little snow on the windward side, allowing a draft to go up behind the lining. When you use a lining with the extra door flap, it can be closed and the outer door raised, so that fresh air enters behind the lining without creating a draft inside" (p. 133).

16.   Account by Dr. Mackenzie, in J. Arthur Thomas, "The Physical Welfare of Mothers and Children in Scotland" (1918), p. 152. See photographs of "Typical Black House in the Hebrides, without chimney or windows" (p. 152) and of "One of the older houses in Ben Decula" of dry-stone walls without rendering or whitewash (p. 153).

17.   Innocent concisely treats the historical developments of chimneys in Britain, pp. 264–70. His coverage begins with the statement: "There is hardly any [material] for the study of the opening which served in early times for the double purpose of letting in light and as an outlet for smoke. This opening became specialized as the window when it was situated in the wall, and when in the roof, it was developed in one direction into the rooflight, louvre, or skylight, and in another direction into the modern chimney." Continental Europe appears to have lagged behind England in the adoption and development of fireplaces and chimneys. Numerous references to early fireplaces (not all of which are listed in the index) are found scattered throughout T. Hudson Turner [and John Henry Parker], *Some Account of Domestic Architecture in England* (1851–59). Recently, Dr. LeRoy J. Dresbeck of Western Washington State College has carried on considerable research into the evolution of the fireplace in medieval times.

18.   *A New Concordance of the American Revised Bible,* standard ed. (New York, 1903), s.v. "lamp."

19.   Edward W. Clark, "Roman Terra-Cotta Lamps" (1906), pp. 171, 178.

20.   "Use of Ancient Lamps" (1909), p. 215.

21.   Tomlinson, p. 52.

22.   See John Henry Middleton, "The Temple and Atrium of Vesta and the Regia" (1886), pp. 391–423, with numerous illustrations showing hypocausts with vent-flue pipes on the exhaust side of the *suspensura.* Also see Middleton, "Construction in Ancient Rome," pp. 41–60. Pl. 3 shows details of hypocausts from the Baths of Caracalla and the Baths of Severus in Rome. A well-known and often illustrated example of a Roman domestic hypocaust, discovered at Lincoln in England, is shown in Tomlinson, p. 53, figs. 2 (plan) and 3 (section). Many drawings of various layouts and details are given in the section on Roman hypocausts in Josef Durm, *Die Baukunst der Römer* (1905), pp. 357–61, figs. 395–98.

23.   For a concisely informative statement about Roman hypocausts see Anderson, Spiers, and Ashby, *Ancient Rome,* p. 106. It reads in part: "For the halls which required an exceptional heat the walls were virtually lined with [flues consisting of] socket-jointed clay pipes. . . . In rooms of smaller size the tile piers were sometimes dispensed with altogether, the whole of the concrete floor resting on ledges or corbels in the wall. Middleton gives one instance in the house of the Vestals where there is a concrete floor 14 inches thick with a bearing of 20 feet. In such cases the floors were filled in on some temporary support of wood planking, which will naturally have left an impression on the under surface of the concrete."

24. "Underground heating pipes, starting from the kitchen, heat the different rooms from below and debouch eventually into a kind of chimney erected partly against and partly outside the house. . . . This underground heating system has the great advantage of permitting the room to remain clean and comparatively free from dust." Andreas Eckardt, *History of Korean Art* (1929), p. 15.

25. Jesse Walter Fewkes, *Antiquities of the Mesa Verde National Park* (1909). See p. 18 for description and pl. 15, diagram of Kiva, for details of construction.

26. For occurrences in natural caves, see Louis N. Forsyth, "Archaeological Remains in the Mazatec Country" (1910), pp. 328–34.

27. See Rees, *Cyclopaedia*, vol. 40. The author of the article on "Wells, in Rural Economy" devotes a long paragraph to each of three wells dug in England during the last decade of the eighteenth century to depths of 167, 394, and 236 feet; the nature of the soils through which the well was excavated is reported along with the volume and level of the water in the well and other pertinent data.

28. "Well-digging" in Rees, vol. 40. The article goes on to describe, in thorough and specific detail, the installation and operation of an effective ventilating apparatus for eliminating the noxious air encountered in well digging. The device consists of lengths of metal pipe (that may be "carried to any distance") and a fire pan so arranged as to create rarefied air in the pipe in order to draw off the noxious air that accumulates in the excavation.

29. See Huss, *Rational Building,* pp. 294–5. For the entire account of the Abbey of Ste. Marie de Breteuil see Huss, pp. 292–300 (or Viollet-le-Duc, *Dictionnaire,* pp. 223–31) and fig. 123a (plan), fig. 123b (longitudinal section), and fig. 123c (two transverse sections).

30. The Flavian Amphitheater is shown in section in Durm, p. 676, fig. 745.

31. In addition to reproducing many of the revealing drawings of Gaudet's remarkable series on the Coliseum (including those which reconstruct the rope platform on which the *velarium* was supported and hauled about), Durm delineates in specific detail similar rope platforms used in the Roman theater at Orange (p. 655, fig. 731) and the amphitheater at Nîmes (p. 688, fig. 755).

32. *Vitruvius, the Ten Books on Architecture,* trans. by Morris Hicky Morgan (1914). See bk. 1, chap. 6, in which Vitruvius states that "the lines of houses must be directed away from the quarters from which the winds blow so that as they come in they may strike against the angles of the blocks and their force thus broken and dispersed" (p. 27).

33. From annotated photographs in Rudofsky, *Architecture without Architects,* figs. 82–86.

34. Ibid., figs. 113–15. In another part of the world wind towers and other systems effectively use the energy of the environment to cool buildings. This traditional scheme is thoroughly investigated and explained in Mehdi N. Bahadori, "Passive Cooling Systems in Iranian Architecture" (1978), pp. 144–50, 152, 154.

35. Anderson, Spiers, and Dinsmoor, *Ancient Greece* pp. 23–25, including fig. 6, "Detail Plan of Domestic Quarter at Cnossus."

36. A prime example is that of the "House of the Faun" at Pompeii, the plan of which is given in Robertson, *Greek and Roman Architecture,* p. 306 fig. 128.

37.   See Joseph Thatcher Clarke, *The Hypaethral Question* (1879). This is the best and fullest account to date of the complex problems of ventilation encountered by the classical Greeks in their temples. Humidification with respect to the monumental employment of ivory is given some treatment in Anderson, Spiers, and Dinsmoor, pp. 61 and 112, and more recently in Orlandos, *Les Matériaux de construction,* pt. 1, fasc. 16, chap. 4, pp. 131–34.

38.   This drawing, "Passages in the Great Pyramid," is found in Walter Woodburn Hyde, "A Visit to the Pyramids of Gizeh" (1910), p. 261. The section drawing reproduced here, together with some of the specific information in Hyde's account, are from W. M. Flinders Petrie, *The Pyramids and Temples of Gizeh* (London, 1883).

39.   Perhaps the first of many illustrations that show this customary method of lowering a giant granite plug into its ultimate position is that representing the South Pyramid of Dashur in G. Perrot and C. Chipiez, *L'Égypte,* vol. 1 of *Histoire de l'art dans l'antiquité* (1882), fig. 150.

40.   The length of the air shafts are cited in Karl Baedeker, *Egypt,* 4th ed. (1898), p. 114.

41.   Even in the last decade of the nineteenth century, millennia after the dust of excavation had settled and the workers had reverted to dust themselves, tourists were warned that a visit to the interior would find it "fatiguing; travellers who are in the slightest degree predisposed to apoplectic or fainting fits and ladies travelling alone should not attempt to penetrate into these stifling recesses; the explorer has to crawl and clamber through low and narrow passages; . . . the stones on the floor are often extremely slippery, and the close air smells strongly of bats; [finally] the temperature of the interior is 79° Fahrenheit." Ibid., p. 113.

42.   The lower end of this larger shaft terminates to one side of the descending passageway, from which access to it was blocked up and concealed behind a wall slab inconspicuously lining the smooth side of the passageway.

Chapter 13

1.   Quoted from the preface of *The Builder's Dictionary* (1734).

2.   In *Our Primitive Contemporaries,* Murdock lists in great detail the division of labor by gender among each of the large number of native peoples he discusses. For example, among the Haidas of British Columbia (p. 251), the Iroquois of northern New York (p. 301), and the Witotos of northwestern Amazonia (p. 466), the men build the houses; whereas the women build and repair the houses among the Hopi of Arizona (p. 334), the Kalmucks of central Asia, and the Hottentots of southern Africa. On the other hand, both sexes participate in the erection of the dwelling among the Ainus of northern Japan (p. 168). Sometimes, too, both sexes contribute to the building operation, but are traditionally assigned different phases of the task.

3.   In Samoa, "though women prepare the thatch, plait the screens, and fetch the gravel, the actual construction of the house falls to a specialized and highly honored craft of male artisans. The carpenters are organized into guilds, each with its chief, its masters and apprentices, its trade-mark and its special ceremonial. . . . A ceremony of consecration, with prayers to the tutelary divinity of the family and the carpenters' guild, marks the completion of the building." Ibid., p. 54.

4.   For variety of house types in a single area of Africa, see L. W. G. Malcolm, "Huts and Villages in the Cameroon, West Africa" (1923), pp. 21–27. See also MM. Augustin Bernard and Edmond Doutte, "Types of Rural Dwellings in Algeria," *Scottish Geographical Magazine* 34(1918): 29–30. See Alfred C. Haddon, "Studies in the

Anthropogeography of British New Guinea" (1900), pp. 422–24, for brief descriptions of a large number of different house types, from marine villages to the tree houses of the hill tribes.

5.   A very elaborate, twelve-day ceremony of founding a native temple in Hawaii is recounted in great detail in Wilkes, *Narrative*, vol. 4, appendix 3, pp. 506–8. Dedicatory ceremonies of other kinds were scrupulously observed in connection with the placing of foundation deposits in ancient Egyptian temples. The practice is analogous to the hermetically sealed box of documents and memorabilia customarily set in a hollowed-out cornerstone in many important buildings of the Western world in later centuries and continuing into the present. A thorough and detailed account of the origins, symbolic meanings, locales and variants of the "house-tree" or "topping out" ceremony—fixing a green branch at the topmost peak of a newly framed structure—is given in John R. Stilgoe, "Topping Out" (1980), p. 63.

6.   Edwin H. Gomes, chap. 3 of *Seventeen Years Among the Sea Dyaks of Borneo* (1911), p. 47. See photograph of native house under construction, facing p. 44. (The same author's "Notes on the Sea Dyaks of Borneo" [1911], pp. 695–723 consists of extensive excerpts from the book.)

7.   Nicholas Pike, "The Hottentots of Southern Africa" (1893), p. 14773.

8.   This account of the application of different kinds of grasses is from Bentley, *Pioneering in the Congo*, vol. 1, p. 146. Throughout, Bentley includes much information on the great variety of house types in the Congo River basin and on native house building, all from firsthand observation and, in most cases, participation in their construction.

9.   Quoted from Murdock, pp. 297–98; pages include a plan and sketch of an Iroquois Long House. Another type of American Indian dwelling—rather more like some native African houses in both construction and appearance—is described in Melicent Humanson Lee, "The Ancient House of the San Diegueno Indians" (1928), pp. 100–105, 108. See also Oliver G. Ricketson, Jr., "American Nail-less Houses in the Maya Bush" (1927), pp. 27–36.

10.   Wilkes, pp. 146–47, including woodcut of "Samoan Faletele."

11.   See *Encyclopaedia Britannica,* 11th ed., s.v. "tent."

12.   Quoted from Murdock, pp. 140–41. For further description and comment on a yurt, see J. Kopernicki, "Characteristics of the Calmucks" (1872), pp. 429–31. Kopernicki states that "the entire arrangement of the tent, both outside and inside, is the affair of the women. The husband only charges himself with the construction of the framework, and with some definite corrections which may be necessary" (p. 430).

13.   "To make felt, wool is spread in two layers on a straw mat, sprinkled with water, rolled up with the mat, and tied. A number of people form in two parallel lines, pushing the roll back and forth between them with their feet until the wool is sufficiently pressed. Then the roll is undone, and the women, sitting in a circle, beat the fabric between the palms of their hands for two or three hours. The native felt is sometimes wonderfully light and beautiful, and is frequently embroidered with much skill and taste." Murdock, p. 146.

14.   Laubin and Laubin, *Indian Tipi,* p. 157.

15.   Ibid., pp. 63–65.

16.   "Extensive remains of prehistoric lake dwellings exist in the bed of the River Save, near Dolina, in northern Bosnia, which fall in no way behind the better known remains in Switzerland. . . . Four dwelling houses built on piles—three of which are well preserved, while one has been buried—have been laid bare. . . . The remains of these researches have a special value, in that they have determined the architectural construction of the pile dwellings with an accuracy which has seldom been attainable." *Records of the Past* 1(1902): 126–27.

17.   "The lake dwellings discovered at Roulers in Belgium are of special interest because of the great variety in the remains found, which indicate that the locality was inhabited by Lake Dwellers from Neolithic to quite modern times. . . ." Ibid., p. 184.

18.   The standard works, gathering together reports of all discoveries up to the time of their publication, are Robert Munro, *Lake Dwellings of Europe*—the Rhind Lectures in Archaeology for 1888—(1890) and the same author's *Palaeolithic Man and Terramare Settlements in Europe*—the Munro Lectures in Anthropology and Prehistoric Archaeology in connection with the University of Edinburgh—(1912). The latter includes photographs of prehistoric pilings preserved in the mud of former lake bottoms.

19.   T. M. Coan, "Prehistoric Times" (1872), p. 107.

20.   See text and photograph in Marion Lowndes, "Black Hell in the Pacific" (1940), p. 9.

21.   Thomas Barbour, "Notes on a Zoological Collecting Trip to Dutch New Guinea" (1908), p. 473. A photograph of the end view of a communal "Longhouse" near Dorey, on stilts over the water, is captioned "One wonders how it is possible to use the bridge [running from land to the dwellings]; the poles roll about and there is no handrail; still it is done, and even by young children," p. 479.

22.   Thomas Barbour, "Further Notes on Dutch New Guinea" (1908), p. 527. Photographs of native Dutch New Guinea houses and temples built over water appear on pp. 528, 530, 533, 534, and 539. At the time the pictures were taken, the platforms appear to be about five feet or so above water.

23.   Displayed in the Museum of Science and Industry in Chicago are comparative scale models, created in the 1930s, of pile-driving practices in the past. The series starts with a depiction of two Stone-Age men, perched on a temporary circular platform of boards that is fixed to the pile it girdles. The men are in a position to raise and drop a heavy cylinder of wood, serving as a hammer. Furnished with short horizontal rods to right and left by way of handles, the cylinder is kept on target by a vertical rod passing through it that projects upward from the top of the pile into which it is inserted. Mortar-and-pestle schemes very similar to this device are used by the modern Dyaks for hulling rice (see illustrations in both the article and the book by Gomes). But it seems somewhat doubtful that Paleolithic men would have gone to the trouble—with the tools at their disposal—to fashion such a device when clubs or mauls would have been a much easier and quicker means of driving their piles.

24.   In coastal waters, the length of the piles above water level was, of course, affected by the tides, whose daily fluctuations could be considerable. The actual depth of coastal waters may, and often does, change from year to year due to either shoal formation or scouring action. But the extent of tidal fluctuations—that is, the differential between mean low and mean high water—is quite constant and varies but little for a given locale. So a fifty-five-year-old publication will be sufficiently accurate, for our purposes, in designating two figures (in feet); namely, the Mean Range of Tide and the Spring Range of Tide. The following data is from Department of Commerce, *Tide Tables: U.S. and Foreign Ports for the Year 1930* (1929). For New Guinea and Papua, the figures are strikingly different between the island's northern coast (where most of the native dwellings over water are found) and its southern coast. Thus:

The northern coast	Mean Range–Spring Range
Port Constantine	2.5–3.1
Rooke Island	2.4–3.0
Parsee Point	2.6–3.2
Kiriwina (largest of Trobriand Islands)	2.4–3.0
Cape Vogel, Ward Hunt Strait	1.9–2.4
The southern coast	
Su-a-u Harbor	6.6–8.1
Port Moresby	6.5–8.0
Fly River Entrance	10.9–13.5

25. For two similar types of houses built by the same natives—those constructed over water and those over land—see Barbour, "Zoological Collecting Trip," p. 473.

26. George N. Curzon, "Journeys in French Indo-China" (1893), p. 100.

27. The most specific and thorough account of igloos and igloo construction is found in a five-part article by Frederick Schwatka, "The Igloo of the Innuit" (1883), pp. 182–84, 216–18, 259–62, 304–6, 347–49. This quotation is from his section on the procedure used to locate the kind of snow required. What follows is a condensed paraphrasing of Schwatka's coverage of the actual construction of a snow igloo, in all its carefully worked out steps and sequences, and a quotation from his section describing the chinking of the snow-block structure.

Chapter 14

1. Personal correspondence, letter of 21 March 1982, from JTT. Much has been written on Egyptian constructional practices, but most writers have either ignored significant problems or glossed over the details. They have therefore proposed misleading solutions to the difficulties the ancient builders met and overcame. The present chapter—which appeared in a slightly different form as an article under the same title in the *Journal of the Society of Architectural Historians* 37(March 1978): 3–12—attempts to explain some of the considerations heretofore passed over.

2. With respect to the Egyptians' possible use of tackle and pulleys, Clarke and Engelbach, in *Ancient Egyptian Masonry,* state unequivocally that no pulleys were used in the rigging of Egyptian ships. In chap. 4, "Transport Barges," these authors assert that "at the only place where a pulley would be expected none exist" and that "although hundreds of models and pictures of sailing boats are known, a pulley occurs in none of them, at any rate in dynastic times, and the evidence brought forward suggests that pulleys were unknown. Further, if they had been used, in building, for lifting blocks of stone, it would be expected that a model pulley would have been found . . . yet none is found" (p. 44). If pulleys were not used in connection with the relatively light requirements of sailing vessels, it is inconceivable that they would have been used for lifting heavy stones. In any case, pulleys appear to be entirely foreign to the constructional practices of ancient Egyptians.

3. Choisy, *L'Art de bâtir chez les Égyptiens,* p. 80, contains much about rockers and their operation ("Montage par l'ascenseur oscillant"). But some of this distinguished engineer's theories and suppositions are suspect. For example, it seems most unlikely that the rockers were ever rotated about a vertical peg (p. 84 fig. 69) or that the ends of the rockers' runners were ever fashioned to such thin and sharp points as his drawings indicate.

4. Engineer Olaf Tellefsen, *Natural History* 79(November 1970): 10, presents drawings and comments on the use of the balance beam—he calls it the "weight arm"—which he admits "has been the workhorse of peoples ever since man learned to build with heavy stones" (page 16). He states that the apparatus lifts a big stone "about a foot," enough to have "planks, rollers, and a pair of runners under it" (page

12). So far, so good. But most of the operations and applications the author goes on to claim for this device are either patently impracticable (like his double weight arm for both raising a block and moving it laterally in one operation) [page 18] or unresolved with respect to problems of construction that his theories cannot encompass (such as how the capstone of the pyramid was raised and installed in place).

5.   Modern representations of ancient timber sleds are based upon mural relief carvings, particularly those showing the transport of a colossal statute of Djehuty-hotep of the twelfth Dynasty at El Bersheh in Egypt (often described and frequently illustrated) and the gigantic winged bulls for the palace of Sennacherib at Nineveh during his reign beginning in 705 B.C. (discovered by Layard and described and pic-tured, *inter alia,* by Pinches, "Assur and Ninevah," pp. 23–41). A timber sled having fourteen-foot-long runners with four stout crosspieces mortice-and-tenoned to the run-ners, and with many notches and sinkages to accommodate secondary pieces and at-tachments, is shown in clear detail in a scale drawing in Clarke and Engelbach, p. 89 fig. 85.

6.   Erectional bosses left on column drums as well as stylobate and wall stones (to accommodate lifting slings) are familiar enough in classical Greek construction. Their use by the ancient Egyptians (to receive the lifting points of levers) is substan-tiated by the survival of unremoved projections on the casing blocks of the Third Pyramid at Giza and on the temples of the Theban area. See R. Engelbach, *Problem of the Obelisks* (1923), p. 56.

7.   Clarke and Engelbach, p. 92, comment in considerable detail on construction ramps used in Egyptian temple building, particularly in the case of the pylon towers, but their book has little to say about other construction ramps. But notices of exten-sive ramps—from quarry to river and from river to pyramid—are given in Englebach, p. 70, including fig. 26 (for ramps at Aswan), and in Baedeker, *Egypt,* p. 121 (for the Third Pyramid at Gizeh). Baedeker, p. 109, also quotes Herodotus's figures concerning the construction ramp for the Great Pyramid at Gizeh. "They first made the road for the transport of the stones from the Nile to the Libyan Mountains; the length of the road amounts to five stadia (1017 yds.), its breadth is ten fathoms (60 ft.), and its height, at the highest places, is eight fathoms (48 ft.), and it is constructed entirely of smoothed stone with figures engraved on it. Ten years were thus consumed in making this road and the subterranean chambers. . . ." Baedeker remarks that this route is still traceable and indicates it on his map as approaching the east face of the pyramid at an angle (pp. 132–33). When the Arabs removed the casing blocks to Cairo in the Middle Ages, they partially restored this ramp.

8.   The distinguished Egyptologist Edwards, *Pyramids of Egypt,* p. 270, acknowl-edging that "it must be admitted that Pyramid construction is a subject on which the last word has certainly not yet been written," asserts that "only one method of raising heavy weights was open to the ancient Egyptians, namely by means of ramps com-posed of brick and earth which sloped upwards from the level of the ground to what-ever height was desired." Edwards devotes a number of pages (269–83) to describing "foothold embankments" and "supply ramps," which, he says (p. 276), "would be raised to [each] new level of the Pyramid" as the work progressed; "so the building continued to grow course by course until lastly the capstone . . . would be placed on the apex. . . . It may therefore be deduced that the capstone, already shaped but still in the rough, was taken to the top of the Pyramid on its sledge. . . ."
    The amount of work and materials involved in providing embankments and a supply ramp to the top of a 480-foot-high structure—all to be subsequently discarded and removed—staggers the imagination. Surely the Egyptians had a less prodigal means of utilizing both manpower and materials on such vast falsework constructions than to squander them on these enormous transient earthworks. Furthermore, the long, long supply ramp would have served most inefficiently. For, in order to maintain the proper gradient, the ramp would have had to be constantly lengthened, its height augmented, and a smooth pavement of stones laid down at each new increment of

height. All these interferences would have interrupted the constant traffic of hauling up the blocks.

9.   Egyptologists generally have no training or experience—or even interest, judging by their scholarly output—in the matters discussed in this study. Apparently it was ever thus. "There is quite a considerable literature on the subject, mostly done either by engineers (on a brief visit) with no knowledge of archaeology to enable them to control their assertions, or by archaeologists to whom engineering is a sealed mystery. While the publication of a new grammatical form or historical point will evoke a perfect frenzy of contradiction in the little world of Egyptology, the most absurd statements on a mechanical problem will be left unquestioned, and, what is worse, accepted. In most branches of modern archaeology the alleged savant must work in conjunction with the specialist, and the specialist needed for the subject under discussion is the foreman quarryman. This was brought home to me with great force when I was at work on the obelisk, and I shall never forget the ease nor the contempt with which an old Italian quarryman disproved some of my then most cherished theories. His range of knowledge may have been limited, but it was painfully accurate." Engelbach, p. 22. A case in point is the unmistakably non-Egyptian procedure advocated by a modern engineer, published in the *Journal of the American Institute of Architects* 56(August 1971): 50, claiming that the stones of the Great Pyramid were raised to their positions at successive levels on large counterbalanced elevator platforms.

10.   For a photograph of this rocker, see Clarke and Engelbach, fig. 89 facing p. 93. To be sure, this rocker and a few others like it date from the New Kingdom, some 1,100 years after the Great Pyramid was built. But we are extremely fortunate in having even these few authentic examples of a constructional device, whatever their ancient dynastic date. For although the Egyptians preserved in their tombs and foundation deposits countless examples of household objects and artifacts of all sorts (either the objects themselves, models of them, or murals depicting their use), no utensils employed in building construction other than hand tools were preserved. It seems reasonable to assume that in tradition-dominated Egypt a device as simple as a rocker must have been in use with little if any change for millennia.

11.   In this connection Clarke and Engelbach, p. 128, report that "in the Great Pyramid, as possibly in certain others, a large depression in the packing blocks runs down the middle of each face, implying a line of extra thick facing there. . . ." But whether this was done as a feature of the original construction or in connection with the stripping of the casing blocks by the Arabs in the Middle Ages is unclear.

12.   As is so often the case in mechanical processes, the description and explanation of the various operations outlined above take considerably more time—and make the procedures seem much more complicated—than the operations would be in practice.

13.   It should be acknowledged that Clarke and Engelbach, p. 121, declare that the case against the Egyptians ever having used the rocker device to raise the stones of the Great Pyramid is "proved" by the negative evidence of the unfinished casing blocks of the Third Pyramid (which are not, they say, in the form of "a series of steps") and by "all other known examples of unfinished masonry." Yet these thorough and reasonable writers admit that the limestone casing of the Third Pyramid "is now broken up" (p. 128); so more positive evidence should be sought for dismissing the use of the rocker. Clarke and Engelbach conclude that "the foregoing notes on pyramid construction are not to be regarded as a complete and final exposition of the many problems hitherto unexplained, but rather as preliminary deductions which seem to follow from the information at present available, and which may have to be considerably modified in the light of future research" (p. 129).

Part of the reluctance to accept the rocker device may be due to the exaggerated claims that some have made for it and to the rather sketchy idea of its operation as given by some writers. For example, even W. M. F. Petrie *Arts and Crafts of An-*

cient Egypt (1909), p. 75, who was probably the first to suggest its use, mentions shims that are wedge-shaped in section for the rocker's runners to ride up on, to right and left. These tapered shims were not only unnecessary in the operation but would have considerably complicated the work of the men who inserted them. For besides slowing down the procedure, they would have required the men levering the blocks to expend a much greater effort in rocking the stone and in holding it tilted until the next layer of shims could be shoved into position.

14.   Baedeker, *Egypt*, p. 134, gives an English translation of the account by Herodotus (the earliest writer on the subject) of the construction of the Great Pyramid. Here is the passage that pertains to the raising of stones in stepped sequence by means of small "machines" that may have been rockers: "This pyramid was first built in the form of a flight of steps. After the workmen had completed the pyramid in this form, they raised the other stones (used for the casing) by means of machines, made of short beams, from the ground to the first tier of steps; and after the stone was placed there it was raised to the second tier by another machine; for there were as many machines as there were tiers of steps; or perhaps there was but one machine, easily moved, that was raised from one tier to the other, as it was required for lifting the stones." (A somewhat differently worded translation is given in Clarke and Engelbach, p. 120.) It is understandable that Herodotus's account of the Great Pyramid's erection seems garbled, contradictory, and questionable with respect to some of its supposed facts; for by the time the Greek historian received his information from the local guides, the Great Pyramid was already many, many centuries old. In any case, the procedures discussed above are consistent with either of the alternatives put forward in Herodotus's account.

15.   Accustomed as they were to vast building projects that required thousands of workers, the men in charge of these undertakings were exceptionally skilled in the efficient organization and administration of the work force. This ability to organize and deploy great numbers of workers was, in fact, one of the most remarkable achievements of the Egyptian builders. For, on the one hand, it involved logistical problems as general as housing and victualing very large numbers of workmen at the quarries and at the building sites. On the other hand, it required making such detailed arrangements as the specific allotment of space (some $22'' \times 22''$) to each of the stonecutters quarrying a granite obelisk. For these and other instances of administrative efficiency in building operations see, for example, Engelbach, p. 43; James Henry Breasted, *History of Egypt* (1905), p. 414; and E. Baldwin Smith, *Egyptian Architecture*, p. 236. "We cannot help admitting that they were perhaps the best organizers of human labour the world has ever seen, and their method of carrying out a task always appears to be the most efficient and economical, in principle at any rate, when we take into account the appliances which they knew and the methods of transport at their disposal." Clarke and Engelbach, p. 3.

16.   The extent to which the practice of quarrying stones oversized was widespread throughout ancient times (and even in the medieval period) is neither generally appreciated nor adequately acknowledged in print. Certainly, most of the practices employed by Greeks during the classical period are familiar, such as the oversized diameters of the column drums to protect them from injury in transit and during erection before the flutes were cut and the bosses left on these same drums to accommodate hoisting slings in setting them accurately in place. But the extent to which the Romans and, above all, the Egyptians utilized oversized and/or projecting features has not been sufficiently reported or properly studied.

17.   Clarke and Engelbach fig. 96 facing p. 98, note that the joints between the granite casing blocks that survive *in situ* at the base of the Great Pyramid never gap more than one fiftieth of an inch. Any practice mason knows that it is impossible to set rectangular blocks of stone—even ones far smaller in their areas of contact than these—with such astonishing tightness by slipping them between others already in place. Hence it appears undeniable that the big casing blocks were juxtaposed to right and left, beginning with a block at or near the middle of each course. The corner blocks, by being drawn diagonally inward against the completed runs on two adjacent faces of the pyramid, acted as terminal closures.

18. A shallow hole in the excess stock, with wooden plug inserted, is shown in Choisy, *Histoire,* vol. 1, p. 34 fig. 21. The author asserts that auger holes can be found in the stones of the Great Pyramid, where, in all probability, these plugs were implanted. He fails, however, to identify which stones or which of their faces possess these holes.

19. Both maintaining accuracy of batter in the faces of the pyramid and avoiding twist in the salient angles where a pair of these faces intersect are dealt with in considerable detail by Clarke and Engelbach, pp. 124–29.

20. Ibid., chap. 9, "Dressing and Laying the Blocks," pp. 96–116. Vertical joints —though slightly oblique in plan—are documented and illustrated with respect to some of the casing stones of the Great Pyramid and elsewhere.

21. "It was the presence of the mortar in the bedding joints which enabled the blocks to be laid. Without it, the Egyptians could not have laid them at all. . . . Mortar is made use of to form an even bed and to facilitate 'setting,' which is the technical term for getting a block exactly into place; the mortar being, practically speaking, a lubricant. It is obvious that, unless a stone of considerable weight is laid on a bed of such a nature, so that it can be adjusted hither and thither, a good setting cannot be obtained. For masonry of any fineness, a layer of some sort must be used having the consistency of butter—in other words, a lime-cream, which as a cement is without value. . . ." Ibid., p. 78.

22. Hyde, "Pyramids of Gizeh," p. 318, states that "vast quantities of chips—estimated at one half the bulk of the pyramid—were thrown over the cliff to the north and south of the 'Great Pyramid,' thus forming an artificial enlargement of the plateau, extending for some hundreds of yards outwards from the rock's edge. These masses of chips are very interesting; for they show peculiar stratification, according to the kinds of refuse thrown out at different times, strata composed of large chips, alternating with those of smaller ones. . . ." Of course, most of this accumulation would have already been built up from the extensive operations of the stonecutters, both those who had excavated innumerable tombs in the bedrock around the pyramids and those who had been charged with accurately shaping blocks at the site previous to their incorporation in the pyramid. But there would have been much additional debris as a result of the stripping process, particularly the large fragments Hyde mentions, which might have come from hewing off the steps of the access stairways.

Bibliography

Ackerman, James S. "Ars sine scientia nihil est: Gothic Theory of Architecture at the Cathedral of Milan." *Art Bulletin* 31(1949): 85–111.

Adler, F. "Der Pharos von Alexandria." *Zeitschrift für Bauwesen* 51(1901): 169–98, with 17 text figures and plates 19–21 in atlas.

Agricola, Georgius. *De re metallica*. Basle, 1556. Translated from the Latin by Herbert Clark Hoover and Lou Henry Hoover. London, 1912.

Anderson, William J., R. Phené Spiers, and Thomas Ashby. *The Architecture of Ancient Rome*. New York: Charles Scribner's Sons, 1927.

Anderson, William J., R. Phené Spiers, and William Bell Dinsmoor. *The Architecture of Ancient Greece*. London: B. T. Batsford, 1927.

Andrews, Francis B. *The Mediaeval Builder and His Methods*. Oxford: Oxford University Press, 1925.

Architectural Association Sketch Book. First Quarterly Part. London: The Architectural Association, 1913.

Arnold, Hugh. *Stained Glass of the Middle Ages in England and France*. New York: Macmillan, 1913. Reprint. 1956.

Bacon, Benjamin W. "Among the Sun-Temples of Coele-Syria." *Records of the Past*. 5(1906): 66–83, with 13 illustrations.

Baedeker, Karl. *Egypt: Handbook for Travellers*. 4th ed. Leipsic: Karl Baedeker, 1898.

Baedeker, Karl. *Greece*. 2d rev. ed. Leipsic: Karl Baedeker; London: Dulan & Co., 1894.

Baedeker, Karl. *Palestine and Syria*. 3d ed. Leipsic: Karl Baedeker, 1898.

Bahadori, Mehdi N. "Passive Cooling Systems in Iranian Architecture." *Scientific American* 238(February 1978): 144–50, 152, 154, with eight drawings and three plates.

Bailey, Truman. "Trained Tuskers of the Teak Forests." *Natural History* 50(December 1942): 228–37, with 17 photographs.

Baines, F. *Westminster Hall. Report to the First Commissioner of H.M. Works, &c., on the Condition of the Roof Timbers of Westminster Hall, with Suggestions for Maintaining the Stability of the Roof*. London: HMSO, 1914, with 39 text figures and 12 large-scale, mainly foldout drawings.

Banham, Rayner. *The Architecture of the Well-tempered Environment*. Chicago: University of Chicago Press, 1969.

Bannister, H. M. "The Esquimaux Dog." *American Naturalist* (Salem, Massachusetts: Peabody Academy of Science) 3(December 1869): 522–30.

Barbour, Thomas. "Notes on a Zoological Collecting Trip to Dutch New Guinea." *National Geographic* 19(1908): 469–84, with twelve illustrations and two maps.

Barbour, Thomas. "Further Notes on Dutch New Guinea." *National Geographic* 19(1908): 527–45.

Barbour, Thomas. "Notes on Burma." *National Geographic* 20(October 1909): 841–66, with 34 illustrations.

Bartlett, James. "Shoring." *Encyclopaedia Britannica*. 11th ed., with eight illustrations.

Batchelder, John M. "The Lamprey as a Builder." *Science* 4(21 November 1884): 469–70.

Beckett, Sir Edmund. *A Book on Building: Civil and Ecclesiastical: including Church Restoration* . . . 2d ed., enl. London: Crosby Lockwood and Co., 1880.

Bell, George Joseph. *Segmental and Elliptical Oblique or Skew Arches: A Practical Treatise*. 2d ed. Carlisle: Charles Thurnam & Sons, 1906.

Benson, Adolph B. *The America of 1750: Peter Kalm's Travels in North America*. The English version of 1770. 2 vols. New York: Wilson-Erickson, 1937.

Bentley, W. Holman. *Pioneering on the Congo*. 2 vols. New York: Fleming H. Revell Co., 1900, with 206 illustrations.

Berg, Gösta. *Sledges and Wheel-less Vehicles*. Uppsala: Almqvist & Wiksell, 1935.

Bickmore, Albert S. *Travels in the East Indian Archipelago*. London: John Murray, 1868.

Boëthius, Gerda. *Den Nordiska Timmerbyggnadskonsten*. Stockholm: Fritzes Hovbokhandel, 1927.

Bordeaux, Jean Hippolyte Raymond. "Des voûtes en bois et leur réparation." *Revue de l'art chrétien* 6(1862): 35–70.

Borgera, William C. "Nias—The Island of Gold." *Travel* 67 (June 1936): 23–25, 48.

Bosse, Abraham. *La Pratique du trait à prevves de M. Desargues, Lyonnois, pour la coupe des pierres en l'architecture*. Paris: Pierre des-Hayes, 1643, with 114 engraved diagrammatic plates.

Brandon, Raphael, and J. Arthur Brandon. *The Open Timber Roofs of the Middle Ages*. London: David Bogue, 1849.

Breasted, James Henry. *A History of Egypt*. New York: Charles Scribner's Sons, 1905.

Breeks, James Wilkinson, *An Account of the Primitive Tribes and Monuments of the Nilagiris*. London: India Museum, 1873.

Brindley, William. "Marble: Its Uses as suggested by the Past." *Transactions: Royal Institute of British Architects*, n.s. 3(1887): 45–55, with six plates.

Brindley, William. "Ancient Quarries in Egypt, with an Account of a Recent Journey across the Eastern Desert." *Transactions: Royal Institute of British Architects*, n.s. 4(1887–88): 5–26, with six plates.

Brown, G. Baldwin. *From Schola to Cathedral: A Study of Early Christian Architecture and its Relation to the Life of the Church*. Edinburgh: David Douglas, 1886.

Buchanan, John. "The Industrial Development of Nyasaland." *Geographical Journal* 1(January–June 1893): 245–53, with a map.

The Builder's Dictionary: or, Gentleman and Architect's Companion. 2 vols. London, 1734. Reprint. Washington: Association for Preservation Technology, 1981.

Building Code Recommended by the National Board of Fire Underwriters, New York: An Ordinance providing for fire limits, and regulations governing the construction, alterations, equipment, repair, or removal of buildings or structures. 4th ed., rev. New York, 1922.

Burdsall, Richard L., Arthur B. Emmons, 3d, Terris Moore, and Jack Theodore Young. *Men Against the Clouds.* Harper & Brothers, 1935. Rev. ed. Seattle, Washington: The Mountaineers, 1980.

Burges, William. "Architectural Drawing in the Middle Ages." *Transactions: Royal Institute of British Architects,* n.s. 3(1887): 235–45, with five examples illustrated and an addenda listing numerous publications.

Burns, Justin. "The Actual Building of a Chinese Railway." *Engineering Magazine* 28(December 1904): 380–401, with 30 illustrations.

Busch, Moritz. *Travels between the Hudson and the Mississippi 1851–1852.* Translated and edited by Norman H. Binger. Lexington, Kentucky: The University Press of Kentucky, 1971.

Caroe, Alban D. R. *Old Churches and Modern Craftsmanship.* London: Oxford University Press, 1952.

Cassinello, Fernando. *Bóvedas y cúpulas de ladrillo . . . .* 2d ed., Madrid: T. Graf Torroba, 1964.

Castellano, Mimmo. *La Valle dei Trulli.* Bari: Leonardo da Vinci Editrice, 1968, with many photographs plus technical drawings.

The Century Dictionary: An Encyclopedic Lexicon of the English Language. 10 vols. New York: The Century Co., 1889–95, s.v. "ladder" and "scaling ladder."

Charles, F. W. B. *Medieval Cruck-Building and Its Derivatives: A Study of Timber-Framed Construction based on Buildings in Worcestershire.* The Society for Medieval Archaeology Monograph Series, no. 2. London, 1967.

Choisy, Auguste. *L'Art de bâtir chez les Romains.* Paris: Ducher et Cie., 1873.

Choisy, Auguste. *L'Art de bâtir chez les Égyptiens.* Paris: Librairie G. Baranger Fils, 1904.

Choisy, Auguste, *Histoire de l'architecture.* 2 vols. Paris: Librairie George Baranger, 1929.

"City of San Salvador Destroyed by an Earthquake." *American Journal of Science & Arts,* 2d ser., 18(November 1854): 277–84.

Clark, Edward W. "Roman Terra-Cotta Lamps." *Records of the Past* 5(1906): 170–86, with 32 examples illustrated.

Clarke, Joseph Thatcher. *The Hypaethral Question.* Papers of the Harvard Club, no. 1. Cambridge, Massachusetts, 1879.

Clarke, Joseph T., Francis H. Bacon, and Robert Koldeway. *Investigations at Assos: Drawings and photographs of the Buildings and Objects Discovered during the Exca-*

vations of 1881–1882–1883. Cambridge, Massachusetts: Archaeological Institute of America, 1902–21.

Clarke, Somers, and R. Engelbach. *Ancient Egyptian Masonry*. London: Oxford University Press, 1930.

Coan, T. M. "Prehistoric Times." *Appleton's Popular Science Monthly* 1(May–October 1872): 101–112.

"The Complete Engineer of Three Hundred Years Ago," Editorial in the Engineering Literature Supplement of *Engineering News* 63(17 February 1910): 17. (Based on *A Practical Abstract of the Arts of Fortification and Assailing . . . Written for the benefit of such as delight in the Practice of those Noble Arts*. London: R. Austin, 1645.)

Conant, Kenneth John. Review of *The Construction of Gothic Cathedrals*, by John Fitchen. *Journal of the American Institute of Architects* 42(November 1964): 50.

Cordingley, Reginald A. "British Historical Roof-Types and Their Members." *Transactions of the Ancient Monuments Society*, n.s. 9(1961): 73–117.

Corlett, Dudley Stuart. "The Sacred Cities of Ceylon." *Art and Archaeology* 13(April 1922): 151–68, with 19 photographs.

Cranage, D. H. S. *Cathedrals and How They Were Built*. Cambridge: Cambridge University Press, 1948.

Crossley, Fred H. *Timber Building in England from Early Times to the End of the Seventeenth Century*. London: B. T. Batsford, 1951.

Curman, Sigurd, and Johnny Roosval. *Sveriges Kyrkor: Konsthistoriskt Inventarium Gotland, II Rute Setting*. Stockholm, 1935.

Curzon, George N. "Journeys in French Indo-China (Tongking, Annam, Cochin China, Cambodia)." *Geographical Journal* 2(July–December): 97–111; 193–210.

Czarnowsky, Charles. "Engins de levage dans les combles d'églises en Alsace." *Les Cahiers techniques d'art* (Strasbourg: Éditions F.-X. Le Roux) 2(January–August 1949): 11–27 fasc. 1–2, with 25 illustrations.

Davis, Arthur P. "Use of Concrete for Dams, Tunnels, Culverts and Canals." *Proceedings of the Twentieth Annual Convention, American Concrete Institute* 20(1924): 89–95, with four photographs.

Day, Arthur L. "Earthquakes and Their Effect on Buildings." *Proceedings of the Twenty-Second Annual Convention, American Concrete Institute* 22(1926): 72–78.

Deimal, Richard F. "Strength of materials." *Encyclopedia Americana*. 1949.

Denby, Minister. *Journal of the Society of Arts* (London) 40(1892): 166.

Desgodets, Antoine. *Les Lois des bâtimens suivant la coutume de Paris*. Paris, 1768.

Dibner, Bern. *Moving the Obelisks: A chapter in engineering history in which the Vatican obelisk in Rome in 1587 was moved by muscle power, and a study of more recent similar moves*. Cambridge: MIT Press, 1970.

Drachmann, A. G. *The Mechanical Technology of Greek and Roman Antiquity*. Madison: University of Wisconsin Press, 1963.

Drexler, Arthur. *The Architecture of Japan*. New York: The Museum of Modern Art, 1955.

du Colombier, Pierre. *Les Chantiers des cathédrales*. Paris: Éditions A. & J. Picard, 1953.

Dupree, Hunter. "The Pace of Measurement from Rome to America." *The Smithsonian Journal of History* 3(1968): 19–40, with 11 figures and 12 tables.

Durm, Josef. *Die Baustile. Historische and Technische Entwickelung. Des Handbuches der Architektur Zweiter Theil*. 1. Band: *Die Baukunst der Griechen*. Zweite Auflage. Darmstadt: Verlag von Arnold Bergsträsser, 1892.

Durm, Josef. *Die Baustile. Historische und Technische Entwickelung. Des Handbuches der Architektur Zweiter Teil*. 2. Band: *Die Baukunst der Etrusker. Die Baukunst der Römer*. Zweite Auflage. Stuttgart: Alfred Kroner Verlag, 1905.

Eckardt, Andreas. *A History of Korean Art*. London: Edward Goldston, 1929.

Edmunds, Charles K. "Shantung—China's Holy Land." *National Geographic* 36 (July–December 1919): 231–52, with 21 illustrations and a map.

Edwards, I. E. S. *The Pyramids of Egypt*. Rev. ed. London: Penguin Books, 1972.

Emy, A. R. *Traite de l'art de la charpenterie*. Paris: Dunod, 1878.

Encyclopedia Americana. 1949, s.v. "building regulations" and "strength of materials."

Encyclopaedia Britannica. 11th ed., s.v. "ladder," "shoring," and "tent."

Engelbach, R. *The Problem of the Obelisks*. London: Fisher Unwin, 1923.

Enlart, Camille. *Manual d'archéologie française depuis le temps mérovingiens jusqu'à la renaissance*. Part 1, *Architecture religeuse*. Paris: Alphonse Picard et fils, 1902.

Eton, William. *A Survey of the Turkish Empire*. 2d ed. London: Printed for T. Cadell, jun. & W. Davies, 1799.

Fairchild, David. "Madeira on the Way to Italy." *National Geographic* 18(December 1907): 751–71, with 20 illustrations.

Farabee, William Curtis. "A Pioneer in Amazonia: The Narrative of a Journey from Manos to Georgetown." *Bulletin of the Geographical Society of Philadelphia* 15(1917): 57–103, with 14 photographs.

Fathy, Hassan. *Architecture for the Poor*. Chicago and London: University of Chicago Press, 1973.

Ferrare, Sig. Abate. "An Account of the Earthquake which occurred in Sicily, in March, 1823." Translated by W. S. Emerson. *American Journal of Science* 9(1825): 216–39.

Fewkes, Jesse Walter. *Antiquities of the Mesa Verde National Park: Spruce-Tree House*. Smithsonian Institution, Bureau of American Ethnology Bulletin 41. Washington, D.C.: Government Printing Office, 1909, with 21 plates.

Fitch, James Marston, and Daniel P. Branch. "Primitive Architecture and Climate." *Scientific American* 203(December 1960): 134–44.

Fitchen, John. "A Comment on the Function of the Upper Flying Buttress in French Gothic Architecture." *Gazette des Beaux-Arts,* ser. 6, 45(February 1955): 69–90, with eight line drawings and two appendices.

Fitchen, John. "A House of Laminated Walls." *Society of Architectural Historians Journal* 16(May 1957): 27–28.

Fitchen, John. "Architecture: the Optimistic Art." *American Institute of Architects Journal* 42(December 1964): 47–48.

Fitchen, John. "Some Contemporary Techniques of Arch Construction in Spain." *American Institute of Architects Journal* 34(December 1960): 32–34, with three photographs and a line drawing.

Fitchen, John. *The Construction of Gothic Cathedrals.* Oxford: Clarendon Press, 1961; Chicago: University of Chicago Press, Midway Reprints, 1977; Phoenix Books, 1981.

Fitchen, John. *The New World Dutch Barn.* Syracuse: Syracuse University Press, 1968. Reprint. 1975.

Fitchen, John. Review of *The Development of Carpentry, 1200–1700: An Essex Study,* by Cecil Alec Hewett. *Bulletin for Preservation Technology* 3(1971): 8–9.

Fitzrandolph, Helen E., M. Dorial Hay, and Anna M. Jones. *The Rural Industries of England and Wales: A Survey Made on behalf of the Agricultural Economics Research Institute, Oxford.* 4 vols. Oxford: Clarendon Press, 1926–27.

Fletcher, Alice C. "An Average Day in Camp among the Sioux." *Science* 6(July–December 1885): 285–87.

Forbes, R. J. *Notes on the History of Ancient Roads and Their Construction.* Amsterdam: Allard Pierson Stichting, 1934.

Forrest, George. "The Land of the Cross-bow." *National Geographic* 21(1910): 132–56.

Forsyth, Louis N. "Archaeological Remains in the Mazatec Country." *Records of the Past* 9(1910): 328–34, with three photographs.

Fort, George F. *A Historical Treatise on Early Builders' Marks.* Philadelphia: McCalla & Stavely, 1885.

Fox, William F. "History of the Lumber Industry in the State of New York." In the *Sixth Annual Report of the Forest, Fish and Game Commission of the State of New York,* 237–305. Albany: James B. Lyon, 1901, with nineteen photographs and a two-page map.

Furnfijelm, E. F. de. Letter translated from the Russian. In *American Journal of Science and Arts* 11(May 1851): 136–37.

Gabe, R. M. *Karel'skoe derevyannoe Zodchestro* (Wooden architecture of Karelia). Gosudarstvennoe architekturnoe isdatel'stvo. Moscow: Akademii Architektury CCCP, 1941, with many drawings and photographs, plus a bibliography.

Gamio, Manuel. "Cultural Evolution in Guatemala and Its Geographic and Historic Handicaps." Part 2, "Colonial and Modern Evolution." *Art and Archaeology* 23(January 1927): 17–32, with 29 illustrations. (See also Part 3, "Technical data on which the Previous Articles have Been Premised." 23(February 1927): 70–78.)

Ghosal, S. "The Buddhist Relic Mound at Sopara." *Records of the Past* 2(1903): 297–307.

Gibbon, J. H. "A Visit to the Salt Works of Zipaquera, near Bogota, in New Grenada." *American Journal of Science and Arts* 32(July 1837): 89–95.

Gibbs, G. "Observations on the Dry Rot." *American Journal of Science and Arts* 2(1820): 114–17.

Gide, André. *Travels in the Congo.* Translated by Dorothy Bussy. New York: Alfred A. Knopf, 1937.

Gilliss, J. M. "On the Earthquake of April 2, 1851, in Chile." *American Journal of Science & Arts,* n.s. 21(May 1856): 388–99.

Gimpel, Jean. *The Medieval Machine.* New York: Holt, Rinehart and Winston, 1976.

A Glossary of Terms Used in Grecian, Roman, Italian, and Gothic Architecture. 5th ed., enl. 1 vol., text; 2 vols., plates. Oxford: John Henry Parker, 1850.

Golding, William. *The Spire.* New York: Harcourt Brace & World, 1964.

Gomes, Edwin H. *Seventeen Years Among the Sea Dyaks of Borneo.* London: Seeley & Co., 1911, with 40 illustrations and a map.

Gomes, Edwin H. "Notes on the Sea Dyaks of Borneo." *National Geographic* 22 (August 1911): 695–723, with 26 illustrations.

Gorringe, Henry H. *Egyptian Obelisks.* New York: the author, 1882.

Gorsky, Bernard. *Island at the End of the World.* Translated from the French by Alan Houghton Brodrick. London: Rupert Hart-Davis, 1966.

Grant, Anne. *Memoirs of an American Lady, with Sketches of Manners and Scenery in America, as they existed previous to the Revolution.* New York: D. Appleton & Co., 1846.

Greenwell, G. M. "The Strange Beehive Village of Talbeseh." *Travel* 67(September 1936): 20–21, 58.

Guastavino, R. *Essay on the Theory and History of Cohesive Construction Applied to the Timbrel Vault.* Boston: Ticknor and Co., 1892, with 62 figures.

Haddon, Alfred C. "Studies in the Anthropogeography of British New Guinea." *Geographical Journal* 16(1900): 265–91, 414–41.

Hadley, H. M. "How Structures Withstood the Japanese Earthquake and Fire." *Proceedings of the Twentieth Annual Convention, American Concrete Institute* 20(1924): 188–208.

Hamlin, Talbot. *Architecture through the Ages.* New York: G. P. Putnam's Sons, 1944.

Harshberger, John W. "Phytogeographic Influences in the Arts and Industries of the American Aborigines." *Bulletin of the Geographical Club of Philadelphia* 4(January 1904–October 1906): 137–53.

Hartman, John M. "Syenite Quarries at Assouan." *Scientific American Supplement* 36(July–December 1893): 14754. (Extract of remarks before the Franklin Institute, 19 April 1893.)

"The Harvard Expedition to Samaria." *Harvard Theological Review* (January 1909); reprinted in *Records of the Past* 8(1909): 175–76.

Harvey, John. "The Masons of Westminster Abbey." *Archaeological Journal* (London: Royal Archaeological Institute of Great Britain and Ireland) 113(November 1957): 82–101.

Harvey, William. *The Preservation of St. Paul's Cathedral and Other Famous Buildings: A Text Book on the New Science of Conservation, including an Analysis of Movements in Historical Structures Prior to Their Fall.* London: The Architectural Press, 1925.

Hatt, W. K. "Note on Fatigue in Mortar." *Proceedings of the Eighteenth Annual Convention, American Concrete Institute* 18(1922): 167–73, with five figures and three tables.

Henson, Llewellyn L. "Researches in Palestine." *Records of the Past* 5(1906): 39–59, with six photographs and a plan.

Hess. "Die Canale des Staates New York, nebst Bemenhaugen den Wasserverbrauch auf Schifffahrtscanälen." *Zeitschrift für Bauwesen* 17(1867): 513–44, with tables and foldout maps.

Hewett, Cecil Alec. *The Development of Carpentry: 1200–1700 An Essex Study.* Newton Abbot: David & Charles, 1969.

Hewett, Edgar L. "Prehistoric Irrigation in the Navaho Desert." *Records of the Past* 4(1905): 322–29, with six illustrations.

Heyman, Jacques. "The Stone Skeleton." *International Journal of Solids Structures* 2(1966): 249–79, with 49 figures.

Heyman, Jacques. "Beauvais Cathedral." *Transactions of the Newcomen Society* 40(1967–68): 15–35, with 13 illustrations.

Heyman, Jacques. "The Safety of Masonry Arches." *International Journal of Mechanical Science* 11(1969): 363–85.

Holt, Elizabeth G. ed. *A Documentary History of Art.* Vol 1, *The Middle Ages and the Renaissance.* Garden City, New York: Doubleday, Anchor Books, 1957.

Hommel, Rudolph P. *China at Work: An Illustrated Record of the Primitive Industries of Chinese Masses, Whose Life is Toil, and thus an Account of Chinese Civilization. Records of Chinese, Oriental and other Primitive Industries, being the results of an Expedition begun in the year 1921, . . . and published for the Bucks County Historical Society, Doylestown, Pennsylvania.* New York: John Day Co., 1937. Reprint. Cambridge: MIT Press, 1970.

"Hong Kong: Scaffolding, Chinese Style." *Construction Methods and Equipment* 52(July 1970): 137–38.

Horn, Walter, and Ernest Born. *The Plan of St. Gall: A Study of the Architecture and Economy of, and Life in a paradigmatic Carolingian Monastery. . . .* 3 vols. Berkeley: University of California Press, 1979.

Hose, Charles. "A Journey up the Baram River to Mount Dulit and the Highlands of Borneo." *Geographical Journal* 1(January–June 1893): 193–208.

Howard, F. E. "On the Construction of Mediaeval Roofs." *Archaeological Journal* 71(1914): 293–352.

Hubbard, George D. "The Geographical Setting of Chengtu." *Bulletin of the Geographical Society of Philadelphia* 21 (January–October 1923): 109–32, with four maps and thirteen photographs.

Hunt, Casper. "The Empire of Darkness." *Travel* 53(October 1929): 37–39, 49. (A review of André Gide, q.v.)

Huss, George Martin. *Rational Building*. New York: Macmillan, 1895. (A translation of Viollet-le-Duc, "Construction," in *Dictionnaire raisonné de l'architecture française,* q.v.)

Huth, Hans. *Observations Concerning the Conservation of Monuments in Europe and America*. Washington, D.C.: National Park Service, 1940.

Hyde, Walter Woodburn. "A Visit to the Pyramids of Gizeh." *Records of the Past* 9(1910): 246–64, 313–27, with 13 illustrations.

Innocent, C. F. *The Development of English Building Construction*. Cambridge: Cambridge University Press, 1916. Reprint. Cambridge: MIT Press, 1971.

Irving, Robert. *Hurricanes and Twisters*. New York: Scholastic Book Service, 1961.

James, George Wharton. "Primitive Inventions." *The Craftsman* 5(October 1903–March 1904): 124–37, with 13 illustrations.

James, John. *The Contractors of Chartres*. 2d ed., rev. 2 vols. Wyong, Australia: Mandorla Publications, 1981.

Janson, H. W. *History of Art*. Englewood Cliffs, N.J.: Prentice Hall; New York: Harry N. Abrams, n.d. [ca. 1962].

Jope, E. M. "Vehicles and Harness." Chapter 15 of Part 4, "Transport," in *The Mediterranean and the Middle Ages, c. 700 B.C. to A.D. 1500*. Vol. 2 of *A History of Technology,* edited by Singer et al. Oxford: Clarendon Press, 1956.

Kerr, Robert. "Observations on the Architect's Functions in Relation to Building Contracts." *Transactions: Royal Institute of British Architects,* N.S. 3(1887): 128–40.

Kopernicki, J. "Characteristics of the Calmucks, An Ethnological Study." Translated from the Russian. *Appleton's Popular Science Monthly* 1(May–October 1872): 419–34.

Kramrisch, Stella. *The Hindu Temple*. 2 vols. Calcutta: University of Calcutta, 1946.

Kreuger, Henry. "The Tote Road and the Pung." *The Conservationist* (Albany, NY: New York State Conservation Department) 24(February–March 1970): 29–31.

Kubler, George. "A Late Gothic Computation of Rib Vault Thrusts." *Gazette des Beaux-Arts,* ser. 6, 26(July–December 1944): 135–48.

Kuhn, Albert. *Roma: Ancient, Subterranean, and Modern Rome.* New York: Benziger Brothers, 1916.

Kumm, Karl W. "From Hausaland to Egypt." *Scottish Geographical Magazine* 27(1911): 225–42.

Kyle, M.G. "Bricks Without Straw at Pithom: A Reëxamination of Naville's Works." *Records of the Past* 8(1909): 304–7.

Lake, Harry. "Jahore." *Geographical Journal* 3(January–June 1894): 281–302.

Landels, L. G. *Engineering in the Ancient World.* Berkeley and Los Angeles: University of California Press, 1978.

Lassaulx, M. F. "Notes on the Churches of the Rhine." In *Architectural Notes on German Churches, with Notes Written during an Architectural Tour in Picardy and Normandy,* edited by William Whewell. 3d ed. Cambridge: J. & J.J. Deighton, 1842.

Laubin, Reginald, and Gladys Laubin. *The Indian Tipi: Its History, Construction and Use.* New York: Ballantine Books, 1971.

"The Laws of Hammurabi, King of Babylonia." Translated in *Records of the Past* 2(1903): 66–96, with seven photographs.

Lee, Melicent Humanson. "The Ancient House of the San Diegueno Indians." *Art and Archaeology* 25(February 1928): 100–105, 108, with seven progress photographs of steps in its construction.

Leon, Paul. *La Vie des monuments français: destruction, restauration.* Paris: éditions A. & J. Picard, 1951.

Lethaby, W. R. *Architecture.* New York: Henry Holt & Co., 1912.

Lhote, Henry. *The Search for the Tassili Frescoes: The Story of the Prehistoric Rock-paintings of the Sahara.* Translated from the French by Alan H. Brodrick. New York: E. P. Dutton, 1959.

Littledale, St. George R. "A Journey Across Central Asia." *Geographical Journal* 3(January–June 1894): 445–72.

Longfellow, William P. P., ed. *A Cyclopaedia of Works of Architecture in Italy, Greece, and the Levant.* New York: Charles Scribner's Sons, 1903.

Lopez, Frank G. "Building regulatins." *Encyclopedia Americana.* 1949.

Lord, Arthur R. "Notes on Concrete—Wacker Drive, Chicago." *Proceedings of the Twenty-Third Annual Convention, American Concrete Institute* 23(1927): 28–78, with five figures.

Lorentz, H. A. "An Expedition to the Snow Mountains of New Guinea." *Scottish Geographical Magazine* 27(1911): 337–59, with a foldout map and six photographs.

Lowndes, Marion. "Black Hell in the Pacific." *Travel* 75(October 1940): 4–9, 39, 40.

Lucas, A. *Ancient Egyptian Materials & Industries.* 2d ed., rev., London: Edward Arnold & Co., 1934. (See particularly chap. 3, "Building Materials," and chap. 14, "Wood.")

M'Adam, John Loudon. *Remarks on the present System of Road Making; deduced from Practice and Experience with a view to a revision to the existing laws, and the introduction of improvement in the Method of Making, Repairing and Preserving Roads . . . .* 4th ed., rev. London: Longman, Hurst, Rees, Orme, & Brown, 1821. (See particularly 'Directions for Repair of an old Road." [pp. 38–43] and "Report from the Select Committee on the Highways of the Kingdom" [pp. 60–195].)

Mainstone, Rowland J. "The Springs of Structural Invention." *Royal Institute of British Architects Journal* 70(February 1963): 57–71, with 54 illustrations and bibliographical notes.

Mainstone, Rowland J. "On Construction and Form." *Columbia University School of Architecture Program,* no. 3(Spring 1964): 51–70, with 12 figures.

Mainstone, Rowland J. "The Structure of the Church of St. Sophia, Istanbul." *Transactions of the Newcomen Society* 38(1965–66): 23–49, with twelve text illustrations plus nine additional plates comprising twelve (mainly photographic) illustrations.

Mainstone, Rowland J. "Brunelleschi's Dome." *Architectural Review* 162 (September 1977): 156–66, with 27 illustrations, both photographs and drawings, and bibliographical notes.

Malcolm, L. W. G. "Huts and Villages in the Cameroon, West Africa." *Scottish Geographical Magazine* 39(1923): 21–27.

Mark, Robert. "The Structural Analysis of Gothic Cathedrals." *Scientific American* 227(November 1972): 90–99, with twelve figures.

Marshall, William B. "Useful Products of the Century Plant." *Journal of Geography* 1(1902): 6–17, with five photographs.

Martin, Roland. *Manuel d'architecture grecque.* Paris: A. & J. Picard, 1965.

Mason, Otis T. *The Origins of Invention: A Study of Industry among Primitive Peoples.* London: Walter Scott, 1895. Reprint. Cambridge: MIT Press, 1966.

Matthews, Kenneth D. "Roman Aqueducts: Technical Aspects of Their Construction." *Expedition: The Bulletin of the University Museum of the University of Pennsylvania* 13(Fall 1970): 2–16, with ten drawings and seven photographs.

Maunsell, F. R. "Kurdistan." *Geographical Journal* 3(January–June 1894): 81–93 plus two pages of discussion.

McBride, Harry A. "The Land of the Free in Africa." *National Geographic* 42(October 1922): 410–30, with 22 photographs.

McCullough, David G. *The Great Bridge.* New York: Simon & Schuster, [1972].

McGee, W. J. "Some Features of the Recent Earthquake in and around Charleston, S.C." *Science* 8(September 24, 1886): 271–75.

McIntyre, Loren. "The Lost Empire of the Incas." *National Geographic* 144(December 1973): 729–87.

McMaster, John B. *Bridge and Tunnel Centres.* Science Series, no. 20. New York: D. Van Nostrand, 1875.

Mease, James. "On Some of the Vegetable materials from which Cordage, Twine and Thread are Made." *American Journal of Science* 21(1832): 27–38.

Mercer, Henry C. *Ancient Carpenters' Tools*. 3d ed. Doylestown, Pa.: The Bucks County Historical Society, 1960.

"The Messina Earthquake." *Scottish Geographical Magazine* 26(1910): 95–96.

Mézieres, le Camus de. *Le Guide de ceux qui veulent bâtir; Ouvrage dans lequel on donne les renseignmens nécessaires pour réussir dans cet Art, & prévenir les fraudes qui pourroient s'y glisser*. 2 vols. Paris: Benoit Morin, 1781. (See particularly 1:47–60, "Choix des Entrepreneurs . . . . "; 1:244–53, "Des vieux Bois, des Etaiemens, des Cintres de Charpente les voûtes, & des Etresillons pour les terres"; and 2:216–54, "Des Devis.")

Middleton, John Henry. "The Temple and Atrium of Vesta and the Regia." *Archaeologia* 49, pt. 2(1886): 391–423, with ten text figures, three photographs, and six plates.

Middleton, John Henry. "On the Chief Methods of Construction Used in Ancient Rome." *Archaeologia* 51, pt. 1(1888): 41–60, with nine text figures and three color plates.

Moles, Antoine. *Histoire des charpentiers: leur travaux*. Paris: Libraire Gründ, 1949.

Morris, Thomas. *British Carpentry: History and principles of Gothic Roofs*. London: Simpkin, Marshall & Co., 1871.

Mortet, Victor. "L'Expertise de la cathédrale de Chartres en 1316." *Congrès archéologiques,* 1900, pp. 308–29.

Les mosquées de Samarcande. Fascicule 1, *Gour-Émir*. Expédition pour la confection des papiers. St. Petersbourg: Commission Impériale Archéologique, 1905.

Muirhead, Findlay, ed. *Southern Italy, including Rome, Sicily, and Sardinia*. The Blue Guides/Italian Touring Club. London: Macmillan, 1925.

Munro, Robert. *Palaeolithic Man and the Terramara Settlements in Europe*. New York: Macmillan, 1912, with 75 plates and 174 text figures.

Munro, Robert. *The Lake Dwellings of Europe*. London: Cassell, 1890.

Murdock, George Peter. *Our Primitive Contemporaries*. New York: Macmillan, 1934.

Needham, Joseph, with the collaboration of Wang Ling. *Science and Civilization in China*. Vol. 4, *Physics and Physical Technology;* pt. 2, "Mechanical Engineering." Cambridge: Cambridge University Press, 1965.

Nicholson, H. J. B. *The Abbey of Saint Alban: Some Extracts from its Early History and a Description of its Conventual Church*. 3d ed. London: George Bell & Sons, 1876.

O'Callaghan, E. B. *The Documentary History of the State of New York*. Vol. 3. Albany: Weed Parsons & Co., 1850.

L'Oeuvre des Compagnons du Devoir. 3d ed. Paris: Librairie du Compagnonnage, 1961.

Oldquist, Andrew. "On Belonging to Tribes." *Newsweek*, 5 April 1982, 9.

Orlandos, A. K. *Les Matériaux de construction et la technique architecturale des anciens Grecs*. 2 vols. Paris: E. de Boccard, 1966–68.

Orr, John B. "Artistic Stucco." *Proceedings of the Thirteenth Annual Convention, American Concrete Institute* 13(1917): 262–71, plus discussion, 272–74.

Panofsky, Erwin. *Abbot Suger on the Abbey Church of St. Denis and Its Treasures*. Princeton: Princeton University Press, 1946.

Papworth, Wyatt. "Notes on the Superintendents of English Buildings in the Middle Ages." *Transactions: Royal Institute of British Architects,* n.s. 3(1887): 185–234.

Parsons, William Barclay. *Engineers and Engineering in the Renaissance*. Baltimore: Williams & Wilkins, 1939.

Partington, C. F. *The Builder's Complete Guide* . . . London: Sherwood, Gilbert, & Piper, 1825.

Pearson, J. C. "Shrinkage of Portland Cement Mortars and Its Importance in Stucco Construction." *Proceedings of the Seventeenth Annual Convention, American Concrete Institute* 17(1921): 133–49, with 11 figures and a summary.

Penrose, Francis Cranmer. *Investigation of the principles of Athenian architecture; or, The results of a . . . survey conducted . . . with reference to the optical refinements exhibited in the construction of the ancient buildings at Athens*. London: Society of Dilettanti, 1851.

Perrault, C., trans. *Marcus Vitruvius Pollio: Les dix livres d'architecture, corrigés et traduits . . . en français, avec des notes et des figures . . . .* Paris, 1673.

Perrot, G. and C. Chipiez, *Histoire de l'art dans l'antiquité. Vol. 1, L'Éypte*. Paris, 1882.

Petrie, W. M. Flinders. *Ten Years' Digging in Egypt, 1881–1891*. New York and Chicago: Fleming H. Revell Co., n.d.

Petrie, W. M. Flinders. *The Arts and Crafts of Ancient Egypt*. Edinburgh and London: T. N. Foulis, 1909.

Petroski, Henry. "When Cracks Become Breakthroughs: Structural failure, not success, improves the evolution of a design." *Technology Review* 85(August–September 1982): 18–30, with 14 illustrations.

Pike, Nicholas. "The Hottentots of Southern Africa." *Scientific American Supplement* 36(July–December 1893): 14772–73.

Pinches, Theophilus G. "Assur and Ninevah." *Records of the Past* 12(1913): 23–41, with seven illustrations.

Plummer, John T. Brief Strictures on Rainey's Article . . . ." *American Journal of Science and Arts* 42(April 1842): 197–200.

Pomeroy, Samuel Wyllys. "Remarks on the Coal Region between Cumberland and Pittsburgh, and on the Topography, Scenery, etc. of that Portion of the Alleghany Mountains." *American Journal of Science and Arts* 21(1831): 342–47.

Porphyrios, Demetrius. "Traditional Earthquake Resistant Construction on a Greek Island." *Society of Architectural Historians Journal* 30(March 1971): 31–39, with seven drawings and seven photographs.

Porter, C. H. *Paper on Building Stones: Addressed to the New Capitol Commissioners.* Albany: Joel Munsell, 1868.

Powys, A. R. *Repair of Ancient Buildings.* London: J. M. Dent & Sons; New York: E. P. Dutton, 1929.

Prentis, Edmund Astley, and Lazarus White. *Underpinning: Its Practice and Applications.* 2d ed., rev. New York: Columbia University Press, 1950.

Price, Francis. *A Series of . . . Observations . . . upon . . . the Cathedral Church of Salisbury.* London: C. and J. Ackers, 1753.

Rackham, R. B. "The Nave of Westminster." In *Proceedings of the British Academy 1909–1910,* pp. 33–96. London: Henry Frowde, Oxford University Press, 1910.

Rainey, Phineas. "On the Dry Rot." *American Journal of Science and Arts* 34(July 1838): 169–79.

Ramée, Daniel. *Dictionnaire général des termes d'architecture en français, allemand, anglais, et italien.* Paris: C. Reinwald, Libraire-éditeur, 1868.

Ramsay, Dr. W. M. "The Early Christian Art of Nova Isaura." *Records of the Past* 3(1904): 318–20.

Rauline, Henri. "The Church of the Sacred Heart at Montmartre: Its Origin and Construction." *Architectural Record* 3(July–September 1893): 3–28, with 20 illustrations.

Rees, Abraham. *The Cyclopaedia; or, Universal Dictionary of Arts, Sciences, and Literature.* 47 vols., including 6 vols. of plates. First American edition, revised, corrected, enlarged, and adapted to this country. Philadelphia: Samuel F. Bradford & Murray, Fairman & Co., [1810–24]. Unpaginated.

Regnault, Dr. F. "The Prehensile Function of the Foot." *Scientific American Supplement* 36(July–December 1893): 14868–69, with four figures.

Rempel, John I. *Building With Wood.* Toronto: University of Toronto Press, 1967.

Richardson, Charles H. *Building Stones and Clays.* Syracuse: the author, 1917.

Ricketson, Oliver G., Jr. "American Nail-less Houses in the Maya Bush." *Art and Archaeology* 24(July–August 1927): 27–36, with 16 pen-and-ink drawings of details and scheme of construction.

Robertson, D. S. *A Handbook of Greek and Roman Architecture.* 2d ed. Cambridge: Cambridge University Press, 1943, with an extensive bibliography.

Roebuck, Carl, ed. *The Muses at Work: Arts, Crafts, and Professions in Ancient Greece and Rome.* Cambridge: MIT Press, 1969. (See chap. 1, "Greek Building" by Robert Scranton; chap. 2, "Roman Imperial Building" by James E. Packer; chap. 4, "Stone Carving: Sculpture" by Brunilde Sismondo Ridgway; and chap. 7, "Sailing" by Lionel Casson.)

Rondelet, J. *Traité théorique et pratique de l'art de bâtir.* 6 vols., text; 2 vols., plates. Paris: the author, 1812–17.

Rudofsky, Bernard. *Architecture without Architects*. New York: The Museum of Modern Art, 1965. Unpaginated.

Salzman, L. F. *Building in England Down to 1540: A Documentary History*. Oxford: Clarendon Press, 1952.

Schaffer, R. J. *The Weathering of Natural Building Stones*. Department of Scientific and Industrial Research, Building Research Special Report, no. 18. London: HMSO, 1933.

Schmidt, Karl. *Die Baugerüste: Arbeits-und Schutzgerüste im Hochbau*. Munchen: Verlag Hermann Rinn, 1949.

Schwatka, Frederick. "The Igloo of the Innuit." *Science* 2 (July–December 1883): 182–84; 216–18, with two woodcuts; 259–62, with nine woodcuts; 304–6, with plan and section; 347–49, with three woodcuts.

Scott, George Gilbert. *Gleanings from Westminster Abbey*. 2d ed. Oxford: John Henry and James Parker, 1863.

Seddon, J. P. "On the Shoring of Grosmont Tower." In *Papers Read at the RIBA Session, 1872–73*, pp. 101–10, with many details on one plate. London: Royal Institute of British Architects, 1873.

Shaw, Edward. *Civil Architecture, being a complete theoretical and practical System of Building, containing the fundamental principles of the art . . . .* 6th ed. Cleveland, Ohio: Jewett, Proctor, & Worthington, 1852.

Shelby, Lon R. "Setting out the Keystones of Pointed Arches: A Note on Medieval Baugeometrie." *Technology and Culture* 10(October 1969): 537–48, with eight figures.

Shelby, Lon R. "The Education of Medieval English Master Masons." *Pontifical Institute of Medieval Studies* 32(1970): 1–26.

Shelton, A. L. "Life among the People of Eastern Tibet." *National Geographic* 40(July–December 1921): 295–326, with 36 illustrations and a map.

Sibree, James. *A Naturalist in Madagascar . . . .* London: Seeley Service & Co., 1915. (Reviewed in *Scottish Geographical Magazine* 32(1916): 255–56.)

Sih-Gung Cheng. "China's Geography: Historical and Social." *Scottish Geographical Magazine* 34(1918): 281–94, with a map, illustrations, and an extensive bibliography.

Simms, Frederick Walter. *Practical Tunnelling; explaining in detail the Setting out of the Works; Shaft Sinking and Heading Driving; Ranging the Lines and Leveling Under Ground; Sub-Excavating, Timbering, and the Construction of the Brickwork of Tunnels . . . .* 2d ed., rev. London: Lockwood & Co., 1860, with additinal plates, by W. Davis Haskoll.

Simpson, F. M. *A History of Architectural Development*. Vol. 1, *Ancient, Early Christian, and Byzantine*. London: Longmans, Green & Co., 1921.

Simpson, William. "Mud Architecture: Notes Made in Persia and Other Countries." *Transactions: Royal Institute of British Architects*, n.s. 3(1887): 57–80, with eight illustrations.

Smith, Alfred Charles. "On the Method of Moving Colossal Stones, as practiced by some of the more advanced Nations of Antiquity." *Wiltshire Archaeological and Natural History Society* 10(1865): 52–60.

Smith, C. H. "Lithology; or, Observations on Stone Used for Building." Part 1, "Treating chiefly of the Sandstones." Part 2, "Treating Chiefly of the Oölites." *Transactions of the Royal Institute of British Architects of London* (Longman, Brown, Green & Longmans) 1, pt. 2(1842): 129–68.

Smith, E. Baldwin. *Egyptian Architecture as Cultural Expression.* New York: D. Appleton-Century Co., 1938.

Smith, G. E. Kidder. *Italy Builds.* New York: Reinhold, 1955.

Smith, J. T. "Medieval Roofs: A Classification." *Archaeological Journal* 115(1960): 111–49.

"A Spider's Device in Lifting." *Science* 3(January–June 1884): 432–33.

Starr, Frederick. *Indians of Southern Mexico: An Ethnological Album.* Chicago, 1899, with 141 plates.

Statham, H. Heathcote. *Architecture for General Readers.* 2d ed., rev. New York: Charles Scribner's Sons, 1897.

Stephens, J. L. *Incidents of Travel in Central America, Chiapas, and Yucatan.* 2 vols. New York, 1841, with drawings by Catherwood.

Stilgoe, John R. "Topping Out." *Harvard Magazine* (March–April 1980): 63.

Street, George Edmund. *Some Account of Gothic Architecture in Spain.* London: John Murray, 1865.

Struik, Dirk J. *Yankee Science in the Making.* rev. ed. New York: Collier Books, 1968.

Strzygowski, Josef. *Early Church Art in Northern Europe.* London: B. T. Batsford, 1928.

Tavernier, Jean Baptiste, Baron d'Aubonne. *Voyages en Turquie, en Perse, et aux Indes.* England, 1678; Germany, 1684.

Thatcher, A. G. H. *Scaffolding: A Treatise on the Design and Erection of Scaffolds, Gantries and Stagings . . . .* London: B. T. Batsford, 1904.

Thomas, J. Arthur. "The Physical Welfare of Mothers and Children in Scotland." *Scottish Geographical Magazine* 34(1918): 147–54.

Thunnissen, Ir. H. J. W. *Gewelven: Hun Constructie en toepassing in de historische en hedendaagse bouwkunst.* Amsterdam: J. Ahrend & Zoon, 1950.

Toglietta, Guido Ubaldo. *Discorso del mattonato e selicato di Roma.* Vol 1. Rèal Società di Storia Patriae, 1878.

Tomlinson, Charles. *Rudimentary Treatise on Warming and Ventilation.* London: John Weale, 1850.

Torell, Clark A. "Development of the Project Site to Support the Construction Activity." Part of chapter 12, "Preconstruction Activities," in *Planning, Engineering, and Construction of Electric Power Generation Facilities,* edited by Jack H. Willenbrock and H. Randolph Thomas. New York: John Wiley, 1980.

"Travel and Traffic in China." *Journal of Geography* 2(1903): 31–33. (Abstract from *Monthly Summary of Commerce & Finance*, June 1901.)

Travelli, Joseph S. "Manilla Hemp." *American Journal of Science and Arts* 41(October 1841): 200–203.

Tredgold, Thomas, with J. T. Hurst. *Carpentry and Joinery* . . . . 8th ed. London, 1892.

Trouvelot, Jean. "De la restauration des monuments historiques." *Techniques et architecture*, 9th ser., nos. 11–12(November 1950): 38–50, with 45 illustrations.

Tschopik, Harry, Jr. "At Home in the High Andes." *National Geographic* 107(January 1955): 133–46, with a map and ten illustrations.

Turner, T. Hudson. *Some Account of Domestic Architecture in England*. 3 vols. in 4. Oxford: John Henry Parker, 1851–59.

Uhde, Constantin. *Baudenkmaeler in Spain und Portugal*. Berlin: Ernst Wasmuth, 1892.

U.S. Bureau of Standards. *Code for Protection against Lightning*. Handbook No. 17, part 2 and appendix A. Government Printing Office, 1932.

U.S. Department of Commerce. *Tide Tables: U.S. and Foreign Ports for the Year 1930*. U.S. Coast and Geodetic Survey Series, no. 439. Government Printing Office, 1929.

U.S. Department of the Interior, Bureau of Reclamation. *Thermal Properties of Concrete*. Bulletin 1 of *Cement and Concrete Investigations, Boulder Canyon Project Final Reports*, pt. 7. Denver, Colorado, 1949.

"Use of Ancient Lamps." *Records of the Past* 8(1909): 215.

van Ravenswaay, Charles. "America's Age of Wood." *Proceedings of the American Antiquarian Society* (Worcester, Massachusetts), April 1970, pp. 49–66.

Viala, Pierre. *Le village des Bories à Gordes dans le Vaucluse*. 6th ed. Gordes, 1981, with sixteen photographs, two drawings, and a plan.

Viollet-le-Duc, [Eugène Emmanuel] *Dictionnaire raisonné de l'architecture française du XIe au XVIe siècle*. 10 vols. Paris: Libraires-Imprimeries Réunies, 1858–68.

Viollet-le-Duc, [Eugène Emmanuel] *Discourses on Architecture*. Translated by Benjamin Bucknall. 2 vols. London: George Allen & Unwin, 1959.

Vitruvius, the Ten Books on Architecture. Translated by Morris Hicky Morgan. Cambridge: Harvard University Press, 1914.

von Frisch, Karl. *Animal Architecture*. New York: Harcourt Brace Jovanovich, 1974.

von Schenck, Natalie. "The 'Cenotes' of Yucatan." *Records of the Past* 6(1906): 90–92.

Ward, F. Kingdon. *In Furthest Burma*. London: Seeley Service & Co., 1912. (Reviewed in *Scottish Geographical Magazine* 37(1921): 277–78.)

Warland, E. G. *Modern Practical Masonry*. London: Batsford; New York: Dodd Mead & Co., 1929

Watson, Thomas Lennox. *The Double Choir of Glasgow Cathedral: A Study of Rib Vaulting.* Glasgow: James Hedderwick & Sons, 1901.

Weir, James, Jr., "Animal Intelligence." *Scientific American Supplement* 36(July–December 1893): 14997–98.

Whewell, Rev. William. *Architectural Notes on German Churches, with Notes Written during an Architectural Tour in Picardy and Normany, to which are added "Notes on the Churches of the Rhine" by M. F. Lassaulx.* 3d ed. Cambridge: J. & J. J. Deighton; London: John W. Parker, 1842.

White, John Claude. "Castles in the Air: Experiences and Journeys in Unknown Bhutan." *National Geographic* 25(1914): 365–455.

Wilkes, Charles. *Narrative of the United States Exploring Expedition . . . . 1838–1842.* 5 vols. and an atlas. Philadelphia: Lee and Blanchard, 1845.

Williams, Christopher, with photographs by Charlotte Williams. *Craftsmen of Necessity.* New York: Random House, Vintage Books, 1974.

Williams, J. C. "Effect of the Time of Cutting Timber." *Engineering News* 63(3 February 1910): 121.

Williams-Ellis, Clough, John Eastwick-Field, and Elizabeth Eastwick-Field. *Building in Cob, Pisé, and Stabilized Earth.* 3d ed., rev. and enl. London: Country Life, 1950.

Willis, Robert. "On the Construction of the Vaults of the Middle Ages." *Transactions of the Royal Institute of British Architects.* (London: Longman, Brown, Green, and Longmans). 1(1842; Reprint, 1910): 1–69, with twenty-two text figures and three plates.

Wilson, Ernest H. "The Kingdom of Flowers—China." *National Geographic* 22(November 1911): 1003–35, with 24 photographs.

Wright, Frederick Bennett. "The Fortress of Masada." *Records of the Past* 5(1906): 368–72.

Wulff, Hans E. *The Traditional Crafts of Persia.* Cambridge: The MIT Press, 1966.

Zabaglia, Niccola. *Castelli e ponti di Maestro Niccolo Zabaglia con alcune ingegnose pratiche, e con la descrizione trasporto dell' obelisco Vaticano e di altri del Cavaliere Domenico Fontana.* 2d ed., published simultaneously in Latin and in Italian. Rome, 1824, with many large, engraved plates of details and ensembles alike.

Indexes

General Index

Photographs as sources of information on building practices of the past, 19, 20, 250n16

Pile-supported structures
pile dwellings over water, 20, 220–222 (quoted), 252n22, 289nn16–24
piles as sub-grade supports, 254n19

Pisé construction, 266n22 (quoted), 266n23 (quoted)

Pit-sawing, 20, 136, 251n17, 274n10

Quality performance of vernacular buildings in some native cultures: granite farm buildings of N. Portugal, corbeled stone trulli of SE Italy, squared log habitations of Sweden, Switzerland, the Balkans, New World Dutch barns of eastern New York State, 41

Rafts: of inflated skins, of logs, of grass, 180

Ramps (*See also* "Ground levels") 177, 229, 230

Revival of interest in handicraft methods of building construction, 13–14

Rituals (*See also* Building regulations)
Dyak communal house under construction, 214, 215
making bricks in India, 40
temple building in Egypt, 41
"topping out" ceremonies, 288n5
twelve-day ceremony founding a Hawaiian temple, 288n5

Roads
access roads, 177
famous routes of the past, 175–176
ordinary roads in China, including their pavement, 176

Rope knots
instances of where not intended to be untied, 117
nature, purposes, security from working loose, ease of untying, 117

Rope lashing
kept tight by long wedges, 90
for scaffolding, 53, 86, 90, 91
universal among indigenous peoples, 118

Rope making, 118

Rope, uses of, applied to buildings and related activities
many thatched roofs, 117
repairing the breach in a Chinese river's dike, 186–187
Spanish windlass device, 237
stone-weighted rope device, 112
suspension bridges, 68–69, 115, 116
towing and/or lifting, 118 (quoted), 120, 122–123
various mechanical operations, 118 (quoted), 119

Scaffolding
atypical prodigality in Sacré Coeur church, Paris, 87 (quoted)
of bamboo, in the Far East, 90
conjectural scheme of, for finishing the Great Pyramid, 290
definition and terminology, 85
part of the building itself serving as, 90
permanent, as in Salisbury Cathedral's spire, 150–151
putlogs, 86
Viollet-le-Duc's schemes of, 89, 90

Setting stone blocks
blocks of ice, 5
Egyptian mortar used primarily as a lubricant, 237
handling and positioning bosses, 161
pry-bars, 156
Spanish windlass device, 237

Shoddy building due to
sometimes, competitive bidding (stucco), 42 (quoted)
faulty ingredients (mortar), 43 (quoted)
inferior materials (crooked tiles), 43 (quoted)
unseasoned wood, 44

Shoring
definition and purposes, 97
extensive shoring, E end of Winchester Cathedral, 99 (quoted)
major shoring executed in Partishow Church, 97, 99 (quoted)
sapling poles used to shore formwork for floors in multistoried modern Spanish building, 98

Shrinkage in building materials
in the curing of concrete, 81
in medieval mortar joints, 80
in timber construction, across the grain, 81

Site selection
Christian churches, 48, 258n5 (quoted)
conditions and requirements, 48, 214
Dyaks of Borneo, via a building committee, 214
overall layout, plan of St. Gall, 48

Stone blocks roughed out oversized at the quarry
as protection against injury in setting column drums, 159
as protection against injury in transit, 157 (quoted), 158
as temporary corbels to support falsework, 162

Stresses during construction, reduction of
Egyptians' non-use of rollers explained, 79
movement of huge lintel without rollers, 79

movement of obelisks via levers, jacking, and series of ramps, 79

Stresses which act *on* buildings
aerodynamic oscillation, 64, 68–69. (*See also* Suspension bridges)
dead load vs. live loads, defined, 64
endemic, and hence cannot be ignored, 83
lightning strokes, 74–75
no records kept, in the past, 63
seismic forces, 74 (quoted)
wind action from any direction, including upward, 64

Stresses which act *within* buildings
domes subject to centrifugal outward forces, 72, *73*
fatigue, 75–76
kinetic stresses, 71
lateral thrust in arches, 71–72. (*See also* Arch terminology and Catenary curve)
partial loadings, 71
shear stresses, 66–67 (quoted), *70*
shrinkage, 80–81
thermal stresses, 80

Surveys
for network of Roman roads, 48, 258n4
for property boundaries in Egypt, 48, 258n3
for Roman aqueducts, 47, 258n2

Thatching, 117, 216, 217, 221, 249n12, 251n20, 269n9

Tradition, persistence of, in building practices and forms
common building practices recognized and accepted by the whole tribe or community, 35, 86, 213
fixity of life-pattern, 35, 256n31 (quoted)

Transportation by land
by beasts of burden, 173 (quoted)
by draft animals, 174
by human carriers, 172 (quoted) (*See also* Carrying devices)
by long files of human haulers, 177
for obelisks, sequential series of mounded-up slopes, 178
by rolling heavy blocks, 174

Transported: examples of what is required to be
building materials *to* the site, 169
excavated materials *from* the site, 171, 172 (quoted)
whole dwellings (tepees, yurts, Bedouir tents, African huts), 172

Undulating masonry courses, *82,* 264n33

Vault construction
of hollow pots, 256n31 (quoted)
Roman concrete, 106, *107*
stone-weighted rope device, 111, *112*
timbrel system, 106, 108

Vegetation, harmfulness of, 255n20, 255n21 (quoted)

Ventilation
artificial illumination and its effect on, 189–190 (quoted)
charcoal braziers, a health hazard, 195, 196 (quoted)
Coliseum, passages and stairs in, 200, 201, *202–205*
Great Pyramid during construction, 207, 210–211, *208–209*
humidification, 206, 207
hypocausts: separation of smoke from warmed air, 197, *198*
kiva: circulation of fresh air, 197
monastic kitchen, 200
purposes of, 189
Roman velarium and other sun-shades, 201
roof-top lanterns for, 191–192
roof-top wind deflectors, 287nn33,34
smoke-filled interiors, 192–193 (quoted), 194

Water transport
canals, first used world-wide for irrigation, 183
China's Grand Canal, 183 (quoted)
Egyptian obelisks, method of shipping, 179
major break in dikes, repair of, 184–185 (quoted), *186–187*
quicker and easier than by land, 178

Water wells
excavating procedures, *132*
noxious air encountered, 199

Wedges
to maintain strict horizontality at intermediate supports of centering frames, 100, 163 (quoted), 266n18
to permit controlled, gradual decentering, 100, 266n16 (quoted)
to split logs and crucks longitudinally, 135
to tighten lashings, 90

Wood
advantages and versatility of, 131, 134
charring to preserve timber from decay, 133–134 (quoted)
practical indestructability of, if remaining below the ground water table, 132
a technique of hand-digging water wells, *132*

Index of Authors Quoted

Index of References to Illustrations

Masonry techniques, Egyptian (cont.)
  laying and dressing the blocks, 294n20
  rough facing the blocks before dressing,
    276n5
  tightness of joints, 294n17
Metallic fatigue in buildings, disastrous
  consequences of, 262n22
Mud plastering, 251n19
  execution of, 273n37

Native vernacular houses
  building practices of, 250n12
  Dyak, under construction, 288n6
  North American, under construction,
    288n9
  Samoan, 288n10
  variety of, 288n4, 250n16
Notched logs
  as fixed ladders, 273n34
  as movable aids in construction, 273n35

Occupancy, structural modifications due
  to changes in, 259n19, 260n22
One-man conveyance of heavy loads,
  278n11, 278n12
Open timber roofs in England, 275n18

Passive cooling systems in Iranian
  architecture, 287n34
Piles, buildings on, over water, 252n22,
  289n20, 289n21, 289n22, 289n25
Pinnacles, 249n10, 260n2
Pisé construction, 266n22, 267n23
Pit sawing, 274n10
Portcullis plugs in Egyptian pyramids,
  259n21, 287n39

Quarries
  and building stones, 249n6
  descent of blocks from Greek, 280n29
  on the island of Portland, England, 276n6
  worked in Roman times, 277n2

Rafts of inflated skins, 282n42
Raising holes, 264n6
Ramps, construction, 291n7
Repairs and reconstructions, 250n14
Rollers as aids in moving huge blocks,
  262n25
Rocker device, 291n3, 292n10
Roman concrete
  barrel vault, 267n26
  materials and methods, 259n17
  ressaults, 259n18
  wall construction, 267n24, 267n25
Rope
  knots, 270n10
  Manilla hemp, 269n5
  methods of fabrication, 269n6, 270n15
  rope platform for supporting velarium,
    286n31

St. Gall, plan of, 258n6
Salisbury Cathedral, 260n8, 264n5,
  275n23
Scaffolding
  Chinese, 265n9
  common practices, 251n21
  in general, 264n3
  for hay storage, 284n3
  Thatcher's, 264n8
  Viollet-le-Duc's, 264n7
Shoring
  as carried out at Partrishow Church,
    England, 265n13
  as undertaken at Winchester Cathedral,
    254n19, 265n14
Steeple, Church
  blasted by lightning, 254n15, 262n2
  overturned by high winds, 253n14
Sun-shades in hot climates, 287n33
Surveying in Ancient Egypt, 258n3

Tepee (or tipi), American Indian,
  289n14, 289n15
Thatching
  process of, 251n20
  tied down types of, 269n9
Tilt-up operations, 275n21
Timber structures, numbering and test
  assembling, 275n20
Tools
  native handicrafted, 257n10
  traditional timber-working, 274n8
Treasury of Atreus, 277n16
Trulli of southern Italy, 257n8
Tunneling, 268n30

Undulating courses in Egyptian walls of
  masonry, 264n33

Vault
  timbrel, 268n27
  without formwork, 268n33
Vehicles and harnesses, 279n19
Ventilated walls, 284n3
Ventilation
  artificial, in mines, 284n5
  within an igloo, 285n13
  lack of, 285n16
  via louvered lanterns, 284n9
  within a medieval abbey's kitchen,
    286n29
  within a tepee, 285n15
  within a yurt, 285n14

Water transport
  ancient sailing vessels, 282n48
  of Egyptian obelisks, 281n37
  with heavy loads suspended immersed,
    281n38